Minding the House:

A Biographical Guide to
Prince Edward Island MLAs

1873–1993

Minding the House:
A Biographical Guide to
Prince Edward Island MLAs

1873–1993

General Editor
Blair Weeks

Written & Researched by
Blair Weeks
Sue Connolly
Natalie Munn

The Acorn Press
&
The Association of Former Members of the Legislative Assembly of Prince Edward Island

Charlottetown
2002

Minding the House: A Biographical Guide to Prince Edward Island MLAs, 1873-1993
ISBN 1-894838-01-7
© 2002 by the Association of Former Members of the Legislative Assembly of Prince Edward Island

Fact Checking: Jannah McCarville, Doug Weeks, Natalie Munn, Sue Connolly
Editing: Jeff Bursey
Bibliography: Sharon Clark
Cover Photos: Brian Simpson
Book Design: Heather Mullen
Publication Co-ordination: Laurie Brinklow
Printing: Williams & Crue Ltd., Summerside, Prince Edward Island

A co-publication of
The Acorn Press
P.O. Box 22024
Charlottetown, PE C1A 9J2
www.acornpresscanada.com

and

The Association of Former Members of the Legislative Assembly of Prince Edward Island
P.O. Box 338
Charlottetown, PE C1A 7K7

We gratefully acknowledge the funding support of the Government of Prince Edward Island, including the Department of Education and the Department of Community and Cultural Affairs; and the Millennium Bureau of Canada.

National Library of Canada Cataloguing in Publication Data

Weeks, Blair, 1963
Minding the house: a biographical guide to Prince Edward
Island MLAs, 1873-1993

Co-published by the Association of Former Members of the
    Legislative Assembly of Prince Edward Island
Includes bibliographical references.
ISBN 1-894838-01-7

I. Prince Edward Island. Legislative Assembly Biography.
2. Politicians Prince Edward Island Biography. 3. Prince
Edward Island Politics and government Biography. I. Connolly,
Susan, 1976 II. Munn, Natalie, 1973 III. Association of Former
Members of the Legislative Assembly of Prince Edward Island. IV.
Title.

FC2605.W44 2002   324'.22'0924   C2002-903697-3
F1046.8.W44 2002

Dedication

Frederick Leo Driscoll
(1932-2000)

It is most fitting that this important book dealing with Prince Edward Island's political history is dedicated to Fred Driscoll. It was Fred's idea to publish this collection of biographical sketches of every person who served as a Member of the Legislative Assembly of Prince Edward Island from 1873 to 1993. He was the driving force that propelled this project from the idea stage.

Fred Driscoll was a school teacher, a university professor, a Member of the Legislative Assembly, a Member of Executive Council, and a Government Leader in the Legislature. He had a varied career, which interwove history and the politics of the day.

It was my good fortune to represent 3rd Queens for three terms with Fred, as well as to sit in Cabinet with him. But it was his performance in the role of representative from Prince Edward Island at the federal-provincial Constitutional conferences for which I shall most remember him. During those private and public discussions and debates he excelled, and demonstrated great analytical skills.

Fred Driscoll had a brilliant mind and a keen intellect. He always advocated that people put their positions in writing, which, of course, meant that these positions would be subjected to his ability to penetrate both the weakest and strongest points.

With his passing, Prince Edward Island lost one of the most brilliant political minds that our province was blessed to have serve as an MLA and as a Cabinet Minister. It was a privilege to have been one of his colleagues and friends.

Fred Driscoll is survived by his wife Bernie, his children Jamie and Jennifer, his grandchildren Cait, William, and Cameron, and his brothers Wilfred, Robert, Lawrence, and Gerald.

Horace B. Carver, Q.C.

Message from the Honourable Herb Gray,
Former Deputy Prime Minister and
Minister responsible for the Government of Canada's
Millennium initiative

Association of Former Members of the Legislative Assembly,

I am pleased to offer my sincere congratulations to Association members on the publication of their guide. The collection of biographies of members who served in Prince Edward Island's Legislative Assembly is an important document, both for its historical content and political record. Canadians are proud of their history and of the people who serve political office. Undoubtedly, the guide will serve to inspire others on a political path, and become a valuable resource of information on the Island's history and culture.

The Government of Canada proudly supported this publication with a financial contribution through the Canada Millennium Partnership Program. We were pleased to have this unique opportunity to work in partnership on this publishing venture with the Association of Former Members of the Legislative Assembly. It is an important document for the 21st century and a link to the past for future generations.

You have joined the thousands of Canadians who contributed to the millennium legacy in the spirit of our national millennium theme, "Sharing the Memory, Shaping the Dream." Your contribution to Prince Edward Island's heritage, and in fact to all of Canada, has helped to make this special time in our history a memorable one!

Best Wishes,

The Hon. Herb Gray, M.P.
Deputy Prime Minister

Contents

Foreword

Even those who serve have dreams.

And so it was when the Association of Former Members of the Legislative Assembly was formed in 1988 with its primary goal: "...to put its members' knowledge at the service of the Island community and elsewhere by sharing their experience through educational institutions and other forms." Having stated the goal, and understanding its inherent challenges, the thoughts of the Association turned toward how to achieve it. In response to this goal, one suggestion was to publish a collection of biographies chronicling the lives of the 418 members who served in the Prince Edward Island Legislature from 1873 until a general election was held on 18 November 1996. The election was a benchmark in the history of the Prince Edward Island Legislature as the number of members was reduced from 32 to 27, and the electoral boundaries between ridings were redrawn.

In 1990 an independent Management Committee was established to accomplish the task of publishing the biographies. Leading the Management Committee was Fred Driscoll, a former Member of the Legislature and history professor at the University of Prince Edward Island. In 1996 the biography project was given a higher priority by the Association of Former Members of the Legislative Assembly due in part to the urging of Fred Driscoll to have the project completed. In 1999 staff resources were provided to the project by the provincial government under the supervision of Fred Driscoll. In November 2000, Fred Driscoll, the driving force behind the biography project, died. Blair Weeks, previously seconded from the Department of Education, took on the duties of project coordinator. In December 2000, former Member Roberta Hubley agreed to oversee the project on behalf of the Association of Former Members of the Legislative Assembly.

As the project has come to a conclusion, the Association of Former Members of the Legislative Assembly now enjoy a measure of accomplishment of the original goal. The completed biographies will be a standard reference work for provincial libraries and research libraries throughout the country. This book is a piece of history long in the making and a tribute to those who have served in the Legislature. It is also a fulfilment of the dream of Fred Driscoll and other former Members who shared his vision.

The publication of this book is a fulfilment of the dream of the Association of Former Members of the Legislative Assembly. The Association would like to provide the deepest thanks and appreciation to the University of Prince Edward Island and the project team, and to the provincial and federal governments for their support. The Association of Former Members of the Legislative Assembly is indebted to Fred Driscoll.

The men and women presented in this book dreamed big, and our beloved Island has benefitted greatly as these dreams were fulfilled.

Marion Murphy
President

Albert Fogarty
Past President

The Association of Former Members of the Legislative Assembly

Provincial Election Results: 1996

Members of the Legislative Assembly elected in the general election held 18 November 1996 and winner of subsequent by-election:

District 1 Souris-Elmira	Andy Mooney (Conservative)
District 2 Morell-Fortune Bay	Kevin MacAdam (Conservative)
District 3 Georgetown-Baldwin's Road	Michael Currie (Conservative)
District 4 Montague-Kilmuir	Jim Bagnall (Conservative)
District 5 Murray Harbour-Gaspereaux	Pat Binns (Conservative)
District 6 Belfast-Pownal Bay	Wilbur MacDonald (Conservative)
District 7 Glen Stewart-Bellevue Cove	Pat Mella (Conservative)
District 8 Tracadie-Fort Augustus	Mildred Dover (Conservative)
District 9 Stanhope-East Royalty	Jamie Ballem (Conservative)
District 10 Sherwood-Hillsborough	Elmer MacFadyen (Conservative)
District 11 Parkdale-Belvedere	Chester Gillan (Conservative)
District 12 Charlottetown-Kings Square	Wayne Cheverie (Liberal)*
District 13 Charlottetown-Rochford Square	Paul Connolly (Liberal)
District 14 Charlottetown-Spring Park	Wes MacAleer (Conservative)
District 15 Winsloe-West Royalty	Don MacKinnon (Conservative)
District 16 North River-Rice Point	Ron MacKinley (Liberal)
District 17 Crapaud-Hazel Grove	Norman MacPhee (Conservative)
District 18 Park Corner-Oyster Bed	Beth MacKenzie (Conservative)
District 19 Borden-Kinkora	Eric Hammill (Conservative)
District 20 Kensington-Malpeque	Mitch Murphy (Conservative)
District 21 Wilmot-Summerside	Greg Deighan (Conservative)
District 22 Saint Eleanors-Summerside	Nancy Guptill (Liberal)
District 23 Cascumpec-Grand River	Keith Milligan (Liberal)
District 24 Evangeline-Miscouche	Robert Maddix (Liberal)
District 25 West Point-Bloomfield	Herb Dickieson (New Democrat)
District 26 Alberton-Miminegash	Hector MacLeod (Liberal)
District 27 Tignish-Deblois	Robert Morrissey (Liberal)

Conservative 18 Liberals 8 New Democrats 1

*Wayne Cheverie resigned on 25 September 1997. Richard Brown was elected in District 12 Charlottetown Kings Square on 17 November 1997.

Provincial Election Results: 2000

Members of the Legislative Assembly elected in the the general election held 17 April 2000:

District 1 Souris-Elmira	Andy Mooney (Conservative)
District 2 Morell-Fortune Bay	Kevin MacAdam (Conservative)*
District 3 Georgetown-Baldwin's Road	Michael Currie (Conservative)
District 4 Montague-Kilmuir	Jim Bagnall (Conservative)
District 5 Murray Harbour-Gaspereaux	Pat Binns (Conservative)
District 6 Belfast-Pownal Bay	Wilbur MacDonald (Conservative)
District 7 Glen Stewart-Bellevue Cove	Pat Mella (Conservative)
District 8 Tracadie-Fort Augustus	Mildred Dover (Conservative)
District 9 Stanhope-East Royalty	Jamie Ballem (Conservative)
District 10 Sherwood-Hillsborough	Elmer MacFadyen (Conservative)
District 11 Parkdale-Belvedere	Chester Gillan (Conservative)
District 12 Charlottetown-Kings Square	Bobby MacMillan (Conservative)
District 13 Charlottetown-Rochford Square	Jeff Lantz (Conservative)
District 14 Charlottetown-Spring Park	Wes MacAleer (Conservative)
District 15 Winsloe-West Royalty	Don MacKinnon (Conservative)
District 16 North River-Rice Point	Ron MacKinley (Liberal)
District 17 Crapaud-Hazel Grove	Norman MacPhee (Conservative)
District 18 Park Corner-Oyster Bed	Beth MacKenzie (Conservative)
District 19 Borden-Kinkora	Eric Hammill (Conservative)
District 20 Kensington-Malpeque	Mitch Murphy (Conservative)
District 21 Wilmot-Summerside	Greg Deighan (Conservative)
District 22 Saint Eleanors-Summerside	Helen MacDonald (Conservative)
District 23 Cascumpec-Grand River	Phillip Brown (Conservative)
District 24 Evangeline-Miscouche	Wilfred Arsenault (Conservative)
District 25 West Point-Bloomfield	Eva Rodgerson (Conservative)
District 26 Alberton-Miminegash	Cletus Dunn (Conservative)
District 27 Tignish-Deblois	Gail Shea (Conservative)

Conservative 26 Liberals 1

* Kevin MacAdam resigned his seat for District 2 Morell-Fortune Bridge in the Legislative Assembly on 19 October 2000 to contest the riding of Cardigan in the federal election of that year. A by-election was held in Morell-Fortune Bridge on 26 February 2001 and Kevin MacAdam was re-elected to his former seat.

Acknowledgements

The Association of Former Members of the Legislative Assembly and the authors of this book had a great deal of assistance in its preparation. The two most significant sources of primary material for the project were the Prince Edward Island Public Archives and Record Office and the Prince Edward Island Collection of the Robertson Library at the University of Prince Edward Island. Members of the staff at the Public Archives who provided their professional support were Charlotte Stewart, Jannah McCarville, Kevin MacDonald, John Boylan, Jill MacMicken-Wilson, Lynda Callbeck, and Marilyn Bell. The Prince Edward Island Collection staff includes Simon Lloyd, Crystal Gavard, Leo Cheverie, Chris MacLauchlan, and Liz Statts. Prince Edward Island is very fortunate to have these two resources and their professional staff; many provinces are not.

Edward MacDonald's *If You're Stronghearted: Prince Edward Island in the 20th Century*, was a godsend to the project. This comprehensive and readable history of the province in the 20th century was used frequently as a resource for political commentary and assisted in defining many of the significant acts of provincial politicians. Additional acknowledgement must go to Edward MacDonald for his guidance and enthusiastic assistance.

Fred Driscoll (deceased), Edward MacDonald, Andy Robb, and Harry Holman served on the project's editorial board, which provided the framework and historical compass for the biographies, and frequent and wise advice which was greatly appreciated. Roberta Hubley, in addition to serving on the editorial board, assisted in the writing, researching, and editing process. She acted as a liaison to the Association of Former Members of the Legislative Assembly and worked closely with the project staff. Thanks for the great help and good humour.

Marion Murphy, the president of the Association of Former Members of the Legislative Assembly, played an important role by lending the unquestioned support of the Association to the project.

The assistance of Albert Fogarty was instrumental to the success of the project. While serving as president of the Association of Former Members of the Legislative Assembly, he obtained financial assistance from the Millennium Bureau and the Government of Prince Edward Island. As past-president, Fogarty made a successful appeal to the Government of Prince Edward Island for sufficient additional funds to allow the project to be completed. He also contributed to the editing and proofreading process.

Laurie Brinklow and her colleagues at The Acorn Press played a fundamental role in the production of the book. Their experience was greatly appreciated by the less experienced writing team.

Bill Arsenault, Neil Morrison, and Jamie Driscoll contributed to the research effort in the early stages of the book.

The administration of a book of this scope would not have been possible without the guidance of Anna Fisher, Secretary of the History Department of the University of Prince Edward Island. The Association of Former Members of the Legislative Assembly would like to thank the History Department for its support and for allowing the opportunity to work with such a helpful individual. The staff of the Business Office at the University of Prince Edward Island provided a great deal of professional support. The staff was also extremely considerate of the financial challenges that the project experienced.

Elections PEI gave the project a foundation on which to build, and we thank Lowell Croken and Merrill Wiggington for their dedication to the political and electoral history of the province.

The Association of Former Members of the Legislative Assembly would like to thank the many people, particularly local genealogists, who provided historical information about particular Members. Those thanked include Donna Collings, Kay Nicholson, Christine Gorman, Evelyn MacLure, Sasha Mullally, Julie Jackson, Nichola Cleaveland, Lynn Ellsworth and the PEI Executive Council Staff, Daryl MacDonald, Gary Carroll, Myron and June Weeks, Danny Keoughan, Ron Gauthier, Alan Hubley, Paul Connolly, Sheldon Coffin, Garth Turtle, Mike Proud, Sandra Sheidow, Donald MacKenzie, Dr. Malcolm Beck, and Paul Jenkins. Others who helped in a variety of ways include Doug Boylan, Catherine Hennessey, Shelley Muzika, Sandi White, and Ross Young. A great deal of gratitude is due to Waldron Leard for filling a number of holes in the research. Katherine Dewar made some important clarifications of the history of her relatives. Georges Arsenault contributed valued information on the Acadian Members. Aaron Gauthier, Fred Horne, and Susan Rodgers of the Wyatt Heritage Properties in Summerside revised the Lefurgey and Wyatt biographies. Virginia Flood, Administrative Assistant for the Lieutenant-Governor, provided protocol information on honours and degrees.

In conclusion, thank you to the Prince Edward Island Department of Education for its contribution of staff and financial support, the Department of Community and Cultural Affairs for providing a Cultural Development Grant to the project during its early stages, and the Government of Prince Edward Island for its significant financial support to the project. Publication of this book was also made possible through a Millennium Grant provided by the Millennium Bureau of Canada. Prince Edward Island's Members of Parliament were also supportive of the effort to secure federal funding.

Lastly, the staff would say the obvious, that any faults in the book are attributable to them, not to those named above. In a project of this complexity and scope, carried out under certain time constraints, there are bound to be errors, for which the staff take full responsibility.

Blair Weeks
Susan Connolly
Natalie Munn

Key to Abbreviations

* = A Member of the Legislative Assembly and whose biography is included in this book

A. and A.S. Rite = Ancient and Accepted Scottish Rite

A.F. and A.M. = Ancient Free and Accepted Mason

Acadians = Blanchard, J. Henri. *The Acadians of Prince Edward Island, 17201964.*

Acadiens = Blanchard, J. Henri. *Acadiens de L'Île du Prince Edouard.*

CCB = *Cyclopedia of Canadian Biography...*

C.M.B.A. = Catholic Mutual Benefit Association

COR = Stamp, Robert. *Canadian Obituary Record...*

CPG = *Canadian Parliamentary Guide*

CWW = *Canadian Who's Who...*

DCB = *Dictionary of Canadian Biography*

EC = *Encyclopedia Canadiana*

ECB = *An Encyclopedia of Canadian Biography...*

ECO = Prince Edward Island. Executive Council. Orders

Eminent Men = *Canadian Biographical Dictionary and Portrait Gallery of Eminent...*

Family Files = see Archival and Manuscript Collections, PARO

HFER = History of the Federal Electoral Ridings, 1867-1992.

L.O.L. = Loyal Orange Lodge

Meacham's Atlas = Allen, C.R. *Illustrated historical atlas of Prince Edward Island...*

MNI = *Master Name Index, see Archival and Manuscript Collections, PARO*

MWOT = *Canadian Men and Women of the Time...*

PARO = Public Archives and Records Office (P.E.I.)

PPMP = *Canadian Publicity Company. Prominent People of the Maritime Provinces.*

RG = Record Group see Archival and Manuscript Collections, PARO

WWC = *Who's Who in Canada...*

WWCL = *Who's Who in Canadian Law*

WWPEI = *Who's Who on PEI*

Explanatory Notes

The discovery of every pertinent detail about each Member of the Legislative Assembly from 1873 to 1993 was the ultimate goal of this volume. What has been achieved is obviously something less. Nonetheless, a diligent effort was made to better know each subject. In one sense, it was less difficult to find out what was needed about modern and living subjects. From another perspective, living subjects have lives after their political careers end and continue to make history. To this end, a questionnaire was circulated to the former Members of the Legislative Assembly to update the events and involvements in which they are presently engaged. It was assumed that the former Members are still involved in the activities they reported.

Information about former Members, particularly those who have died, for the most part was obtained from materials available in the public domain: archival records; birth, death, and marriage records; newspapers; biographical compilations; and family and community histories. For those interested in reviewing the research, references have been included for each biography.

Efforts were made to keep the form of each biography standard. The format for the biographies was based in part on that utilized in the *Dictionary of Canadian Biography*, published by University of Toronto Press. The aim was to provide the name and titles of the Member, the Member's birthdate (b.), parents, marriage date (m.) and spouse, children, religion, and, finally, date (d.) and place of death. The spouse's last name, previous to marriage, is mentioned in the first paragraph wherever possible. In the final paragraph, the married name of the spouse is used. Due to time constraints, locating all information concerning the spouse was not a primary goal of the research. Instead, any material easily or quickly located regarding the spouse was included. In some cases, the authors were not certain whether the parents of Members' spouses were still living. Efforts were made to include all named children of Members. The record of children who died in infancy should not be viewed by readers as complete.

The title Honourable is used frequently. The criteria for the use of this term is based on convention. As a result, opinions on the convention vary.

According to the Centennial Protocol Handbook for Canada, published by the Department of Canadian Heritage (for the purposes of this book), Honourable is awarded to present and former Lieutenant-Governors, PEI and Federal Supreme Court Judges, Members of the Privy Council of Canada, and Senators. Current Premiers and Cabinet Ministers are granted the title while in office, as are Provincial Speakers.

Readers may assume that a Member of the Legislative Assembly represented the riding stated in the first line of the second paragraph (political history paragraph) throughout his or her career, unless otherwise stated in the sentences immediately following. At times the common name of the Member is used at the beginning of the third paragraph, with the exception of Premiers, as more than one paragraph has been devoted to the political career of the people who held this office. In general, the biography of Members was limited to 250 words, Members of Executive Council 500 words, and Premiers 1,000 words. There are some exceptions to this guideline. In some cases, there was more biographical material available.

The terms councillor and assemblyman were designations used, in part, to distinguish the two Members from the riding. These terms were not used in the biographies. For a more sufficient description of the history of the terms, and the role the designations played, the reader is directed to Paul Connolly's Afterword, a concise history of the Legislative Assembly.

Readers will observe that Members appointed to Executive Council (Cabinet) in the late 19th and early 20th centuries were required to run a second time following their election. The subsequent by-election occurred in the appointed Member's riding. This practice was discontinued at an undetermined point early in the 20th century.

Throughout the book, the two traditional parties in the province are referred to as Conservative and Liberal. This is for simplicity's sake so as to avoid confusion. Liberal-Conservative, a term common in the late 19th and early 20th centuries, and Progressive Conservative, the modern term, fall under the umbrella term of Conservative.

In September 1873, a special federal election was held to determine the six Members of Parliament to represent Prince Edward Island as a result of the colony becoming a Canadian province. Many members of the provincial House of

Assembly resigned to participate in the election. The special federal election was not a general election.

The provincial ridings have changed a number of times since Confederation. For more information on the evolution to the present makeup of the Legislative Assembly, the reader is once again directed to the Afterword. For quick reference, an outline of the evolution of the riding system in the province is provided below:

1873–1893: 15 ridings with two members representing each riding

1st Prince
2nd Prince
3rd Prince
4th Prince
5th Prince

1st Queens
2nd Queens
3rd Queens
4th Queens
Charlottetown Royalty

1st Kings
2nd Kings
3rd Kings
4th Kings
Georgetown Royalty

1893–1966: 15 ridings with one Councillor and one Assemblyman representing each riding

1st Prince
2nd Prince
3rd Prince
4th Prince
5th Prince

1st Queens
2nd Queens
3rd Queens
4th Queens
5th Queens

1st Kings
2nd Kings
3rd Kings
4th Kings
5th Kings

1966–1996: 16 ridings with one Councillor and one Assemblyman representing each riding

1st Prince
2nd Prince
3rd Prince
4th Prince
5th Prince

1st Queens
2nd Queens
3rd Queens
4th Queens
5th Queens
6th Queens

1st Kings
2nd Kings
3rd Kings
4th Kings
5th Kings

1996–present: 27 ridings with one member representing each riding

Number 1	Souris-Elmira
Number 2	Morell-Fortune Bay
Number 3	Georgetown-Baldwin's Road
Number 4	Montague-Kilmuir
Number 5	Murray River-Gaspereaux
Number 6	Belfast-Pownal Bay
Number 7	Glen Stewart-Bellevue Cove
Number 8	Tracadie-Fort Augustus
Number 9	Stanhope-East Royalty
Number 10	Sherwood-Hillsborough
Number 11	Parkdale-Belvedere
Number 12	Charlottetown-King's Square
Number 13	Charlottetown-Rochford Square
Number 14	Charlottetown-Spring Park
Number 15	Winsloe-West Royalty
Number 16	North River-Rice Point
Number 17	Crapaud-Hazel Grove
Number 18	Park Corner-Oyster Bed
Number 19	Borden-Kinkora
Number 20	Kensington-Malpeque
Number 21	Wilmot-Summerside
Number 22	St. Eleanors-Summerside
Number 23	Cascumpec-Grand River
Number 24	Evangeline-Miscouche

Number 25	West Point-Bloomfield
Number 26	Alberton-Miminegash
Number 27	Tignish-Deblois

A number of Members of the Legislative Assembly of Prince Edward Island also served as Members of Parliament. As the names and number of ridings have changed significantly since Confederation, it is worthwhile reviewing the history of federal ridings in the province. At Confederation, Prince Edward Island had six MPs in three dual-member ridings. In 1892 the number was reduced to five and reduced again to four in 1903. In 1911 it was lowered to three. In 1915 the number of federal ridings in the province was fixed at four, through amendment to the British North America Act. The amendment stated that no province will have less seats in the House of Commons than it has in the Senate.

1873-1892: 6 seats, 2 in each riding

Prince County
Queen's County
King's County

1892-1903: 5 seats

West Prince
East Prince
West Queen's
East Queen's
King's

1903-1911: 4 seats, 2 in Queen's

Prince
Queen's
King's

1911-1915: 3 seats

Prince
Queen's
King's

1915-1966: 4 seats, 2 in Queen's

Prince
Queen's
King's

1966 to present: 4 seats

Egmont
Malpeque
Hillsborough
Cardigan

Finally, as Patrick Binns* is, as of this publication, an active politician, it seemed prudent that an assessment of his political program should occur following his career as Premier.

Biographies

A

ACORN, HERBERT HUNT, merchant, lumber manufacturer, mayor, and member of fishermen's loan board; b. ca. 10 August 1868 in Lower Montague, son of Charles Acorn and Caroline Sabine; m. 7 February 1894 Harriet Ann Sellar, and they had seven children, Harry (died early in life), Marjorie (died early in life), Dorothy (died early in life), Clarence, George, William A.*, and Wanda; United; d. 6 December 1939 in Charlottetown.

Acorn, a Liberal, was first elected to the Legislative Assembly in the 1935 general election for 1st Kings. He was re-elected in the general election of 1939 and died while a Member. From 1920 to 1921, Acorn was the Mayor of Souris. His son William represented 1st Kings from 1951 to 1959, and from 1965 until his death in 1966.

Acorn was educated at the local school in Lower Montague and later at the Charlottetown Business College. He began his working life in 1884 as an employee of Daniel Gordon*, joining the Georgetown mercantile firm of Westaway and McDonald – Lewis Westaway* and Malcolm McDonald* were both politicians – two years later. In 1888 Acorn moved to Charlottetown and was employed by Prowse Brothers Limited, one of the larger mercantile enterprises in the province. This firm was owned by Lemuel Prowse*, an MLA and MP. In 1896 Acorn opened a general store in Souris, which a fire destroyed a few years later. Acorn then built the successful Klondyke Lumber Mill, which he operated until his death.

His other involvements included serving as a member of the Advisory Committee of the Federal Salt Fish Board and, from at least 1936 to 1939, as a member of the Fishermen's Loan Board. While on this board, Acorn travelled the Island extensively, and was responsible for overseeing the construction of several buildings used to store fish or supplies. He also worked toward the diversification of the number of species of fish caught by Island fishermen. Acorn contributed to the busi-ness life of his own community by serving as a board member and president of the Souris Board of Trade. Herbert Acorn, while still a resident of Souris, died 6 December 1939 at the Prince Edward Island Hospital.

Harriet Acorn, the daughter of Henry and Mary Sellar of Charlottetown, was born in 1870 and died in 1936.

References
CPG 1936, 1939, 1940; Townsend p. 138; *Beacon* no. 15 1993; *Guardian* 19 April 1938, 7 December 1939; *Patriot* 7 December 1939; PARO: Acc. 2323, Leard Files Reel #1; MNI-Cemetery Transcripts.

ACORN, WILLIAM A., automobile dealer; b. 10 January 1915 in Souris, son of Herbert H. Acorn* and Harriet Ann Sellar; m. 1938 Ann Selina MacIsaac of Hermanville, and they had five children, Shirley Ann (died 15 July 1947), Robert, Earl, Barbara, and Shirley; United; d. 25 May 1966 in Souris.

Acorn, a Liberal, was first elected to the Legislative Assembly in the general election of 1951 for 1st Kings. He was re-elected in the general election of 1955 and in a by-election held 9 February 1965. Acorn was defeated in the general elections of 1959 and 1962. Acorn won the nomination for 1st Kings in the general election of 1966, but died during the campaign. The general election held 30 May had resulted in a tie. The vote in 1st Kings was deferred until 11 July 1966 and decided the overall election winner, the Liberals.

Acorn's father also served in the Legislative Assembly for 1st Kings, serving the district from 1935 until his death in 1939.

Acorn, a lifelong resident of Souris, operated a sub-agency for a Charlottetown automobile dealer. He was a member of the Eastern Kings Board of Trade and served as the vice-president of Souris Lions Club. William Acorn died of a heart attack on 25 May 1966 at his home.

Ann Acorn was born in 1915 and died in 1967. She was the daughter of Angus Dan MacIsaac and Flora MacIntyre of Hermanville.

References
CPG 1959; Elections PEI; *Beacon* no. 15 1993; *Guardian* 26 May 1966; PARO: Acc. 2323, Leard Files; MNI-Cemetery Transcripts.

AGNEW, JOHN, clerk, fish and meat packer, produce exporter, and fox breeder; b. 22 August ca. 1853 in Glasgow, Scotland, son of John Agnew and Jean McCulloch or McCullogh; m. 22 December 1882 Agnes St. Clair Ireland, and they had at least 10 children, Annie Florence, Alexander, William, John, George, Amy, Belle, Daisy Irene, Helen, and Effie Jean; Presbyterian; d. 26 October 1928 in Charlottetown.

Agnew, a Liberal, was first elected to the Legislative Assembly in the general election of 1904 in 1st Prince. He was re-elected in the general election of 1908. Acorn was defeated in the general election of 1912. Appointed Speaker in 1909, Agnew held this position until the termination of the Liberal government of that period. In 1908 he moved a resolution to prohibit the use of automobiles on Island roads. Agnew was the first Mayor of Alberton, serving from 1913 to 1917. A strong proponent of temperance, he was appointed Chairman of the Prohibition Commission in June 1927.

Agnew lived in Scotland until about 1876, and attended the Free Church School in Glasgow. He first emigrated to Richibucto, New Brunswick, and lived there for one or two years. Agnew resided in Alberton from 1877 to 1916, when he moved to Charlottetown. Upon his move to Alberton from Richibucto, Agnew clerked for Robert Bell at his store and in his lobster factory. Soon he bought the factory, and later opened others at North Cape and Miminegash. Agnew had a meat cannery in Alberton, canned mackerel as well, and owned a shop where cans and boxes were made. He had schooners trading with the West Indies, and to support his shipping endeavours bought and exported produce. A fox breeder, Agnew was president of the Provincial S. B. Fox Co. Ltd., John Agnew Fur Farms Ltd., and the Prince Edward Island Black Fox Co. He had fox ranches in Ontario and British Columbia, as well as on the Island. In 1903 Agnew was elected as the first president of the Alberton and West Prince Board of Trade.

His social activities included membership in the Independent Order of Oddfellows and the Independent Order of Foresters. While in Alberton, Agnew was an elder and chairman of the Board of Trustees in the Presbyterian Church. Upon his move to Charlottetown, he was elected elder of St. James Presbyterian Church, where he taught bible class. John Agnew died 26 October 1928.

Agnes Agnew, the daughter of Capt. James Ireland, an Islander, and Ann McLeod, died in Orangeville, Ontario, 7 January 1938.

References
CPG 1910, 1912; *Canada's Smallest Province* p. 350; Green, pp. 13, 225; *Past and Present* p. 328; *Prominent Men* p. 410; *Guardian* July 1915 (Supplement), 27 October 1928; *Maple Leaf Magazine* December 1928 p. 374, February 1938 p. 34; *Patriot* 26 October 1928; PARO: MNI-Census 1881; Marriage Register.

AITKEN, GEORGE BEAIRSTO, farmer, justice of the peace, and railway valuator; b. ca. 20 May 1836 in Lower Montague, son of Johnson Aitken and Elizabeth Beairsto; m. ca. 14 February 1870 Jane D. Shaw, and they had six children, Ben Oswald (died at eight years on 25 July 1879), William Eldred (died at six years on 20 July 1879), George Russell, John Wallace, Henry Merrill, and Elizabeth Jane (Bessie); Presbyterian; d. ca. 18 February 1909 in Lower Montague.

Aitken, a Liberal, was elected to the Legislative Assembly in the 1893 general election for 4th Kings. He was defeated in the general elections of 1886 and 1897, and in the election for Legislative Council in 1890. During the time he represented 4th Kings, the government carried out repairs on the road leading to the ferry in Lower Montague, constructed a steel bridge in Montague, and repaired Aitken's Wharf in Lower Montague.

Aitken was born and educated in Lower Montague, where he lived all his life. During the construction of the Murray River Railway, Aitken was one of the valuators. He was an active worker in his church and community.

Aitken died ca. 18 February 1909 after a two-week battle with pneumonia. His brother James died 19 February 1909 while viewing the remains.

Jane Aitken, the daughter of Neil Shaw of Montague, died 5 March 1921.

References
CPG 1887, 1891, 1897; Fraser, pp. 52-53; *Examiner* 16 October 1881, 19 February 1909; *Guardian* 19 February 1909, 20 February 1909; *Islander* 18 March 1870; *Patriot* 18 February 1909; PARO: Baptism Record, RG 19 Vital Statistics, Series 3 Volume 7; Aitken Family File; MNI-Census 1881; Census 1901.

ALLEN, LUCAS R., merchant, food plant manager, and corporate board member; b. 17 July 1878 in St. Nicholas, son of Benjamin C. Allen and Melvina Goodwin, both of New Brunswick; m. 16 June 1903 Winnifred Brace, and they had five children, Irene, Florence, Edith, Mildred, and Margaret; Methodist/United; d. 7 April 1964 in Summerside.

Allen, a Liberal, was first elected to the Legislative Assembly in the general election of 1927 for 5th Prince. He was re-elected in the general elections of 1931 and 1935. He was appointed as a Minister without Portfolio in August 1935. Allen also served on the Summerside Town Council.

Allen received his primary education in St. Nicholas until he was 12. Later he attended school in Summerside. His introduction to the workplace began ca. 1893 as a delivery person for Brace, McKay and Company, which was owned by John A. Brace, later Allen's father-in-law. Allen worked there for many years and became manager of the grocery department. In 1901 he made an investment in the company when it became a joint stock company, and a year later was appointed to its board of directors. In 1926 Allen became president of Brace, McKay and Company, a position he held until 1939 when he became vice-president and took on reduced duties. He remained as vice-president until 1958. Allen had business interests beyond Brace, McKay and Company. During the Second World War Allen was secretary-treasurer and plant manager of Island Foods Incorporated, which manufactured dehydrated potatoes for the forces overseas. He served on the board of directors of Pure Canadian Black Fox Company, The Malpeque Oysters Limited, Royal Silver Black Fox Company, Island Terminals Incorporated, and Northumberland Ferries Limited.

Allen had a number of other involvements in the community. He served as a president of the Summerside Board of Trade and helped found the Associated Board of Trade of Prince Edward Island. He was active in the International Order of Foresters, Knights of Pythias, Y's Men's Club, the L.O.L., and King Hiram & Mt. Lebanon Lodges of the A.F. and A.M. in Summerside. Allen, a skilled hockey player and rifle shot, was also a member of the Summerside Golf Club, the Summerside Curling Club, and the Summerside Quoit Club. He served as trustee on the board of directors of the Falconwood Hospital, Prince County Hospital, the YMCA, and the People's Cemetery. In 1914 Allen was a member of the board of trustees of Summerside Methodist Church, and he acted as the secretary-treasurer of the Methodist Sunday school in Summerside for 13 years. In 1930 Allen was elected as an elder of Trinity United Church in Summerside. He was awarded the King's Jubilee Medal in 1935. Lucas Allen died 7 April 1964.

Winnifred Allen was the daughter of John A. Brace from Summerside and Margaret Howatt from Tryon.

References
CPG 1928; *Maritime Reference Book* 1926 pp. 63–64, 410; *WWC* 1936 II p. 3; *Guardian* 9 May 1938, 8 April 1964; *Journal-Pioneer* 8 April 1964; PARO: RG 19: Vital Statistics series 3; Marriage Records subseries 4; Marriage licenses.

ANNEAR, THOMAS MONTAGUE, farmer; b. 3 November 1872 in Lower Montague, son of John A. Annear and Hannah Poole; m. 16 December 1897 Mary Jane Beck of Murray Harbour, and they had seven children, Janet Eileen (died 30 August 1905 at six years and 10 months), Chessels, John A., Thomas Montague, Cameron, Inez Jean, and Agnes; United; d. 18 October 1947 in Lower Montague.

Annear, a Liberal, was first elected to the Legislative Assembly in the general election of 1931 for 4th Kings. He was re-elected in the general elections of 1935 and 1939.

Annear was a farmer who owned a 270-acre farm where he raised pigs, cattle, and horses. Montague Annear died 18 October 1947 of a heart attack.

Mary Jane Annear, the daughter of Thomas Beck and Mary Hawkings, died in January 1946.

References
Guardian 28 January 1914, 20 October 1947; *Maritime Advocate and Busy East* vol. 33 no. 9 April 1943; *Patriot* 20 October 1947; PARO: RG 19 Vital Statistics series 3; Marriage records subseries 4.

ARSENAULT, ADRIEN F., lawyer; b. 12 April 1889 in Egmont Bay, son of Etienne J. Arsenault and Philomene Pitre; m. first 27 October 1920 Bernice A. MacDonald, and they had two children, Leonce and Adrien; m. secondly 4 September 1935 Ellen MacNeill, and they had three children, Leonard, Helen, and John; Roman Catholic; d. 28 June 1941 in Summerside.

Arsenault, a Conservative, was first elected to the Legislative Assembly in a by-election held 30 August 1922 for 3rd Prince. He was re-elected in the general elections of 1923, 1927, and 1931. He was appointed to Executive Council from 1923 to 1927. From 1931 to 1935, Arsenault once again served on Executive Council as Minister without Portfolio. In addition to being an effective speaker, well-read, and fluent in both French and English, he also had a gift for humour and storytelling.

Arsenault received his primary education at the local school in St. Chrysostome. Later he attended St. Joseph's University in New Brunswick and was awarded a Bachelor of Arts in 1912. Arsenault studied law in the office of Albert C.

Saunders* from December 1912 until 1916. Following his admission to the Bar, he worked with Neil McQuarrie and Aubin Arsenault* in the firm of McQuarrie and Arsenault. When both McQuarrie and Aubin Arsenault were called to the bench, Arsenault took over the practice.

Arsenault had a busy life outside of politics and the law. He was a leader of the Société Saint-Thomas-d'Aquin, and was its first secretary-treasurer. Arsenault was a member of the golf and curling clubs in Summerside, a member of the Knights of Columbus, the C.M.B.A., and La Société L'Assomption, and was the leader of the male choir at St. Paul's Roman Catholic Church in Summerside. Adrien Arsenault died 28 June 1941.

Bernice Arsenault was the daughter of John A. MacDonald* of Indian River, who represented 3rd Prince in the House of Assembly and the Legislative Assembly, and Anne C. McKelvie. She died 4 September 1935. Ellen Arsenault was a native of Travellers Rest.

References
CPG 1883, 1923, 1924, 1928, 1933, 1936; *Acadiens* p. 84; Elections PEI; *WWC* 1934-1935 p. 1714; *WWC* 1943-1944 p. 686; *Patriot* 30 June 1941 p. 5; PARO: RG 6.1 Series 19 Bar Admittances.

ARSENAULT, LL.D., M.A., HONOURABLE AUBIN EDMOND, teacher, lawyer, and judge; b. 28 July 1870 in Abrams Village, son of Joseph Octave Arsenault* and Gertrude Gaudet; m. firstly Anita, native of Ireland, marriage annulled; m. second 5 November 1907 Bertha Rose Gallant and they had 11 children, Iphigenie, Cyril, Catherine, Regis, Valerie, Marie, Laure-Jeanne, Patricia, Felice, Paula, and Lois; Roman Catholic; d. 27 April 1968 in Charlottetown.

Arsenault, a Conservative, was first elected to the Legislative Assembly in the general election of 1908 for 3rd Prince. He was re-elected in the general elections of 1912, 1915, and 1919. In January 1912 he was appointed to Executive Council as a Minister without Portfolio. Upon the resignation of Premier John A. Mathieson* in 1917, Arsenault became Premier and Attorney-General. In the 1919 general election, the Conservatives were defeated, yet Arsenault remained Leader of the Opposition until his appointment to the Prince Edward Island Supreme Court in 1921. In 1906 Arsenault was elected to the Summerside town council, and, while councillor, helped launch a campaign for the advocacy of sewage and water systems.

In September 1919, Premier Arsenault passed an Order-in-Council which enabled motor vehicles to use Island roads on all days of the week, subject only to the restrictions of the Motor Vehicle Act. Earlier in his political career, in 1909, Arsenault was one of only three Members to vote against a bill to prohibit automobiles from running on the streets and public highways.

Prohibition had begun in the province more than 20 years previous to Arsenault becoming premier. Though privately opposed to Prohibition, rather than advocate his own view regarding the consumption of alcohol, Arsenault amended Prohibition legislation to provide for a plebiscite to ascertain the will of Islanders in regard to the continuance of the Prohibition Act. He was defeated before the plebiscite could be held. The Conservative loss in the 1919 general election came about partly due, according to the *Canadian Annual Review*, to Arsenault's supposed favouritism toward fellow Roman Catholics and the negative feelings this generated in Protestants. In his memoirs, Arsenault indicated that the defeat was more likely due to his advocacy of a uniform education tax. According to Edward MacDonald's *If You're Stronghearted*, there was general discontent in the Island populace at the time, in part due to high inflation, and the Arsenault Administration became a victim of this popular dissatisfaction.

Arsenault's father, initially a Liberal and later a Conservative, was a Member of the House of Assembly from 1867 to 1895 for 3rd Prince, served on Executive Council, and was the first Island Acadian to be appointed to the Senate. One of Arsenault's brothers, Joseph Felix*, represented 3rd Prince from 1897 to 1904, when he was defeated by Joseph F. H. Arsenault*.

Arsenault received his education in Abrams Village. In 1885 he entered St. Dunstan's College and obtained a second class teaching license, going on to teach for two years at a country school and one year at St. Joseph's College. Subsequently Arsenault returned to St. Dunstan's College for one year, following which he articled at the law firm of McLeod, Morson and McQuarrie – Neil McLeod* and Walter Morson* were also politicians – for four years, and was admitted to the Bar as an attorney. The next year he went to London, England, to article with the Honourable Charles Russell. When these studies were completed, Arsenault returned to Charlottetown and started a law firm there in association with H. R. MacKenzie. After some months he moved to Summerside and continued in private practice for one year. He then entered into a partnership with Neil McQuarrie. He served as a director of the Canadian Bar Association. On 1 May 1921, Arsenault was named the successor to Justice Fitzgerald, Associate Judge of the Supreme Court of Prince Edward Island, and he served on the bench for 25 years.

Outside of his legal and political careers, Arsenault had numerous interests. He was the first director of the Prince Edward Island Travel Bureau, a director of the Good Roads Association, a director and executive member of the Canadian Geographical Society, president of the Canadian Association of Tourist and Publicity Bureau, and a Fellow of the Royal Society for the Encouragement of Arts in England. In the early 1920s, he accepted the position of president of the Prince Edward Island Tourist Association. On 16 February 1929, Arsenault prepared and presented a brief to Sir Henry Thorton of Canadian National Railway. He was part of a delegation sent by the Island Tourist Bureau and the Charlottetown Board of Trade. The brief urged Canadian National Railway to build a first-class hotel in Charlottetown. The company voted to assign $1 million to the project.

Additionally, Arsenault was president of the Acadian National Society of the Maritime Provinces, and one of the founders of the Société Saint-Thomas-d'Aquin. He was awarded a Doctor of Laws degree from Laval University and St. Dunstan's University, and a Master of Arts degree from St. Joseph's University.

Arsenault was a trustee of the Lady Wood Fund, a trust fund to be used for the benefit of aboriginal peoples, for over 20 years, beginning in 1931. He was a member of the Knights of Columbus and achieved the rank of 4th degree Knight. Aubin Arsenault died 27 April 1968. On 15 March 2001, the provincial government named Charlottetown's refurbished Nurses Residence, home of the Public Education Branch of the Department of Education, the Aubin Arsenault Building.

References
Acadiens pp. 84–85; Arsenault, Aubin; *CPG* 1910 p. 436; *DCB* XII 1891–1900 p. 39; MacDonald *Stronghearted* pp. 112, 138–39; *PPMP* p. 13; *WWC* 1943–1944 pp. 16, 916; *Guardian* 29 April 1968, 28 July 1973, 15 March 2001; *Journal-Pioneer* 23 and 27 September 2000; *Patriot* 30 June 1941; PARO: RG 6.1 Series 19: Bar Admittances 31.

ARSENAULT, JOSEPH FÉLIX, businessman and office holder; b. 16 October 1865 in Abrams Village, son of Joseph Octave Arsenault* and Gertrude Gaudet; m. 26 September 1892 Gertrude Cormier, and they had 11 children, Alyre, Ermalie, Irene, Louise, Ulric, Jacqueline, Edouard, Alfreda, Auldine, and two unnamed children (died in infancy); Roman Catholic; d. 27 February 1947, in Summerside.

Arsenault, a Conservative, was first elected to the Legislative Assembly in the general election of 1897 for 3rd Prince. He was re-elected in the general election of 1900. He was defeated in the general election of 1904 by Joseph F. H. Arsenault*.

Arsenault's father was a Member of the House of Assembly and served on Executive Council, eventually becoming the first Island Acadian in the Senate. Aubin Edmond*, one of Arsenault's brothers, was premier from 1917 to 1919.

"Joe-Félix," as he was known in his community, attended the local school in Abrams Village, St. Joseph's College in Memramcook, New Brunswick, and the Commercial College in Charlottetown. In 1897 he became a partner in his father's general store in Wellington. The firm, J. O. Arsenault and Sons, appears to have prospered in the 1890s. In 1899 it built a three-and-a-half-storey general store, one of the largest on the Island, and, for a time, Wellington's biggest attraction. In 1900 Arthur Rogers of Summerside joined the new firm, J. O. Arsenault, Son and Company. The partnership expanded into buying and selling livestock and agricultural produce, operating a brick kiln, and entered the lobster industry. It shipped lobster by sea and rail to off-Island markets. In December 1901, the business declared bankruptcy. In 1902 Arsenault organized a joint stock company in the same area, but, by 1903, H. S. Sharp Ltd. of Summerside acquired a controlling interest. Later that year, Herb Sharp sold J. O. Arsenault, Son and Company Limited to his son James. Arsenault maintained an association with his former business until 1905, when he left for the United States.

In Coleraine, Minnesota, Arsenault worked for the Oliver Mining Company. Except for two years spent managing a general store in Grand Rapids, Michigan, he lived in Coleraine until 1913. That year he moved to Quebec, and from there to Summerside in 1914. Arsenault relocated to Charlottetown in 1917 when he joined the Department of Internal Revenue. In 1922 he returned to Abrams Village to manage a general store, moving back to Summerside in 1925 to manage a similar business. From 1930 to 1945, Arsenault served as Deputy Prothonotary and Clerk of the County Court.

Arsenault was an active member of the Société l'Assomption, and he was a member of the Société Saint-Thomas-d'Aquin and the Knights of Columbus in Summerside. Joe-Félix Arsenault died 27 February 1947.

Gertrude Arsenault of Sackville, New Brunswick, daughter of Vital Cormier and Celina Bourque, died 1 December 1940.

References
Acadiens p. 85; *CPG* 1899, 1901, 1908; *DCB* XII 1891-1900 pp. 39-41; *By the Old Mill Stream* pp. 142-47, 197; *Guardian* 1 March 1947; *Patriot* 27 February 1947.

ARSENAULT, JOSEPH FÉLIX H., merchant, post-master, lobster canner, and justice of the peace; b. 15 February 1866 in Urbainville, son of Hubert Arsenault and Sophie Arsenault; m. 24 November 1892 Emélie Bernard, and they had six children, none of which are known; Roman Catholic; d. 28 January 1946 in Charlottetown.

Arsenault, a Liberal, was elected to the Legislative Assembly in the general election of 1904 for 3rd Prince. Previously he had been defeated in the general election of 1900, and was defeated in the general election of 1908.

Arsenault received his education at the school in Egmont Bay, following which he moved to the United States, remaining there for a few years. Upon returning to the Island, Arsenault opened a successful general store and operated a lobster cannery. He also served as postmaster and Justice of the Peace. At this time he lived on Higgins' Road in Lot 13. J. F. H. Arsenault died in Charlottetown on 28 January 1946.

Emélie Arsenault was the daughter of Joseph Bernard and Lisette Gallant. She died in Charlottetown on 13 December 1935.

References
Acadiens p. 86; *CPG* 1901, 1905, 1909; Elections PEI; *Past and Present* pp. 608-609; *Guardian* 29 July 1983.

ARSENAULT, HONOURABLE JOSEPH OCTAVE, farmer, teacher, and merchant; b. 5 August 1828 in Cascumpec, son of Meleme Arsenault and Bibienne Poirier; m. 15 April 1861 Gertrude Gaudet, and they had five sons and four daughters, including Joseph Felix* and Aubin Edmond*; Roman Catholic; d. 14 December 1897 in Abrams Village.

Arsenault, initially a Liberal and later a Conservative, was first elected to the House of Assembly in the general election of 1867 for 3rd Prince. He was re-elected in the general elections of 1870, 1872, 1873, 1876, 1879, 1882, 1886, and 1890. He was elected to the Legislative Assembly in the general election of 1893. In August 1870 Arsenault broke with the Liberal Party to join the Conservatives under the leadership of James C. Pope*. He did this in protest of the government's refusal to give Catholic schools the financial grants that Peter McIntyre, the Bishop of Charlottetown, had requested. Several other Catholic Liberals defected, the Liberal administration was ended, and a coalition government was formed. Arsenault remained a Conservative and was appointed to Executive Council by Premier Pope, where he served from 25 July 1873 to 4 September 1876. Later he was appointed to Executive Council by Premier W. W. Sullivan and Premier Neil McLeod and served between 11 March 1879 and 21 April 1891. On 18 February 1895, he became the first Island Acadian to be appointed to the Senate, where he served until his death.

Two of Arsenault's sons followed in his political footsteps. Joseph Félix* was a successful candidate for the Conservatives in 3rd Prince in the general elections of 1897 and 1900, and Aubin Edmond* was premier from 1917 to 1919.

A resident of Abrams Village, Arsenault was first educated in the local schools of Urbainville and Miscouche. Later he attended Central Academy in Charlottetown and achieved his first class teaching certificate. Around 1847, Arsenault began a teaching career that lasted 18 years. In 1865 Arsenault left teaching and opened a general store in Abrams Village, where he had taught for 12 years. In 1874 he expanded his business and opened a store in Wellington. This new store became his commercial base.

In the 1870s, Arsenault bought a fish plant. He first concentrated on processing mackerel, extending his interests into lobster in the 1880s. He built a plant at Cape Egmont and soon became one of the leading packers in the region. In an international competition held in Jamaica in 1891, he won the gold medal for his canned lobster. On 23 May 2001, Arsenault was inducted, posthumously, into the Junior Achievement Prince Edward Island Business Hall of Fame.

Arsenault did not lose his interest in education and French-language instruction once he entered the business and political worlds. In 1868, while serving as a Member of the House of Assembly, he obtained the Assembly's approval for a £5 bonus to be paid to any teacher competent to teach French. He also served as a member of the Board of Education from 1879 to 1891.

The advancement of the Acadian people was one of Arsenault's major concerns. He was on the committee that organized the first national convention of Acadians in 1881. At that convention, Arsenault was elected second vice-president of the colonization society. This body was set up to encourage Acadians to settle on unoccupied land in Quebec and New Brunswick so that they could enjoy a more prosperous life. Joseph Arsenault died 14 December 1897.

Gertrude Arsenault was the daughter of Felix Gaudet and Marine Poirier. She died in Summerside on 18 March 1919.

References
Acadiens p. 86; *DCB* XII 1891-1900 pp. 39-41; *Guardian* 24 May 2001; *Island Magazine* 33 1993.

ARSENAULT, JOSEPH WILFRED, school teacher, college professor, school supervisor, and president of Fishermen's Loan Board; b. 5 March 1906 in St. Raphael, son of Joseph H. Arsenault and Marie Pitre; m. 6 September 1950 Yvonne Gaudet, and they had one child, Jean-Paul; Roman Catholic; d. 19 April 1971 in Montreal.

Arsenault, a Liberal, was first elected to the Legislative Assembly in the general election of 1947 for 3rd Prince. He was re-elected in the general election of 1951. In 1948 he was appointed as a Minister without Portfolio. On 12 February 1949, Arsenault was appointed Provincial Secretary, which he held until 1954, when he was again appointed Minister without Portfolio. He resigned his seat in 1954.

Arsenault, known as "Willie," received his primary education at St. Raphael School. Later he attended Queen Square School in Charlottetown, and in 1928 went to St. Dunstan's College. Arsenault was a public school teacher and Supervisor of Acadian schools in the province. He later taught French and physics at Prince of Wales College. Arsenault served as president of the Fishermen's Loan Board. In 1955 he moved to Montreal and

taught school. Wilfred Arsenault died 19 April 1971.

Arsenault's mother was a native of Hope River. Yvonne Arsenault was the daughter of Emanuel Gaudet of Miscouche and Mannie Cormier of Sackville, New Brunswick.

References
Acadiens pp. 86–87; *By the Old Mill Stream* pp.198–99, 370; *PEI. Journal of the Leg. Assembly* 1953 p. 2, 1954, p. 2; *Maritime Advocate and Busy East* January 1950; *Patriot* 23 April 1971.

ARSENAULT, PROSPER A., school teacher and vice-principal; b. 25 May 1894 in Howlan, son of Julitte Arsenault; Roman Catholic; d. 28 October 1987 in Woodstock.

Arsenault, a Liberal, was first elected to the Legislative Assembly in the general election of 1955 for 1st Prince. He was re-elected in the general elections of 1962 and 1966. He was defeated in the general election of 1959. In 1958 Arsenault was appointed to Executive Council as a Minister without Portfolio, and in 1966 he became Speaker, serving in this position until 1970.

Arsenault received his education in Howlan from 1906 to 1914. From 1918 to 1920, and again from 1930 to 1932, he attended St. Dunstan's College. Arsenault taught school for many years, in the communities of Howlan, Bloomfield, Roxberry, Conway, Unionvale, and Inverness. Between 1941 and 1946, Arsenault was vice-principal of the largest Aboriginal school in Canada at LeBret, Saskatchewan. From 1946 to 1948, he took summer courses at St. Joseph's University in New Brunswick and received a teaching diploma. In 1949 Arsenault obtained a certificate of child psychology from the University of Ottawa. The following year, he received a first class teaching diploma from Prince of Wales College. Arsenault could speak French, English, Spanish, and Latin. Prosper Arsenault died 28 October 1987 in O'Leary.

References
Acadiens p. 87; *CPG* 1961 p. 701; *Guardian* 9 March 1970, 30 October 1987; *Journal-Pioneer* 17 November 1987; PARO: St. Anthony's Catholic Church Records; Leard Files.

B

BAGNALL, C.M., FLORA MINNIE LEONE, teacher; b. 20 July 1933 in Springfield, daughter of John Sutherland MacKay and Margaret Mayne; m. 29 July 1953 Erroll Bagnall, and they had five children, Elaine, Carol, Donna, Lloyd, and John; United.

Bagnall, a Conservative, was first elected to the Legislative Assembly in the general election of 1979 for 1st Queens. She was re-elected in the general elections of 1982, 1986, and 1989. Bagnall served as the Minister of Education from 28 October 1982 until 1986. She also served as the Minister Responsible for the Status of Women, and was the first female Conservative in the province to hold a Cabinet post. Bagnall and Marion Reid* were the first female Conservatives elected to the Legislative Assembly. Bagnall was the first female to have responsibility for the Status of Women, the first female leader of the Conservatives (interim) and the first female Leader of the Official Opposition of any province in Canada. In 1979 Bagnall represented the Legislature at the Commonwealth Parliamentary Conference in Wellington, New Zealand. During the 1980 session, Bagnall chaired the Select Standing Committee on Fisheries, and was a member of the Select Standing Committee on Agriculture and Forestry. She served on the Policy and Priorities Board and was a member of the Community Affairs, Fisheries and Labour, Highways and Public Works and Justice committees. While Minister of Education, Bagnall represented Canada at the Commonwealth Education Ministers Conference in Nicosia, Cyprus, in 1984. In 1992 she represented the province for a second time at the Commonwealth Parliamentary Conference in the Bahamas.

Bagnall's grandfather, Donald Newton MacKay*, was a Liberal MLA who represented 1st Queens from 1935 until 1943.

Leone Bagnall received her primary education at the Springfield school and later attended Prince of Wales College. From 1971 to 1973, Bagnall studied at the University of Prince Edward Island and obtained a Diploma in Education. She graduated from the University with a Bachelor of Arts in 1978 and a Bachelor of Education in 1979. She worked as both a teacher and a housewife. Bagnall taught school at Breadalbane and Stanley Bridge, and in Kensington at Queen Elizabeth Elementary. She was president of the Hazel Grove Women's Institute and president of Central Queens Home and School. Bagnall was a charter member of the Prince Edward Island Association for Children with Learning Disabilities and a member of Eastern Star. She belongs to the Crystal Chapter #1, the Alpha Chapter of Delta Kappa Gamma, the Hunter River United Christian Women, and the Lucy Maud Montgomery Land Trust. Additionally, Bagnall is a member of the Queen Elizabeth Hospital Foundation and chair of the Advisory Committee for the Order of Prince Edward Island.

She received the Estelle Bowness Award from the University of Prince Edward Island for inspirational teaching. In 1992 Bagnall received the Canada 125 medallion and in 1995 she was invested in the Order of Canada. Leone Bagnall and her husband live on the family farm in Hazel Grove.

Bagnall's father was a native of Springfield and her mother was born in Summerfield. Her husband, Erroll Bagnall, the son of J. C. Pope Bagnall and Annie Pound, was born 9 May 1931.

References
PEI ECO 717/82; *WWPEI* p. 8; *Common Ground* vol. 2 no. 5 October 1983, vol. 11 no. 4 September/October 1992; *Guardian* 11 April 1986, 29 May 1986, 13 June 1988, 5 January 1995, 18 March 1996; *Islander* 19 September 1992.

BAKER, CHESTER CLEVELAND, farmer, fox breeder, and government fox inspector; b. 14 April 1886 in Margate, son of Richard Herbert Baker and Evelyn England Tuplin; m. first 15 July 1911 Ethel M. Johnson, and they had six children, Donald R., Mildred, Gladys, Audrey, Dorothy, and Marjorie; m. secondly 25 July 1934 Winnifred Gertrude Thompson, and there were no children; United; d. 22 July 1967 in Margate.

Baker, a Liberal, was first elected to the Legislative Assembly in the general election of 1935 for 4th Prince. He was re-elected in the general elections of 1939, 1947, 1951, 1955, and 1959. He was defeated in the general election of 1943. In 1949 he was appointed Minister of Agriculture and remained in that position until 1955.

Baker received his primary education at the school in Margate, and later attended the Truro Agricultural College. He was a farmer and fox breeder. From 1925 until 1929, Baker held the position of fox inspector for the Dominion Department of Agriculture. In 1929 he was elected to the board of directors of the Canadian Fox Breeders Association and served as president for one year. Baker acted as a superintendent of Margate Sunday School at the United Church, and was a member of the Mount Zion Masonic Lodge, Prince Edward Chapter No. 12. A hockey fan, Baker donated trophies to the North Shore and South Shore hockey leagues. Chester Baker died 22 July 1967 as a result of an accident with highway maintenance equipment.

Baker's father was a native Islander while his mother was born in Boston. Ethel Baker, the daughter of Rev. W. E. Johnson who resided in both Kensington and Calgary, was born in 1883 and died in 1923. Winnifred Baker, the daughter of H. D. Thompson, was born in Margate.

References
CPG 1960 p. 670; *History of Margate* pp. 37, 61; *PEI Journal of the Leg. Assembly* 1955, p. 2; *Guardian* 24 July 1967; *Maritime Advocate and Busy East* March 1943, January 1950.

BARBOUR, HONOURABLE GEORGE HILTON, labourer, farmer, fox rancher, constable, chief prohibition inspector, chief of customs and excise department, insurance salesperson, and civil servant; b. 5 September 1878 in Alma, son of Thomas Archibald Barbour and Mary Currie; m. 24 April 1907 Carrie Elora Casely, and they had two children, Greta Mary and Wendell George; United; d. 6 February 1962 in Ottawa.

Barbour, a Liberal, was first elected in the general election of 1935 for 2nd Prince. He was re-elected in the general elections of 1939, 1943, and 1947. Barbour resigned his seat in 1942 when he was selected as the prices and supplies representative to the regional office of the Wartime Prices and Trade Board in Charlottetown. Upon re-election in 1943, Barbour was appointed to Executive Council as Minister of Public Works and Highways. On 6 July 1949 he was appointed to the Senate.

Barbour received his primary education in Alma, and at the age of 17 moved to Boston. While residing in Massachusetts, he attended educational upgrading classes and worked at a company that sold ice. In 1907 Barbour returned to the Island and settled in Bloomfield where he farmed and bred foxes. He relocated in 1913 to Alberton and was employed there as a constable. While in this position, his barn was burned and shots were fired at him. In 1923 Barbour moved to Howlan. While he lived there, another of his barns burned down under suspicious circumstances. From 1918 until 1927, Barbour was chief prohibition inspector, and while on duty took an active part in the seizure of the *Nellie J. Banks*, a famous rum-runner. He moved to Summerside in 1923 and resided there until 1927. In that year, after resigning as prohibition inspector, Barbour moved to Charlottetown and became the district chief of the Customs and Excise Department. In 1934 he moved to the Brae, purchased a farm, and grew seed potatoes and raised dairy cows. Barbour returned to Charlottetown in 1942 and built a house at 130 Upper Prince Street. He maintained ownership of the Brae farm but had someone manage it for him until 1945, when he sold it. Barbour also worked with the Dominion Life Insurance Company. George Barbour died 6 February 1962 in the Senate Chamber in Ottawa, shortly after giving a speech.

Carrie Barbour, the daughter of William Samuel Casely of Kensington and Mary Ann Moase, was born 20 November 1886 and died 26 July 1970.

References
Barbour pp. 4, 9–10, 14–18, 24–25; *CDP* p. 21; Elections PEI; MacNevin pp. 255–57; *WWC* II 1936–1937 p. 54; *Guardian* 7 February 1962, 8 February 1962; *Debates of the Senate* 5th Session, 24th Parliament: vol. CXI no. 9: Wed. 2 February 1962.

BEER, HENRY, merchant, postmaster, and justice of the peace; b. 7 June 1835 in Charlottetown, son of George Beer and Mary Ann Holland; m. ca. 3 August 1857 Amelia Ings of Pownal, and they had four children, Henry Herbert, Annie Augusta, Emma, and Frank Alfred; Methodist/United; d. 2 August 1886 in Charlottetown.

Beer, a Liberal, was first elected to the House of Assembly for 3rd Queens in 1870. He was re-elected in the general elections of 1872, 1873, and 1876. He was defeated in the general election of 1879. At the formation of the Haythorne-Palmer government in 1871, Beer was appointed to Executive Council, but resigned in January 1873. He opposed the construction of the railway and Confederation. Beer resigned his seat in 1872 when a delegation left for Ottawa to negotiate terms of union. He served as Speaker of the Assembly under Premier L. H. Davies* in 1877.

Beer's father had represented 2nd Queens, then Charlottetown and Royalty, in the House of Assembly, and later represented 2nd Queens in the Legislative Council until the time of his death in 1872.

Born in Charlottetown, Beer received his early education at Central Academy, where he was awarded prizes in arithmetic at various times, including 1845. From 1855 to 1881, he and his family operated a general store in Southport. Beer dealt in produce, imported goods, and owned a brickyard. The first post office in Southport was operated from his store, and Beer served as postmaster from 1860 to 1873, and from 1875 to 1876. He was Justice of the Peace around 1870. Beer moved part of his store to Charlottetown in 1881, but the business was destroyed in the fire of February 1884.

Beer was active in the local militia, attaining the positions of Captain of "G" Company (Southport) and Captain of the "Dundas Rifles" (Southport) — a company of the Queens County Brigade — and rising to the rank of Lieutenant-Colonel of the 82nd Battalion of Volunteer Militia, Colonel of the 82nd Queens County Battalion of Infantry, and Colonel of the Queens County Regiment. Beer was present at the formation of the Provincial Rifle Association. He was a prominent Mason and a past master of St. John's Lodge A.F. and A.M.

In 1885 Beer was elected Mayor of Charlottetown. He was a strong proponent of a waterworks program and a civic building for Charlottetown, but did not live to see these plans come to fruition. In 1885 a smallpox epidemic erupted. Beer, who during his term chaired the Board of Health, received credit from the *Examiner* and the *Herald* for his work on behalf of the sick. It is perhaps this contact with the disease that led to his death on 2 August 1886. As a measure of respect for Beer's dedication to Charlottetown, local stores and businesses closed during his funeral.

Amelia Beer, born 10 July 1832, was the daughter of John Ings and Sarah Wood. Ings was prominent in public affairs as publisher of a Conservative-supporting newspaper, the *Islander*. Beer's daughter Annie Augusta married William Stewart*.

References
Bremner *Scrapbook* Appendix p. iii; *Checklist and Historical Directory* pp. 48, 118; *CPG* 1879, 1880; Elections PEI 1998; *Past and*

Present p. 510; Polland p. 176; *Charlottetown Herald* 8 September 1886; *Examiner* 2 September 1886, 3 September 1886; *Islander* 16 July 1847; *Patriot* 4 September 1886; *Royal Gazette* vol. 15 30 December 1845; *Summerside Journal* 9 September 1886; PARO: RG 19 Vital Statistics series 3; Acc. 3979 Colonel Henry Beer Biography p. 1; Henry Herbert-Baptismal record 6 June 1859; MNI; Ings Family File.

BELL, JOHN HOWATT, teacher and lawyer; b. 13 or 25 December 1846 in Cape Traverse, son of Walter Bell and Elizabeth Howatt; m. ca. 7 July 1882 Helen Howatt of St. Eleanors, and there were no children; Methodist; d. 29 January 1929 in Los Angeles, California.

Bell, a Liberal, was first elected to the House of Assembly for 4th Prince in the 1886 general election. He was re-elected in the general election of 1890. He was elected to the Legislative Assembly in the general election of 1893. He was re-elected in the general elections of 1897, 1915, and 1919. He was defeated in the general election of 1923. Bell resigned at the end of the legislative session in 1898 to run successfully in a federal by-election in East Prince held 14 December. He was defeated in the federal election of 1900.

Following the 1915 provincial election, Bell was chosen as Leader of the Opposition. He became premier by winning the 1919 general election when the Liberals took 24 seats to the Conservatives' six. Elected as Premier at age 72, he remains the oldest premier to take office in the province's history. Premier Bell raised taxes to, among other things, increase teachers' salaries. At the time, teachers were in short supply and poorly paid. They were also threatening to go on strike. In 1920 his government raised teachers' salaries between 46 and 60 per cent. His government also enacted a Highways Bill in 1922 to take advantage of the Federal Highways Act of 1919. The Federal Act offered assistance for highway improvements, which was a responsibility of provincial governments. After settling the conflict over teachers' salaries, Bell's government imposed a poll tax to pay for the salary increase and road improvements. With the Conservatives promising to rescind the tax levy, there was little hope of Bell surviving for another term. The Liberals suffered a devastating defeat in the 1923 general election, with the Conservatives winning 25 seats to the Liberals' five.

Bell was an advocate of women's suffrage in the 1890s. In 1922 his government introduced voting rights for women.

Though born in Cape Traverse, Bell resided in Summerside for the majority of his adult life.

He was educated at the public school in Cape Traverse, Prince of Wales College, and Albert College in Belleville, Ontario. He received a Bachelor of Arts in 1868 and a Master of Arts in 1869 at Albert College. While at Albert College, Bell involved himself with local matters and spoke out in favour of temperance legislation. After graduation he taught in several Ontario schools, including one in Beamsville.

From 1870 to 1874, Bell studied law in Ontario with the firms of Ferguson, Bain and Myers and later with James, McDonald and Ingerson. He was admitted to that province's Bar in 1874, and began practising law in Ottawa with the firm Bradley and Bell, where he remained for approximately eight years. In 1882 he moved to Emerson, Manitoba. He was admitted to the Manitoba Bar and practised law there until 1884. When Bell returned to the Island in 1884, he was admitted to the Bar and established an independent practice. Later he became a partner with B. W. Tanton in the firm of Bell and Tanton. Bell was awarded the designation of King's Counsel sometime between 1910 and 1912.

Bell was well-known as an outdoors man who liked fishing, long walks, and golf. He travelled extensively, and toured Egypt, Palestine, Greece, and Italy on foot for the majority of the journey. After retiring from politics, he made yearly trips to California where he had relatives and friends. He was made an honourary president of the Canadian Tourist Society of Southern California and spoke at various British and Canadian gatherings. Bell was elected R. W. Grand Master of the Grand Orange Lodge for Prince Edward Island in 1891.

Bell died 29 January 1929 after being struck by an automobile while in California on an extended visit. His death was ruled an accident by a coroner's jury.

Helen Bell was the daughter of Cornelius Howatt*, a former Speaker of the House of Assembly and an outspoken critic of Confederation.

References
Bell History; CDP pp. 32-33; *DCB* XII 1891-1900 p. 452-53; *EC* 1975 p. 361; MacDonald *If You're Stronghearted* pp. 113-14, 121; *Provincial Premiers Birthday Series; Examiner* 8 May 1895; *Guardian* 7 August 1891, 30 January 1929, 2 February 1929, 8 February 1929, 11 February 1929; *Island Magazine* no. 43 Spring/Summer 1998; *Pasadena Star News* 30 January 1929; *Patriot* 22 February 1924, 30 January 1929; PARO: Acc. 3043/28a; Acc. 2323 Leard Files, Reel #2; RG 6.1 series 19 Bar Admittances.

BELL, Q.C., MORLEY MYERS, lawyer; b.14 January 1894 in Tryon, son of Donald Bell and Eva Myers; m. 21 June 1922 Floyde "Flora" Lena Robinson, and there were no children; United; d. 2 July 1976 in Summerside.

Bell, a Liberal, was first elected in a by-election held 19 December 1945 for 5th Prince. He was re-elected in the general election of 1955. He was defeated in the general election of 1959. He was a member of the Summerside Town Council from 1940 to 1943.

He received his early education at Tryon Consolidated, and later attended Prince of Wales College. He served with the 10th Overseas Battalion from 1918 until his discharge one year later. Bell articled at Bell and Tanton, under the supervision of his uncle John H. Bell*, who was premier from 1919 to 1923. Bell was admitted to the Bar in 1918 and later became a partner in his uncle's law firm. From 1926 to 1973, he practised law without a partner. In 1973, at the time of his retirement, Bell was the oldest practising member of the province's Law Society.

Bell involved himself in a number of community activities. He served as president of the Summerside Curling Club from 1949 to 1950. He was a trustee of the Prince County Hospital and served on its board for over 45 years. Bell was a member of the Masonic Lodge and the Summerside YMCA, and served as president of the Summerside Rotary Club. In 1964 he was appointed to the National Library Advisory Committee by the federal Cabinet. Morley Bell died 2 July 1976.

Floyde "Flora" Bell, the daughter of G. W. Robinson of Summerside, died 20 April 1965.

References
CPG 1956; Elections PEI; *Guardian* 20 April 1965, 3 July 1976; PARO: RG 6.1 series 19 Bar Admittances; Bell Family File.

BELL, K.C., HONOURABLE RICHARD REGINALD, lawyer, judge, and farmer; b. 5 December 1901 in Charlottetown, son of Arthur J. Bell and Sarah MacKenzie; m. 5 June 1934 Helena L. Rogers, and they had two children, Richard and Carolyn; United; d. 24 March 1980 in Charlottetown.

Bell, a Conservative, was first elected to the Legislative Assembly in the general election of 1943 for 2nd Queens. He was re-elected in the general elections of 1947, 1951, 1955, and 1959. Bell was elected Conservative party leader in 1950 and held the post until 1957. Because of his party's poor showing in the elections of 1951 and 1955, Bell resigned as leader of his party. In 1959 Bell was appointed Attorney and Advocate General in the government of Premier Walter Shaw. He resigned in 1960 upon his appointment to the province's Supreme Court. Bell was a former secretary of the provincial Conservative party and former leader of the Young Conservatives.

"Reg" Bell received his primary education at West Kent School, and later attended Prince of Wales College. Following college, he articled with Judge G. S. Inman and was called to the Bar in 1927. In 1928 Bell became a partner in the firm of Bell, Mathieson and Foster, to which David L. Mathieson* belonged. In 1946 Bell was granted the designation of King's Counsel. In 1960 he was appointed to the Supreme Court. Bell was a Lieutenant in the 204th Battery Reserve from 1942 until 1945. He became owner of Highland View Farms ca. 1947, and specialized in Shorthorn cattle, Yorkshire hogs, and Cheviot sheep. He was a president of the Prince Edward Island Shorthorn Breeders Association, the Maritime Provinces' Director of the Dominion Shorthorn Association, and a national director of the Shorthorn Association. Bell was also a president of the Charlottetown Board of Trade and the Prince Edward Island Law Society.

Bell was president of the Charlottetown Curling Club, and a director of the Charlottetown Driving Park and the Provincial Exhibition Association. Bell was a member of the Charlottetown Club, the United Services Officers Club, and the Charlottetown Rotary Club. He served on the board of stewards of the Trinity United Church for many years. Reginald Bell died in Charlottetown 24 March 1980 while a resident of Stanhope.

Helena Bell was the daughter of Benjamin Rogers, Jr., and Winnie Collings. Her grandfather was Benjamin Rogers, Sr.*, of Charlottetown.

References

CPG 1960; *Past and Present* pp. 521–22; *WWC* 1936-1937 pp. 75–76; *Guardian* 15 January 1966, 24 March 1980; *Maritime Advocate and Busy East* November 1951; PARO Acc. 3043/29.

BENNETT, O.C., LL.D., D.C.L., M.SC., HONOURABLE GORDON LOCKHART, teacher and educational administrator; b. 10 October 1912 in Charlottetown, son of J. Garfield Bennett and Annie Lockhart; m. first 10 August 1937 Doris L. Bernard, and they had one child, Frances Diane; m. secondly 20 August 1985 Muriel Emily Deacon, and there were no children; United; d. 11 February 2000 in Charlottetown.

Bennett, a Liberal, was first elected to the Legislative Assembly in the general election of 1966 for 5th Queens. He was re-elected in the general elections of 1970 and 1974. He was appointed Minister of Education and President of Executive Council in July 1966. On 24 September 1970, Bennett became Minister of Justice, Attorney-General, and President of Executive Council. He also served as Provincial Secretary from 1972 to 1974. Bennett resigned from politics on 2 May 1974 to accept the position of Lieutenant-Governor, and was sworn in to this office on 24 October of that year. He served in that position until 1980.

Bennett received his early education at Charlottetown elementary schools. Later he attended Prince of Wales College and Acadia University, where he earned a Bachelor of Science in 1937. In 1947 he earned a Master of Science in Chemistry, also from Acadia University. He began teaching in St. Eleanors in 1931, but three years later returned to university. Bennett resumed teaching at West Kent School in Charlottetown in 1937, and in 1939 he was appointed to the faculty of Prince of Wales College as a member of the chemistry department. As well, Bennett served as registrar of the College. From 1985 to 1992, he was chancellor of the University of Prince Edward Island. On 11 February 1984, he was sworn in as an Officer of the Order of Canada.

Bennett was president of the Prince Edward Island Music Festival, the Canadian Bible Society, the Dominion Curling Association and the Prince Edward Island Branch of the Council of Canadian Unity, and provincial president of the Terry Fox Centre. He chaired the United Way Campaign and the Prince Edward Island 1973 Centennial Committee. Bennett coached the hockey and football teams at Prince of Wales College and was an official in English rugby across the Maritimes. He was a director of the Prince Edward Island Symphony Orchestra, and was a member of the Canadian Club, the Rotary Club of Charlottetown and the Masonic Order. Bennett was awarded a Doctorate of Civil Laws from Acadia University and an honourary degree from the University of Prince Edward Island. He was a Paul Harris Fellow, and was inducted as a builder to the Canadian Curling Hall of Fame. Gordon Bennett died 11

February 2000.

Doris Bennett was the daughter of H. Bruce Bernard.

References

CPG 1979; *CWW* 2000 p. 99; Elections PEI; *WWPEI* p. 13; *Atlantic Advocate* January 1975; *Guardian* 16 May 1990, 12 February 2000; *Journal-Pioneer* 11 April 1990; *Patriot* 12 April 1984.

BENTLEY, GEORGE WHITEFIELD

WHEELOCK, merchant and farmer; b. 1 December 1842 in Margate, son of Thomas Bentley and Hannah Smith; m. 9 February 1870 Emma Jane Dennis, and they had 11 children, Annie Ermina (died at one year and four months), George Harwood (died at five years and four months), Lorena Maude (died at 24), William, Mary E., Lorena, James A., Georgeanna, Thomas Whitefield*, Charles W., and one other child; Methodist; d. 8 April 1909.

Bentley, a Conservative, was first elected to the House of Assembly in the general election of 1879 for 4th Prince. He was re-elected in the general elections of 1882, 1886, and 1890. He was defeated in the general election of 1893. In 1887 he was appointed to Executive Council as Commissioner of Public Works. The appointment necessitated a by-election and Bentley was returned despite determined opposition. The debate over the need for legal control of alcohol consumption was one of the most significant issues of the late 19th and early 20th centuries in the province. Bentley's position on the issue was clear as he was a lifelong advocate of temperance.

Bentley was educated in Margate, and lived either there or in Kensington throughout his life. He owned a general store and was a farmer. For a number of years, Bentley was involved with the temperance movement, and eventually served in the office of Grandworthy Patriarch of the Grand Division of Prince Edward Island. He was also a Member of the National Division of the Sons of Temperance of North America and travelled throughout eastern Canada and the United States, participating in the activities of this organization. George Bentley died 8 April 1909.

Bentley's father emigrated from Yorkshire in 1817, while his mother, Hannah Smith, was born during passage to the Island in 1800. Emma Bentley, the daughter of William Dennis of Margate, was born 15 February 1849 and died 21 May 1910. Thomas Whitefield Bentley*, George Bentley's son, was elected to the Legislative Assembly for 4th Prince in 1923.

References

CCB 1888, pp. 259-60; *CPG* 1891, 1897; Elections PEI; *Meacham's Atlas*; PARO: MNI-Mercantile Agency Reference Book September 1876; MNI-Cemetery Transcripts; MNI-Census 1881, 1891; Marriage Book 11 p. 297.

BENTLEY, THOMAS WHITEFIELD, manager and provincial supervisor of life insurance company; b. 5 July 1884 likely in Margate or Kensington, son of George Whitefield Wheelock Bentley* and Emma Jane Dennis; m. Linda Irene Moore, and they had six children, George Haley, Jack, May, Marge, Helen, and Jean; United; d. 12 June 1952 in Charlottetown.

Bentley, a Conservative, was elected to the Legislative Assembly in the general election of 1923 for 4th Prince, a riding which his father represented from 1879 to 1893 in the House of Assembly.

A resident of Kensington, Bentley was the branch manager of the Maritime Life Assurance Company. Following his retirement in 1952, he was retained by the company in the capacity of Supervisor for the Province. Bentley was a member of the Trinity United Choir in Charlottetown for many years, and was a member of the Masonic Lodge and the Oddfellows. He and his wife intended to move to Montague in 1952. A heart ailment eventually precluded the resettlement plans. Thomas Bentley died 12 June 1952 at the Prince Edward Island Hospital.

Linda Bentley, the daughter of John A. Moore, was born 12 June 1882 and died 27 May 1961.

References

CPG 1924; *Guardian* 13 June 1952; PARO: MNI-Cemetery Transcripts.

BERNARD, HONOURABLE

JOSEPH ALPHONSUS, clerk and merchant; b. 27 March 1881 in Tignish, son of Theodore Bernard and Anne Perry; m. 21 September 1909 Zoë Chiasson, and they had 17 children, Timothy, Walter, Elphege, Harold, Ralph, Omer, Cecil, Edith, Letitis, Marcella, Joan, Gloria, Norma, and four others who are unnamed (died in infancy); Roman Catholic; d. 7 September 1962 in Sherwood.

Bernard, a Liberal, was elected to the Legislative Assembly in the general election of 1943 for 1st Prince. He resigned in 1945, and on 30 May of that year was appointed Lieutenant-Governor, serving in that position until 1950. Bernard was vice-president of the West Prince Liberal Association from 1920 to 1943.

Bernard received his primary education at the school in Sea Cow Pond and at the Tignish Grammar School. He went on to attend a school in Amawalk, New York, run by the Christian Brothers and Union Commercial College in Charlottetown. Bernard also lived in Boston and a number of other locations in Massachusetts. Late in life he resided in Charlottetown and Parkdale. For the majority of his life, he was a merchant in Tignish, but prior to this he worked in Massachusetts. In 1897 he worked as clerk for J. H. Myrick and Company. In 1899 he worked for Dunkel and Company. In Boston in 1907 Bernard was a street car conductor, but by 1911 he had returned to Tignish and was employed as a bookkeeper for J. J. Arsenault. In 1920 he became a partner in the firm of Morris and Bernard, general merchants of Tignish, one of the most successful businesses in the town. In 1925 Bernard became vice-president of the firm, and president in 1940. From 1930 to 1946, he was president of the Tignish Hall Company Limited. He was secretary-treasurer of the Palmer Road Dairying Association from 1923 to 1943. Bernard was chairman of the Tignish Library and was a member of the Tignish Merchants' Association. He was a member of the 4th degree Knights of Columbus, and until late in his life was active in the affairs of the Roman Catholic Church, the Société Saint-Thomas-d'Aquin and the Catholic Mutual Benefit Association.

Bernard's family made a substantial contribution during the Second World War. He served as a civilian recruitment director, while five of his sons, one daughter, and two sons-in-law enlisted. Joseph Bernard died 7 September 1962 at the Livingston-MacArthur Nursing Home in Sherwood.

Zoë Bernard, the daughter of Joseph M. Chiasson and Catherine DesRoches of Tignish, died in 1952. Joseph Bernard's maternal grandfather, Stanislaus F. Perry*, was a prominent politician.

References
Acadiens p. 88; *CPG* 1945, 1947, 1950; *WWC* 1958-1960 p. 83, 1960-1961 p. 1213; *Guardian* 8 September 1962; PARO: St. Simon and St. Jude Roman Catholic Church Records.

BERNARD, HONOURABLE JOSEPH GERARD LÉONCE, manager of tourism complex, manager of credit union, executive director of venture capital group, and chair of village commission; b. 23 May 1943 in Abrams Village, son of Joseph Antonin Bernard and Marie Emma Cormier; m. 27 July 1968 Florence Gallant of Cape Egmont, and they had four children, Michel, Pierre, Francine, and Charles; Roman Catholic.

Bernard, a Liberal, was first elected to the Legislative Assembly in a by-election held 3 November 1975 for 3rd Prince. He was re-elected in the general elections of 1978, 1979, 1982, 1986, and 1989. On 2 May 1986 he was appointed Minister of Industry and Minister Responsible for the Prince Edward Island Development Agency. From 1989 to 1991, Bernard served as Minister of Community and Cultural Affairs and Minister of Fisheries and Aquaculture. On 15 November 1991 he resigned from Executive Council to accept a position as general manager of Le Village de L'Acadie, but remained a Member of the Legislative Assembly until 1993. On 28 May 2001 Bernard was sworn in as Lieutenant-Governor. He is a former chair of the Village of Wellington and also chaired the Wellington Housing and Planning Committee. In 1991 Father Eloi Arsenault, president of the Société Saint-Thomas-d'Aquin, stated that "Léonce has helped tremendously in bringing the concerns of the Acadian people to the top levels of government. His honesty and hard work have not only earned him a great deal of respect, but have brought respect to the Acadian community."

From 1949 to 1960, Léonce Bernard attended the school in Mont Carmel, and, from 1960 to 1962, studied at Evangeline Regional High School in Abrams Village. From 1963 to 1967, Bernard served in the Royal Canadian Air Force. From 1970 to 1986, he was manager of the Evangeline Credit Union. Bernard was an executive director of the Baie Acadienne Venture Capital Group, a president of the Conseil Co-operative de l'Île-du-Prince-Edouard and was the province's representative on the Canadian Council of Co-operatives. He was a member of the executive of the Federation of Municipalities, a president of the Credit Union Managers' Association, and a treasurer of the Evangeline Tourism Association. Bernard served as director of the Centre Goëland, the Baie Acadienne Industrial Commission, the League Data Computer Company, and the Prince Edward Island Credit Union Stabilization Board. He was district chairman of the Co-operators Advisory Committee Board. Bernard held the positions of a director of the Unit 5 School Board and a vice-president of the United Way. He served as treasurer of the local Minor Hockey Association and the Wellington Boys and Girls Club. Bernard was a member of the Wellington Club, the Wellington Firemen, and the Wellington Royal Canadian Legion.

In 1987 he was recognized by *Atlantic Insight*, Atlantic Canada Plus, and the Atlantic Provinces Economic Council as Innovator of the Year in 1987. Bernard was given the award in recognition for the work he carried out with his constituents to set up a locally owned co-op potato chip factory, Olde Barrel. Léonce Bernard and his wife reside in Charlottetown at Fanningbank, the official residence of the Lieutenant-Governor.

Florence Bernard is the daughter of Albenie Gallant and Alina Arsenault.

References
Atlantic Guidebook p. 30; *CPG* 1977, 1996; *WWPEI* p. 14; *Atlantic Insight* 10 (1) January 1988; *Guardian* 4 April 1986, 15 November 1991, 16 November 1991; *Journal-Pioneer* 30 December 1987, 14 November 1991, 15 November 1991, 13 February 1993.

BETHUNE, DAVID F., politician; b. 6 November 1886 in Charlottetown, son of David Bethune and Mary Bethune; Baptist; d. 1960.

Bethune, a Conservative, was elected to the Legislative Assembly in the general election of 1931 for 2nd Queens. He was defeated in the general elections of 1935 and 1939.

Bethune's father was born in Scotland. His mother was a native of Prince Edward Island. David Bethune died in 1960.

References:
CPG 1932, 1936, 1941; PARO: MNI-Census 1881, 1891; Census 1901; Charlottetown Protestant Cemetery Records.

BINNS, M.A., HONOURABLE
PATRICK GEORGE, development officer, civil servant, farmer and businessperson; b. 8 October 1948 in Weyburn, Saskatchewan, son of Stanley Ernest Binns and Phyliss Mae Evans; m. 8 May 1971 Carol Isobel MacMillan of Stratford, and they had four children, Rob, Mark, Brad, and Lilly; Roman Catholic.

Binns, a Conservative, was first elected to the Legislative Assembly in the general election of 1978 for 4th Kings. He was re-elected in the general elections of 1979 and 1982. He served as Minister of Industry, Municipal Affairs, Fisheries, Environment, Labour and Housing from 1979 to 1984. In 1984 Binns resigned his seat in the Legislature to run successfully for Cardigan in that year's federal election. While a Member of the House of Commons, Binns served as the Parliamentary Secretary for the Minister of Fisheries and Oceans, and was a member of the Standing Committees of Fisheries and Forestry, Miscellaneous Estimates, Agriculture and Parliament. He was defeated in the federal election of 1988. Binns was re-elected provincially in the general elections of 1996 and 2000 for Murray River-Gaspereaux. In 1981 he ran for the leadership of the Conservatives upon the resignation of Premier John Angus MacLean*, but lost to James M. Lee*.

Binns returned to Island politics in 1996 when he ran for the leadership of the provincial Conservatives and was elected leader on 4 May. Following 10 years of Liberal rule, he became Premier when the Conservatives formed a government after the general election on 18 November 1996, winning 18 of 27 seats in the newly reformed Legislature. In the general election of 2000, the Conservatives received a second mandate from voters by winning 26 of the 27 seats in the Legislature.

Binns received his early education at St. Dominic Savio in his home town. Subsequently he attended Meridian School in Lloydminster, Saskatchewan, and the University of Alberta, where he earned a Bachelor of Arts and a Master of Arts in Community Development. In his early career, he worked as a development officer for the Government of Alberta.

In 1970 Binns came to the Island on a student exchange program. Binns worked for the Rural Development Council of Prince Edward Island in 1972 and 1974, and from 1974 to 1978 he worked for the provincial government. Binns established a sheep farm in Hopefield and was a coordinator for the Regional Services Centres in Montague and Souris. In 1978 he left his private career to enter the political arena. In 1988, when Binns returned to a private career after his time in federal politics, he took up bean farming, and formed the companies Island Bean Limited and Pat Binns Associates. Binns is a founder and has served as an organizer for the Northumberland Fisheries Festival. He was vice-president of the Northumberland Recreation Association. In 1978 Binns received the Jubilee Medal for Outstanding Public Service. Patrick and Carol Binns live on the family farm in Hopefield.

Carol Binns is the daughter of M. J. (Buster) and Claire MacMillan of Stratford.

References
CPG 1998–1999; *CWW* 2000 p. 116; *WWC* 2000 pp. 43–44; *Guardian* 31 March 1978, 17 November 1988.

BIRCH, JAMES EDWARD, merchant; b. 29 July 1849 in Port Hill, son of Thomas Birch and Agnes Ellis; m. 20 November 1901 Isabel Currie of Elmsdale, and there were no children; Anglican and Episcopalian; d. 6 December 1941 in Alberton.

Birch, a Conservative, was elected to the Legislative Assembly for 1st Prince in the 1897 general election. He was defeated in the general elections of 1893 and 1900.

After finishing his education in Port Hill, Birch moved to Alberton. In the partnership of Birch and Dyer he opened a general store in Alberton, which he operated for 40 years. He was secretary of the West Prince Board of Trade for three decades and participated in the Associated Board of Trades in the province for many years.

Birch devoted much time and energy to the temperance movement. A Son of Temperance and a lifelong abstainer, he was widely known for his efforts to curtail alcohol consumption. He was also a Forester and a Member of the Masonic Order. In 1935 he received a gold emblem in recognition of his long membership in the Masonic Lodge. An avid reader, Birch possessed an extensive library, which included volumes on history and the classics. James Birch died 6 December 1941.

Birch's father was born near Vale of Avoco in Ireland. His mother was born on the Island. Isabel Birch died 27 August 1950.

References
CPG 1897, 1899, 1901; *Herald* 27 November 1901; *Maple Leaf Magazine* January/February 1942; *Summerside Journal* 10 December 1941; PARO: MNI-Census 1881, 1891; St. James Anglican and Elmsdale Cemetery Transcripts.

BLAKE, PATRICK, merchant, butcher, and exporter; b. 8 March 1846 in Charlottetown, son of John Blake and Catherine Keoughan; m. first 20 February 1870 Annie Bell Inman, and they had four children, Ethel W., Frank, Florence, and one other daughter; m. secondly 15 April 1901 Emma Gertrude Quirk, and they had no children; d. 20 November 1909 in Charlottetown.

Blake, a Conservative, was first elected to the House of Assembly in the general election of 1882 for Charlottetown Royalty. He was re-elected in the general elections of 1886 and 1890. On 27 March 1890, Blake was appointed Speaker. In 1891 he resigned from the Assembly and was defeated in the House of Commons by-election in Queen's County held that year. In his early political career he was elected to the municipal council of Charlottetown in January 1880, and was re-elected for two years in 1881.

Blake attended the public schools in Charlottetown. At an early age, ca. 1856, he served as a librarian for the Catholic Young Men's Literary Institute in Charlottetown. In 1865 Blake and his brother Maurice joined their father in partnership in his successful butchering business. Later he became a senior partner in the firm Blake and Brothers Wholesale Merchants, exporters of cattle to Great Britain. Blake served as a judge at the Provincial Exhibition and as a director. Blake was a founding member of the Charlottetown Board of Trade and served as vice-president from 1893 to 1896. In 1901 he was a member of the Board of Trade's Council. In 1902 Blake left the Island to live in Sydney, Nova Scotia. There he established a provisioning firm, P. Blake and Company. When he left the province, the respectful send-off given him demonstrated that he was appreciated not only as a politician but as a valued citizen. Patrick Blake died 20 November 1909 in Charlottetown.

Blake's parents were born in Ireland. His father was from Tipperary County. Annie Blake, the daughter of William Inman of Desable, England, was born ca. 1845.

References
CPG 1889, 1891; *DCB XIII* pp. 86–87; Elections PEI; *Examiner* 16 April 1881 p. 3; *Islander* 4 March 1870 p. 5; PARO: MNI-Census, 1881, 1891; MNI-Hutchinson's p. 261; Charlottetown Roman Catholic Cemetery Records.

BLANCHARD, Q.C., J. ELMER, lawyer; b. 6 March 1927 in Charlottetown, son of J. Henri Blanchard and Ursule Gallant; m. 17 September 1955 Jean Aylward of Tignish, and they had four children, Yvette, Denyse, Adrienne, and Alfred; Roman Catholic; d. 20 September 1970 while tuna fishing off the coast of eastern Prince Edward Island.

Blanchard, a Liberal, was first elected to the Legislative Assembly in the general election of 1966 for 5th Queens. He was re-elected in the general election of 1970. He was defeated in the general election of 1962. On 28 July 1966, Blanchard was appointed Minister of Labour and Manpower Resources. He was appointed Minister of Justice and Attorney General in 1969, and died while in office.

Blanchard's grandfather, Jeremiah Blanchard*, also served in the Legislative Assembly, and was appointed a Minister without Portfolio. His father, Dr. J. Henri Blanchard, was a well-known Acadian historian and vice-principal and professor at Prince of Wales College.

Blanchard received his early education at the Model School and the Queen Square School. He then attended Prince of Wales College and St. Dunstan's University. Following university he studied law in the office of H. F. MacPhee. Blanchard was admitted to the Bar in 1953 and was named Queen's Counsel in 1966. He served in a variety of executive positions with the Prince Edward Island Law Society and the Canadian Bar Association. Blanchard served as president of the Charlottetown Junior Board of Trade and was Private Secretary to Lieutenant-Governor W. J. MacDonald. He was a member of the Charlottetown Club, the United Services Officers Club, the Knights of Columbus, and the Charlottetown Board of Trade. He also held the rank of Captain of the Supplementary Reserve Canadian Army. He died suddenly on 20 September 1970 while tuna fishing in waters off eastern Prince Edward Island, in the company of then-premier Alex Campbell* and Minister of Fisheries Bruce Stewart*.

Jean Blanchard was born on 26 November 1931 and is the daughter of Austin Aylward and Alma Donahue of Pleasant View. She resides in Charlottetown.

References
CPG 1964, 1970; *Guardian* 21 September 1970; Interviews: Alfred Blanchard, Jean Blanchard, and Yvette Blanchard.

BLANCHARD, JÉRÉMIE "JEREMIAH,"
farmer; b. 27 September 1859 in Rustico, son of Sylvestre Blanchard and Virginie Doucette; m. first 1 June 1880 Domitilde Gallant, and they had 11 children, J. Henri, Ignace, André, Félix, Pierre, Jérôme, Urbain, Angéline, Alvina, Emilie, and Domitilde; m. secondly 1921, Léonie (DesRoches) Gomeau of Miscouche, and they had seven children, Jerôme, Yvonne, Ernestine, Pius, Antoine, Ephrem, and Marie-Agnès; Roman Catholic; d. 17 March 1939.

Blanchard was first elected as a Conservative to the Legislative Assembly in the general election of 1893 for 1st Prince. He was re-elected in 1922, in a by-election, and was re-elected as a Liberal in the general elections of 1923 and 1927. Blanchard was defeated in the general election of 1890 and in a by-election in 1891. He was defeated in the general election of 1919 for 3rd Prince by Premier Aubin E. Arsenault. In 1890 Blanchard was defeated in the Legislative Council election for 1st Prince. Blanchard was appointed to Executive Council as a Minister without Portfolio in 1927 and again in 1930.

Blanchard received his education in the public schools of the Rustico area. Though primarily a farmer, he learned the trade of carpentry with his father. In 1882 he moved from Rustico to the Duvar Road in the western part of the Island. Jeremiah Blanchard died 17 March 1939.

Domitilde Blanchard, the daughter of Ignace Gallant and Domitilde Buote of Rustico, was born in 1855 and died 9 January 1918. J. Henri Blanchard's son, J. Elmer Blanchard*, also served in the Legislative Assembly.

References
CPG 1931; *Patriot* 17 March 1930; PARO: Marriage Register No. 13 1873–1887; St. Anthony's Church Cemetery Records.

BONNELL, M.D., JOHN CRANSTON,
physician and orthopaedic surgeon; b. 23 January 1929 in Hopefield, son of Henry (Harry) George Horace Bonnell and Charlotte Matilda MacEachern; m. 1957 Cathy Craig, and they had four children, Elizabeth, Mary, John, and Bill; Presbyterian; d. 31 May 1980 in Murray River.

Bonnell, a Liberal, was elected to the Legislative Assembly in a by-election held 4 December 1972 for 4th Kings. Bonnell served as a Member until the general election of 29 April 1974 was called. The by-election resulted from the vacancy caused by the resignation of Bonnell's brother Mark Lorne* after his appointment to the Senate. Their grandfather, Mark H. Bonnell*, was elected to the Legislative Assembly in 1922 for 4th Kings and served until 1923.

Bonnell received his primary education at West Kent School. He attended Prince of Wales College and later graduated from Dalhousie University in 1960 with a medical degree. Following his medical training he carried on a family practice in Bedeque and Montague. Later Bonnell completed post-graduate training in general surgery in St. John's and in Orthopaedic Surgery at the Royal Victoria Hospital and Shriners Hospital for Crippled Children in Montreal. On completion of post-graduate training in 1969, he returned to Charlottetown to practise medicine and specialized in the treatment of arthritis. Bonnell became the director of the Prince Edward Island Rehabilitation Centre. In August 1979 he moved to Okolona, Mississippi, where he practised medicine until April of 1980. At that time Bonnell suddenly became very ill and he returned to the province. John Bonnell died 31 May 1980 in Murray River.

Bonnell served as director of the Gencheff Camp for Crippled Children, the director of the Prince Edward Island Rehabilitation Council, as an advisor to the Prince Edward Island Division of the Canadian Rheumatoid and Arthritis Society, and as provincial surgeon for St. John Ambulance. He was a member of the Masons and the Shriners. Bonnell was honoured by Queen Elizabeth II during her Silver Jubilee, and the Governor General honoured him on several occasions for his work with St. John Ambulance.

Cathy Bonnell is the daughter of John Wilfred Craig and Isabel Martin of Middleton. She was born 6 May 1935 in Middleton, and resides in Ottawa.

References
CPG 1973, 1974, 1997; WWC 1999 p. 133; Guardian 18 April 1978, 2 June 1980, 2 August 1980.

BONNELL, CAPTAIN MARK H., ship's captain and farmer; b. ca. 7 June 1860 in Lamaline, Newfoundland, son of Robert Bonnell, Jr., and Ann Hillier; m. ca. 1882 Margaret McDonald, and they had four children, Jane C. (died at 18 months on 6 December 1889), Mary E., Clara A., and Henry "Harry"; Presbyterian; d. 22 March 1945 in Murray River.

Bonnell, a Liberal, was elected to the Legislative Assembly in a by-election held 30 August 1922 for 4th Kings. He was defeated in the general election of 1923.

Bonnell resided in Murray Harbour, and was a sea captain and a farmer. Mark Bonnell died 22 March 1945.

Margaret Bonnell was born 5 November 1860 and died 8 March 1929. Two of Harry Bonnell's children, Mark Lorne* and John Cranston*, served in the Legislative Assembly, with the former also serving as a Senator.

References
CPG 1923, 1924; Elections PEI; Patriot 23 March 1945, 21 April 1951; PARO: Bonnell Family File; MNI-Census 1891; Census 1901; Little Sands Cemetery Index.

BONNELL, M.D., (C.M.), LL.D., L.M.C.C., HONOURABLE MARK LORNE, physician; b. 4 January 1923 in Hopefield, son of Henry (Harry) George Horace Bonnell and Charlotte Matilda MacEachern; m. 6 July 1949 Ruby Jardine, and they had two children, Mark Lorne and Linda Florence; Presbyterian.

Bonnell, a Liberal, was first elected to the Legislative Assembly in the general election of 1951 for 4th Kings. He was re-elected in the general elections of 1955, 1959, 1962, 1966, and 1970. From 1955 to 1959, he served as Minister of Health. In 1965 he was appointed Liberal House Leader and acting Leader of the Prince Edward Island Liberal Party. In December 1965 Bonnell was a candidate for the leadership of the Liberal Party, won by Alexander B. Campbell*. He served as Minister of Welfare from 1966 to 1970, and Minister of Tourism Development from 1966 to 1971. Bonnell served as Minister Responsible for Housing from 1970 to 1971. On 15 November 1971, he was appointed to the Senate. Bonnell was a member of the Standing Senate Committee on Social Affairs, Science and Technology, and he chaired the Sub-Committee on Post-Secondary Education and served as deputy chair of the Sub-Committee on Veterans Affairs. Senator Bonnell opposed Bill C-22, the Drug Patent Act, as he was concerned that jobs would be lost and the cost of drugs would increase.

Bonnell's elevation to the Senate meant that a by-election was needed in 4th Kings. Held 4 December 1972, it was won by his brother, John Cranston*, also a Liberal. Their grandfather, Mark H. Bonnell*, was elected to the Legislative Assembly in 1922 for 4th Kings and served until 1923.

Bonnell was educated at Hopefield school beginning in 1929. In 1934 he attended West Kent School and from 1939 to 1943 Prince of Wales College. In 1949 Bonnell graduated from the medical school of Dalhousie University. He practises as a physician and surgeon in Murray River and Montague, and he was a member of the Medical Staff of Kings County Memorial Hospital in Montague. Bonnell was also a member of the Charlottetown Hospital Medical Staff and an Associate of the Queen Elizabeth Hospital. He was also president of Island Cablevision Limited.

Bonnell is a member of the Prince Edward Island Medical Society and the Canadian Medical Society. He is an honourary member of the Prince Edward Island Tourist Association and a Past Master of St. Andrew's Lodge No. 13, and Philae Temple Halifax. He is a past member of the Kings County Board of Trade. In May 2001 Bonnell received an Honourary Doctorate of Laws from the University of Prince Edward Island. Mark Lorne Bonnell is a resident of Murray River.

Ruby Bonnell, the daughter of John Jardine of Charlottetown and Freetown, died 17 December 1979.

References
CPG 1997; *CWW* 2000 p. 137; *WWPEI* p. 18; *Capital List* p. 56; *Guardian* 17 August 1987, 14 May 2001.

BOWLEN, PATRICK DENNIS, farm equipment salesperson, rancher, and oil company president; b. 24 May 1879 in Cardigan, son of Michael Bowlen and Marie Casey; m. Olive Kemper, and they had four children, Evelyn, Betty, Paul, and William Michael; Roman Catholic; d. 21 September 1946 in Toronto.

Bowlen, a Liberal, was elected to the Legislative Assembly in the general election of 1904 for 3rd Kings. Bowlen served on the Board of Hospital Commissioners for the province. His brother, John James, was a Member of the Legislative Assembly of Alberta, Leader of the Alberta Liberal Party, and Lieutenant-Governor of Alberta.

Bowlen received his early education at Glennfanning and Cardigan, later attending Prince of Wales College and Commercial Business College in Charlottetown. He began a successful career in business and agriculture, working as an assistant manager for an agricultural implements firm around 1908. Following his brief political career, Bowlen moved to Alberta where he was owner of the 30,000-acre "Bar C" ranch near Marley. He was one of Canada's largest horse dealers and provided a significant number of the horses used on the Western Front during the First World War. In 1918 the *Patriot* published an article recognizing his success in Alberta. Around 1926 Bowlen sold the ranch and organized an oil company, eventually known as the Texas-Canadian Oil Company, which he headed until about 1944. His brother John was also a successful rancher in Alberta. At the time of Patrick Bowlen's death on 21 September 1946, John had recently purchased a 2,217-acre ranch in the Carseland-Blackie district.

William Michael Bowlen was killed in 1945 during the Second World War while fighting with the Royal Canadian Air Force.

References
Canada: Veterans Affairs; *CPG* 1908; *Globe and Mail* 23 September 1946; *Island Patriot* 31 December 1918; *Summerside Journal* 26 September 1946.

BRADLEY, WALTER, teacher and school principal; b. 29 September 1945 in St. Theresa's, son of Chester Bradley and Florence Kelly; m. 27 July 1968 Janet MacLeod, and they had eight children, Jocelyn, Darrell, Amy, Matthew, Lana, Monica, Stacy, and Carl; Roman Catholic.

Bradley, a Liberal, was first elected to the Legislative Assembly in the general election of 1989 for 2nd Kings. He was re-elected in the general election of 1993. Bradley was defeated in the general election of 1996 for Morell-Fortune Bay. On 15 April 1993 Bradley was appointed Minister of Agriculture, Fisheries and Forestry. He served as chair of the Canadian Council of Forestry Ministers. While a Member of the Legislative Assembly, The Links at Crowbush Cove golf course was constructed at Lakeside in his riding. Other major government initiatives that occurred in his riding during his tenure were improvements in the park in St. Peters, the addition of an extension to the Legion in Morell, and the relocation of the Provincial Library Headquarters to Morell. While he was Minister of Agriculture, Fisheries and Forestry, the Department of Agriculture administered the compensation process for losses incurred to potato farmers due to the PVY-n virus.

Bradley received his primary education at St. Teresa's School, and later attended St. Dunstan's High School and St. Dunstan's University. He graduated from the University of Prince Edward Island with a Bachelor of Education degree. In 1985 he graduated from Dalhousie University with a Master of Education. Bradley began teaching in the late 1960s, eventually becoming vice-principal and later principal of Morell Regional High School. Bradley served as chair of the Morell Village Commission. He was a member of the Morell Legion and the Morell and Area Recreation Committee. He was a president of the Prince Edward Island Baseball Association and was an accomplished athlete who excelled in baseball and track and field.

Walter Bradley lives in Morell with his wife Janet and their family.

References
CPG 1996, 1997; *Guardian* 14 April 1989, 10 March 1992, 8 March 1996, 8 November 1996; *Patriot* 7 March 1994.

BRECKEN, Q.C., FREDERICK DE ST. CROIX, lawyer, public servant, and business person; b. 9 December 1828 in Charlottetown, son of the Honourable John Brecken and Margaret Leith de St. Croix; m. 28 September 1858 Helen Leith Boyd Emslie of Kingston, Ontario, and they had five children, Fred K., Arthur, Leith, Helen Amelia, and Fanny Constance (died in infancy); Anglican; d. 14 October 1903 in Charlottetown.

Brecken, a Conservative, was first elected to the House of Assembly in the general election of 1863 for the district of Charlottetown Royalty. He was re-elected in the general elections of 1867, 1870, 1872, and 1873, and in a by-election held in September 1873. He was defeated in the general election of 1876. He served as Attorney-General and Advocate General from April 1859 to January 1863. He again served as Attorney-General from September 1870 to April 1872 and from April 1873 to August 1876.

When the Island joined Confederation in 1873, a special federal election was held to determine Members of Parliament for the new province. Brecken was unsuccessful as a candidate for Kings County. However, in the 1878 federal election, he was elected to the House of Commons for the district of Queen's County. Although Brecken was initially declared elected in the general election of 1882, his opponent, John T. Jenkins*, was declared elected following an official recount. Brecken subsequently won the seat due to a decision of the provincial Supreme Court in February 1883. Brecken resigned his seat in 1884 to accept an appointment as Postmaster and Assistant Inspector for Prince Edward Island.

Brecken came from a family with a long political history. His father, John Brecken, served as a Member of the House of Assembly from 1830 to 1834, and as a member of Executive Council and Legislative Council from 1834 until his death. Brecken's grandfather, Ralph Brecken, served as a Member and as the Speaker of the House of Assembly. Col. Joseph Robinson, Brecken's great-grandfather, an Assistant Judge of the province, was Speaker of the House of Assembly in 1790.

For most of his life Brecken lived in Charlottetown, although he did reside for a time in London, England, and Ottawa. He was educated at Central Academy in Charlottetown. Brecken studied law with Sir Robert Hodgson before attending Lincoln's Inn and the Inner Temple in London. He was called to the Bar in 1852. Until 1874 he was a partner with the firm Haviland* and Brecken, and later a partner with the firm Brecken and Fitzgerald. In 1884 Brecken became the postmaster of Charlottetown and provincial post-office inspector, serving in this position until his death. He was also a director of the Charlottetown Gas Company.

Throughout his life Brecken attended the Anglican Church, and became a member of the Executive Committee of the Diocesan Church Society. Additionally, he was a Trustee and Governor of Prince of Wales College, and served as a Trustee of the Lunatic Asylum. Frederick Brecken died 14 October 1903.

Brecken was married in Saint John, New Brunswick. Helen Brecken, the daughter of Captain Emslie of Her Majesty's 83rd Regiment, was born in 1839 and died 3 October 1906.

References
CDP pp. 70–71; *CPG* 1876, 1879; *DCB XIII*, p. 110; *Daily Patriot* 3 October 1906; *Islander* 4 November 1859; PARO: Brecken Family File; MNI Commission Book #2558-5 p. 97; MNI-Census 1881; MNI-Charlottetown Manuscript p. 14; MNI-Hutchinson's pp. 83, 259, 260.

BRODIE, PETER, farmer and auctioneer; b. 9 March 1857 in Stanhope, son of George Brodie and Louisa Ann Rielly; m. first ca. 24 December 1897, Janie Ann Court of Donaldston, and there were no children; m. secondly Nina Bernard of North Rustico, and there were no children; Presbyterian; d. 3 June 1945.

Brodie, first a Liberal and later an Independent, was elected in the general election of 1919 for 3rd Queens. He was defeated in the general election of 1923 as an Independent candidate.

Brodie received his early education at the local school in Stanhope. Later in life he moved to York where he farmed and was an auctioneer. He was a member of the Farmers Institute and Stock Breeders Association, as well as president of the Swine Breeders Association of Prince Edward Island. Brodie was also a director of the Farmers Cooperative Association and a director of the Egg Circle of Prince Edward Island. He was awarded a long service medal in Number 6 Company of the Prince Edward Island Volunteers, which was trained for service in the North West Rebellion. Peter Brodie died 3 June 1945.

Janie Brodie was born ca. 1875 and died in 1898 at the age of 24. Nina Brodie was born 14 July 1869 and died 5 July 1953.

References
CPG 1921, 1924; *Patriot* 4 June 1945; PARO: Marriage License Book #16, 1882–1923 pp. 80, 92; Donaldston United Church Cemetery Records; York United Church Cemetery Transcripts.

BROWN, BETTY JEAN, registered nurse; b. 31 October 1937 in Charlottetown, daughter of Gordon and Dorothy Roberts; m. 9 September 1960 Murdo M. Brown, and they had two sons, Bruce McQueen and Stephen Andrew; United.

Brown, a Liberal, was first elected to the Legislative Assembly in the general election of 1986 for 3rd Queens. She was re-elected in the general election of 1989. Brown was defeated in the general elections of 1982 and 1993. On 2 May 1986, Brown was appointed Minister of Education in the Joseph A. Ghiz* Administration and served in that Ministry until 1989 when she was appointed Liberal caucus chair.

Brown was elected to the Southport Village Commission in 1973 and served as the chair in 1976. In 1977 she was elected to the executive of the Prince Edward Island Federation of Municipalities and became its first female president in 1979. She served on the executive of the Canadian Federation of Municipalities from 1979 to 1980.

Brown received her early education at the Southport School. She then attended Prince of Wales College in Charlottetown and the Prince Edward Island Hospital School of Nursing. Brown was a trustee of the Southport School Board, a member of the Bunbury-Southport Planning Board, and a director of the Community Improvement Committee. She was a member and secretary-treasurer of the Prince Edward Island Fur Breeders Association. Brown was a member of the Southport Women's Institute and the Prince Edward Island Women's Institute. She helped operate the family fur farm in Southport and worked as a nurse part-time at the Garden of the Gulf Nursing Home. Betty Jean Brown and her husband reside in Stratford.

Murdo Brown is the son of William and Norma Brown.

References
Atlantic Guidebook p. 31; *CPG* 1993; *History of Southport* p. 55; *WWPEI* p. 20; *Common Ground*, September/October 1982.

BRUCE, ALEXANDER FRASER, farmer and wholesale merchant; b. 10 May 1857 in Heatherdale, son of John Bruce and Anne Finlayson; m. 24 December 1884 Mary Isabella MacKinnon of Uigg, and they had seven children, Callum, John Callum*, Willard, Fraser, Barbara, Catherine, and Munro; Presbyterian/United; d. 28 November 1927 in Valleyfield.

Bruce, a Liberal, was declared elected to the Legislative Assembly by two votes in the general election of 1900 for 4th Kings. He was sworn in and served in the Legislature during the 1901 session. Eventually a recount and a judicial appeal of the 4th Kings election resulted in Murdoch McKinnon* being declared elected. McKinnon took his seat in the Legislative Assembly in May 1902.

Born in Heatherdale, Bruce was a farmer in Valleyfield on the Douse Road. Later he operated a wholesale business in Montague. As a result of his success in business, he retired to enjoy travelling, studying, and working on his Montague property. Alexander Bruce died 28 November 1927.

Mary Bruce, the daughter of William MacKinnon, was born 2 January 1854 and predeceased her husband. John Callum Bruce* served in the Legislature for 4th Queens from 1928 until his death in 1933.

References
CPG 1901 p. 362; Elections PEI; *Meacham's Atlas*; *PEI Journal of the Legislative Assembly* 1901 pp. 3, 89, 1902 pp. 6–7, 9, 17–18, 89; *Examiner* 29 December 1884; *Patriot* 29 November 1927; PARO: Marriage License Book RG 19 series 3 subseries 1 volume 5; MNI-Census 1891; Census 1901; Montague United Church Records.

BRUCE, JOHN CALLUM, farmer and fox breeder; b. 25 November 1885 in Valleyfield, son of Alexander Fraser Bruce* and Bella MacKinnon; m. first Christie A. MacDonald; m. secondly 5 March 1924 Effie McLeod; Bruce's one child, Isabel, was likely the daughter of his first wife; United; d. 26 May 1933 in Charlottetown.

Bruce, a Liberal, was first elected to the Legislative Assembly in a by-election held 16 August 1928 for 4th Queens. He was re-elected in the general election of 1931, and died while serving as a Member of the Legislative Assembly.

Bruce's father served in the Legislature during the 1901 session. Eventually a recount and a judicial appeal of the 4th Kings election resulted in Murdoch McKinnon* being declared elected. Donald A. MacKinnon*, Bruce's uncle, was Lieutenant-Governor from 1904 to 1910.

Bruce received his early education at Valleyfield School, and later attended Nova Scotia Agricultural College. He was a farmer and fox breeder and resided in Vernon River. John Bruce died 26 May 1933. His body was discovered floating by the dock at the foot of Queen Street. The death was ruled by a coroner's jury to be an accidental drowning.

Christie Bruce was born in 1885 and died in 1922. Effie Bruce, the daughter of John F. McLeod, was born in 1885 and died in 1971. Isabel Bruce died several years before her father, as a result of an accident. Isabel and three friends, who also died, were travelling in a car that collided with a train on Mount Edward Road, near Charlottetown.

References
CPG 1931, 1932; *Maple Leaf Magazine* June/July 1933; *Patriot* 26 May 1933 p. 1; PARO: Vernon River Memorial Cemetery Transcripts.

BRUCE, STANLEY, farmer and teacher; b. 29 March 1937 in Heatherdale, son of John Bruce and Margaret Belle MacPhee of Heatherdale; m. 30 June 1967 Anne Louise Thorbourne, and there were no children; Protestant.

Bruce, a Liberal, was first elected to the Legislative Assembly in a by-election held 26 November 1984 for 4th Kings. He was re-elected in the general elections of 1986, 1989, and 1993. He was defeated in the general election of 1982. While in Opposition, Bruce served as forestry critic. In 1986 he was appointed Chair of the Standing Committee on Energy and Forestry. He was a member of the Standing Committees on Agriculture; Energy and Forestry; Education, Community Affairs and Justice; Fisheries, Industry and Tourism; and Labour and Agriculture; and the Special Standing Committee on Maritime Economic Integration.

Bruce has resided in Heatherdale throughout his life. He was educated at the public school in Heatherdale and Montague High School from 1943 to 1956, following which he attended Prince of Wales College during the summers of 1957, 1958, and 1959, where he obtained a teaching certificate. An educator for 11 years, he taught in Montague area schools. He was also a director of the Federal Dairy Company and operated a small mixed farm prior to his election to office in 1984. In addition to his involvement in provincial politics, Bruce served as a member of the Valleyfield Community Council. Bruce is a celebrant of his Scottish heritage and enjoys playing traditional Highland music.

Anne Bruce is the daughter of Bruce and Marianna Thorbourne of Liverpool, Nova Scotia.

References
CPG 1982–83, 1986, 1996; Elections PEI; *WWPEI* p. 20; *Guardian* 17 March 1993.

BUCHANAN, M.A., ALAN GILMORE, university lecturer, government policy advisor, corporate development manager, and director of government relations; b. 28 October 1952 in Belfast, son of Samuel Buchanan and Mae Gilmore; m. 1 September 1978 Deborah Ann Watts of Grand Tracadie, and they have four children, Sam, Alison, Hannah, and Colin; Presbyterian.

Buchanan, a Liberal, was first elected to the Legislative Assembly in the general election of 1989 for 4th Queens. He was re-elected in the general election of 1993. On 15 April of that year, he was appointed Minister of Health and Social Services and on 9 June 1994 became Minister of Provincial Affairs and Attorney-General. Buchanan was a member of the Municipal Management Board. As Minister of Health and Social Services, he guided the health reform law through the Legislature. The bill restructured the health care system and provoked some protest from the health care unions' membership. Buchanan served on the Cabinet Committee on Rural Development, as well as a number of other legislative and standing committees. On 21 May 1996 he resigned from Cabinet and the Legislative Assembly.

Buchanan graduated from the University of Prince Edward Island with a Bachelor of Arts and from Queen's University with a Master of Arts. He was a lecturer in political studies and Canadian Studies at the University of Prince Edward Island and a senior economic policy advisor with the provincial government. In 1996, following his political career, he accepted the position of corporate development manager with Island Telephone, and currently works as director of government relations for Aliant Incorporated, Island Telephone's parent company.

Buchanan contributed to the establishment of the advisory board of the Institute of Island Studies. He was a member of the Board of Theatre Prince Edward Island, a president of the Belfast Historical Society, and a director of the Belfast Pipe and Drum Band Incorporated. Buchanan was a member of the Unit Four school board and the publications committee of the Prince Edward Island Museum and Heritage Foundation. In April 1997 Buchanan was appointed to the Law Commission of Canada. He has published articles in the journal *Canadian Ethnic Studies,* and contributed text on the Prince Edward Island Development Plan to the social studies textbook *Maritimes: Tradition, Challenge and Change.*

Alan Buchanan and his family reside in Belfast.

References
CPG 1996; *Maritimes: Tradition, Challenge and Change,* pp. 169-171; *Guardian* 18 March 1993, 18 May 1996, 23 May 1996, 17 August 1996: appointment announcement, Island Telephone, 25 April 1997 p. A4, 6 June 2001 p. C2.

BUNTAIN, JOHN HOWARD, teacher, farmer, stock raiser, fox breeder, and telephone company manager; b. 14 November 1866 in Rustico, son of John Buntain and Amelia MacNeill; m. 15 June 1904 Alberta E. Coles, and they had four children, Victor Charles, Helen Amelia, John Howard, and Doris Constance; Presbyterian; d. 1952.

Buntain, a Conservative, was first elected to the Legislative Assembly in the general election of 1912 for 2nd Queens. He was re-elected in the general election of 1923. He was defeated in the general elections of 1915 and 1927.

Buntain attended the public schools in the Rustico area, later attending Prince of Wales College. Throughout his life, he lived in the Rustico-Wheatley River area. In 1891, at age 25, he was living with his parents and in 1901 was still residing with his father. Early in his adult life, certainly in 1891, Buntain taught school. By 1901, he was operating a farm. He served as president of Oyster Bed Bridge Black Fox Limited as well as manager of Rustico Rural Telephone Company Ltd. John Buntain died in 1952.

Buntain's father was born in Scotland, where his ancestors took an active part in political affairs. Alberta Buntain, the daughter of Charles Coles of Milton, was born in 1880 and died 22 July 1945.

References
CPG 1916, 1926, 1928; PARO: Buntain Family File; MNI-Census 1891; Census 1901; St. Mark's Anglican Church Cemetery Records.

BURGE, RICHARD LOUIS, farmer, potato and fertilizer dealer, and manager of potato marketing commission; b. 13 June 1898 in Five Houses, son of Michael Burge and Catherine Flynn; m. 2 March 1924 Theresa Whitty, and they had 7 children: Dr. Francis "Frank," Alban, Dr. Irene, Claire, Bernadette, Marie, and Michael; a niece, Noreen Whitman, became a member of the family in 1947 when her mother died; Roman Catholic; d. 26 June 1990 in Souris.

Burge, a Conservative, was elected to the Legislative Assembly in the general election of 1947 for 2nd Kings, He was defeated in the general elections of 1935, 1939, 1943, and 1951.

"Lou" or "R. L." Burge resided in Five Houses, east of St. Peters Bay, and was educated locally. Burge was interested in furthering his education, but was needed on the family farm as all his brothers had left the area. As a result, Burge read widely in an effort to educate himself while farming. He bred Holstein cattle and was a dairy producer. Later Burge became a potato and fertilizer dealer, under the name of R. L. Burge Produce. Burge was president of the Canadian Horticultural Council and a founding board member of the Prince Edward Island Elite Seed Farm. He also served as the general manager and chairman of the board of the Prince Edward Island Potato Marketing Board. In 1992, he was given, posthumously, an award honouring his dedication to the agriculture industry in the province. R. L. Burge died 26 June 1990 at Colville Manor in Souris.

Theresa Burge was born on 2 February 1900 and was the daughter of Peter Whitty and Mary Anne Power of Charlottetown. She died on 7 January 1964.

References
CPG 1938, 1941, 1947, 1948, 1952; *Guardian* 27 June 1990, 28 June 1990, August 1990; PARO: Burge History - Burge, Irene.

BUTLER, WALLACE BRUCE, farmer; b. ca. 3 August 1883 in Peters Road, son of William Butler and Mary Honor Jenkins; m. 20 July 1902 Thelda Blanche Poole, and they had four children, May, Olia, Howard, and Ethel; Presbyterian; d. 2 September 1952.

Butler, a Liberal, was first elected to the Legislative Assembly in the general election of 1919 for 4th Kings. He was re-elected in the general elections of 1923 and 1927.

Butler was educated at the Alma School. He resided in Murray Harbour where he worked as a farmer, and was a member of the Freemasons. Wallace Butler died 2 September 1952.

Thelda Butler, the daughter of James F. Poole of Roseneath, was born 25 June 1882 and died 27 April 1961.

References
CPG 1921, 1928; PARO: Census 1901; Murray Harbour North Cemetery Records.

C

CALHOUN, JOHN R., merchant; b. in New Brunswick.

Calhoun, a Liberal, was elected to the House of Assembly in the 1876 general election for 4th Prince. He served on several committees, including the Public Accounts Committee. Calhoun chaired the Special Committee to Report Standing Rules and Orders for the governance of the House of Assembly. In 1877 he presented a petition to the House on behalf of the citizens of Summerside, which stated that the Act for the Better Government of Towns and Villages was inadequate. The petition further requested an Act of Incorporation for Summerside to enable the residents to govern the town in an efficient manner. Calhoun's support of the petition was derived, in part, from his having been a member of the first town board of Summerside in 1875, a position which he held for two years.

Born in New Brunswick, Calhoun spent a significant part of his adult life in Summerside. In 1871 he was listed as an employee of J. L. Holman. At the same time, he operated a general store and sold lumber and flour. In 1878 he carried out business on the shore-front at Queen's wharf in Summerside. An 1878 Summerside map locates a sawmill and warehouse on the east end of the waterfront belonging to him. In the 1880–1881 Teare Directory of Prince Edward Island he was listed as a lumber merchant located on Eustance Street. It is known that John Montague Clarke* worked for Calhoun in Summerside.

References
CPG 1879; *Meacham's Atlas, Roads to Summerside* pp. 69, 88; PEI *Journal of the House of Assembly* 1877; *Examiner* 19 April 1875; PARO: RG 19 series 3 subseries 1 volume 4 1871–1881 License Cash Books; *Lovell's PEI Directory* 1871; *McAlpine PEI Directory* 1870–71 p. 1362; *MNI-Mercantile Agency Reference Book* 1876; *MNI-Teare Directory of PEI* 1880–81.

CALLBECK, LL.D., HONOURABLE CATHERINE SOPHIA, businessperson; b. 25 July 1939 in Central Bedeque, daughter of Ralph R.

Callbeck and Ruth Campbell; United.

Callbeck, a Liberal, was first elected to the Legislative Assembly in the general election of 1974 for 4th Prince. She was re-elected in the general election of 1993 for 1st Queens. She served as Minister of Health and Social Services and Minister Responsible for the Disabled from 1974 to 1978. In the federal election of 1988, Callbeck was elected to the House of Commons as the representative for Malpeque and remained there until 1993 when she resigned her seat to seek the leadership of the Prince Edward Island Liberal Party. While in Ottawa she served as the Official Opposition critic for consumer and corporate affairs, energy, mines and resources, and financial institutions, and as the associate critic for privatization and regulatory affairs. Callbeck was the vice-chair of the Caucus Committee on Sustainable Development. In 1993 she returned to the provincial scene, becoming Liberal leader on 23 January 1993 upon the resignation of Premier Joseph Ghiz*. She was sworn in as Premier and President of Executive Council on 25 January 1993. In that year's general election, Callbeck led the Liberals to victory, winning 31 of 32 seats. She became Canada's first elected female premier.

Following the 1993 general election, despite winning a large majority, Callbeck faced a difficult task. The provincial debt was high and the country was in the midst of a recession. Furthermore, federal transfer payments had declined and the interest on the provincial debt was inhibiting government initiatives.

Callbeck felt strongly that the province's financial house needed to be returned to good order. In 1993 she began a program of government reform. Government departments, crown corporations, and agencies were consolidated. The provincial health care and education systems were rationalized. Beyond these initiatives, Callbeck believed that the deficit problem had to be addressed. The Callbeck Administration legislated a 7.5 per cent wage rollback for provincial public sector employees. Over 12,000 public sector employees were affected. The rollback saved $24.6 million, but it also required breaking several collective agreements.

As historian Dr. Edward MacDonald states in his book, *If You're Stronghearted*, "The 7.5% Solution proved to be a fiscal success but a political disaster." Public servants were angry with the government and were vocal in their criticism. The Callbeck Administration's attempts to rationalize the health care system further alienated the populace. During her time as premier, the government also undertook a far-reaching reform of the provincial electoral system. The 16 dual-member ridings were abolished in favour of 27 new single-member constituencies. These changes in the electoral map were implemented in the 1996 general election. She resigned as premier in August 1996. In the general election held in November 1996, the Liberals suffered defeat under the leadership of Keith Milligan*.

On 23 September 1997, Callbeck was appointed to the Senate by Prime Minister Jean Chrétien. She served as a Member of the Senate Standing Committee on Banking, Trade and Commerce, and is presently a member of the Social Affairs, Science and Technology Committee, and the Transportation and Communications Committee.

Premier Callbeck was a trailblazer for women in politics, provincially and nationally. At the time of her 1974 election, she became the second woman to be elected to the provincial Legislature, and was the youngest woman to be appointed a provincial Cabinet minister and only the second woman to be appointed to the provincial Cabinet.

Callbeck received her early education at the Central Bedeque School and then attended Summerside High School. Subsequently she studied at Mount Allison University in Sackville, New Brunswick, and earned a Bachelor of Commerce in 1960. In 1963 Callbeck earned a Bachelor of Education from Dalhousie University and then went on to complete post-graduate courses in business administration at Syracuse University. She was the recipient of an honourary Doctorate of Laws from Mount Allison University in 1996.

In her early career Callbeck was a business teacher in both New Brunswick and Ontario. She moved back to the Island to work in the family retail business, Callbeck's Limited, and continues to play a large role in the business today. Callbeck was chair of the board at the Confederation Centre of the Arts and was a member of the board of regents at Mount Allison University and the board of governors at the University of Prince Edward Island. She was also a member of the Maritime Provinces Higher Education Commission and of the board of the Institute for Research in Public Policy. Senator Callbeck was named a director of the Mutual Fund Dealers Association in 1998.

Callbeck has served as a director of the Prince Edward Island United Way Fund and the Canadian Heart and Stroke Foundation, and has been a member of the board of the Prince County Hospital and of the Red Cross Sustaining Membership Program. She has co-chaired Meals-on-Wheels and chaired the Bedeque Area Centennial Days. Callbeck was a member of the Provincial Committee for the International Year of the Disabled and was a director of the Atlantic Canada Institute. She has also been a board member and elder at the Bedeque United Church. Catherine Callbeck lives in the family home in Central Bedeque.

References
CPG 1998-1999; MacDonald *If You're Stronghearted* pp. 363-65, 369, 372, 374; *WWPEI* p. 21; *Guardian* 24 October 1986, 30 March 1993, 29 August 2002; *Journal-Pioneer* 7 February 1975, 7 August 1996.

CALLBECK, HENRY JOHN, merchant, agent, justice of the peace, shipbuilder, and sheriff; b. 25 February 1818 in Tryon, son of Philip M. Callbeck and Ann (Nancy) Warren; m. 15 August 1843 Charlotte Amelia Robinson of Charlottetown, and they had nine children, Ann, Eleanor, Selina, Myra, Charlotte, Thomas, Philip, John, and Matilda; Methodist; d. 29 January 1898 in Charlottetown.

Callbeck, a Liberal, was first elected to the House of Assembly in the general election of 1867 for 2nd Queens. He was re-elected in the general elections of 1870, 1872, and 1873. He served on Executive Council from 1867 to 1870.

Callbeck spent the early years of his life in Tryon, remaining on the family farm until 1838. He was educated at the local school. After leaving home, he and his brother became coastal traders on a schooner. In 1840 he opened a general store in Tryon and operated it for 11 years. During the same period, he was a shipbuilder, producing several vessels for the Newfoundland and English markets. While on a business voyage to Liverpool, England, in 1844, he was shipwrecked and barely escaped death, spending 12 hours in the cold water during a violent storm. Compounding the physical damage he suffered, Callbeck lost $3,000 in uninsured cargo. He moved to Charlottetown in 1851, where he opened a store and conducted a general retail business. During his last 30 years of business operations, Callbeck dealt largely in the purchase and sale of wool sheared on Prince Edward Island. He also acted as agent for Tryon Woolen Factory, later Stanfield and Lord Woolen

Mills, which eventually became the Stanfield Mill in Truro.

In addition to a busy mercantile and political career, Callbeck served as a Justice of the Peace and High Sheriff for Queens County in 1881 and 1882. He also was a governor of Prince of Wales College, director of the Merchant's Bank of Prince Edward Island, president of the Mutual Fire Insurance Company for nine years, and city treasurer of Charlottetown from 1856 to 1867. His benevolent activities included being a trustee of the Lunatic Asylum and the Poor House, membership in the Charlottetown Fire Department for eight years, and serving as a member of the Methodist Board of Management. Henry Callbeck died 29 January 1898.

Charlotte Callbeck, daughter of Thomas Robinson and Eleanor McConnell, was born 11 December 1815 and died 27 September 1875. Henry John Callbeck was a brother of former Premier Catherine Callbeck's* great-great-grandfather.

References
Callbeck p. 54; *CPG* 1874; Elections PEI; *Patriot* 31 January 1898; PARO: RG 19 Marriage Bond, Accession # 2810, St. Paul's Anglican Church Record; MNI-Mercantile Agency Reference Book 1876; MNI-Hutchinson's; MNI-Census 1861; Sherwood Cemetery Records.

CAMERON, DONALD, farmer, postmaster, and court commissioner; b. ca. 1836, in Springton, son of John Cameron and Mary Stuart; Methodist; d. ca. 1882.

Cameron, a Conservative, was first elected to the House of Assembly in the general election of 1867 for 1st Queens. He was re-elected in 1871 and in the general election of 1879. He was defeated in the general election of 1873, a by-election held in September of 1873, and in the general election of 1882. He participated in the debate over the prohibition of alcohol and supported the temperance movement.

Educated in Springton, Cameron remained there throughout his life. He was primarily a farmer, but also served as postmaster for Township 67 and Commissioner for Taking Affidavits in Supreme Court.

Cameron's father emigrated from Invernesshire, Scotland, and was a descendant of the Camerons of Lochiel. His mother was a descendant of the Stuarts, the Royal Family of Great Britain. Cameron lived with his mother and sister. Donald Cameron died ca. 1882.

References
CPG 1880, 1881, 1885; Elections PEI; PARO: MNI-Census 1891.

CAMPBELL, P.C., Q.C., LL.D., HONOURABLE ALEXANDER BRADSHAW, b. 1 December 1933 in Summerside, son of Thane Alexander Campbell* and Cecilia Lillian Bradshaw; m. 19 August 1961 Marilyn Ruth Gilmour, and they had three children, Blair Alexander, Heather Kathryn, and Graham Melville; United.

Campbell, a Liberal, was first elected to the Legislative Assembly in a by-election held 9 February 1965 for 5th Prince. He was re-elected in the general elections of 1966, 1970, 1974, and 1978. He was elected party leader in December 1965 and became Leader of the Opposition in 1966. On 28 July 1966, at the age of 32, Campbell became premier. He served as Attorney-General from that date until 1969. He became a member of the Privy Council on 5 July 1967. From 1969 to 1972, he was Minister of Development and, from 6 September 1972 to 2 May 1974, served as Minister of Agriculture and Forestry. Campbell held the positions of Minister of Justice and Attorney and Advocate General from 2 May 1974 to September 1978. He added the Ministry of Cultural Affairs on 1 July 1976. He led the Liberals to four consecutive victories in general elections, the only premier to accomplish this feat. Campbell resigned in September 1978, five months after leading the Liberals to a narrow victory in that year's general election.

Campbell's father represented 1st Prince from 1931 to 1943, and served as premier from 1936 to 1943.

"Alex" Campbell's premiership is inextricably linked with the Comprehensive Development Plan. He recognized the need for federal support if the province was to survive as a viable economic entity. Campbell believed in the necessity of change and the value of new ideas. To address the need for economic growth, the Development Plan was conceived. Due to the unprecedented financial support from Ottawa, the Campbell government set the province on a path of economic development and social and cultural change never before seen in the province.

The effects of the Comprehensive Development Plan cannot be diminished. A greatly increased provincial civil service was created, and it rose in numbers from 1,435 in 1966 to 2,658 in 1974. The population of the urban areas greatly increased and was paralleled by an increase in the rural non-farm population. Holland College and the University of Prince Edward Island were created, the public education system was restructured from 370 local school boards to five consolidated school boards, and many new educational facilities were built or were improved significantly. The agriculture industry was radically changed, first as a result of education programs for agriculture producers, and subsequently by encouraging producers to organize producer-owned marketing agencies. The Campbell Administration created the Land Development Corporation and the Prince Edward Island Lending Authority to ensure that farmers would continue to have affordable access to land, given the finite nature of the resource in the province. Industrial development was also a major emphasis of the Plan. To this end, industrial parks were constructed in West Royalty and Summerside, and efforts were made to attract manufacturing companies to the province. Economic development grants to local entrepreneurs were also a focus of the government. The Plan had many other effects as well, such as improvements to the provincial health and welfare system and to the tourism industry.

Though the Plan accelerated the decline of rural institutions, Campbell sought to offset the social upheaval it created. He instituted the Family Farm Capital Grants Program to slow the decrease in the number of family farms. He made efforts to ensure that Islanders continued to maintain control of their land base by implementing legislation restricting non-resident land ownership. During Campbell's term as premier, the Prince Edward Island Heritage Foundation was created. The Institute of Man and Resources was created with the mandate to explore alternative energy sources.

In retrospect, the Plan certainly did not improve the economy to the degree to which it was intended. Upon his resignation, Campbell lamented the degree to which the province continued to depend on the federal government. Nonetheless, Islanders enjoy the benefits of, for example, a well-trained professional civil service, greatly improved educational facilities, and a better-organized agriculture industry. The Campbell government entrenched these institutions into Island society.

Alex Campbell graduated from Summerside High School in 1951, following which he attended Dalhousie University, graduating in 1959 with a Bachelor of Arts and with a Bachelor of Law. Later that year he was called to the provincial Bar. Campbell practised law in Summerside from 1959

until he took up politics full-time. He was awarded the designation of Queen's Counsel in 1966. In 1978 Campbell resigned as premier and was later appointed to the Supreme Court. He retired from the Court in 1994.

Campbell was involved in a number of community activities. In 1952 he was the skip of the Prince Edward Island Schoolboy curling champions. Following university he was a secretary of the Summerside Board of Trade. Campbell was a member of the Summerside Y's Men's Club and served as president of the YMCA from 1980 to 1991. He was an elder at Trinity United Church in Summerside. In 1982 Campbell was appointed Prince Edward Island coordinator of the Governor General's Canadian Study Conference held in 1983. He was the Prince Edward Island chairman of the Duke of Edinburgh Awards from 1984 to 1990. Campbell served as chairman of the Institute of Man and Resources and as a board member of the Prince Edward Island Museum and Heritage Foundation. From 1983 to 1990, he chaired the Summerside and Area Historical Society. In 1976 he was awarded a Doctor of Laws degree from McGill and in 1979 a Doctor of Laws degree from the University of Prince Edward Island. Alex Campbell and his wife reside in Stanley Bridge.

Marilyn Ruth Campbell is the daughter of Melville A. Gilmour of Guelph, Ontario.

References
CPG 1966, 1978; *CWW* 1999 p. 192; MacDonald *If You're Stronghearted* pp. 285, 310–11, 336, 342; PEI ECO 738/72, 727/78, 603/76; *Provincial Premiers Birthday Series*; WWPEI p. 22; *Atlantic Advocate* January 1971; *Canada and the World* December 1972; *Canadian Magazine* 3 April 1976; *Guardian* 12 September 1978; *Journal-Pioneer* 1 December 1978; *Toronto Star* 18 May 1972, 23 May 1972.

CAMPBELL, JAMES WILLIAM DON, merchant and farmer; b. 30 July 1910 in South Kildare, son of David Campbell and Eliza Martha Hardy; m. 21 October 1939 Corean MacPhee of Lot 11, and they had two children who were twins, Don Hardy Bryan and James William Barry; United; d. 7 April 1993 in O'Leary.

Campbell, a Conservative, was first elected to the Legislative Assembly in the general election of 1951 for 1st Prince. He was re-elected in the general election of 1959. He was defeated in the general elections of 1955 and 1962.

Don Campbell was educated at the Montrose School. From 1937 to 1988, he owned and operated Campbell's Store in Alberton. He also maintained a farm in Kildare, specializing in pigs, potatoes, and cattle. Campbell was the first farm equipment dealer in Prince County, and also the first farmer in Alberton to ship cattle out of the area by train. A strong advocate of a ferry to West Prince, Campbell made efforts to keep the issue alive. He was a member of West Point Ferries Limited, the Alberton Prince County Exhibition, the Land Use Commission, and the Chamber of Commerce, and served as president and director of the Alberton Seed Cleaning Plant. Campbell was a member of the Zetland Masonic Order, the Albert Edward Lodge of Perfection, the Sovereign Consistory, the St. Lawrence Chapter of the Rose Croix, and St. Peter's Anglican Church. He was a member of the Alberton Curling Club. Don Campbell died 7 April 1993 at the Community Hospital in O'Leary.

Corean Campbell died in October 1990.

References
CPG 1952, 1956, 1962, 1963; *Journal-Pioneer* 7 April 1993, 8 April 1993; *West Prince Graphic* 8 February 1984.

CAMPBELL, JOHN ARCHIBALD, farmer; b. 4 May 1879 in Heatherdale, son of Donald S. Campbell and Flora McLeod; m. first Annie Martin, and they had one child, Mrs. Winston King; m. secondly 24 August 1917 Christine Anne McKinnon, and they had four children, Donald A., Florence E., Jessie K., and Charles J.; Presbyterian; d. 4 October 1969 in Charlottetown.

Campbell, a Liberal, was first elected to the Legislative Assembly in the general election of 1927 for 4th Kings. He was re-elected in the general elections of 1931, 1935, 1939, 1943, and 1947. On 15 August 1935, he was appointed as a Minister without Portfolio in the government of Premier Walter Lea*, and held this post in the governments of Thane A. Campbell* and Walter Jones*. Campbell resigned in 1949.

He received his early education in Heatherdale, where he lived for the majority of his life, with the exception of a short period of time when he lived in the United States. Campbell was a farmer and, according to the *Maritime Advocate and Busy East*, a leader in the agricultural community. John Campbell died 4 October 1969 at the Prince Edward Island Hospital.

Christine Campbell, the daughter of Charles McKinnon of Heatherdale and Jessie MacKinnon, was born 7 June 1879 and died 21 January 1966.

Their daughter, Mrs. Winston King, eventually settled in Medford, Massachusetts. Charles J. Campbell was killed in action in Belgium in 1944 during the Second World War.

References
CPG 1936, 1944, 1945, 1949, 1950; *CWW* 1936–1937 p. 166; *Maritime Advocate and Busy East* August 1941; *Patriot* 6 October 1969; PARO: Census 1901; Valleyfield Presbyterian United Cemetery Records.

CAMPBELL, JOSEPH G., carpenter; b. 19 March 1893 in Poplar Point, son of John William Campbell and Mary Campbell; m. Janet MacDonald; Roman Catholic; d. 1974 in Montague.

Campbell, a Liberal, was first elected to the Legislative Assembly in the general election of 1947 for 3rd Kings. He was re-elected in the general election of 1955. Campbell was defeated in the general elections of 1943, 1951, 1959, and 1962. On 13 October 1949, he was appointed as a Minister without Portfolio.

When Campbell was not in the Legislature, he worked in a carpentry shop in Poplar Point, where he built and sold wood sleighs, driving sleighs, carts, and driving wagons. He also operated a forge, where he made metal wheels for wagons, runners for sleighs, and shoes for horses. Because of poor health, he retired and moved to Montague, where he lived in a senior citizens' home until his death.

Joseph G. Campbell was the uncle of former Premier W. Bennett Campbell*. He was instrumental in Bennett Campbell's decision to enter politics.

References
CPG 1949, 1953, 1958, 1961, 1967; PARO: Leard Files.

CAMPBELL, ROBERT ERSKINE, farmer and automobile salesperson; b. 27 April 1922 in Alberton, son of Keir Fraser Campbell and Eliza Mae Haywood; m. 27 November 1943 Georgie Ona Lewis, and they had eight children, Dianne, David, Donald, Elizabeth, Elda, Gwenda, Robert, and Margaret; Church of the Nazarene; d. 31 May 1992 in Charlottetown.

Campbell, a Liberal, was first elected to the Legislative Assembly in the general election of 1962 for 1st Prince. He was re-elected in the general elections of 1966, 1970, 1974, 1978, 1979, 1982, 1986, and 1989. He served as a Minister without Portfolio from November 1966 to 1972. From October 1972 to May 1974, and again from September 1978 to May 1979, Campbell was Minister of Fisheries.

He was a member of Treasury Board, a member of Policy Board, and a member of the Welfare Advisory Board. Campbell died while serving as a Member of the Legislative Assembly. Campbell was considered a tireless advocate of his constituents. His loud, impassioned speeches in the Legislature and around the Island earned him the affectionate title of the "Great West Wind," a title in which he took great pride.

"Bob" Campbell was educated in the Union School, and served in the Merchant Navy overseas from 1941 to 1942 before he established a farming operation in Alberton. He was a farmer and livestock dealer, specializing in cattle and hogs. In his early career, Campbell sold used cars. He was a trustee of the Alberton Regional High School and of the Elmsdale School, as well as vice-president of the Children's Association for the Mentally Challenged and chair of the Alberton Museum. Campbell was a director of the Prince County Exhibition and was a member of the West Prince Board of Trade. He was also a trustee of the Western Hospital. "Bob" Campbell died 31 May 1992.

Georgie Campbell is the daughter of Theodore C. Lewis of Alberton. Elizabeth Campbell married Hector MacLeod*, who served in the Legislative Assembly from 1993 to 2000.

References
COR 1992 p. 33; CPG 1992; Elections PEI; WWPEI p. 24; *Eastern Graphic* 11 May 1983; *Guardian* 8 January 1987, 1 June 1992, 29 August 2002; *Journal-Pioneer* 1 June 1992; *Monitor* 17 March 1976; *West Prince Graphic* 3 June 1992.

CAMPBELL, C.C., K.C., LL.D., M.A., HONOURABLE THANE ALEXANDER, lawyer and judge; b. 7 July 1895 in Summerside, son of Alexander Campbell and Clara Tremaine Muttart; m. first 28 February 1930 Cecilia Lillian Bradshaw, and they had four children, Virginia Tremaine, Alexander Bradshaw*, James Melville, and Harriet Isabelle; m. secondly 18 June 1970 Paula Agnes Champ, and there were no children; United; d. 28 September 1978 in Ottawa.

Campbell, a Liberal, was first elected to the Legislative Assembly in the general election of 1931 for 1st Prince. He was re-elected in the general elections of 1935 and 1939. He had been defeated in a by-election held 21 October 1930. Before his first election win, Campbell held the position of Attorney-General for a year. When the Liberals formed a government after the 1935 election, he was appointed Attorney and Advocate General by Premier Walter M. Lea*. Campbell led the Liberals during the 1935 election campaign due to the illness of Premier Lea. Upon Lea's death, Campbell became Premier on 14 January 1936. He held this office until 1943, when he resigned to take the position of Chief Justice of the Prince Edward Island Supreme Court.

Premier Campbell created a provincial police service which would later be absorbed by the Royal Canadian Mounted Police. He was premier during the creation of a National Park in the Dalvay-Cavendish area, and when the province's Travel Bureau was incorporated into the provincial government. Campbell was the first premier to enact public service legislation, and he developed sound budgeting control of the Island's finances. He devoted much time and energy to the province's role in the Second World War. Campbell was popular with Island voters throughout his time in office.

In 1966, Campbell was the only Island premier to see a son, Alexander, sworn in as premier of the province.

Campbell received his early education in public schools. He later attended Prince of Wales College in Charlottetown, and in 1915 earned a Bachelor of Arts from Dalhousie University in Halifax. In 1917 Campbell earned a Master of Arts, also from Dalhousie University. In 1918 he served with the 9th Canadian Siege Battery. Campbell then attended Oxford University as a Rhodes Scholar, where in 1922 he earned a Bachelor of Arts and in 1926 a Master of Arts. In 1922 Campbell returned to the province where he read law with former Premier Albert C. Saunders* in Summerside. He was called to the Bar in 1927 and went into practice with Saunders at that time. Campbell continued in his private practice until 1943, when he was appointed Chief Justice of Prince Edward Island, a position he held until 1970. He also served as Chief War Claims Commissioner of Canada from 1952 to 1970. In 1970 Campbell was appointed Chief Commissioner of the Foreign Claims Commission in Ottawa and held this position until his death.

Campbell was actively involved in his community. He was a member of the National Historic Sites and Monuments Board and the National Library Council. He was a member of the board of governors for St. Dunstan's University and was the first non-Catholic to serve as Chair. He served as a member of the board of Dalhousie University and as chancellor of the University of Prince Edward Island. Campbell was a member of the Dominion Curling Association, chairman of the board of trustees of the Macdonald Brier, and vice-president and president of the Royal Caledonian Curling Club of Scotland. He was inducted into the Canadian Curling Hall of Fame as a builder. Campbell was the first chair of the Prince Edward Island Heritage Foundation. He was president of the Rotary Club of Charlottetown, the Charlottetown Canadian Club, and the Dominion Curling Association. Campbell received an Honourary Doctorate of Laws from Dalhousie University in 1938 and from St. Dunstan's University in 1962. In 1973 he was appointed a companion of the Order of Canada. Thane Campbell died 18 September 1978 at the Ottawa-Carleton Hospital.

Cecilia Campbell was the daughter of Melville L. Bradshaw and Elytha Dorothy Reade of Summerside. She died on 29 September 1968.

References
CPG 1940; *CWW* 1973-75 p. 158; *Premiers Gallery*; *Journal-Pioneer* 29 September 1978; PARO: Leard Files.

CAMPBELL, P.C., HONOURABLE W. BENNETT, teacher and civil servant; b. 27 August 1943 in Montague, son of Wilfred Campbell and Edith Rice; m. 1 August 1970 Margaret Shirley Chiasson of Bear River, and they had eight children, Kelly, Colin, Grant, Sherri, Grace, Brad, Carmel, and John Paul; Roman Catholic.

Campbell, a Liberal, was first elected to the Legislative Assembly in the general election of 1970 for 3rd Kings. He was re-elected in the general elections of 1974, 1978, and 1979. Campbell was defeated in the general election of 1986 by 18 votes and A. A. Joey Fraser* claimed the riding. In 1981 he was a successful candidate in a federal by-election held 13 April for Cardigan. Campbell was appointed to the Privy Council and served as Minister of Veterans Affairs. He was defeated in the federal election of 1984. From 10 October 1972 to September 1978, Campbell occupied the position of Minister of Education. He was chairman of the Council of Ministers of Education from 1975 to 1976, and Provincial Secretary from 1974 to 1976. On 18 November 1976, Campbell was appointed Minister of Finance. In September 1978, following the appointment of Premier Alexander Campbell* to the Supreme Court, he was elected interim leader. On 9 December 1978, Campbell won the Liberal

leadership. From 18 September 1978 to 3 May 1979, he was Premier and President of Executive Council and Minister of Finance. He also served as chairman of the Regional Treasury Board for the Council of Maritime Premiers. After the Liberal defeat in the 1979 general election, from May of that year to January 1981 Campbell held the position of Leader of the Opposition.

Campbell's time as premier lasted less than a year. He inherited the difficult task of trying to rebuild the Liberal party, which had maintained power for 12 years, and which had been led by the very popular and dynamic Premier Alexander Campbell. The task was made more daunting because the Liberals possessed a mere two-seat majority following the May 1978 general election, which then fell to a one-seat majority with the resignation of Premier Alexander Campbell. Given the circumstances, Premier Bennett Campbell called an election for April 1979, and the Conservatives gained power by winning 21 seats. Despite the defeat under his leadership, Campbell is more closely identified with the Alexander Campbell era, the Development Plan, his years as a provincial minister, and his stint as federal Minister of Veterans Affairs than with his short period as premier and leader of the Liberals. The small Liberal majority after the 1978 election perhaps contributed more to Campbell's brief time in the premier's office than any fault of his leadership in the 1979 election campaign.

Campbell received his primary education at the Poplar Point School, and in 1960 he graduated from St. Dunstan's High School. He attended St. Dunstan's University and completed the two-year education program. From 1962 to 1972, Campbell taught in Montague and Montreal. On 6 August 1986, he became a civil servant with the Prince Edward Island government. Campbell served as Superintendent of Insurance and Public Trustee until 11 February 2000. On 14 February of that year, he was appointed Family Law Coordinator in the Department of Community Services and Attorney-General. Campbell was a member of the Prince Edward Island Teacher's Federation and the Lions Club, and is an honourary member of the Royal Canadian Legion. W. Bennett Campbell and his family reside in Cardigan.

Shirley Campbell, the daughter of Joseph Chiasson and Margaret Gallant, was born 26 September 1947.

References

CPG 1984, 1987; *CWW* 1986 p. 199; *HFER* Cardigan p. 2; PEI ECO 1048/76; *WWC* 1982-1983 p. 663; *WWPEI* p. 23; *Globe and Mail* 18 September 1978, 17 December 1978; *Guardian* 6 August 1986.

CAMPBELL, WILLIAM, farmer and mill owner; b. 12 January 1836 in Park Corner, son of James Campbell of Park Corner and Elizabeth Montgomery; m. first 1 March 1863 Elizabeth McLeod, and they had three children, Hugh M., John E., and Elizabeth A.; m. secondly 2 January 1874 Elizabeth Sutherland, and they had five children, Jane W., William W., James A., Robert S., and Lorne; Presbyterian; d. 15 December 1909 in Seaview.

Campbell, a Conservative, was first elected to the House of Assembly in an 1873 by-election held in September for 1st Queens. Campbell was re-elected in the general elections of 1876, 1879, and 1882. He was defeated in the general election of 1886. He was elected to the Legislative Assembly in a by-election held in 1896 for 4th Prince. He was re-elected in a by-election held in 1898 for 1st Queens. He was defeated in the general election of 1897 for 4th Prince and the general election of 1900 for 1st Queens.

In 1879 Campbell was appointed to the Executive Council as a Minister without Portfolio. A year later, Campbell became Commissioner of Public Works and, on appealing to his constituents, was re-elected by acclamation. In 1882 he again was appointed Commissioner of Public Works and continued in this position until 1 February 1887, when he resigned to run, unsuccessfully, for the House of Commons in the Queen's County riding. He was a supporter of free schools in the 1876 election, and was a member of the coalition party, made up of both Conservative and Liberals, in support of the Free School Act. He took an active part in the debates over the land question, free schools, and the reduction of provincial expenditure.

Campbell received his education in New London. Professionally he was a farmer and mill owner. During different periods of his life, Campbell lived in New London, Melville, and Charlottetown. While involved in politics, Campbell was Commissioner of the government stock farm. He was a Lieutenant-Colonel in the Queens County Militia.

Campbell's second wife, Elizabeth Sutherland, the daughter of John S. Sutherland of Park Corner, was born ca. 1851.

References

CCB p. 473; *CPG* 1885, 1887, 1903; Elections PEI; *Meacham's Atlas*; *Island Argus* 10 February 1874; PARO: RG Vital Statistics, Vol. 12 1855-1865; RG Vital Statistics series 3 subserie 3 volume 9 1871-1878; MNI-Census 1881, 1891.

CANFIELD, ELLA JEAN, merchant; b. 4 October 1919 in Westmoreland, daughter of Everett Garrett and Lydia Granville McVittie; m. 30 June 1939 Parker Ellsworth Canfield, and they had one child, Mildred Joyce; Anglican; d. 31 December 2000 in Charlottetown.

Canfield, a Liberal, was first elected to the Legislative Assembly in the general election of 1970 for 1st Queens. She was re-elected in the general elections of 1974 and 1978. She was defeated in the general elections of 1966 and 1979. Canfield's election in 1970 marked a milestone in provincial history, as she was the first woman elected to the Legislative Assembly and the first woman to serve on Executive Council. On 10 October 1972, she was appointed Minister without Portfolio and Minister Responsible for the Prince Edward Island Housing Authority. Canfield served in these positions until 2 May 1974. She also served as the chair of the Advisory Committee on the Status of Women.

Jean Canfield received her primary education at Crapaud Elementary School. When her family moved to Cambridge, Massachusetts, she attended Cambridge High and Latin School. Canfield also attended Union Commercial College in Charlottetown and the Lincoln School of Nursing in Los Angeles. For 15 years she and her husband ran a general store in Crapaud.

Canfield was involved in a number of community activities. She was chair of the management committee of the Crapaud Exhibition, a member of the Home and School Association, and secretary-treasurer of the Englewood School Board. Canfield was an organizer of the Community Schools, served as president and treasurer of the Crapaud Women's Institute, and was a secretary of the St. John's Anglican Church Women's Organization. In 1977 she was awarded the Queen's Jubilee Medal. Canfield was a member of the Crapaud Community Curling Club, the Zonta Club, the Canadian Club, and the Chamber of Commerce of Crapaud and Victoria. Ella Jean Canfield died 31 December 2000 at the Queen Elizabeth Hospital.

Parker Canfield, the son of Alfred A.

Canfield of Westmoreland, died in July 1971.

References
CPG 1966, 1978, 1979, 1980; *WWPEI* p. 25; *Atlantic Advocate* 63 (5) January 1973; *Guardian* 24 April 1974, 16 April 1979, 2 January 2001.

CARR, C.L.U., HOWARD BENNETT, insurance brokerage owner and property developer, school teacher and principal; b. 21 December 1929 in Wheatley, son of J. Howard Carr and May L. Crabbe; m. 11 May 1957 Mary Jean Coffin MacKay, and they had five children, Deborah Ann, Clive H. R., Alexis Jean, H. Darke, and B. Mark; Anglican.

Carr, a Conservative, was elected to the Legislative Assembly in a by-election held 4 December 1972 for 2nd Queens. He was defeated in the general election of 1974. He served as the Opposition critic for Education, Labour and Housing. Carr was president of the Conservative party at the provincial and national levels. He was also the President of the Young Conservative Association of Canada. Carr served for over 20 years as a municipal councillor, treasurer, and chairman for the community of West Royalty.

From 1935 to 1945, Carr received his early education at Wheatley School, and continued his studies at Prince of Wales College where he studied from 1946 to 1948. In 1951 Carr graduated from the Royal Canadian Armoured Corps School in Camp Borden, Ontario, and was commissioned as a Lieutenant in the Canadian Army. He served as an officer in the Prince Edward Island 17th Regiment RECCE and as a call-out officer in New Brunswick. In 1952 Carr returned to Prince of Wales College and graduated in 1953. He became a teacher and school principal. In 1977 he graduated from the University of Toronto's Institute of Chartered Life Underwriters of Canada and was granted the C.L.U. designation. Later Carr was the founder and general manager of Bennett Carr Insurance Limited. He opened Seawood Marina Ltd. (1971), a property ownership business. Carr has served as president of both the PEI Life Underwriters Association and the PEI Federation of Agents and Brokers, and as a director of both these national professional bodies. He co-authored an insurance textbook used in the Associate Insurance professional designation program, which was administered by the Insurance Brokers Association of Canada.

Carr involved himself in community activities. He was a president of the Canadian Cancer Society, served as the provincial campaign chairman and was awarded the Terry Fox Marathon of Hope Citation. He was a member of the United States Trotting Association and served a double term as president of the Charlottetown Driving Park and the Provincial Exhibition Association. He served as a school board trustee for Charlottetown Rural High School. In 1960 Carr was the Canadian representative to the World Assembly of Youth in Africa. He was awarded the Canadian Commemorative Medal from the Governor General. In 1989 he was honoured as Citizen of the Year of West Royalty, and was declared Mr. West Royalty in his citation.

Bennett Carr is a member of the Victoria Lodge of Charlottetown and a 32nd degree Scottish Rite Mason. He has been head of both the Lodge and Chapter in the Summerside Valley of the Rite. He is a Shriner, a member and former president of the Commonwealth Society, a member of Charlottetown Rotary, the PEI Symphony Society, the University of Prince Edward Island Alumni Association, and a former L.O.L. member. Bennett Carr and his wife reside in West Royalty.

Jean Carr, the daughter of Reginald Coffin and Sadie Jane MacKenzie, was born in Rollo Bay.

References
CPG 1974, 1975; *WWPEI* p. 26; *Guardian* 3 May 1993; *Journal-Pioneer* 25 April 1974; *Patriot* 10 March 1989; Questionnaire to Former MLAs.

CARROLL, M.B.A., TIMOTHY, manager and professor; b. 17 January 1951 in Charlottetown, son of Claude Carroll and Mary Dooley; m. 28 November 1978 Kathy Jenkins, and they had four children, Melissa, Esther, Patrick Joseph, and Daniel; Roman Catholic.

Carroll, a Liberal, was first elected to the Legislative Assembly in the general election of 1986 for 5th Queens. He was re-elected in the general elections of 1989 and 1993. On 2 May 1986, he was appointed Minister of Agriculture in the Joseph Ghiz* Administration. Carroll resigned as Minister on 25 October 1988, but remained a Member of the Legislative Assembly.

Tim Carroll received his secondary education at Charlottetown Rural High School. He attended the University of Prince Edward Island where he earned a Bachelor of Business Administration in 1973. In 1974 Carroll earned a Master of Business Administration from the University of

Saskatchewan. In his early career he held numerous managerial positions with, among other organizations, the Ontario Vegetable Growers' Marketing Board, the Alberta Agricultural Products Marketing Board, and the Prince Edward Island Market Development Centre. Carroll was assistant professor of marketing at St. Francis Xavier University in Antigonish, Nova Scotia, before he returned to Charlottetown after accepting the position of assistant professor of marketing at the University of Prince Edward Island. In 1984 he was the research coordinator for the Maritime provinces on the Royal Commission of Inquiry into Marketing Practices for Potatoes in Eastern Canada. Carroll was a member of the Charlottetown Winter Carnival Committee and the Charlottetown Diocesan Committee on Christian Unity. Timothy Carroll and his wife reside in Parkdale.

Kathy Carroll, the daughter of Lawson Jenkins and Eileen MacKenzie, was born 4 October 1956.

References
CPG 1996; *Atlantic Guidebook* p. 31; *Guardian* 26 October 1988.

CARVER, Q.C., HORACE BOSWELL, lawyer; b. 29 December 1948 in Charlottetown, son of Gordon Russell Carver and Cecelia Mae White; m. 19 May 1973 Lucile Barbara Conrod, and they had four children, Jonathan Boswell (died in infancy), Julie, David, and Michael; Protestant.

Carver, a Conservative, was first elected to the Legislative Assembly in the general election of 1978 for 3rd Queens. He was re-elected in the general elections of 1979 and 1982. He was defeated in the general elections of 1974 and 1986. On 3 May 1979, he was named Minister of Justice and Attorney-General, and he served in these positions until 1981. Carver was appointed Minister of Public Works from 3 May 1979 to 1980, and Minister of Community Affairs from 1981 to 1982. From 1979 to 1982, he was Government House Leader, and in March 1986 was appointed Deputy Speaker. He served as one of the province's representatives during the constitutional conferences of the early 1980s.

Carver received his early education in the Hazelbrook and Bunbury Schools. He attended Charlottetown Rural High School and Prince of Wales College. Carver studied at Dalhousie University in Halifax where he received a Bachelor of Arts in 1970 and a law degree in 1973. Following

university he returned to Charlottetown where he practised law. On 24 January 1980, he was designated Queen's Counsel. Carver has been a member of the Canadian Law Society and the Prince Edward Island Law Society. He was chair of the Queen Elizabeth Hospital Foundation and the Prince Edward Island Rural Beautification Society. He was a president of the Protestant Family Service Bureau and served as honourary chairman of the St. John Ambulance finance campaign. Horace Carver and his family reside in Charlottetown.

Lucile Carver is the daughter of Laurie Conrod and Sadie Peppard of Dartmouth, Nova Scotia.

References
CPG 1986; *WWPEI* p. 27; *Guardian* 4 December 1979; PEI Cabinet Biographic Summary 1980.

CHAPPELL, PROWSE GORRILL, farmer; b. 30 September 1928 in Kitchener, Ontario, son of Alexander Chappell and Pearl Gorrill of Summerside; m. 25 April 1951 Ethelbert Dawson, and they had four children, Ronald, Wayne, Deborah, and Cindy; United Baptist.

Chappell, a Conservative, was first elected to the Legislative Assembly in the general election of 1978 for 4th Prince. He was re-elected in the general elections of 1979, 1982, and 1986. He was defeated in the federal election of 1988 in Egmont. On 3 May 1979, he was appointed Minister of Agriculture and Forestry and, on 28 October 1982, Chappell was named Minister of Agriculture. He was a member of Treasury Board and was responsible for the Prince Edward Island Land Development Corporation and the Grain Elevator Corporation. He was proud of the fact that the School Milk Program was introduced while he was Minister of Agriculture. Chappell chaired the Conservative caucus and acted as Opposition spokesperson on agriculture.

Chappell attended Summerside High School. In 1952 he took over his father's farm in Sherbrooke and raised beef and dairy cattle. He was a president of the Prince Edward Island Federation of Agriculture and a provincial director of the Canadian Federation of Agriculture. He was a member of the Summerside Regional Planning Board, a chair of the Sherbrooke Community Improvement Committee, and a Sherbrooke School Trustee.

Bertie Chappell is the daughter of Rex

Dawson of Albany.

References
CPG 1988; *HFER* Egmont p. 3; *WWPEI* p. 28; *Guardian* 12 April 1978, 17 October 1985, 1 October 1988; *Journal-Pioneer* 31 March 1989; PEI Cabinet Biographic Summary 1980.

CHEVERIE, Q.C., HONOURABLE WAYNE, lawyer, lecturer, regulation commission chair, and judge; b. 19 May 1950 in Charlottetown, son of Charles George Cheverie of Souris and Clara Austin of Tracadie; m. 8 March 1975 Theresa ("Terri") Bennett, and they had two children, Jared Anthony and Joslin Nicolle; Roman Catholic.

Cheverie, a Liberal, was first elected to the Legislative Assembly in the general election of 1986 for 5th Queens. He was re-elected in the general elections of 1989 and 1993. He was elected to the Legislative Assembly in the general election of 1996 in the new electoral district of Charlottetown-King's Square. On 2 May 1986 he was assigned three Ministries, Attorney-General, Justice, and Labour. In 1989 Cheverie became Minister of Health and Social Services and Government House Leader. He was again named Minister of Justice and Attorney-General in January 1993. On 15 April of the same year, Cheverie was appointed Provincial Treasurer. He was named Opposition House Leader and Opposition critic for finance in November 1996. In 1994 he was serving as Provincial Treasurer when a bill was passed to impose a 7.5 per cent salary and wage rollback for all provincial public sector employees. Cheverie ran for the Liberal leadership in 1996, but finished second to Keith Milligan* at the largest political convention in Island history. Following the convention and his election in the 1996 general election, Cheverie resigned his seat upon appointment as chair of the Island Regulatory and Appeals Commission. On 31 August 2001, Cheverie was appointed to the Supreme Court of Prince Edward Island.

Cheverie received his primary education at Queen Square School. He subsequently attended Birchwood High School and St. Dunstan's University. In 1971 Cheverie graduated from the University of Prince Edward Island with a Bachelor of Arts. Three years later he graduated from Dalhousie University with a Bachelor of Law. He became a partner in Campbell, Lea, Cheverie and Michael. From 1977 to 1983, he lectured in business law at the University of Prince Edward Island. He was a council member of the province's Law Society and

a member of the Rules Committee of the Family Division of the Supreme Court. Cheverie served as an executive member of the provincial branch of the Canadian Bar Association.

Cheverie was a director of the Catholic Family Services Bureau and served as a member of the Parish Council and lecturer at St. Pius X.

Wayne Cheverie and his wife reside in Parkdale. Terri Cheverie is the daughter of William Bennett of Gander, Newfoundland, and Mary Bennett of Charlottetown.

References
Atlantic Guidebook p. 31; *CPG* 1997; *WWPEI* p. 28; *Guardian* 26 September 1997, 27 September 1997, 1 September 2001; *Maclean's* 8 September 1986.

CLARK, M.Th., BARRY ROY, college instructor, youth director, teacher, minister, and counsellor; b. 5 July 1948 in Charlottetown, son of Roy Leard Clark and Irene Blanche MacPherson; m. 20 August 1973 Judith Ann Kerrick, and they have three children, Amie Charissa, Jeremy Roy "Jay," and Ashley; Church of Christ.

Clark, a Conservative, was first elected to the Legislative Assembly in the general election of 1978 for 6th Queens. He was re-elected in the general election of 1979. He was defeated in the general election of 1982. On 3 May 1979, Clark was appointed as a Minister without Portfolio and Minister Responsible for the Housing Corporation. On 1 April 1980, he was named Minister of Tourism, Industry and Energy. Clark was the first ordained person appointed to the provincial Cabinet, and one of the first two members of the clergy elected to the Legislature. He made two unsuccessful bids for the leadership of the Conservative party, the first in 1981 and the second in 1990.

Clark received his primary education at Sherwood School. At the age of 14, he worked in the sports department of Canadian Tire. The following year he travelled to Banff, Alberta, to obtain employment. The next summer he fished lobster in Murray Harbour. Clark attended Prince of Wales College and Maritime Christian College, and from 1968 to 1969 Lincoln Christian College. In 1970 he graduated from the University of Prince Edward Island with a Bachelor of Arts in Psychology. That same year, Clark graduated from Maritime Christian College and was awarded a Bachelor of Arts in Theology. From 1971 to 1974, Clark ministered at the Metro Toronto Church. On 26

August 1973 he was ordained at the Sherwood Church of Christ. Following the ordination he moved to Toronto to minister at Keele Street Church, located in the city's west end. Clark obtained a Master's degree in counselling, and a diploma in practical theology from the University of Edinburgh in Scotland. For one year he taught at Montague High School. His ministries have included a year as Youth Minister at the Tinley Park Church of Christ in Chicago, a year at the Montague Church of Christ, a summer at the Central Christian Church in Charlottetown, and supply preaching at the Fredericton and Glasgow churches. While in Edinburgh, Clark served as assistant minister at the Liberton Kirk of the Church of Scotland. In 1974 he was the Red Cross Youth Director for the province. Clark worked as a community development facilitator and business instructor at the Leadership Institute of Holland College. For a period of time he operated the Shining Waters Lodge in Cavendish. Clark was the minister at New Glasgow Church of Christ. For five years he did missionary work in Thailand, returning to Prince Edward Island in the middle of 2001. Clark now resides in New Glasgow and is working as a counsellor.

Judith Clark is the daughter of Merrit Kerrick of Elizabethtown, Kentucky.

References
CPG 1981, 1982-1983; PEI Cabinet Biographic Summary 1980. *Guardian* 23 August 1973, 8 April 1978, 16 April 1979, 22 October 1981, 8 October 1985, 8 April 1989, 7 September 1990; 21 October 2002; *Journal-Pioneer* 5 November 1981; UPEI: Robertson Library: PEI Collection.

CLARK, RUSSELL CHARLES, merchant and board member; b. 22 December 1878 in Mount Stewart, son of Solomon C. Clark and Hannah Newberry; m. 14 September 1901 Marion J. McKay, and they had three children, Stirling K., William Keir*, and one unnamed (died in infancy); United; d. 15 July 1964 in Charlottetown.

Clark, a Liberal, was first elected to the Legislative Assembly in the general election of 1927 for 3rd Queens. He was re-elected in the general elections of 1935, 1939, 1943, 1947, 1951, and 1955. He was defeated in the general election of 1931. On 30 September 1930, he was appointed as a Minister without Portfolio.

Clark's son Keir* served in the Legislative Assembly from 1947 to 1959 and from 1966 to 1970.

Clark attended Mount Stewart School, Prince of Wales College, and Charlottetown Business College. He was a merchant in Mount Stewart and held directorships with the Charlottetown Can Company, Charlottetown Fur Sales, Associated Shippers Incorporated, McDonald V. Rowe Woodworking Company, and Island Foods of Summerside. Russell Clark owned and operated lobster factories in Mt. Stewart and Blooming Point. He owned and operated a blueberry processing plant in Mt. Stewart. He owned a 600-acre farm, a fox ranch, and was a partner in a car dealership in Charlottetown. Russell Clark died 15 July 1964 at the Prince Edward Island Hospital.

Marion Clark, the daughter of Kenneth McKay of Mount Stewart, was born in 1877 and died in 1975.

References
CPG 1936, 1940, 1948, 1956, 1970; Elections PEI; *Guardian* 16 July 1964; PARO: Mount Stewart People's Cemetery Records.

CLARK, WILLIAM EDWARD, farmer and director of livestock testing station; b. 24 March 1932 in Summerside, son of Ivan Leroy Clark and Maisy Laura Miller; m. 21 June 1958 Ruby Ida Best, and they had three children, Colleen Laura, Catherine Erma, and Edith Lynne; United.

Clark, a Liberal, was first elected to the Legislative Assembly in the general election of 1970 for 3rd Prince. He was re-elected in the general elections of 1974, 1978, 1979, 1982, 1986, 1989, and 1993. He served as Minister of Agriculture and Forestry from 27 April 1978 to 3 May 1979. On 15 June 1989, Clark was appointed Speaker and served in that position until 15 April 1993. He was named chair of caucus in the same year. He was an executive member of the Commonwealth Parliamentary Association.

"Eddie" Clark received his primary education at the school in Central Lot 16. Later he attended basic training in the Royal Canadian Navy at the Cornwallis Naval Base, and enrolled in agricultural courses in Charlottetown. From 1951 to 1952, Clark served in the Royal Canadian Navy. He is a beef farmer and was director of the beef testing station in Nappan, Nova Scotia. He was president of the Prince Edward Island Junior Farmers, a leader of the 4-H Club for 25 years, a president of the Prince Edward Island Shorthorn Breeders' Association, a member of the Federation of Agriculture, a member of the Rural Development

Council, chairman of the Family Farm Program, and a board member of the Farm Credit Corporation. Clark served on the board of directors of the Summerside Co-op and was a trustee of Athena Regional High School. He was a member of the Prince Edward Island Heritage Foundation and the Summerside Chamber of Commerce. Clark is a member of the Miscouche Royal Canadian Legion. Clark is chairman of the Lot 16 United Church Congregation and secretary of the Lot 16 Cemetery Committee. Eddie Clark and his wife reside in Belmont Lot 16.

Ruby Clark is the daughter of Harry Best of Belmont and Erma MacLaurin.

References
CPG 1971, 1996; *ECO* 290/78; *WWPEI* p. 29; *Guardian* 14 March 1979, 15 October 1985, 4 April 1986, 16 August 1986, 27 April 1989, March 1993, 8 February 1994, 15 February 1996, 15 May 1996, 31 May 1996; *Journal-Pioneer* 5 December 1992, 12 December 1992, 21 November 1995, 10 May 1996, 31 May 1996.

CLARK, WILLIAM KEIR, merchant; b. 30 May 1910 in Mount Stewart, son of Russell Charles Clark* and Marion J. McKay; m. 17 June 1940 Anna I. McLaren of Georgetown, and they had three children, Gwen, Marion, and Marjorie; United.

Clark, a Liberal, and later an Independent Liberal, was first elected to the Legislative Assembly in the general election of 1947 for 3rd Kings. He was re-elected in the general elections of 1951, 1955, and 1966. He was defeated in the general election of 1959. He was appointed as a Minister without Portfolio on 6 June 1951. On 11 June 1953, he was named Minister of Education and served in that Ministry until 1959. From 1954 to 1955, Clark served as Provincial Treasurer, and, from 28 July 1966 to 7 February 1969, he was Minister of Health and Municipal Affairs. He resigned that position on 7 February 1969 because he "did not agree with certain programs in the provincial government's multi-million dollar development program, and the delegation of government responsibility to the Economic Improvement Corporation, a government-appointed body, charged with the implementation and operation of the plan." Clark did not resign as a Liberal Member and continued sitting in the Legislature. On 3 March 1970, he crossed the floor of the Legislature to sit as an Independent Liberal, stating, "I am no longer connected to the party of the plan." He was referring to the Comprehensive Development Plan administered by the Economic Improvement Corporation. Clark's switch to Independent Liberal ended the Liberal majority, leaving the Legislature with 16 Liberals, one of whom was Speaker, 15 Conservatives, and one Independent. Premier Alexander Campbell* called a general election shortly thereafter, in which the Liberals won 27 seats and the Conservatives five. Prior to his time in provincial politics, Clark was elected Mayor of Montague in 1940.

Clark's father served in the Legislative Assembly from 1927 to 1931 and from 1935 to 1959. Thus, father and son served in the Legislative Assembly concurrently from 1947 to 1959.

Clark attended Prince of Wales College. In 1934 he graduated from Dalhousie University with a Bachelor of Commerce degree and that same year opened a store in Montague. Clark was a merchant until 1979. He was also a director/owner of Clark Bros. and, with his family, had interests in Clark Brothers in St. Peters Bay and Mount Stewart. Clark was born in Mt. Stewart, into a family involved in the general merchant business for more than 100 years. William Keir Clark resides in Montague.

Anna Clark was the daughter of William W. McLaren and Flora MacKenzie of Georgetown.

References
CPG 1956, 1960, 1970; *Eastern Graphic* 4 July 1979; *Guardian* 8 February 1969, 4 March 1970, 7 March 1970, 18 March 1970.

CLARKE, JOHN MONTAGUE, clerk, lumber merchant, contractor, and civil servant; b. ca. 8 October 1854 in Bedeque, son of Theophilus DesBrisay Clarke of Bedeque and Eleanor Clarke of Darnley; m. 8 May 1877 Sarah M. Reeves of Freetown, and they had seven children, Eleanor, Margaret, Peter, Theophilus, William, Annie, and Horace Easter; Methodist; d. 25 May 1936 in Edmonton, Alberta.

Clarke, a Liberal, was elected to the Legislative Assembly in the general election of 1904 for 5th Prince. He was defeated in the general election of 1908. From February to November of that year, he served on Executive Council as a Minister without Portfolio. Clarke advocated temperance and took part in the passing of the Prohibition Law.

He received his education in the public schools of Bedeque. Early in adult life Clarke trained in business while working with John R. Calhoun*, a Summerside lumber merchant. Later he moved to Colorado where he remained for five years. Upon his return to the Island, he started a lumber business in Kensington. Following this, Clarke, with Major Schurman and Nathan McFarlane, began another lumber company. Clarke remained associated with the business until 1907, when he sold it to M. F. Schurman. He became involved in general contracting and his new company constructed buildings across the Island, including Zion Church in Charlottetown. In 1916 he moved to Edmonton with his family. Until his retirement a few years before his death, Clarke held the position of Supervisor of Agriculture for Alberta.

Beyond his mercantile and political activities, Clarke had other interests. He served as a member of the Summerside school board and on the Summerside Town Council. He was a prominent member of the Masonic Order and Independent Order of Foresters. As a Forester he received special recognition by his selection to serve as a delegate to the Supreme Court meeting in England, as well as to meetings in Toronto in 1898 and in San Francisco in 1902. John Clarke died 25 May 1936.

Sarah Clarke was born 27 February 1855 and died in 1931.

References

CPG 1908, 1909; Elections PEI; *Patriot* 3 June 1936; PARO: RG 19 series 3 subseries 3 Marriage Registers Vol. 9 1871-1878; MNI-Census 1891; Census 1901; Bedeque United Church Book 1 p. 58.

CLEMENTS, HONOURABLE GILBERT RALPH,

electrical contractor, merchant, realtor, and insurance agent; b. 11 September 1928 in Victoria Cross, son of Robert Kelly Clements of Yarmouth, Nova Scotia, and Mary Ruth Stewart of Kensington; m. 8 July 1953 Wilma Catherine MacLure, and they had three children, Robert, David, and Gail; United.

Clements, a Liberal, was first elected to the Legislative Assembly in the general election of 1970 for 4th Kings. He was re-elected in the general elections of 1974, 1979, 1982, 1986, 1989, and 1993. He was defeated in the general election of 1978. From 1974 to 1978, Clements served as Minister of Municipal Affairs, Environment, Tourism, Parks and Conservation. He served as Opposition critic for finance and energy from 1979 to 1986. From 1986 to 1989, Clements was Minister of Finance and Minister of Community and Cultural Affairs. He held the positions of Minister of Finance and Minister of the Environment from 1989 to 1993. For two terms Clements chaired the Canadian Council of Environment Ministers. While Minister of the Environment, he received the Crandall Award from the Travel Industry Association of Canada for the greatest contribution by an elected person to preserving the environment in Canada. In 1992 Clements was an official member of the Canadian delegation to the Earth Summit in Rio de Janeiro. During his time in government he attended conferences on the environment in England, the USSR, Venezuela and Alaska. In 1981 Clements served as interim Leader of the Liberal Party, and in October of the same year ran for the Liberal leadership, but lost to Joseph Ghiz*. He served on the Montague Town Council for two terms prior to 1970 and twice ran unsuccessfully for the Mayor's seat. He also served as a President of the Prince Edward Island Young Liberals Association. Clements was appointed Lieutenant-Governor 30 August 1995, and served until May 2001.

He received his early education at Montague Memorial School, and, from 1944 to 1945, attended Mount Allison Academy. In 1944 Clements was employed by the Canadian General Electric Company Limited in Halifax, and a year later was transferred to Toronto. From 1949 to 1970, he operated and owned the Montague Electric Company Ltd., a successful electrical contracting and appliance sales business. Clements has worked as a fire and automobile insurance agent, and owned and operated Southern Kings Real Estate Incorporated.

In 1970 Clements was appointed magistrate for the town of Montague, and in 1972 he was appointed a notary public. He served as a school trustee on the boards of the regional high school, elementary school, and the consolidated school in Montague. Clements was a firefighter, a president and founding member of the Garden of the Gulf Museum Incorporated, and assisted in the establishment of the Montague Junior Chamber of Commerce. He was a member of the Prince Edward Island Fish and Wildlife Association, a Red Cross volunteer, and a volunteer for the Montague Community Welfare League. In August 1996 Clements was appointed Chancellor of the Order of Prince Edward Island, and in October of that year he was made a Knight of the Order of Saint John. Clements belongs to the St. Andrews Masonic Lodge No. 13 A.F. and A.M. and the United Church Men's Club. Gilbert Clements and his wife reside in Montague.

Wilma Clements is the daughter of Benjamin MacLure and Mary "Mamie" MacKinnon of Montague.

References

Atlantic Guidebook p. 31; *CPG* 1979, 1998-1999; *CWW* 2000 p. 246; *WWC* p. 116; *WWPEI* p. 30; *Atlantic Insight* vol. 3 no. 3 April 1981; *Eastern Graphic* 14 October 1981; Questionnaire to Former MLAs.

CLOW, JAMES, merchant, farmer, and justice of the peace; b. 1837, in Murray Harbour North, son of Benjamin Clow; m. 17 March 1857 Lucy Graham of Gaspereaux, and they had five children, Lucy, Benney, Margaret, Willie, and Stephen; Presbyterian; d. 1 April 1901 in Murray Harbour North.

Clow, a Conservative, was elected to the House of Assembly in the 1890 general election for 4th Kings. He was defeated in the general election of 1897. Clow was elected to the Legislative Council in 1882 for 2nd Kings and served there until 1890.

A farmer, merchant, and exporter in Murray Harbour North, Clow also ran a general store there, and served as a Justice of the Peace. James Clow died 1 April 1901.

Lucy Clow, the daughter of William Graham, was born ca. 1832 and died 2 June 1905. James Clow's mother was born in Scotland.

References

CPG 1887, 1891, 1897; *Meacham's Atlas*; *Charlottetown Herald* 10 April 1901; *Islander* 20 March 1857; PARO: MNI-Hutchinson's p. 160; MNI-Census1881, 1891; Montague Funeral Home Records.

COMPTON, DANIEL JAMES, general merchant, exporter, and forester; b. 28 January 1915 in Belle River, son of Benjamin Compton and Sarah Elizabeth; m. 24 November 1947 Mary Agnes Compton, and they had five children, Patricia, Daniel James, Susan Jean, George, and Richard Paisley; Church of Scotland; d. 18 April 1990.

Compton, a Conservative, was first elected to the Legislative Assembly in the general election of 1970 for 4th Queens. He was re-elected in the general elections of 1974, 1978, 1979, and 1982. He was defeated in the general election of 1966. Compton was elected Speaker on 29 June 1979, and served in this position until 1983. He had a particular interest in the province's forestry policy, in part due to many years working as a forester.

Compton was educated in Belle River from 1921 to 1932, and resided there most of his life, living in the house in which he was born. He left Belle River during the Second World War. Compton was the Leading Supply Assistant on the HMCS *Swansea* and a member of the EG 9 Striking Force Group. Compton was awarded the 1939 to 1945 Star, the France and Germany Medal with Atlantic Bar, the Voluntary Service Medal, the George VI Medal, and the Queen Elizabeth Medal. Following the war, he went into the business of cutting pulpwood and lumber, and did so for much of his adult life. He also ran a general store in Belle River and did some exporting.

In 1988 Compton was named Citizen of the Year in Belfast at the Winter Carnival. The recognition was due in part to his many years of assistance with the area's Alcoholics Anonymous organization. Compton also involved himself in a number of other community activities, including serving as vice-president of the Belfast Historic Society, and he was a member of the Royal Canadian Legion, Eldon Branch. He was known for his rich knowledge of local history and his enjoyment of storytelling. Daniel Compton died 18 April 1990.

Compton's mother was a native of Brandon, Manitoba. He had two stepsons, George and Richard Paisley of Florida. Mary Compton was the daughter of James E. Compton of Cambridge, Massachusetts.

References

COR 1990 pp. 49-50; *CPG* 1967, 1986; *CPR* vol. 2 no. 4 1979 p. 53; *WWPEI* p. 31; *Guardian* 11 April 1978, 19 April 1979, 8 February 1988, 19 April 1990; Interview: James E. Compton.

CONNOLLY, JOHN PAUL, educator and investment counsellor; b. 22 June 1946 in Charlottetown, son of Stephen Peter Connolly and Eulalia Catherine McNally; m. 20 May 1972 Etta Blanche MacLean, and they had four children, Susan Maureen, Nancy Mary, Heather Patricia, and John Paul; Roman Catholic.

Connolly, a Liberal, was first elected to the Legislative Assembly in the general election of 1982 for 6th Queens. He was re-elected in the general elections of 1986, 1989, and 1993. In 1996 he was elected for the new riding of Charlottetown-Rochford Square. Connolly was defeated in the general election of 1979 for 3rd Queens. From 1982 to 1986, he was Opposition critic for Health, Social Services, and the Status of Women. In 1986 he co-chaired the Liberal Task Force on Job Creation and chaired Policy Board. In 1989 Connolly was appointed Minister of Education, Minister Responsible for Native Affairs, and Minister Responsible for the Status of Women. In 1992 he vice-chaired the Council of Ministers of Education, Canada. While Minister of Education, Connolly initiated significant reform within the provincial education system. In 1993 he served on the Cabinet Committee for Public Consultation, and in 1996 he was appointed Minister of Higher Education. Connolly was a Commissioner for the Prince Edward Island Electoral Boundaries Commission which produced a new electoral map for the province, reduced the number of seats in the Legislature from 32 to 27, and eliminated the dual member system. From 1999 to 2000, he served as Leader of the Opposition.

Paul Connolly received his primary education at Queen Square School. Later he attended Birchwood High School. Connolly graduated from St. Dunstan's University with a Bachelor of Arts in 1968. In 1971 he graduated from the University of Prince Edward Island with a Bachelor of Education. A teacher by profession, Connolly has been involved in adult education at Holland College, and has worked at all levels within this institution, having served at different times as instructor, head instructor, chairman, and principal. While at the senior management level, he chaired a number of Holland College committees, one of which was a committee to revise the College Admissions Policy. Connolly presently is a member of the National Parole Board of Canada.

Connolly served on the Maritime Municipal and Training Development Board, was public education chair for the Canadian Heart Foundation, was a camp director for summer camp programs for mentally challenged children, and was a president of the University of Prince Edward Island Panther Booster Club. For three years he was a member of the board of directors of United Way. In 2000 and 2001 he was a co-chair of the Canadian Mental Health Golf Classic. Paul Connolly and his family reside in Charlottetown.

Etta Connolly is the daughter of Willard and Blanche MacLean of Peters Road.

References
CPG 1998-1999.

CONROY, NICHOLAS, farmer, justice of the peace, and officeholder; b. 1816, in Rathdowney, Barony Forth, Wexford, Ireland, son of Thomas Conroy and Christine Herron; m. 7 July 1851 Catherine MacDonald, and they had nine children, Dr. Peter, Tilly, George, Fred, Margaret, Mary, James, Rosetta, and Fannie; Roman Catholic; d. 13 October 1879 in Tignish.

Conroy, a Liberal, was elected to the House of Assembly in a by-election held in 1873 for 1st Prince. He was re-elected in the general election of 1876. He resigned his seat in 1879 to accept an appointment as Register of Deeds for the province.

Conroy was known as a member who was capable of disagreeing with his party's policies. He was in favour of religious education, and was well-liked and respected within many Island communities.

Conroy was educated in Ireland before immigrating to the Island in 1835. He was appointed a Justice of the Peace ca. 1840, and became a Collector of Customs in both Cascumpec and Tignish. He was the Sergeant-at-Arms in the Assembly and was twice appointed High Sheriff of Prince County. Additionally, Conroy served as a trustee and governor of Prince of Wales College in Charlottetown. Nicholas Conroy died on 13 October 1879.

Catherine Conroy, the daughter of John and Sarah MacDonald, and the niece of Peter McIntyre, Bishop of Charlottetown, was a native of Goose River. She was born in 1826 and died 11 December 1903.

References
CPG 1876; DCB X 1871–1880, pp. 194–95; *Meacham's Atlas*; *Royal Gazette* 14 May 1835; *Patriot* 14 December 1903 p. 6; PARO: MNI-Census 1881; MNI-Hutchinson's pp. 249, 252, 259; Conroy Family File.

COOKE, RANDY ELLWOOD, comptroller and fish plant manager; b. 4 July 1961 in O'Leary, son of Elwood Cooke and Shirley MacKinnon; m. 28 June 1985 Adele Buchanan, and they had three children, Kate, Jane, and Benjamin; Nazarene Church.

Cooke, a Liberal, was elected in the general election of 1993 for 2nd Prince. He resigned on 21 August 1995.

Cooke received his primary education at Bloomfield Elementary. Later he attended O'Leary High School and graduated in 1978. In 1982 Cooke graduated from the University of Prince Edward Island with a Bachelor of Business Administration, and became the comptroller at Howard's Cove Seafoods Limited. Since 1993 Cooke has been general manager of Howard's Cove Shellfish.

Cooke was general manager of the Howard's Cove Seafoods Maroons Hockey Team and was a director of the O'Leary Athletic Association. He served on the executive of the Prince Edward Island Senior Hockey League and on the executive of the Prince Edward Island Junior Hockey League.

Randy Cooke and his family reside in Cape Wolfe. Adele Cooke was born on 28 December 1961 and is the daughter of George Buchanan and Hazel Harris of O'Leary.

References
CPG 1995; *Guardian* 13 February 1993, 5 March 1993, 18 March 1995, 22 August 1995, 24 February 1996, 13 April 1996.

COX, HARRY HOWARD, farmer and merchant; b. ca. 10 June 1874, son of Julius Cox and Jane Ellen Jeffs; m. first 1905 Margaret Florence MacLaine; m. secondly Lottie A. MacLaine; m. thirdly Katherine M. Pratt; he had one child, Herbert H.; d. 1950.

Cox, a Liberal, was elected to the House of Assembly in the general election of 1927 for 2nd Kings. He was re-elected in the general elections of 1931, 1935, 1939, 1943, and 1947. He was defeated in the general election of 1923. In 1950 Cox died while serving as a Member of the Legislative Assembly. During his political career, he served as Minister without Portfolio from 1948 to 1950. He also served as Chairman of the Fishermen's Loan Board. As a businessperson, Cox deplored governmental paternalism and applied these beliefs in his day-to-day dealings.

Cox resided in Morell where he was a merchant. As a young man he worked in the general store owned by his uncle, Robert N. Cox*. In 1910 Cox began his own business, which led to many successful ventures, including a lobster factory at Naufrage. He was also the manager and a stockholder of the St. Peters Starch Company Limited and served as vice-president of the Charlottetown Can Company Limited, reportedly the largest of its kind in the Maritimes. In addition, Cox supervised a farm in his home community. Harry Cox died in 1950.

Margaret Cox of St. Peters Bay was born in 1884 and died in 1913. Cox later married Lottie, who died in 1915. Katherine Cox, his third wife, was born in 1882 and died in 1963. Herbert H. Cox went on to become the Chief Engineer with the Malartic Coal Fields in Quebec.

References
CPG 1931, 1944, 1948; MacKinnon *Life of the Party* p. 102; PEI *Journal of the House of Assembly* 1943 p. 3, 1948 p. 3, 1950 p. 3; *Maritime Advocate and Busy East* July 1940; PARO: RG: Vital Statistics Series 3: Marriage Records; 1901 Census; Cemetery Records.

COX, ROBERT N., merchant, manufacturer, lobster canner, and fox breeder; b. 12 October 1850 in Charlottetown, son of John Benjamin Cox and Jane Martha; m. 10 December 1885 Elizabeth Sutherland, and they had six children, Russell, Edith, Lloyd, George, Alice, and Fred; Anglican; d. 19 April 1934 in Charlottetown.

Cox, a Liberal, was first elected to the Legislative Assembly in the general election of 1908 for 2nd Kings. He was re-elected in the general election of 1919. He was defeated in the general elections of 1912 and 1923. On 9 September 1920, Cox was sworn in as a Minister without Portfolio in the government of John H. Bell*.

Cox received his education in Morell and Charlottetown. In his youth he was a clerk with Peake Brothers. Cox resided in Morell for a significant portion of his life and owned a large general store for more than 40 years. His nephew, Harry Howard Cox*, worked in his uncle's store. Cox's business included lobster packing, and he ran two canneries, one at St. Peters Harbour and the other in the Magdalen Islands. He had interests in potato starch manufacturing. In association with Harvey D. McEwen* Cox was involved in two factories, one in St. Peters and one in Lot 40. Cox, like many Island business people following the First World War, was involved in the fox industry. He also spent some time farming. Robert Cox died 19 April 1934 of a stroke at his home on Longworth Avenue in Charlottetown.

Cox's parents were born in Newfoundland. Elizabeth Cox was born in 1858 and died in 1931 of heart failure.

References
CPG 1921; *Maple Leaf Magazine* June 1934; *Patriot* 19 April 1934; PARO: Marriage Register No. 13 1873–1887 p. 104; MNI-Census 1891; St. Paul's Church and Charlottetown People's Cemetery Records.

CRAWFORD, DUNCAN, teacher, farmer, merchant, justice of the peace, and railway appraiser; b. 1837 in Wood Islands, son of Neil Crawford and Mary Sinclair; m. 1864 Mary MacKenzie, and they had four children, Mary J., William, Maggie G., and Donald M.; Presbyterian; d. 1921.

Crawford, a Conservative, was elected to the House of Assembly in a by-election held 21 October 1879 for 4th Queens. He was defeated in the general election of 1882.

Crawford was educated at Central Academy in Charlottetown. He was a licenced teacher and taught at Wood Islands for 12 years. Besides working a farm of 100 acres, Crawford owned a general store. He served as a Justice of the Peace and, in 1871, as a railway appraiser. Duncan Crawford died in 1921.

Crawford's parents both emigrated from Inverary, Argyleshire, Scotland, in 1823. Mary Crawford, of Flat River, was born in 1835 and died in 1919. She was the daughter of Donald MacKenzie of Flat River who had emigrated from Scotland.

References

CPG 1880, 1881, 1883; Elections PEI; *Meacham's Atlas*; MNI-Hutchinson's p. 187; MNI-Census 1861, 1881, 1891; Wood Islands Presbyterian Cemetery Records.

CROSBY, CYRUS WILLIAM, farmer; b. 13 January 1855 in Bonshaw, son of Andrew C. Crosby and Sarah McNeill; m. 16 November 1882 Grace McNeill, and they had three children, Ernest L., Ruth H., and Lawson E.; Baptist; d. 20 January 1936 in Souris.

Crosby, a Liberal, was first elected to the Legislative Assembly in a by-election held for 1st Queens in 1909. He was re-elected in the general election of 1919. He was defeated in the general elections of 1912 and 1915. Following the election, on 8 September 1919 he was appointed to Executive Council as Commissioner of Public Works. Having been appointed to this office, a by-election was held, and Crosby again won the election. He was defeated in the 1923 general election.

While he was Commissioner, the province took advantage of the Federal Highways Act. Under the act, the federal government contributed 40 per cent of the cost of highway construction done by provincial governments. During Crosby's time in office, a significant number of roads were rebuilt and a large number of permanent bridges erected. He became known in political circles as "Good Roads Crosby."

Crosby was educated at the Cavendish Grammar School. He was a farmer and lived in Bonshaw on land known locally as "Alps." He also owned a successful mill in the community. Deeply committed to the Baptist Church in Bonshaw, Crosby served as a deacon and as a clerk. He was a member of the group that worked to build a new church that was eventually completed in November 1893. In 1887 Crosby was a member of the Mutual Improvement Society in the Bonshaw area, whose objective was to raise money for a concert hall. A dairying company was formed in the Bonshaw area in 1898, with Crosby serving as one of the original directors. In 1904 a severe illness caused him to be inactive for a considerable period of time. He sold his farm in 1921, leaving Bonshaw for Charlottetown. The community held a farewell party and presented Crosby and his wife with a token of respect and friendship. It is likely that near the end of their lives, Crosby and his wife moved to the Souris area to live with their daughter, Ruth Matthew. Cyrus Crosby died 20 January 1936.

Grace Crosby, the daughter of James McNeill of Cavendish, was born 9 September 1856 and died in 1934.

References

CPG 1912, 1916, 1921, 1924; Glen pp. 31, 32, 61, 62, 85, 93, 101, 106; *Examiner* 2 March 1904; *Maple Leaf Magazine* February 1936; *Patriot* 3 May 1921, 20 January 1936; PARO: Crosby Family File; MNI-Frederick's PEI Directory pp. 257-58; MNI-Census 1891; Souris West United Church Records.

CULLEN, L.L.D, EUGENE PATRICK, farmer and milk processor; b. 7 August 1905 in Hope River, son of Timothy Peter Cullen and Frances Etta Landrigan; m. 29 July 1942 Gladys Kathleen McCardle, and they had four children, Frances Anne, Mary, Connie, and Tom; Roman Catholic; d. 9 July 1995 in Charlottetown.

Cullen, a Liberal, was first elected by acclamation to the Legislative Assembly in a by-election held 10 July 1944 for 3rd Queens. He was re-elected in the general elections of 1947, 1951, and 1955. He was defeated in the general elections of 1959, 1962, and 1966. In February 1948 he was appointed Speaker and served in this position for two sessions. In 1950 Cullen was Minister of Industry and Natural Resources, and, from 1955 to 1959, he served as Minister of Agriculture.

Cullen's brother Thomas Reid Cullen* also served in the Legislative Assembly, representing 2nd Kings from 1943 to 1947, and again from 1951 to 1955.

Cullen was educated at the Union Commercial College and the Prince Edward Island Agricultural and Technical School. He spent much of his life living on a dairy farm originally owned by his father in Central Royalty, later known as

Sherwood. Between 1922 and 1946, the Cullen family operated a dairy farm and a raw milk route. On 1 February 1946, Cullen founded Purity Dairy Limited on Kent Street in Charlottetown. The dairy met with success and was incorporated in 1953. Purity eventually acquired G and G Dairy Limited. By 1990, Purity Dairy owned nine delivery trucks, employed 25 people, and had 3,500 patrons. It has continued to thrive into the 21st century. Cullen was an integral part of the milk producers' efforts to organize, and was secretary of the Charlottetown Milk Producers and Vendors Association, a director of Prince Edward Island Dairymen's Association, and chairman of the Fluid Milk Association. He also was a member of the Prince Edward Island School Milk Foundation.

Cullen participated in many community activities. He served as chairman of the board of governors of St. Dunstan's University, chairman of the board of management of Prince Edward Island Central School of Nursing, and chairman and board member of Prince Edward Island Health Services Commission. For many years he was a volunteer with United Way and served as president of the Prince Edward Island United Appeal, as a United Way director in the late 1960s to the mid-1970s, and as the provincial campaign chair in 1970. Cullen was a director of the Charlottetown Hospital Board of Management from 1960 to 1980, and a board member of the Queen Elizabeth Hospital from 1981 to 1988. Cullen served on the University of Prince Edward Island Progress Fund and on the board of management of Basilica Recreation Centre. He was honoured by Health Minister Catherine Callbeck* — later a premier of the province — for faithful service to the Hospital Services Commission from 1968 to 1977, and for his help in introducing medicare to the Province in 1970. The University of Prince Edward Island presented Cullen with an honourary degree in recognition of his contribution to the Island. Eugene Cullen died 9 July 1995.

Gladys Cullen was born on 11 April 1919 and died on 13 March 1999. She was the daughter of James McCardle and Annie Duffy of Middleton.

References
CPG 1945, 1958, 1960, 1963, 1967; Elections PEI; PEI *Journal of the House of Assembly* 1950 p. 3, 1959 p. 3; *Guardian* 23 January 1975, 3 December 1977, 25 October 1985, 20 April 1987, 10 July 1995; *Islandside*, July/August 1990.

CULLEN, THOMAS REID, farmer; b. 19 January 1904 in Hope River, son of Timothy Peter Cullen and Frances Etta Landrigan; m. 20 February 1928 Pearl Burke, and there were no children; Roman Catholic; d. 9 December 1984 in Charlottetown.

Cullen, a Liberal, was first elected to the Legislative Assembly in the general election of 1943 for 2nd Kings. He was re-elected in the general election of 1951. He was defeated in the general election of 1947. On 15 February 1944, Cullen was chosen Deputy Speaker, and, on 17 March 1944, became Speaker, serving in that role for four legislative sessions. In 1949 he was appointed Clerk of the General Assembly and acted as Clerk for 13 sessions until 1959. He was reappointed Clerk of the General Assembly in 1966 and remained in this position for 11 sessions.

Cullen's brother Eugene* served in the Legislative Assembly, representing 3rd Queens from 1944 to 1959.

Cullen received his early education at Central Royalty School and later attended Prince of Wales College and St. Dunstan's College. He taught school in West Devon and Suffolk ca. 1921. For the majority of his adult life, Cullen was a farmer. He began farming with his father on the family's dairy farm in Central Royalty, which was later known as Sherwood. In 1928 Cullen moved to Midgell after purchasing a farm on Church Road, and he farmed there until several years before his death. Thomas Cullen died 9 December 1984 at the Queen Elizabeth Hospital in Charlottetown.

Pearl Cullen, the daughter of William P. Burke, was born in Charlottetown.

References
CPG 1946, 1950, 1955; Elections PEI; *Guardian* 10 December 1984.

CUMMISKEY, JAMES H., merchant, trader, and farmer; b. 4 January 1850 in Fort Augustus, son of Hugh Cummiskey and Ellen Mitchell; m. Catherine Woods, and they had seven children, Margaret, Katherine A., James W., Patrick E., Estella F., Hugh Edwin, and Mary Emma Jane; Roman Catholic; d. 5 February 1925, Massachusetts.

Cummiskey, a Liberal, was elected to the House of Assembly in a by-election held in April 1891 for 3rd Queens. He was elected to the Legislative Assembly in the 1893 general election. He was re-elected in the general elections of 1897, 1900, 1904, and 1908, as well as in by-elections held in

1901 and 1905. He was defeated in the general election of 1890. Cummiskey was appointed to Executive Council and served as Commissioner of Public Works in the Donald Farquharson* Administration in December 1900. He was a member of Executive Council in the Arthur Peters* Administration in 1905 and in the Francis Haszard* Administration in 1908 and 1909. From April 1898 to June 1900, he served as Speaker.

Cummiskey's most eventful moments in the Legislature came during the 1900 legislative sessions while serving as Speaker. In 1899 the Liberal government had made efforts to persuade former Liberal Joseph Wise* to resign his seat. He had agreed to do so if a by-election was held before the Legislative Assembly session in the spring of 1900. The by-election was not held and Wise withdrew his resignation. On 8 May 1900, his resignation was announced in the House. This was immediately followed by Wise defiantly taking his seat. In support of the government's desire to maintain a slim majority, Cummiskey did not recognize Wise* when he tried to take his former seat. Amidst pandemonium, Wise's vote with the Conservatives, which would have defeated the government, was not recognized. In the Assembly the following day, Wise again attempted to take his seat, while at the same time Cummiskey entered Wise's resignation into the record. Wise was asked to withdraw, but refused. He was then removed from the Assembly by the Sergeant-at-Arms, with the House Messenger assisting, to be locked in the Speaker's room until the House adjourned. When order was restored, the Liberals held on to power since Henry Pineau*, a sitting Conservative, voted with the government.

Cummiskey lived in the Fort Augustus area for much of his life. Late in his political career he resided in Charlottetown, though he continued to represent his home riding. Cummiskey traded and operated a general store on the Fort Augustus Road at Webster's Corner. He also did some farming. James Cummiskey died 5 February 1925.

Catherine Cummiskey's birthdate remains in question, as it was reported that she was 24 in the 1881 Census and 39 in the 1891. Her father was born in Ireland and her mother was born in Prince Edward Island.

References

CPG 1897, 1909; *Meacham's Atlas*; *Patriot* 31 December 1925; PARO: Census 1881, 1891; MNI-Mercantile Agency Reference Book 1876; St. Joachim's Roman Catholic Church Records Book 1 p. 54; St. Patrick's Roman Catholic Church Records, Fort Augustus; Leard Files.

CURRAN, THOMAS AMBROSE, farmer and carpenter; b. 28 April 1904 in Elliotvale, son of John F. Curran and Jane O'Halloran; m. 12 October 1938 Lauretta Power, and they had seven children, Mary S., Jane, Frank, Anna, Rita, Cathy, and John J. (predeceased his father); Roman Catholic; d. 19 April 1997 in Charlottetown.

Curran, a Conservative, was first elected to the Legislative Assembly in the general election of 1959 for 3rd Kings. He was re-elected in the general elections of 1962 and 1966. He was defeated in the general election of 1970.

Curran was educated at the Baldwin Road Rural School. He took over the family farm after the death of his parents, and continued to work as a farmer and carpenter. He was involved in a number of church and community organizations. He served as a director of the Kings County Memorial Hospital and was a member of the Knights of Columbus. Thomas Curran died 19 April 1997.

Lauretta Curran predeceased her husband.

References

CPG 1961, 1970, 1971; *Guardian* 22 April 1997.

CURRIE, DOUGALD, farmer; b. 22 August ca. 1844 in Fairview, son of Malcolm Currie and Katherine Bell; m. 23 July 1869 Maria Burdette, and they had eight children, Nelson, Katie, Edward, Sophia, Ernest, Brenton, Irene, and Florence; Presbyterian; d. 5 November 1918 in Charlottetown.

Currie, a Conservative, was elected to the Legislative Assembly in a by-election for 2nd Queens held December 1902. He was defeated in the general elections of 1890 and 1904. Currie served as Sergeant-at-Arms in the Legislature for a number of years.

Educated in Fairview, Currie lived there for the majority of his life. He farmed 100 acres, all of which were cultivated. According to *Past and Present*, he was practical and progressive in his farming methods, and stood among the leading agriculturalists of his community. Later in life, he and his family moved to Charlottetown. Dougald Currie died 5 November 1918.

Currie's father was born in Collins, Scotland, and migrated first to Pictou, Nova Scotia, and later to the Island. His mother was also born in Scotland. Maria Currie died 23 June 1923 at the age of 76.

References

CPG 1891, 1903, 1905; Elections PEI; *Past and Present* p. 464;

Guardian 6 November 1918; *Patriot* 6 November 1918; PARO: Marriage Register RG 19 series 3 subseries 3 volume 7 1867–1877; MNI-Census 1891; New Dominion Presbyterian.

CUTCLIFFE, JOHN SINCLAIR, funeral home owner and funeral director; b. 22 August 1930 in Summerside, son of Allie Byron Cutcliffe of Appin Road and Margaret Jean Sinclair of Summerside; m. first 1 May 1954 Anita Lynds, and they had four children, Blair, Douglas, Paul, and Jean; m. secondly 31 January 1986 Norma Jean MacKay, and there were no children; United.

Cutcliffe, a Liberal, was first elected to the Legislative Assembly in the general election of 1966 for 2nd Queens. He was re-elected in the general election of 1970. He was appointed Deputy Speaker on 2 June 1970. Cutcliffe resigned in 1972. He was a President of the Prince Edward Island Liberal Association and a member of the national Liberal executive. In 1972 Cutcliffe was defeated in the federal election in the riding of Malpeque.

Sinclair Cutcliffe received his primary education at West Kent School, and later attended Mount Allison Academy and Union Commercial College. He received his professional training at Embalmers' School in Saint John. In 1952 he worked for his father at the Cutcliffe Funeral Home in Hunter River. A few years later, his father moved the business to Charlottetown. Over a period of years, Cutcliffe purchased the funeral home from his father. In 1976 he purchased the Hennessy and Charlottetown Funeral Homes, and also continued to deliver services under the Cutcliffe name. In 1986 Cutcliffe sold the three funeral homes to an international funeral company. He was a president of the Prince Edward Island Funeral Directors and Embalmers Association and the Canadian Funeral Directors and Embalmers Association.

Cutcliffe acted as a regional vice-president for Eastern Canada International Rescue and First Aid Association and as a field supervisor for the first aid services of the Canadian Red Cross Society. He served as president of Red Cross in the province, as a provincial chief of rescue with the Prince Edward Island Emergency Measures Organization, and as a president of the International Rescue and First Aid Association. Cutcliffe was awarded the Order of Red Cross and numerous other Red Cross Awards. He also won the CJRW and Red Cross Life Saving Award and the Julian S. Wise Heroic Life Saving Award. Cutcliffe was a president of Kiwanis and of Rotary. He was a member of the St. John's Lodge No. 1, and is a Past Master of the A.F. and A.M., a Royal and Select Master of the Cryptic Rite, and a member of the Prince Edward Perceptory, 14th Degree Scottish Rite, Byne L.O.L. No. 614. He was a member of the Belvedere Golf and Winter Club, the Glen Afton Golf Club, and the Charlottetown Yacht Club. Sinclair Cutcliffe and his wife reside in North River.

Anita Cutcliffe, the daughter of Ed Lynds of Kensington and Ruby Lynds, was born 10 November 1936. Norma Cutcliffe, the daughter of Oscar and Winnifred MacKay, was born 29 August 1936.

References
CPG 1972; Elections PEI; *HFER* Malpeque p. 2; *WWPEI* p. 37; *Guardian* 3 October 1970; Questionnaire to Former MLAs.

D

DALTON, K.C.S.G., HONOURABLE CHARLES, druggist, farmer, and fox breeder; b. 9 June 1850 in Tignish, son of Patrick Dalton and Margaret McCarthy, both of Ireland; m. 30 June 1874 Annie Gavin, and they had 12 children, C. Howard M.D., Freda, Nora, Julia P., Florence, Edith, Irene, Gerald, Zita, Joseph Arnold, Catherine, and Mary B.; Roman Catholic; d. 9 December 1933 in Charlottetown.

Dalton, a Conservative, was first elected to the Legislative Assembly in the general election of 1912 for 1st Prince. He was re-elected in the general election of 1915. He was defeated in the general elections of 1908 and 1919. In 1915 Dalton was appointed to Executive Council as a Minister without Portfolio. On 29 November 1930 he was appointed Lieutenant-Governor.

Dalton received his education in the provincial public schools. He lived in Tignish during his childhood and early adult years, and later moved to Charlottetown. Though successful in his political ambitions, it was in the fox breeding industry that Dalton had his greatest achievements. There he was a pioneer, becoming world-renowned and financially prosperous. Nonetheless, financial success did not come easily. In 1890 he was struggling as a farmer and as a druggist. Unknown to the people of the Tignish area, Dalton, in partnership with Robert Oulton, secretly perfected the art of breeding silver foxes. From 1900 to 1914, they bred the most valuable foxes in the world. Dalton became the president of the Charles Dalton Silver Black Fox Company. The effort to develop a rare and distinctive breed of foxes made him a fortune. Dalton and five other fox breeders, Silas and B. I. Rayner, Robert Tuplin, Captain James Gordon, and Robert T. Oulton, forged a pact known as the "Big Six Combine." Its purpose was to limit the number of participants in the business and therefore keep prices soaring. Although the monopoly did not last indefinitely, it survived long enough to enrich Dalton and his associates. From 1912 to ca. 1921, Dalton was the majority owner of *The Guardian.*

Dalton was benevolent to his country and to the Island community. He financed the construction of Dalton Hall at St. Dunstan's College. During the First World War, he donated a fully equipped motor field ambulance to the Canadian Forces. As a result of the death of two of his children from tuberculosis, he built Dalton Sanatorium in North Wiltshire, which was completed in 1916, and donated it to the province. Dalton's local community benefitted from his largesse when he donated the Dalton Normal School to the Parish of Tignish. Dalton donated money to aid in the reconstruction of St. Dunstan's Basilica. He also served as a governor of the Owen Connolly Trust Estate, a trust established for aid in the education of sons of Irish fathers. In 1917 Dalton was bestowed the honour of Knight Commander of the Order of St. Gregory the Great by Pope Benedict XV. Charles Dalton died 9 December 1933 of pneumonia while serving as Lieutenant-Governor.

Annie Dalton, the daughter of Michael Gavin and Catharine O'Neil, was born 12 September 1854 and died 25 December 1938.

References
CPG 1919, 1920, 1933; MacDonald *New Ireland* p. 30; *Prominent Men* p. 572; *Tuplin,* p. 13; *WWC* 1917–1918 p. 1176; *Guardian* 29 August 2002; *Island Magazine,* vol. 3 no. 84 Fall/Winter 1977 p. 20; *Maple Leaf Magazine* January 1939; *West Prince Graphic* 18 October 1995; PARO: MNI-Census 1881, 1891; Baptismal Index; UPEI: Robertson Library: Rankin, pp. 17–18.

DARBY, HARRY ALFRED, farmer, fox breeder, and telephone company president; b. 27 November 1865 in Abrams Village, son of Edwin Darby and Amelia D. Williams; m. first 14 July 1896 Bessie W. Morrison, and they had eight children, Gerald B., Edwin A., Earnest W., G. Arthur, William A., Walter Eric*, Harry B., and Geraldine; m. secondly M. Thelma Allen, and there were no children; Anglican; d. 25 June 1952 in Summerside.

Darby, a Liberal, was elected to the Legislative Assembly in the general election of 1927 for 3rd Prince. He also served as President of the East Prince Liberal Association in 1925 and 1926.

Darby was educated in both Abrams Village and Charlottetown. Later in life he resided near Wellington and on King Street in Summerside. A farmer and fox breeder, Darby was the vice-president and secretary-treasurer of the Egmont Bay

Dairy Company and the president of the Victor Silver Black Fox Company Limited. He was the president of the Rural Telephone Line and was a member of the Masonic Order. In 1917 Darby served on the Military Tribunal. Harry Darby died 25 June 1952 at his home.

Walter Darby*, Harry Darby's son, represented 2nd Prince in the Legislature and served on Executive Council.

Bessie Darby, the daughter of Captain Peter Morrison, was born in 1874 and died in 1930. M. Thelma Darby survived her husband.

References

CPG 1928, 1936; *Patriot* 26 June 1952; PARO: MNI-Keith Compton; MNI-St. Eleanors Anglican Church Records.

DARBY, K.C., HONOURABLE WALTER ERIC,

teacher, lawyer, magistrate, Crown prosecutor, and judge; b. 21 November 1903 in Abrams Village, son of Harry Alfred Darby* and Bessie W. Morrison; m. 1933 Margaret McCreath, and they had four children, Peter, Elizabeth, Cecilia, and Isabel; Anglican; d. 17 March 1980 in Summerside.

Darby, a Liberal, was first elected to the Legislative Assembly by acclamation in a by-election held 18 July 1949 for 2nd Prince. He was re-elected in the general election of 1951. He was defeated in the general election of 1943 for 5th Prince. Darby was appointed Attorney-General, Advocate General, and Provincial Treasurer from 1950 to 1954. Following the death of Premier J. Walter Jones*, Darby ran for leadership of the Liberal party, losing to Alexander W. Matheson* by one vote at the leadership convention.

Darby's father, Harry Darby*, had represented 3rd Prince in the Legislature.

Darby received his primary education at Abrams Village School. From 1917 to 1920, he attended Prince of Wales College, and at that time was the youngest person registered at the College. From 1920 to 1922, Darby taught at O'Leary High School. In 1925 Darby graduated from Dalhousie with a Bachelor of Arts degree and in 1927 with a Bachelor of Law degree. While at Dalhousie, he was president of the Debating Society. From 1927 to 1930, he practised law with the firm Covert, Pearson and Rutledge in Halifax. In 1931 he opened an office in Summerside and carried on a general law practice. He also served as a part-time Stipendiary Magistrate from 1936 to 1944. In 1944 Darby was appointed King's Counsel. He served as a

Crown prosecutor from 1943 to 1948. He appeared before the Supreme Court of Canada on three occasions and represented the province before the Privy Council in London. In 1954 Darby was appointed Judge of the Prince County Court, and in 1975 he was elevated to the Prince Edward Island Supreme Court. Darby retired 21 November 1978 while serving as Chief Justice, at which time he was awarded a plaque by the Summerside Police Force, in appreciation of his support to the police during his time as a judge.

In 1946 and 1947, Darby was president of the Law Society and, in 1948, vice-president of the Canadian Bar Association for the Island. He served as chairman and was the only Canadian member of a Commonwealth Commission established to assist with the reorganization of the Police Force in Trinidad.

During the Second World War, Darby chaired the War Finance Committee for Prince County during nine Victory Loan campaigns. He also served as vice-chairman of the Red Cross War Services Campaigns for a number of years. In 1943 Darby was secretary of Rotary and served as its president in 1944. Later he was made a life member of the Rotary Club. In 1948 he was the first secretary of the Summerside Air Cadet Corps. He served as president of the Prince County Hospital trustees and was a charter member of Summerside Y's Men's Club. Darby was a chair of the Prince Edward Island Milk Board, and in 1964 he was appointed treasurer of the board of governors of Prince of Wales College, a position he held until the formation of the University of Prince Edward Island. Walter Darby died 17 March 1980 at the Prince County Hospital.

Margaret Darby was the daughter of Peter L. McCreath of Halifax.

References

CPG 1946, 1950, 1955; PEI Department of Justice *Annual Report* 1978, p. 10; PEI *Journal of the Legislative Assembly* 1950, p. 2, 1954 p. 2; *Guardian* 18 March 1980; *Journal-Pioneer* 9 September 1978, 18 March 1980; *Maritime Advocate and Busy East* June 1950.

DAVIES, BENJAMIN, merchant, postmaster-general, chairman of the Railway Board, and paymaster of the railway; b. 1813, in Charlottetown, son of Nathan Davies, who emigrated from southern Wales in 1812, and Amelia MacNutt; m. first 2 January 1843 Kezia Attwood Watts, and they had four children, Robert Watts, Louis Henry*, Benjamin, and

Sarah Amelia; m. secondly 18 May 1854 Eliza Frances Townsend Cooke, previously married to Thomas Cooke, M.D., and they had two children, William Lord and Daniel; m. thirdly Mrs. Beal of Tenby, Wales, and there were no children; Anglican; d. September 1904, in Charlottetown.

Davies, a Liberal, was first elected to the House of Assembly in 1850 for 4th Queens. He was re-elected in the general elections of 1867, 1870, 1872, and 1873. He was defeated in the general election of 1855. While in the House of Assembly, he served on Executive Council.

During his time in the Assembly, Davies was particularly concerned with the Land Question, and was an advocate of enabling the tenantry to take ownership from the absentee proprietors. His second son, Louis Henry, would later argue the tenants' case successfully before the Royal Land Commission in 1875 and 1876. Davies and his son Louis* served in the House concurrently from 1872 to 1875.

Davies lived in Charlottetown. He was a merchant and for many years owned B. Davies & Company. He operated shipbuilding yards in Orwell and Rollo Bay and was a ship owner and exporter. Davies had a number of public responsibilities, including serving as a Fire Commissioner in 1843 and councillor for Ward 1 following the incorporation of Charlottetown in 1855. In 1858 Davies was appointed Postmaster-General and served as a Justice of the Peace ca. 1864. In 1869 he became Colonial Secretary. From 1872 to 1873, Davies was chairman of the Railway Board, and later Paymaster of the Railway until 1889.

Davies was a Lieutenant-Colonel in the 1st Queen's Calvary Troop and a Militia Officer of the Old Brigade of Charlottetown. His agricultural interests included membership in the Royal Agricultural Society.

In the winter of 1904, Davies became ill. Later that year, he died in Charlottetown.

Kezia Davies, daughter of Samuel Watts of St. Andrew's, New Brunswick, died in 1853 as a result of burns suffered in a kitchen accident. Eliza Davies was the daughter of Cecil Townsend and Eliza Lea of Charlottetown. Eliza Davies' died on 29 September 1889.

References
CPG 1874, 1876; *Meacham's Atlas*; *Standard Dictionary* pp. 143–46; *Memories of Long Ago* p. 7; *Charlottetown Herald* 21 September 1904; *Colonial Herald* 25 April 1840, 7 January 1843, 14 January 1843, 29 July 1843; *Constitutionalist* 16 May 1846; *Islander* 8 January 1847, 26 May 1854; *Royal Gazette* 25 June 1839, 1 November 1852; PARO: Davies Family File; MNI-Hutchinson's; MNI-Census 1848; MNI-Charlottetown Manuscripts p. 34; MNI-St. Paul's Anglican Church records; MNI-Sherwood Cemetery Records.

DAVIES, P.C., Q.C., RIGHT HONOURABLE SIR LOUIS HENRY, lawyer, judge, business person, and publisher; b. 4 May 1845 in Charlottetown, son of Benjamin Davies* and Kezia Attwood Watts; m. 28 July 1872 Susan Wiggins, and they had seven children, Gertrude, Ethel, Thomas, Mary, Vera, Robert, and Hugh (the latter three did not survive childhood); Anglican; d. 1 May 1924 in Ottawa.

Davies, a Liberal, was first elected to the House of Assembly in the general election of 1872 for Charlottetown Royalty. He was re-elected in the general elections of 1873 and 1876. Davies was defeated in the general election of 1879. In 1869 Davies was appointed Solicitor-General. He served as Leader of the Opposition from 1872 to 1876, and Premier and Attorney-General from 1876 to 1879. Davies was a Member of the House of Assembly concurrently with his father, Benjamin Davies*, from 1872 to 1875.

While Davies was Premier, the Free School Act was passed by the House of Assembly. The Act reconfirmed the non-denominational nature of the province's public school system, ending decades of debate regarding government support for separate schools. This came at a cost, for the process required to pass the legislation proved difficult and socially fractious. Davies united Protestant House of Assembly Members to form the Free Schools Party. This coalition was made up of both Conservatives and Liberals who supported the Free School Act. Davies was also responsible for various reforms in the public service. Following the financial crisis caused by the construction of the railway, the Davies government placed the province upon a sound financial footing. During his years in the provincial legislature, he established a reputation as a capable and committed orator.

In the 1882 federal election, Davies was elected to the House of Commons for Queen's County. He was re-elected in 1887 and 1891. In 1896 Davies was re-elected to the House of Commons representing West Queen's. After accepting an appointment to the Privy Council as Minister of Marine and Fisheries, he was re-elected in a by-election held 30 July 1896. For the fifth consecutive federal general election, Davies was re-elected to the House of Commons in 1900. As federal Minister of Marine and Fisheries, Davies dealt with the Bering Sea sealing controversy. He was responsible for dealing with the control over fishing rights in Canadian waters. Davies also argued Canada's side in the 1899 Alaska Boundary question.

In 1897 during Queen Victoria's Diamond Jubilee, Davies was created a Knight Commander of St. Michael and St. George. On 25 September 1901, he was appointed Puisne Judge, Supreme Court of Canada. He served on the Supreme Court for nearly 23 years, serving as Chief Justice from 1918 until his death. In 1919 he was sworn in as a member of the Imperial Privy Council, at that time the highest court of the Commonwealth.

Davies was educated at the Central Academy and Prince of Wales College in Charlottetown. Later he attended the Inner Temple in London, England, and obtained a law degree. Davies was called to the British Bar in 1866 and to the Bar of Prince Edward Island in 1867. He instructed Alexander Warburton*, a future premier, in the law, as he later did John Whear*. Davies was designated Queen's Counsel in 1880. In November 1890 Francis L. Haszard*, another future premier, joined with Davies in a law practice that continued until Davies' appointment to the Supreme Court.

In Davies' early legal career, he advocated on behalf of the tenantry of Prince Edward Island. For many years the tenants of the province struggled under the system of absentee landlordism imposed when the colony was settled. In 1875 and 1876, Davies argued the tenants' case successfully before the Royal Land Commission. The Commission was responsible for arbitrating the price for the land to be bought by the Island government and then re-sold to the tenants . Davies first gained national recognition in 1877, when he argued successfully on behalf of the British counsel before the International Fisheries Commission. According to the decision of the Commission, Canada and Newfoundland were awarded the sum of $5.5 million as compensation for treatment they received as a result of the Reciprocity Treaty of 1854.

Davies served as president of the Merchant's Bank of Prince Edward Island, as well as the president of Patriot Printing and Publishing Company. Throughout his lifetime he was involved in numerous charitable organizations, serving as president of the Canadian Society of Charities and Correc-

tions and as president of the Canadian Branch of the St. John's Ambulance. Davies was the founder and first president of the Ottawa Tuberculosis Association. During the First World War he also administered the Patriotic Fund. As a member of the Dickens Fellowship, he lectured on various subjects, including the life and works of Charles Dickens. Louis Davies died 1 May 1924, while serving as Chief Justice of the Supreme Court of Canada. He was buried in Beechwood Cemetery, Ottawa.

Susan Davies was the daughter of Reverend Abram Van Gilder Wiggins of St. Eleanors and Helen Diane Townsend.

References

CDP p. 153; MacKinnon *Life of the Party* pp. 57–58; *Prominent Men* p. 461; *Standard Dictionary* pp. 143–46; *Patriot* 1 August 1872; PARO: Davies Family File; MNI-Census 1861, 1881.

DEBLOIS, GEORGE WASTIE, land agent, business person, and justice of the peace; b. 12 July 1824 in Halifax, son of Stephen Wastie and June Catherine DeBlois; m. August 1847 Sarah Frances Haviland, and they had 13 children, Stephen Haviland, Alice R., Robert Fitzgerald, Ada Maria, George Walter, Louis Heath, Elizabeth, Francis, Alfred Ernest, Mary, George Dundes, Laura, and Kathleen; Anglican; d. 14 August 1886 in Charlottetown Royalty.

DeBlois, a Conservative, was first elected in the 1876 general election for the district of Charlottetown Royalty. He was re-elected in the general election of 1879. DeBlois was interested in the education debate waged in the mid-1870s. The Denominationalists or the Sectarian School Party supported government assistance to denominational schools, while the Free School Party or the Non-Sectarian School Party supported free non-denominational schools in the 1876 election. DeBlois was a member of a coalition party, made up of both Conservatives and Liberals, in support of the Free School Act. The 1876 election was fought on the education issue with the candidates aligning themselves as Sectarian or Non-Sectarian. DeBlois was chosen as a candidate for the Free School Party. Following the election, Premier L. H. Davies* appointed DeBlois provincial secretary and treasurer. On the acceptance of this office, DeBlois was elected in a by-election.

After the Public Schools Act was passed in 1877, the coalition weakened. DeBlois and three other Conservatives resigned from Executive Council on 20 August 1878. When the House was called into session in 1879, DeBlois voted with the other Conservatives to bring Davies down. A new government formed in March 1879 under William Wilfred Sullivan*. He called for dissolution, and an election was held in April. DeBlois ran and won as a Conservative. He remained a backbencher for the rest of his political career.

Little is known about DeBlois' early life. An obituary in the *Weekly Examiner and Island Argus* indicates he was educated in Halifax. DeBlois lived there until May 1847, residing after that date in Charlottetown. In his early career DeBlois was a land agent. As a result of being a family friend of Samuel Cunard in Halifax, in 1853 DeBlois became land agent for the extensive Cunard holdings on Prince Edward Island, holding this position until the land was bought by the Island government in 1866. He acted as land agent for landowners Lawrence Sullivan and Lady Cecilia Georgiana Fane. Altogether, he was responsible for estates totalling more than 250,000 acres. This career ended in 1875 when the large estates were purchased with funds supplied by the federal government under terms of Confederation. DeBlois was a business agent for North British Insurance Company, a coal agent for the Sydney Mines Company and the General Mining Association, and a director of the Charlottetown Gas Light Company.

DeBlois also served as a Justice of the Peace for Charlottetown and as Lieutenant-Colonel of the 6th Regiment of Queens County Militia. He was a trustee of Prince of Wales College in 1877 and 1878. George DeBlois died 14 August 1886.

His daughter, Elizabeth, who was deeply attached to her father, died a few hours after viewing his remains, perhaps as a result of the impact his death had on her already weakened heart.

Sarah DeBlois, the daughter of Thomas Heath Haviland, Sr., and Jane Rebecca Brecken, and the sister of Thomas Heath Haviland, Jr.*, was born 23 September 1826 and died in June 1900.

References
DCB XI 1881–1890 pp. 241–42; *Weekly Examiner and Island Argus* 20 August 1886; PARO: DeBlois Family File; MNI-Hutchinson's p. 89.

DELANEY, CARROL WILFRED, fox and mink rancher, farmer, railway ticket agent, and owner of construction and trucking company; b. 20 May 1909 in Summerside, son of Dr. Mark Delaney of Wellington and Mary Cosgrove; m. first 5 November 1930 Josephine Arsenault, and they had four children, Mark A. (died in 1959), Carl, Marie, and Marcia; secondly Alice Toombs, and they had one child, Carol Ann; Roman Catholic; d. 25 June 1971 in Hunter River.

Delaney, a Liberal, was elected to the Legislative Assembly in the general election of 1947 for 5th Prince. He was defeated in a by-election held 26 November 1946 for 5th Prince. He was a town councillor in Summerside with the responsibility for water and sewage.

Carrol W. Delaney had many business interests. He was a fox and mink rancher, a fish broker, owner of County Construction, a potato farmer, and a station agent for Canadian National Railway. He worked as station agent in a number of Island communities, including Hunter River and Summerside. In 1946, according to the *Patriot*, Delaney was operating one of the largest fox ranches in the province. Later in his life he moved to Hunter River and died there on 25 June 1971.

Josephine Arsenault was a native of St. Nicholas.

References
CPG 1947, 1951; *Guardian* 4 November 1947, 26 June 1971; *Patriot* 13 November 1954 p. 1; PARO: Delaney Family File; Interview with Carl Delaney; St. Paul's Roman Catholic Church Records.

DELANEY, MICHAEL C., merchant, b. 20 November 1849 in Malpeque, son of John Delaney and Mary Quigley; m. 4 January 1871 Altimira Jane Robinson, and they had eight children, Annie, Mary A., Martha A., Carry A., Eliza E., Debbie R., Parker, and Claude S.; Wesleyan Methodist and later Baptist; d. 20 January 1918.

Delaney, a Conservative, was first elected to the Legislative Assembly in a by-election held 18 August 1909 for 4th Prince. He was re-elected in the general election in 1912. He was defeated in the general elections of 1904, 1908, and 1915. Following the 1908 election, Joseph Read was declared elected in 4th Prince by a margin of two votes. Later in July 1909, Read was unseated because of a discrepancy over the eligibility of some voters. Some accounts state that Read resigned to allow a by-election. Delaney was successful by a margin of three votes. In 1913 he served as the Conservative whip.

Delaney was educated at the public school in North Tryon. Early in his adult life he started a successful business selling eggs, butter, and general agricultural products. Eventually his two sons entered the business with him and its success continued. Michael Delaney died 20 January 1918.

Altimira Delaney was born 23 December 1849 and died 6 April 1936.

References
CPG 1905, 1915, 1916; Elections PEI; *Maple Leaf Magazine* May 1936; *Patriot* January 1918; PARO: RG Marriage Register series 3 subseries 3 Volume 7 1867–1871 Book 11 p. 524; MNI-Census 1881, 1891; Census 1901; Tryon Church Records.

DENNIS, WILLIAM HENRY, carriage builder, trader, and farmer; b. ca. 20 January 1864 in Port Hill, son of William Henry Dennis, Sr., and Mary Anne Sharpe; m. 14 March 1885 Mary Ann Ellis, and they had seven children, Melbourne, Thomas C., Iva, Milton W., Dana G., Robert C., and J. G.; Presbyterian; d. 15 July 1946 in O'Leary.

Dennis, a Liberal, was first elected to the Legislative Assembly in the general election of 1915 for 2nd Prince. He was re-elected in the general elections of 1919, 1923, 1927, 1931, 1935, 1939, and 1943. He was appointed Minister of Agriculture on 14 January 1936 and served in that ministry until 1943. Dennis believed in working alongside neighbours and members of the community to help them help themselves.

Dennis was educated in the local school. For the most part he worked as a carriage builder, but also traded in agricultural machinery, horses, buggies, wagons, and a variety of other items. Dennis, who did some farming, stayed in close contact with farmers all his life because of his involvement in trading and carriage-building. William Dennis died 15 July 1946.

Mary Dennis, the daughter of John and Margaret Ellis, was born 24 November 1864 and died in 1953.

References
CPG 1920, 1940, 1945; *Maritime Advocate and Busy East,* 31(8) March 1941; *Patriot* 16 July 1946; PARO: RG Marriage License Vital Statistics Box M, 1884; MNI-Census 1891; Census 1901; O'Leary United Church Records; Bloomfield United Church Cemetery Records.

DESROCHES, GILBERT, merchant, shipper, factory owner, contractor, postmaster, farmer, and shoemaker; b. 24 July 1848 in Miscouche, son of Jean DesRoches and Nanette (Nancy) Poirier; m. 21 April 1873 Sophia Poirier, and there were no children; Roman Catholic; d. 2 June 1915 in Miscouche.

DesRoches, a Conservative, was elected to the Legislative Assembly on 2 February 1899 for 5th Prince. He was defeated in the general elections of 1890, 1893, 1897, and 1900.

DesRoches was educated at public schools and resided in his native community. He learned the trade of shoemaker, which he practised for only two years. In 1876, DesRoches went into the mercantile business with his brother-in-law, Joseph Poirier, and in 1880 he established his own business. He became one of the leading merchants in the province. DesRoches was often referred to as the "R. T. Holman of Miscouche." He shipped grain, produce, and eggs, and was the largest shipper of oysters on the Island. He also shipped large quantities of canned lobster to the English market and operated a large factory on the south side of Miscouche. In 1882 he was the contractor for the Miscouche railway station and that same year gained a contract for improvements on the O'Leary station.

Sophia DesRoches, the daughter of Joseph P. Poirier and Barbe Arsenault of Miscouche, was born 2 June 1845. She was educated at Notre Dame Convent and was a prize-winning needleworker and an accomplished gardener.

References
Acadiens p. 90; *CPG* 1901; *DCB* Vol XIV, pp. 292–93; Elections PEI; *Meacham's Atlas*; *Past and Present* pp. 324–25; *Examiner* 22 July 1897; *Summerside Journal* 31 August 1882; PARO: Leard Files; St. John the Baptist Church Records; MNI-Census 1881, 1891.

DEWAR, M.D., C.M., GEORGE FORBES, teacher and physician; b. 12 December 1865 in New Perth, son of Robert Dewar and Jessie Dewar; m. 19 June 1900 Marion Isabella McLeod, and they had two children, Robert Lloyd and Dorothy; Church of Christ; d. 25 November 1961 in Charlottetown.

Dewar, a Conservative, was first elected to the Legislative Assembly in a by-election held 15 November 1911 for 3rd Queens. He was re-elected in the general election of 1912. Dewar's 382-vote by-election defeat of H. J. Palmer*, Premier and Attorney-General, combined with Liberal F. J. Nash's* defeat in another by-election, forced a general election. The two losses created a Conservative majority, and a Conservative government was formed. John Alexander Mathieson*, the Conservative leader, immediately called an election. In the general election of 1912, Mathieson defeated the

Liberals led by Palmer. The victory was historic as it was the first Conservative victory in a general election since 1886, and the first Conservative government since 1891.

Politics was integral to the Dewar family. John Alexander Dewar*, Dewar's brother, was a Member of the Legislative Assembly from 1910 to 1923. One of John's sons, Lloyd George*, later served as a Member of the Legislative Assembly and as a Cabinet Minister.

Dewar was first educated at New Perth School, later attending Prince of Wales College. He taught school in Cardigan before entering McGill to study medicine. Though he struggled financially, Dewar obtained a medical degree and surgical training in 1893, ranking first, academically, among the graduates from the Maritime provinces.

He began practice at Southport, taking over many of the patients from his uncle, Dr. John Knox, who had preceded him in the community. After some time, Dewar moved to 96 Prince Street in Charlottetown where he carried on an extensive practice for years. He was active in the work of the Prince Edward Island Hospital and was highly regarded by his patients, earning the affectionate title, "Dr. Splendid." Dewar remained in the medical profession for close to 50 years, retiring during the Second World War. In 1944 he began spending the winters in Vancouver, in part for the comfort of his chronically ill son, Lloyd. While Dewar was residing in British Columbia, Lloyd died. Late in life Dewar returned to the Island and spent his final years as a resident of the Prince Edward Island Hospital. George Dewar died 25 November 1961.

Marion Dewar, the daughter of Norman McLeod, died in 1942. Dorothy Dewar died in 1904.

References
CPG 1914, 1915; Dewar pp. 28–29; Currie pp. 228–29; PARO: Charlottetown People's Protestant Cemetery Records.

DEWAR, JOHN ALEXANDER, farmer, dairy owner, and fox farmer; b. 7 February 1863 in New Perth, son of Robert Dewar and Jessie Dewar; m. 31 October 1908 Laura MacPhee, and they had five children, John Lincoln, Robert Bruce, Lloyd George*, Gladys Irene, and Olive May; Church of Christ; d. 14 August 1945 in New Perth.

Dewar, a Conservative first and later an Independent Farmer, was first elected to the Legislative Assembly in a by-election held 10 August 1910

for 3rd Kings. He was re-elected in the general elections of 1912, 1915, and 1919. He was defeated in the general election of 1923.

Dewar's first three terms were as a Conservative, but he was not one to toe the party line. In 1912 he broke solidarity by speaking against Premier John A. Mathieson's* decision to increase the horse tax. He also opposed the government's Automobile Act of 1913, which would have enabled an individual community to decide if automobiles would be allowed on its roads. Dewar fought Mathieson the following year over that issue, and tried to introduce a private member's bill regarding the automobile law. The government did not proceed with the legislation at that time. According to Dewar family folklore, his frequent opposition to Conservative initiatives may have stemmed in part from animosity over his exclusion from the Cabinet.

Throughout his career, Dewar opposed the use of the automobile in the province. In 1917 Dewar effectively ended his time as a Conservative when he voted against the party's plan to open all roads seven days a week. The vote on the automobile legislation was close: 15-14. A number of the Government Members, including Dewar, voted against it. Conservative A. P. Prowse cast the 15th vote and the bill was saved. In 1918 Dewar introduced a bill to enfranchise Island women. The bill passed but was not enacted. At the 3rd Kings Conservative nomination convention for the 1919 election, Dewar was defeated by 10 votes. Undaunted, he ran for the Independent Farmers in that riding. The Liberals declined to nominate a candidate and allowed Dewar to run alone against the Conservatives. He won with an increased majority. Dewar also angered the Liberal government with his criticism, and in 1922 fought a highways improvement bill on the grounds that it would put the Island in too much debt and that, furthermore, the public had not endorsed it. Unable to enlist his support, the government nominated a candidate to oppose him in the 1923 election. Dewar, running as an Independent, lost, and his political career ended.

Dewar was joined in politics by both his brother, Dr. George Forbes Dewar*, and eventually by his son, Lloyd George*, who in time would serve as a Member of the Legislative Assembly and as a Member of Executive Council.

Dewar was educated at the local school in New Perth. He inherited the family farm and became a successful farmer. He raised foxes. Dewar helped found the experimental dairy factory at New Perth, and served as president of the Prince Edward Island Dairymen's Association for two terms. He was president of the Maple Leaf Farmers' Institute and director of the National Dairy Council of Canada. Dewar was a director of the Kings County Exhibition Association, the Central Farmers' Institute, the Fruit Growers Association, and the New Perth Egg Circle.

Dewar was a leading speaker for the Temperance Association. In support of that movement, he donated some of his land for the construction of the Phoenix Temperance Hall. Dewar was a member of the Montague Rifle Association and was interested in military matters. John Dewar died 14 August 1945.

Laura Dewar was the daughter of Laughlin MacPhee and Annie Beaton.

References

CPG 1916, 1921, 1925; Dewar; *Guardian* 24 April 1917; *Island Magazine* no. 43 Spring/Summer 1998; *Patriot* 5 April 1918.

DEWAR, C.M., O.P.E.I., M.D., (C.M.), D.P.H., LL.D., F.R.F.P.(C.), LLOYD GEORGE, teacher and physician; b. 20 October 1915 in New Perth, son of John Alexander Dewar* and Laura MacPhee; m. 7 June 1944 Greta Jean Price, and they had two children, Elizabeth Ellen and Brian Lawrence; Church of Christ.

Dewar, a Conservative, was first elected to the Legislative Assembly in the general election of 1955 for 2nd Prince. He was re-elected in the general elections of 1959, 1962, 1966, and 1970, as well as in a by-election held on 8 November 1976. He was defeated in the general elections of 1974 and 1978. He served as interim Leader of the Opposition. In 1957 Dewar contested the Conservative leadership against Walter Shaw*, and lost by two votes. From 1959 to 1966, Dewar served as Minister of Education. From 1965 to 1966, he was Provincial Secretary. Dewar served as a Commissioner of the Village of O'Leary.

Dewar's father served in the Legislative Assembly, as did his uncle, Dr. George Forbes Dewar*.

"Doctor George," as he is known, received his primary education at New Perth school. Between 1931 and 1938, he attended Prince of Wales College for four years in between years of teaching school, first in Brudenell from 1933 to 1934 and 1935 to 1936, and later in New Perth from 1938 to 1939. After 1938 he taught school for another year, and, from 1939 to 1943, attended medical school at Dalhousie University. In 1941 Dewar joined the Royal Canadian Medical Corps, achieving the rank of Captain. He was stationed in Vernon, British Columbia, for two years and later transferred to Halifax until his discharge in 1946. Later that year he studied at the University of Toronto and received a Diploma in Public Health. Dewar returned to the Island and practised medicine in Bedeque for a year. On 15 June 1947, he settled in O'Leary and began a medical practice. He has spent more than 50 years practising medicine in the community and continues to do so at the age of 87. Dewar was a president of the Prince Edward Island Medical Society and a founding director and life member of the College of Family Physicians of Canada.

Dewar has been involved in numerous community activities. He was president of the O'Leary Library Museum association, a director of the Fathers of Confederation Trust, and a director of the Prince Edward Island Museum and Heritage Foundation. Currently Dewar is chair of the Prince Edward Island Potato Museum. He is a member of the Masonic Lodge and served as Master. Dewar is a member of the Royal Canadian Legion, St. John's Ambulance, the Maple Leaf Curling Club, and the Mill River Golf Course. He is active in the Lions Club, the Caledonia Club, and the Prince Edward Island Symphony Society. Dewar has written four books: *The Brothers Dewar* (1976), *The Duvar Diary* (1979), *Life at Leighwood: the Doctor's Home* (1982), and *Prescription for a Full Life* (1993).

Dewar has received many awards and much recognition. Following his military service, he was awarded Canadian Army medals for Volunteer Service and for Long Service. In 1967 he was awarded the Canada Medal and in 1976 Dewar was admitted to the Order of St. John Ambulance as a serving brother. He received the Queen's Jubilee Medal in 1978 and in 1984 was awarded a life membership in the Royal Canadian Legion. The following year the Masonic Lodge presented him with the Masonic Merit Award. Dewar was awarded the Order of Canada in 1989. In 1993 Dewar received the Meritorious Achievement Award from the Prince Edward Island Museum. In 1997 he was named to the Prince Edward Island Order of Merit. Dewar also received a literary award for *Cancer on Mainstreet* and was awarded an honourary doctorate degree from the University of Prince Edward

Island. Dewar was honoured by the Prince Edward Island Potato Board for his work in promoting the industry. He was also honoured for his efforts in promoting the preservation of Scottish culture. George Dewar and his wife reside in O'Leary.

Greta Dewar, the daughter of Laurence Price and Beatrice Storey of Saint John, was born 23 May 1921.

References
CPG 1975, 1978, 1979; WWPEI p. 40; Guardian 22 November 1976, 29 August 2002; Islander 20 October 1990 p. 28; Journal-Pioneer 2 May 1997.

DINGWELL, JAMES WALTER, farmer and carpenter; b. 14 June 1911 in Midgell, son of James E. Dingwell and Eliza Ellen "Nellie" Rogerson; m. 12 July 1939 Phyllis Muriel Webster, and they had seven children, June, Helene, Rodney, Blois, Kevin, Brian, and James (died at eight days); United; d. 19 August 1986 in Midgell.

Dingwell, a Conservative, was first elected to the Legislative Assembly in the general election of 1959 for 2nd Kings. He was re-elected in the general elections of 1962, 1966, 1970, and 1974. He was defeated in the general election of 1955. Dingwell served as farming critic and party Whip during his time in the House. He was a member of many legislative committees, including Agriculture, Education, Public Buildings, and Contingent Accounts. Dingwell attended several parliamentary conferences on behalf of the province.

Dingwell was educated at the Marie School. Following his education he returned to Midgell where he lived the rest of his life. He operated the family farm. Dingwell was a director of the Morell Creamery Co-operative and secretary of the Morell Artificial Insemination Association and chairman of trustees of the Morell United Church. He also worked with his brother Cuyler in a carpentry business for most of his life. James Dingwell died 19 August 1986 at his home.

Phyllis Dingwell was the daughter of Everett and Jennie (Aitken) Webster of Marie.

References
CPG 1958, 1978; Guardian 6 July 1978, 21 August 1986; Journal-Pioneer 25 April 1974.

DOBIE, HECTOR D., farmer and dairy director; b. ca. 7 September 1860 in St. John's, Newfoundland, son of Reverend Robert T. Dobie and his first wife, Elizabeth; m. 1 November 1887 Priscilla Dougherty, and they had five children, Arthur A., John, Howard, Rosamond, and Robert Thomas; Presbyterian.

Dobie, a Conservative, was first elected to the Legislative Assembly in the general election of 1908 for 3rd Prince. He was re-elected in the general election of 1912. He was defeated in the general election of 1915.

Dobie's family moved to the Island in 1875 when his father became the minister at Port Hill Parish, Port Hill. Hector Dobie was a farmer and a director of Grand River Dairying Company Limited in Lot 14.

Priscilla Dobie was born 1 May 1864.

References
Birch-Noye pp. 64–65; CPG 1915, 1916; Elections PEI; PARO: RG 19 Vital Statistics series 3 subseries 3 volume 10 1878-1888; MNI-Census 1891; Census 1901; Summerside People's Protestant Cemetery Records; Crapaud St. John's Anglican Church Records.

DOUCETTE, PETER, carpenter, contractor, road construction foreman, and director and program manager; b. 14 August 1954 in Charlottetown, son of Wilfred Vincent Doucette and Gertrude Margaret Lord; Roman Catholic.

Doucette, a Liberal, was first elected to the Legislative Assembly in the general election of 1989 for 3rd Kings. He was re-elected in the general election of 1993. In April 1993 Doucette was appointed government Whip. He served on a number of legislative committees and chaired the Standing Committee on Justice, Labour and Industry, and the Special Committee on Maritime Economic Integration.

Doucette was educated at the Quincy High School in Quincy, Massachusetts, and Stonehill College in North Easton, Massachusetts. He moved to Quincy with his parents where they had gone to find work. Doucette has worked as a carpenter and a contractor. He carried out his trade as a carpenter with Georgetown Shipyards and various private-sector construction companies. Doucette also worked as a maintenance foreman with the Department of Transportation and Public Works. From 1986 to 1990, he served as a director and chair of the Montague Credit Union. In 1986 he helped found the Southern Kings and Queens Food Bank and served with that organization until 1989. Doucette was chair of the Southern Kings and Queens Advisory Board from 1987 to 1989. He served as secretary-treasurer of the Montague Lions Club from 1987 to 1990.

Peter Doucette is presently government affairs director and program manager for the Regional Co-operative Development Centre in Moncton. He is a member of the Montague Lions Club and is a director with the Riverview Area Community Enhancement Group. Doucette resides in Montague.

References
CPG 1996; *Guardian* 19 April 1989, 13 March 1993, 1 June 1993.

DOUGLAS, M.D., C.M., ALBERT HENRY EDWARD, physician; b. 9 December 1860 in Head of Hillsborough, son of William Henry Douglas and Elizabeth Coffin; m. 1891, Barbara Anderson of Breadalbane, and they had three children, Irene, Alice, and Olive; Presbyterian; d. 6 May 1908 in Hunter River.

Douglas, a Liberal, was first elected to the Legislative Assembly in a by-election for 2nd Queens on 11 July 1900. He was re-elected in the general elections of 1900 and 1904. His victory in the July 1900 by-election gave the Liberals a working majority. The 1900 general election produced a large Liberal majority, in part due to the time and credibility Douglas' by-election victory provided. He served as Speaker from February 1905 until the spring of 1908.

Douglas attended Prince of Wales College, where he obtained a teaching license. After teaching for several years, he attended McGill, eventually receiving his medical degree. Following McGill, Douglas studied at the University of New York. Upon completion of his medical training, Douglas resided in Breadalbane, Charlottetown, and later Hunter River. According to the *Guardian*'s obituary, "his medical skill coupled with close attention to professional duties and an engaging manner soon gained for him an extended practice and with it a large share of personal popularity." Edward Douglas died 6 May 1908 as a result of pneumonia.

Barbara Douglas died at the age of 99 while living with family in Prince Albert, Saskatchewan.

References
CPG 1905; Elections PEI; *Guardian* 7 May 1908; *Patriot* 6 May 1908; PARO: Marriage License Book 16 1882-1923 p. 51; Douglas Family File; Hunter River Presbyterian Church Records.

DOUGLAS, HARVEY OTIS, farmer, potato dealer, and dairy owner; b. 25 November 1901 in Head of Hillsborough, son of Elisha A. Douglas and Emma Louise Coffin; m. 10 August 1927 Edith Elizabeth Pigot, and they had two children, W. Leslie and H. Lane; United; d. 13 September 1975 in Charlottetown.

Douglas, a Liberal, was first elected to the Legislative Assembly in a by-election held 4 December 1950 for 2nd Kings. He was re-elected in the general elections of 1951 and 1955. He was defeated in the general election of 1959. Douglas served on the Town Council of Parkdale for 11 years.

He attended school in Head of Hillsborough. At an early age, Douglas went to Western Canada and resided with his oldest brother Alfred, returning to the Island a few years later. Upon his return, he began farming, and later bought and sold potatoes at the Douglas Co-op Company Limited warehouse in Douglas Station for 13 years. He was a shareholder in the Morell Co-operative Creamery. During the Second World War, Douglas joined the Royal Canadian Air Force and spent almost five years in the service overseas. He landed on the beaches of Normandy on D-Day and continued to fight with the Royal Canadian Air Force until the Allied Forces reached Germany. In October 1945 he came back to his family and to farming. In April 1961 he and his wife moved to Parkdale where he resided until his death.

Douglas was a member of the Caledonia Club, the Canadian Legion, and Park Royal United Church in Parkdale, where he served as both an elder and a steward. Harvey Douglas died 13 September 1975 at the Charlottetown Hospital.

Edith Douglas was the daughter of W. Ross Pigot of Mount Stewart.

References
CPG 1951, 1958, 1960; *Patriot* 13 September 1975.

DRISCOLL, M.A., FREDERICK LEO, teacher, principal, and professor; b. 18 August 1932 in Mount Herbert, son of Joseph J. Driscoll and Isabelle Suzanna Coady; m. 26 October 1957 Bernadette Mary McManus, and they had two children, James William and Jennifer Elizabeth; Roman Catholic; d. 27 October 2000 in Charlottetown.

Driscoll, a Conservative, was first elected to the Legislative Assembly in the general election of 1978 for 3rd Queens. He was re-elected in the general elections of 1979 and 1982. Driscoll was defeated in the general election of 1986. On 3 May 1979, Driscoll was appointed Minister of Education and Minister of Health. On 1 April 1980,

Driscoll was appointed Minister of Education and served until 1982. Following that year's general election, Driscoll became Minister of Energy and Forestry. He was also Minister Responsible for Native Affairs from 1979 to 1986 and Minister Responsible for Trade from 1982 to 1986. Driscoll acted as Government House Leader from 1982 to 1986. He chaired the Policy and Priorities Committee of Cabinet from 1979 to 1982 and the Economic Development Committee of Cabinet from 1982 to 1986. He also served on the Intergovernmental Affairs and the Constitution Committee of Cabinet.

As part of his ministerial responsibility with Intergovernmental Affairs, Driscoll participated in the discussions leading to the patriation of the Canadian Constitution. In 1981, upon the resignation of Premier John Angus MacLean*, Driscoll ran for the leadership of the Conservative party, finishing third behind winner James Lee* and second-place candidate Barry Clark*.

Driscoll received his early education at the Mount Herbert Elementary School. He graduated from St. Dunstan's University with a Bachelor of Arts degree. Driscoll also studied at the University of New Brunswick. Following his graduation from St. Dunstan's in 1953, Driscoll taught in Brackley Point, Southport, Queen Square, and Birchwood. He served as school principal at the Southport School. From 1955 to 1965, he was in the Canadian Army Militia where he reached the rank of Lieutenant. In 1962 Driscoll enrolled at the University of Ottawa where he earned a Master of Arts degree in Canadian history. He returned to the Island and began teaching at St. Dunstan's University from 1965 to 1969. From 1967 to 1969, he was president of the Faculty Association of St. Dunstan's University. From 1969 until he retired on 30 June 1997, Driscoll taught Canadian history at the University of Prince Edward Island, with the exception of the years 1979 to 1986, when he was on leave to accept political office. He served as chair of the Department of History from 1967 to 1968, from 1975 to 1979, and again from 1992 to 1997. Driscoll was faculty representative to the University Senate from 1966 to 1978. From 1971 to 1978, he was the faculty representative to the board of governors of the Canadian Association of University Teachers. He also served on a number of senate, faculty, and faculty association committees.

In October 1986 Driscoll was appointed chair of the Royal Commission on the Prince Edward Island Potato Industry. The report was completed in November 1987. In 1993 he was selected to serve on the Electoral Boundaries Commission of Prince Edward Island, and in September of the same year was appointed to the Federal Electoral Boundaries Commission as the representative for the province. Also in 1993 Driscoll was appointed to the board of the Prince Edward Island Museum and Heritage Foundation. He was a member of the United Services Officers Club, the Belvedere Golf and Winter Club, and the Stanhope Golf Club. Driscoll coached school rugby and minor hockey.

Driscoll had many of his writings published. He wrote articles for the *Dictionary of Canadian Biography* on Daniel Gordon*, Premier Donald Farquharson*, and Donald Ferguson*. In 1998 his article, "History and politics of Prince Edward Island," appeared in *Canadian Parliamentary Review.* Driscoll published several articles in *The Guardian* and wrote a chapter entitled "The Island and the Dominion" in F. W. P. Bolger's book, *Canada's Smallest Province: A History of PEI.* Driscoll also authored the *Prince Edward Island Report of the Royal Commission on the Prince Edward Island Potato Industry* (1987). He was the originator of *Minding the House,* and directed its progression until his death. Frederick Driscoll died 27 October 2000. He is survived by his wife and children.

Bernadette Driscoll is the daughter of William McManus of Charlottetown. J. Russell Driscoll*, who represented 3rd Queens from 1959 to 1970, was Fred Driscoll's cousin and godfather.

References

CPG 1986, 1987; *CWW* 1999 p. 349; *Guardian* 31 October 1981, 5 November 1981, 9 November 1981, 30 October 2000; ECO 240/80; PEI Cabinet Biographic Summary 1980; UPEI: Robertson Library: PEI Collection.

DRISCOLL, JAMES RUSSELL, farmer and produce dealer; b. 4 November 1908 in Mount Herbert, son of Frank Driscoll and Margaret; m. first 15 August 1942 Elizabeth Cecilia MacDonald, and they had five children, Frank, Helene, Sharon, Ann Marie, and Colleen; m. secondly 31 August 1968, Mary Helen MacDonald, and she had six children: Don, Ian, Jenine, Boyd, Howard, and Leanne; Roman Catholic; d. 22 June 1975 in Charlottetown.

Driscoll, a Conservative, was first elected to the Legislative Assembly in the general election of 1959 for 3rd Queens. He was re-elected in the general elections of 1962 and 1966. He was defeated in the general elections of 1955, 1970, and 1974. Driscoll chaired the Southport Village Commission.

Educated in Mount Herbert, Russell Driscoll became a farmer and a produce dealer. Following his second marriage, Driscoll moved from Mt. Stewart to the Keppoch Road. The couple raised the 11 children from their previous marriages. In addition to being a member of the provincial branch of the Canadian National Institute for the Blind, he was a member of the Knights of Columbus and the Lions Club. James Russell Driscoll died 22 June 1975 at the Charlottetown Hospital.

Driscoll's cousin and godson, Frederick L. Driscoll*, was a member of the Legislative Assembly and served as a Cabinet Minister.

Elizabeth Driscoll was the daughter of Hugh Laughlin MacDonald and Mary Ann MacDonald of St. Georges. Mary Helen Driscoll was the daughter of Jeanette Ann Boyd and John Angus MacDonald from Allisary (near Mt. Stewart).

References
CPG 1958, 1970, 1971, 1975; *Patriot* 23 June 1975; PARO: Leard Files.

DUFFY, K.C., CHARLES GAVAN, lawyer and judge; b. 2 November 1874 in Kinkora, son of James Duffy and Elizabeth Smith; m. 25 September 1906 Ethel Mary Eden, and they had one child, Wilfred Francis; Roman Catholic; d. 14 March 1958.

Duffy, a Liberal, was elected to the Legislative Assembly in the general election of 1919 for 5th Queens. He was defeated in the general elections of 1915, 1923, and 1927. On 6 April 1920, he was elected Speaker.

Duffy was first educated at the Kinkora Public School. Later he attended Prince of Wales College and St. Dunstan's College. Following these studies, he read law with Walter A. O. Morson*. Duffy was called to the Bar in 1903, and until 1909 practised law with Morson. After 1909, he practised alone under the firm name Morson & Duffy. In 1921 Duffy was named King's Counsel, and in 1930 he became a Judge of the Queens County Court.

Duffy was a member of the Knights of Columbus. Following his early years in Kinkora, he resided on Brighton Avenue in Charlottetown. Charles Duffy died 14 March 1958.

Ethel Duffy, the daughter of Frank Eden of Halifax, was born ca. 1882 and died 25 January 1953.

References
CPG 1916, 1921, 1923, 1924, 1927; *CWW* 1936-1937 p. 319; PARO: 1901 Census; Charlottetown Roman Catholic Cemetery Records.

DUNPHY, THOMAS JOSEPH, teacher, manager of agricultural exhibition, addictions counsellor, agricultural extension officer, and realtor; b. 12 December 1937 in Peakes Station, son of Thomas E. Dunphy of Peakes and Margaret Curran of St. Teresa's; m. first Rita Kenny; m. secondly 19 May 1978 Marion MacRae-Gillis, and they had four children, Peter, Margaret, Kim Gillis, and Tracey Gillis; Roman Catholic.

Dunphy, a Liberal, was first elected to the Legislative Assembly in the general election of 1986 for 3rd Queens. He was re-elected in the general elections of 1989 and 1993. From November 1991 to 15 April 1993, he held the position of Minister of Transportation and Public Works. Dunphy chaired the Transportation and Public Works Committee, and was a member of the Committee on Education, Community Affairs and Justice, Energy and Forestry, Agriculture, Policy Board, and the Rural Development Board. Upon announcing that he would not be a candidate in the 1996 election, Dunphy reflected that the improvements in the provincial road system while he was Minister were a source of pride. In 1983 he was a candidate for the presidency of the provincial Liberal party eventually won by A. E. "Bud" Ings*.

Dunphy received his early education at the Peakes and St. Teresa's schools, and graduated in 1953. In 1955 he graduated from St. Dunstan's High School. In 1958 Dunphy graduated from the Nova Scotia Agricultural College with a two-year degree in agricultural studies. Two years later he graduated from Macdonald College at McGill with a Bachelor of Science in agriculture. In 1961 Dunphy worked with the Nova Scotia Department of Agriculture and the following year managed that province's Agricultural Exhibition. Dunphy returned to the Island in 1963 and taught at Morell High School. Later Dunphy taught in Quebec, before returning to the Island to teach at Queen Charlotte. He took a two-year leave of absence from his duties at Queen Charlotte to work as an addictions counselor with the Queens County Addiction Services. In 1982 he returned to Queen Charlotte. Following his political career he became a realtor.

Dunphy was a teacher representative to the Home and School Association and a faculty advisor for Queen Charlotte High School Allied Youth. He also served as a director of the York Community Centre. Tom Dunphy and his wife reside in Donaldston.

Marion MacRae-Gillis Dunphy is the daughter of Alex MacRae and Francis Cook.

References
CPG 1996; *WWPEI* p. 45; *Guardian* 24 August 1983, 7 April 1986, 15 November 1991, 18 March 1993, 22 March 1996.

E

ward Island Masonic Lodge A.F. and A.M. He is also a life member of the Lions Club.

Allison and Melba Ellis reside in West Cape. Melba Ellis is the daughter of Benjamin MacIsaac of Dunblane.

References
CPG 1977, 1993; *Guardian* Election Ad 1989, 15 April 1992, 25 January 1993, 16 May 1995; *Western Graphic* 29 July 1992.

ELLIS, ALLISON, farmer, manufacturer of farm machinery, and fisher; b. 19 April 1935 in West Cape, son of Robert Earl Ellis and Clara Barton Dumville; m. 6 November 1956 Elsie Melba MacIsaac, and they had five children, Michael Allison, Sydney Blake (deceased), Amber Melba, Stephen Merle, and Melody Ann; United.

Ellis, a Liberal, and later an Independent Liberal, was first elected in the general election of 1978 for 2nd Prince. He was re-elected in the general elections of 1979, 1982, 1986, and 1989. He was defeated in a by-election held 8 November 1976. From 1978 to 1979, Ellis was a Minister without Portfolio. While in Opposition, he served for a time as House Leader. On 2 May 1986, he was appointed Minister of Energy and Forestry and a member of Treasury Board. Ellis chaired the Standing Committee on Agriculture and Forestry. In April 1992 he became an Independent Liberal after resigning from the party caucus, feeling he had been misled by the Cabinet regarding the construction of the O'Leary Hospital.

Ellis was educated in West Cape, and has worked as a farmer, a fisher, and farm machinery manufacturer. He operated Allison Industries Ltd. He was awarded the Environmentally Friendly Farmer Award from the Atlantic Salmon Federation for Soil Conservation. He served as president of the Acadian Fishermen's Association and as the local president, regional director, and national board member of the National Farmers Union. Ellis was chair of the Prince Edward Island Land Development Corporation and was a director of the Athletic Association in O'Leary. In 1992 he was awarded a commemorative medal for the 125th Anniversary of Confederation from the Canada 125 Committee for his significant contribution to the country, and in the same year he was named Citizen of the Year at the Potato Blossom Festival. Ellis is a member of the Masonic Lodge, and in 1968 was elected Master of the Corinthian Lodge in O'Leary. In 1991 he was elected Grand Master of Prince Ed-

F

FARMER, Q.C., LL.D., MICHAEL ALBAN, school teacher, potato inspector, and lawyer; b. 27 September 1901 in Kinkora, son of Michael Farmer and Margaret Keefe; m. 12 October 1932 Mary Dorothea MacMillan of Charlottetown, and they had four children, William Alban, Mary Honora, Michael Alan, and Elinor Christine; Roman Catholic; d. 27 December 1988 in Charlottetown.

Farmer, a Conservative, was first elected to the Legislative Assembly in the general election of 1959 for 5th Queens. He was re-elected in the general election of 1962. In the general election of 1966, Farmer was elected to the new riding of 6th Queens. He was defeated in the general election of 1970. From 3 January 1963 to 28 July 1966, he served as Provincial Treasurer and Attorney and Advocate General. Farmer represented Ward 2 on the Charlottetown City Council from 1946 to 1952 and made two unsuccessful attempts to become Mayor. From 1935 to 1939, he served as Private Secretary for Lieutenant-Governor George DeBlois.

Alban Farmer received his primary education in the Kinkora school. He attended Prince of Wales College, later teaching school and working as a potato inspector with the federal government. Later he attended St. Dunstan's College, graduating with a Bachelor of Arts in 1925. In 1928 Farmer graduated from Dalhousie University with a Bachelor of Law degree. He articled with J. O. C. Campbell, and was admitted to the Bar in 1930. He began practising law with former premier H. James Palmer*. Farmer served as Crown prosecutor from 1930 to 1934, and, from 1934 to 1968, practised law without a partner. He was awarded the designation of Queen's Counsel. In 1968 he formed a partnership with his son-in-law Ronald V. Dalzell. His son Michael Alan, and his son-in-law Bertrand Plamondon, joined the firm in 1971. In time, the firm became Farmer and Farmer, and in 1984 he joined the partnership of Farmer, Farmer, Fortier and Gregory. In his later years he practised with the firm of Farmer and MacLeod.

Farmer served on the board of many companies and organizations. He was chairman of the board of the Charlottetown Hospital and the Maritime Hospital Service Association—later Blue Cross of Atlantic Canada and now Atlantic Blue Cross Care. From 1936 to 1937, Farmer was president of the Prince Edward Island Law Society. He was a board member and chairman of the Canadian National Institute for the Blind, a board member of the Charlottetown Board of Trade, a board member of the Canadian Bar Association, and on the advisory board of Central Trust. In 1969 St. Dunstan's University awarded Farmer a Doctor of Laws degree. He served as Past State Deputy of the Knights of Columbus and was a 4th degree Knight. Alban Farmer died 27 December 1988 at the Queen Elizabeth Hospital.

Dorothea Farmer, Alban Farmer's wife, was the daughter of William J. P. MacMillan*, a premier of the province. Her sister, Catherine Bernadette, married Charles St. Clair Trainor*. Farmer's son, Michael Alan, was defeated in the 1974 general election for 6th Queens and is presently the Mayor of Stratford.

References
CPG 1970, 1971, 1975; CWW 1988 p. 256; WWCL 1986–87 p. 439; Guardian 10 March 1984, 29 December 1988.

FARQUHARSON, DONALD, teacher, merchant, and newspaper director; b. 27 July 1834 at Mermaid, son of John Farquharson and Frances Stewart; m. first 15 March 1860 Dopsin May Edwards Smith, and they had four children, Laura, Seymour, Alfred, and May (died in 1901); m. secondly 20 October 1870 Sarah Moore, and they had three children, Fanny, Lauretta, and Charles; Presbyterian; d. 26 June 1903 in Charlottetown.

Farquharson, a Liberal, was first elected to the House of Assembly in the general election of 1876 for 2nd Queens. He was re-elected in the general elections of 1879, 1883, 1886, and 1890. He was elected to the Legislative Assembly in the general elections of 1893, 1897, and 1900. He served as a Minister without Portfolio on Executive Council from 1878 to 1879, and from 1891 to 1898. In 1898 he became Premier after Alexander B. Warburton* was appointed as a judge with the court of Kings County. Farquharson served in the Legislature until 1901, when he resigned from the Assembly and the premiership to successfully run for the vacated federal seat of West Queen's in a by-election held

15 January 1902. He died while a Member of the House of Commons, never fulfilling his aim to be in the federal Cabinet.

First elected as a member of the Free School coalition in 1876, Farquharson opposed government funding of denominational schools, but is best-known as the "Prohibition Premier." His attempt to strengthen provincial liquor licensing in 1899 was criticized by temperance supporters and opponents. Prohibitionists thought Farquharson had sold out to the supporters of liquor licensing by allowing licenses, albeit severely restrictive ones, to be issued at all, while incensed licensing advocates complained the legislation was too restrictive. Following the debate that divided his party, he made the legislation less restrictive. Disturbed by the controversy, Farquharson a year later passed the Prohibition Act of 1900, the first of its kind in post-Confederation Canada. The Prohibition Act banned the sale of intoxicating beverages except for industrial, sacramental, or medicinal use.

During the 1899 and 1900 legislative sessions, Farquharson orchestrated a strategy to preserve the Liberal party's slim majority in the Assembly. In 1899 Joseph Wise* broke ranks with the Liberals and voted with the Conservatives. Farquharson eventually persuaded Wise to resign his seat. Later Wise refuted his resignation and attempted to assume his former seat in the Assembly. Amidst pandemonium brought on by Wise's actions, his vote with the Conservatives, which would have defeated the Government, was not recognized by Speaker James Cummiskey*. With order restored on the next day, Farquharson held on to power when Henry Pineau*, a sitting Conservative who had been conspicuously absent from legislative proceedings for some months, switched to the Government side. Seven months later, in December 1900, Farquharson led the Liberals to a 21–9 majority.

In April 1901, in an effort to raise revenues for the province, Farquharson claimed that the federal government owed Prince Edward Island compensation for non-fulfillment of the terms of union regarding transportation. According to Farquharson, the resulting loss of revenue demoralized business, caused many young men to leave home, and devalued farms. The federal government countered that they had met the terms since 1888, but they did agree to increase the Island's subsidy by $30,000 annually, a full and final settlement from the federal government's perspective.

Farquharson attended the local school near Mermaid and Central Academy in Charlottetown. He was a teacher and later a successful businessman. In 1860 he opened a store on the West River at McEwen's Wharf near New Dominion. He and his partner Theophilus Stewart operated the business, and by 1887 their interests included wholesale, milling, and shipping operations. In partnership with his son, Farquharson moved to Charlottetown and operated a general mercantile company. Other business interests included a starch factory at Long Creek and a lobster canning factory at Canoe Cove. He was a founding member, part owner, director, and President of the Patriot Publishing Company, as well as a director of the Merchant's Bank.

For 15 years, Farquharson was a member of the Charlottetown School Board. Additionally, he was a Captain on the General Staff of Militia and Volunteers in 1860, and was responsible for Company H Rifles at Long Creek. Donald Farquharson died 26 June 1903.

Dopsin Farquharson, of Pownal, daughter of Richard Edwards and Magdelen Jenkins, was born 23 July 1834 and died 16 April 1868. Sarah Farquharson, daughter of George Moore of Charlottetown and Elizabeth Chappell, was born ca. 17 October 1843 and died 15 February 1911.

References

CDP p. 197; *CPG* 1901; *DCB* XIII 1901- 1910 pp. 332–33; Pollard p. 109; *Examiner* 27 April 1868 p. 3; *Daily Patriot* 26 June 1903; PARO: MNI-Mercantile Agency Reference Book 1876; MNI-Census 1881; MNI-Farquharson Family File; MNI-Moore Family File; Anglican Church Records, Richmond, Book 1, p. 26; First Methodist, Charlottetown Records, Book 2, p. 29; Charlottetown People's Cemetery Records.

FAY, JAMES BERNARD, farmer, political assistant, goverment inspector, oil company employee, and owner of taxi company; b. 23 September 1947 in Charlottetown, son of John Brady Fay and Margaret Theresa Ellsworth; Roman Catholic.

Fay, a Liberal, was first elected to the Legislative Assembly in a by-election held 8 November 1976 for 1st Kings. He was re-elected in the general election of 1978. He was defeated in the general election of 1979. In 1978 he was appointed Minister Without Portfolio responsible for the Housing Corporation, Cultural Affairs, and as Minister of Justice. He served as a member of the Standing Committees on Agriculture, Labour and Management, and Municipal Affairs. He was a member of the Eastern Kings Community Improvement Commission.

Fay attended East Baltic school and Souris Regional High School. Jim Fay farmed with his brother Joseph at East Baltic. He was employed by the federal government as a potato inspector for Kings County. Following his career as a politician, he moved to Ottawa and worked as a political assistant to Eugene Whelan, federal Minister of Agriculture. He relocated to Fort MacMurray, Alberta. First he worked with an oil company and later he established Fort MacMurray's first taxi company. He was a member of the board of directors of Souris Hospital and Eastern Kings Fire Department. Fay was president of the Basin Head Fisheries Museum and a member of the board of the Eastern Kings Recreation Commission. He was also a member of the board of the Eastern Kings Hockey League. James Fay served as a president of the St. Mary's Church Parish Council.

Fay presently resides in Fort MacMurray, Alberta.

References
CPG 1978, 1979, 1980; PARO: Leard Files.

FEEHAN, HENRY FELIX, fisher, merchant, and farmer; b. ca. 11 July 1854 in Savage Harbour, son of Daniel Feehan of County Tipperary, Ireland, and Mary Mullen of Covehead; Roman Catholic; d. 25 December 1933 in Mount Stewart.

Feehan, a Conservative, was elected to the Legislative Assembly in the 1912 general election for 3rd Queens. He was defeated in the 1908 general election.

Feehan went to public school, going on to attend St. Dunstan's College for one year. Following this he was a lobster fisher. Later, in partnership with his cousin James Feehan, and D. McInnis, he jointly operated a small store in Mount Stewart. According to *Meacham's Atlas*, Feehan was listed as owning a farm on French Village Road in Mt. Stewart in 1880. The Mt. Stewart store was carelessly run and customers often served themselves. To rectify matters, Feehan obtained a loan and bought out his partners, forming H. F. Feehan General Merchant and Dealer, which he operated for many years. In his will he left $4,500 to his niece, Anna Duffy, who kept house for him, but she received little from Feehan as the estate owed

significant amounts. Though he had run a prosperous business, the Depression had taken a toll on his fortunes.

According to one source, Feehan lived his adult life in Mt. Stewart and in 1915 had a comfortable house built on the south side of the Hillsborough River. A second source states that in 1912, at least, he resided in Savage Harbour. In the 1881 Census, Feehan is named as a householder, and indicates that he lived with his mother and a number of brothers and sisters. The 1891 Census recorded that he was living with his mother and four sisters. A different source states that his mother stayed at the family homestead in Savage Harbour. A bachelor, Feehan was quoted as saying, "Well those that would have me, I wouldn't have and those I would have, wouldn't have me." Henry Feehan died 25 December 1933.

References
CPG 1909, 1912; Feehan pp. 195–201; *Meacham's Atlas*; *Maple Leaf Magazine* February 1934; PARO: MNI-Census 1881, 1891; Census 1901; St. Andrew's Roman Catholic Church Records.

FERGUSON, P.C., HONOURABLE DONALD, farmer, journalist, agent, and justice of the peace; b. 7 March 1839 in Marshfield, son of John Ferguson and Isabella Stewart; m. 26 March 1873 Elizabeth S. Scott of Charlottetown, and they had perhaps six children of whom these names are known, J. Helena, R.W., J. Howard, William Scott, Colin Campbell, and Nora Bell; Baptist; d. 3 September 1909 in Marshfield.

Ferguson, a Conservative, was first elected to the House of Assembly in an 1878 by-election for 3rd Kings by acclamation. He was re-elected in the general elections of 1879, 1882, 1886, and 1890 for 3rd Queens. Ferguson's first bid for office was in 1873, when he was defeated in the election for Legislative Council by the anti-railway, anti-Confederation incumbent, Edward Palmer. In 1874 he again was defeated in the Council election. Later that year, Ferguson was appointed Secretary of the Board of Railway Appraisers and served in that role until 1876. In 1879, as Minister of Public Works in the Sullivan* Administration, he was instrumental in passing The Public Roads Act. He resigned in 1880 upon appointment to the position of Provincial Secretary and Commissioner of Lands and was re-elected in a subsequent by-election. He held these positions until 1891. In that year, Ferguson resigned from the Assembly to run in the federal seat of Queen's County, but was narrowly defeated by L. H. Davies*. In 1893 he was appointed to the Senate, where his experience and respected debating skills made him a useful member of the Upper Chamber. Ferguson was appointed in 1894 to the federal Cabinet as a Minister without Portfolio in the MacKenzie-Boswell government, and remained in Cabinet as Minister of Agriculture under Prime Minister Tupper. He left politics upon the defeat of the Conservative government in 1896. Ferguson was a patriotic Conservative, a defender of the Empire, and opposed to American influence. He was an advocate of temperance legislation.

A highlight of Ferguson's career was a March 1886 trip to England as part of a provincial delegation, led by Premier Sullivan, whose objective was to make a formal complaint to the Queen. It was the province's position that the federal government was not meeting its commitments under the Terms of Union regarding the continuous communication between the Island and the mainland. Though not immediately successful, this trip eventually led to improved travelling conditions across the Strait. In 1888 the first steel-screw ship between Charlottetown and Pictou was put in service. Before entering politics, Ferguson took part in the discussions on the problems of Confederation, and championed the cause of union with Canada when it was unpopular in the province. He also promoted the extension of the railway system.

Ferguson resided in Marshfield throughout his life, and was educated at the local school. The private tutoring that supplemented his early schooling spawned a lifelong pursuit of knowledge and self-education. From 1869 to 1870, he was a political writer for the *Island Argus* and frequently contributed to the local press. Later Ferguson worked as an agent for an agricultural implement and farm chemical company. He raised purebred stock. In 1872 Ferguson served as a Justice of the Peace, and in 1873 as Commissioner of Inland Revenue. Further, he was a member of the Board of Commissioners of the Government Poor House, was a member of the board of the Hospital for the Insane, had a managerial post at the Government Stock Farm, and was vice-president of the Dominion Shorthorn Breeders' Association. Besides Ferguson's contribution to local journalism, he had two lectures to local societies published, one of which appeared in *The Prince Edward Island Magazine* entitled "Social Enjoyment in the Old Times."

His other involvement included membership with the Good Templars. He became Grand Secretary of the Good Templars in 1863, and from 1865 to 1867 was the Grand Worthy Chief. Donald Ferguson died 3 September 1909.

Elizabeth Ferguson, the daughter of John Scott, a carriage maker, and Elizabeth Stewart, was born in December 1827 and died in 1927. There is some discrepancy as to the number of children in Ferguson's family. One source indicates the couple raised three sons and two daughters, while census data indicates they had three sons and three daughters.

References
CDP p. 199; Cotton p. 145; CPG 1879; DCB XII 1891-1900 pp. 339-41; *Meacham's Atlas*; *Islander* 4 April 1873; PARO: MNI-Presbyterian Church in Marshfield Record Book p. 146.

FERGUSON, GEORGE JOHNSTON, meat dealer; b. 26 April 1923 in White Sands, son of Ellsworth Ferguson and Minnie MacPherson; m. 4 December 1947 Dorothy Cynthia Stewart of Murray Harbour, and they had three children, Dennis Merton, George Ellsworth, and John Murdock; United.

Ferguson, a Liberal, was first elected to the Legislative Assembly in a by-election held 17 July 1961 for 5th Kings. He was re-elected in the general elections of 1962, 1966, and 1970. On 28 July 1966, he was appointed Minister of Public Works and Highways and served until 2 May 1974.

Ferguson received his education at Prince of Wales College. He worked as a meat dealer. From 1942 to 1946, Ferguson served in the Royal Canadian Navy. He is a member of the Royal Canadian Legion in Montague and the Masonic Order.

Dorothy Ferguson is the daughter of John Murdock Stewart.

References
CPG 1962, 1972; PEI *Journal of the Legislative Assembly* 1974, p. 2.

FOGARTY, M.Ed., ALBERT PRESTON, school teacher, principal, superintendent of education, civil servant, consultant, and executive director of adult education; b. 25 June 1940 in Cardigan, son of James Wilfred Fogarty and Julia Morrison; m. 17 August 1963 Judith Dianne McCabe, and they had five children, Tracey, Albert, Robert, Kelly, and Kerri; Roman Catholic.

Fogarty, a Conservative, was first elected to the Legislative Assembly in the general election of

1979 for 1ˢᵗ Kings, and was re-elected in 1982, 1986, and 1989. In 1974, in his first attempt at public office, Fogarty was unsuccessful in the district of 3ʳᵈ Kings. Fogarty was a provincial delegate to Constitutional conferences, and attended the Canada Round discussions and First Ministers' conference. From 17 November 1981 to 1986, he held the positions of Minister of Health and Social Services and Minister Responsible for Addiction Services and Civil Service. In 1982 he was a United Nations delegate at the Conference on Aging in Vienna, Austria. Fogarty chaired the Cabinet Committee on Social Policy from 1981 to 1986. From 1989 to 1993, he was Opposition House Leader, and, from 1986 to 1993, served as Opposition finance critic. In 1993, upon completion of his term in the Legislature, he became the Provincial Superintendent of Education. This position was created to lead the implementation of education reform in the province.

A native of the Seven Mile Road near Cardigan, Fogarty received his primary education at the school in Glenfanning and in 1958 graduated from Montague Regional High School. In 1962 Fogarty graduated from St. Dunstan's University with a Bachelor of Arts and, in 1966, with a Bachelor of Education. He studied history in graduate school at the University of New Brunswick and was the recipient of a graduate scholarship. In 1977 he graduated from St. Francis Xavier University with a Master of Education. From 1962 to 1964, Fogarty taught at Montague Regional High School. In 1964 he became the principal as well as a teacher at Souris Regional High School, and remained in this position until 1981. He returned as principal and teacher at Souris Regional High School from 1986 until 1993. From 1993 to 1994, Fogarty was the province's Superintendent of Education. Later in 1994 he was a senior policy consultant with the Prince Edward Island Office of Higher Education, Training and Adult Learning. Fogarty opened a professional consulting business, Fogarty Consulting Incorporated, in 1997. The following year he assumed the position of executive director of the Prince Edward Island Institute of Adult and Community Education at Holland College. Fogarty retired from Holland College in December 2001.

Fogarty was a president of the Prince Edward Island Teacher's Federation and a member of the board of directors of the Canadian Teacher's Federation. He was a member of the board of directors of the Canadian Mental Health Association and the Prince Edward Island Arthritis Society. In 1992 he was a member of the Prince Edward Island "Yes" Canada Committee. Fogarty was a member of the board of directors of St. John House Incorporated and chair of the Provincial Advisory Committee of St. John Ambulance. Additionally, he was chair of the board of directors of the Holland College Foundation. Fogarty was a member of the Northern Ireland Children's Event Committee, the Souris Lions Club, and the Souris Knights of Columbus, and is a member of the Rotary Club of Charlottetown. In 1973 he was awarded the Centennial Citizenship Citation and in 1992 received the Commemorative Medal on the 125ᵗʰ Anniversary of Confederation. He also served as president of the Association of Former MLAs.

Fogarty has produced a number of documents, including *Towards Excellence —Final Report of the Structure and Governance of the Prince Edward Island Educational System* (June 1993), *A New Design for School Board Leadership* and *Proposals — Recruitment, Hiring, Induction, Retention and Mobility of School Board Employees* (both June 1994), *Quality and Performance in Post-Secondary Education in Prince Edward Island* (February 1995) and *A Plan for the Future, Adult Literacy* (August 1995), *Eastern Kings: Social and Economic Development — A Different Perspective* (June 1997), *Holland College Professional Addictions Counselor Program — Program Viability Study* (October 1997). With Lorne Amos he co-authored the study *Aerospace Training Needs — Prince Edward Island* (December 1997).

Judith Fogarty was born in Charlottetown on 18 May 1944. Albert Fogarty and his wife reside in Charlottetown.

References
CPG 1976, 1993; *WWPEI* p. 49; *Eastern Graphic* 25 November 1981, 27 January 1993, 3 February 1993; *Guardian* 14 April 1978, 12 April 1979, 15 April 1986, 1 May 1986, 23 January 1993, 8 April 1993, 26 October 1993; *Journal-Pioneer* 23 January 1993; *Royal Gazette* 5 December 1981.

FOLEY, EDWARD P., pharmacist; b. 10 March 1891 in Kildare, son of Patrick Foley and Margaret M. Foley; m. first 11 November 1925 Helen Noonan, and there were no children; m. secondly Margaret Tierney, and there were no children; Roman Catholic; d. 17 October 1980 in Summerside.

Foley, a Liberal, was first elected to the Legislative Assembly in the general election of 1935 for 5th Prince. He was re-elected in the general elections of 1939, 1951, and 1955. Foley was defeated in the general election of 1943. From 1954 to 1958, he served on Executive Council as a Minister without Portfolio. He became Speaker in 1959.

Foley was educated at the local school, Alberton High School, and Prince of Wales College. Following his education, he became a pharmacist in Summerside. He was a member of Summerside's Board of Trade, and was also a member of the Knights of Columbus, the Summerside Curling Club, and the Summerside Golf Club. Edward Foley died 17 October 1980.

Helen Foley, the daughter of J. M. Noonan of Summerside and Margaret Murphy, was born in 1893 and died in 1968.

References
CPG 1936, 1944, 1956; PEI *Journal of the Legislative Assembly* 1959, p. 2 *Guardian* 18 October 1980, 24 October 1980; PARO: Summerside Cemetery Records.

FORBES, GEORGE, merchant, trader, and farmer; b. 25 November 1840 at Marshfield, son of Malcolm Forbes and Christina Scott; m. 22 March 1876 Jessie Isabella Stewart, and they had one child, Wilfred; Baptist; d. 17 December 1925.

Forbes, a Liberal, was first elected to the House of Assembly in the general election of 1886 for 4th Queens. He was re-elected in the general election of 1890. In the general election of 1893, Forbes was elected to the Legislative Assembly. He was re-elected in the general elections of 1897, 1900, and 1915. In 1891 he served on Executive Council in the Frederick Peters* Administration, and again in 1900 in the Donald Farquharson* Administration.

Forbes received his education at the local school in Vernon River. It appears that he spent his adult life living in Vernon Bridge, as he was a merchant and trader in that community from at least 1864. Forbes also was a farmer. George Forbes died 17 December 1925.

Jessie Forbes was born near the Hillsborough River in Frenchfort ca. 1841, and died 1 October 1914. She was the daughter of John Stewart of Frenchfort. Forbes' parents were from Perthshire, Scotland.

References
CPG 1901, 1917; Elections PEI; *Meacham's Atlas*; *Examiner* 27 March 1876; *Patriot* 18 December 1925; PARO: MNI-Mercantile Agency

Reference Book 1876; MNI-Census1881, 1891; Uigg Baptist Church Records.

FORD, DAVID HENRY, dairy worker, butcher, livestock merchant, and farmer; b. 7 September 1920 in Ebenezer, son of Mayus Robert Ford and Matilda Hickox; m. 20 January 1943 Vaunda Jean Saunders, and they had two children, Milton David and Gloria Ann; United.

Ford, a Liberal, was first elected to the Legislative Assembly in the general election of 1974 for 2nd Queens. He was re-elected in the general election of 1978. He was defeated in a by-election held 4 December 1972 and in the general election of 1979. Ford chaired the Municipal Affairs and Housing Committee and was a member of the committees dealing with agriculture and industry, transportation, resources, fisheries, and tourism. He was also a member of the Special Committee on Regulations and chaired the Farm Development and New Farmer Program Advisory and Appeals Board.

Ford received his education at the school in Ebenezer, and in 1940 he volunteered for the armed forces and was declared Category E (medically unfit). Early in his life, Ford moved to Needham, Massachusetts, where he worked for Walker Gordon Dairy. Later, upon his return to the province, he worked buying and selling livestock and had a retail meat business in the old City Market. He purchased livestock both independently and at Canada Packers from 1951 to 1968. In the 1970s, he was a buyer for the NS Abattoir. Ford served as a livestock judge and committee member for the Easter Beef Show and Sale. In the 1980s he was appointed to the Hospital Health Services Commission.

David and Vaunda Ford reside in Warren Grove.

References
CPG 1978, 1980; *Evening Patriot* 12 April 1976; Questionnaire to Former MLAs.

FRANCIS, HARRY S., carriage builder; b. 5 June 1886 in Fortune Bridge, son of John S. Francis and Jane Elizabeth MacKie; m. 11 August 1915 Ethel M. McEwen, and they had six children, Elizabeth, J. Wallace, Hilda, Lorne, Bernice, and Edgar Vernon; United; d. 3 June 1948.

Francis, a Liberal, was elected to the Legislative Assembly in the general election of 1943 for 1st Kings. He was defeated in the general election of 1947.

Francis was educated at the Fortune Bridge School, resided in the community of Fortune Bridge, and was a partner in the firm of J. S. Francis and Sons, carriage builders. Harry Francis died 3 June 1948.

Ethel Francis, the daughter of Wallace McEwen, was born in 1892 and died in 1979.

References
CPG 1947, 1948; PARO: Leard Files; Bay Fortune United Church Cemetery Transcripts.

FRASER, A. A. "JOEY", oil company agent; b. 4 February 1920 in Montague, son of Dr. Albert Joseph Fraser of Vernon Bridge and Mabel Parkman of Alberton; m. 28 December 1945 Mary Elizabeth Gill, and they had seven children, Arthur Richard, Allan Gill, Blair John, Gerard Gordon, Robert James, Mary Noreen, and Rita Elizabeth; Roman Catholic; d. 7 August 2001 in Montague.

Fraser, a Conservative, was first elected to the Legislative Assembly in a by-election held 13 July 1981 for 3rd Kings. He was re-elected in the general elections of 1982 and 1986. He was defeated in the general elections of 1979 and 1989. He served on the Montague Town Council.

"Joey" Fraser, as he was known, graduated from Montague High School and lived in Montague for the majority of his life. A veteran of the Second World War, he served with the North Nova Scotia Highlanders from 1940 to 1945, and was one of the troops that landed in France on D-Day, 6 June 1944. Fraser worked as an agent for Imperial Oil and retired in 1989. For two years he chaired the United Way Appeal and for 20 years served as chairman of the Red Cross Blood Donor campaign. Fraser was a trustee of Montague High School and the Montague school board. He was a member of St. Mary's Parish Council, as well as the Knights of Columbus and the Royal Canadian Legion. Joey Fraser died on 7 August 2001 in Montague.

Mary Fraser, the daughter of Richard Gill of Iona and Maude McGarry, was born 1 November 1919.

References
CPG 1980, 1981, 1989, 1990; *WWPEI* p. 51; *Guardian* 9 August 2001, 17 April 1979.

FRASER, AUSTIN LEVI, teacher, lawyer, and judge; b. 17 March 1868 in Vernon River, son of Edward Fraser and Flora Fraser; m. 25 June 1901 Maud A. Moar, and they had five children, George E., Henry Irving, Vernon, Mildred F., and one other son; Roman Catholic; d. 22 April 1946 in Souris.

Fraser, a Conservative, was elected to the Legislative Assembly in the general election of 1904 for 1st Kings. He resigned his seat in September 1908 to successfully run in the federal election of that year for the riding of King's. He was defeated in the 1911 federal election.

Fraser attended Prince of Wales College and later St. Dunstan's College, where he received a Bachelor of Arts. After graduation he taught school for several years. Following his time in the classroom, Fraser studied law with the partnership of Gaudet and Haszard; Francis L. Haszard* was premier from 1908 to 1911. He was admitted to the Bar on 6 November 1900. Fraser and his wife resided in Souris immediately following their marriage, where he worked as a lawyer. Following his political career, he was appointed Judge of the Kings County Court. Austin Fraser died 22 April 1946, about four years after retiring from the Bench.

Maud Fraser, the daughter of George Moar of Georgetown, died 30 May 1949.

References
CDP p. 215; *CPG* 1908, 1910; Elections PEI; *Charlottetown Patriot* 23 April 1946; *Guardian* 26 June 1901; PARO: 1901 Census; Souris St. Mary's Roman Catholic Church Records.

FRASER, CHARLES J., farmer, investment advisor, theatre owner, salesperson, company director, and feed company owner; b. 11 November 1919 in Montague, son of John Egbert Fraser and Florence May Kennedy; m. 23 June 1948 Ruth Irene MacGregor, and they had three children, John Elliot, Charles Roy, and Donald Harry; United.

Fraser, a Liberal, was elected to the Legislative Assembly in the general election of 1974 for 4th Kings. He was defeated in the general election of 1978 by Pat Binns*. From 1967 to 1973, he was the Mayor of Montague, and while in that office had responsibility for the installation of a primary sewage treatment plant in the community as part of the Comprehensive Development Plan. The plant was the first one installed in the province. Fraser was a Montague councillor from 1955 to 1961. He was also a president of the Prince Edward Island Federation of Municipalities.

Fraser received his education at Montague High School. He was a member of the Royal Canadian Air Force. He operated a large farm on the outskirts of town until he sold the land in the 1960s. In time, Fraser became an investment advisor. Later he was the director and president of the Montague Drive-In Theatre, Limited. He was also a director of Industrial Enterprises Incorporated and a partner in Fraser and Annear Feed Services. Fraser held the position of president of the Atlantic Motion Exhibitors Association and director of the Prince Edward Island Housing Authority. He was a member of the Board of Directors of the Island Telephone Company from 1973 to 1989. He is a member of the Hillcrest United Men's Club. Charles Fraser and his wife reside in Montague.

Ruth Fraser, the daughter of Harry and Edith E. MacGregor, was born 26 March 1921.

References
CPG 1978; *Guardian* 25 January 1967; *Journal-Pioneer* 29 May 1973; Questionnaire to Former MLAs.

G

GALLANT, AMÉDÉE, farmer and fish exporter; b. 24 October 1848 in Bloomfield, son of Fabien Gallant and Tharsile Gallant of Rustico; m. 11 February 1877 Veronique Pineau, and they had nine children, Jean, Marie Eugenie, Josephine, Emmanuel, Zella, Priscilla, Rose, Wilfred, and Christine; Roman Catholic; d. 19 June 1933 in Bloomfield.

Gallant, a Liberal, was elected to the Legislative Assembly in a by-election held 20 July 1898 for 1st Prince. He was elected to fill a vacancy caused by the resignation of Edward Hackett*, who had decided to pursue a career in federal politics.

"Meddie" Gallant, a resident of Bloomfield, was a farmer and operated a fish export business in Miminegash for several years. He was the supervisor of highways for West Prince and had the first telephone installed in his area for better communications in his work.

"Meddie" Gallant died on 19 June 1933 in Bloomfield.

References
CPG 1898-1899; PARO: Leard Files.

GALLANT, BENJAMIN, merchant, fish processor, and brick manufacturer; b. 11 June 1871 in Bloomfield, son of Ebenezer (Eusèbe) Gallant and Martha Arsenault; m. 2 July 1901 Annie M. Gallant, and they had four children, Gertrude, Isadora, W. F., and Louis; Roman Catholic; d. 27 October 1921 in Summerside.

Gallant, a Liberal, was first elected to the Legislative Assembly in the general election of 1900 for 1st Prince. He was re-elected in the general elections of 1904, 1908, 1915, and 1919. On 9 September 1919, Gallant was appointed to Executive Council, where he served until his death.

Gallant received his education at the local school in Bloomfield and at Business and Commercial College in Charlottetown. Following the completion of his education, he returned to Bloomfield and operated a general store and a brick factory, serving as vice-president of Prince Edward Silver Block Company. He was also involved in fish packing, and processed a number of species, including lobster. Gallant's other involvements included membership in the Knights of Columbus and the Catholic Mutual Benefit Association. Benjamin Gallant died 27 October 1921.

Annie Gallant was the daughter of Dr. Isidore Gallant of Rustico and Margaret Campbell.

References
CPG 1916; *Guardian* 31 December 1921 p. 4; *Maple Leaf Magazine* March 1940; *Patriot* 29 October 1921; PARO: MNI-Census 1891; Summerside St. Paul's Roman Catholic Church Records.

GALLANT, ÉTIENNE-É. (Stephen), merchant; b. 6 February 1844 in Egmont Bay, son of Joseph and Marie Arsenault; m. 1 June 1875 Elizabeth McNally of Egmont Bay; there were no children; Roman Catholic; d. in Sydney, Nova Scotia.

Gallant, a Liberal, was elected to the Legislative Assembly in a by-election on 25 July 1895 for 3rd Prince. He was defeated in the general elections of 1890 and 1893.

Gallant operated a store in Richmond before moving to Cape Breton.

Elizabeth Gallant was the daughter of John McNally and Ann Sullivan.

References
Acadiens p. 91; *CPG* 1891, 1897, 1899.

GALLANT, CAPTAIN FRANCIS "François", merchant, trader, and cannery owner; b. 17 March 1841 in Nail Pond, son of Sylvain Gallant and Mary Gaudet; m. 24 October 1870 Katherine McKenna, and they had seven children, Edward, James, Ernest, Emily, Bertha, Mary, and Leo; Roman Catholic; d. 3 October 1905 in Tignish.

Gallant, a Conservative, was elected 17 April 1875 in a by-election for 1st Prince.

Captain Frank Gallant, as he was called, went to sea as a young man, rising to the rank of master mariner, having been captain of several schooners employed in the West Indies and Newfoundland trade. After 14 years on the sea, he engaged in the lobster-packing business in Tignish for some six years. He then went into the general merchandise business. In 1894 he became Tignish's postmaster and operated a small inn. Gallant died in Tignish on 3 October 1905.

Katherine Gallant was the daughter of John

Arnold McKenna of Ireland, later of Charlottetown, and Catherine Mahar. She died in Tignish on 2 June 1892. Frank Gallant's daughter Bertha married Aubin Edmond Arsenault*, Prince Edward Island Premier from 1917 to 1919.

References
Acadiens p. 149; *CPG* 1876; *Meacham's Atlas*; *Past and Present* pp. 333–34; *Daily Examiner* 21 January 1895; *Islander* 28 October 1870; *Journal-Pioneer* 3 December 1899; *Patriot* 16 June 1903; PARO: Marriage Records Book 1867–1871 #11 p. 417; Marriage License Book 1871–1881 #12 pp. 61-2, 71-2; MNI-Census 1881, 1891; Leard Files.

GALLANT, J. AUGUSTIN, teacher, principal, and lawyer; b. 4 August 1916 in Egmont Bay, son of Peter Gallant and Eleanor Arsenault; m. 27 December 1943, Marcella Bernard of Tignish, and they had seven children, Peter, Michael, Carroll, John, Patrick, Richard, and Robert; Roman Catholic; d. 5 May 1994 in Summerside.

Gallant, a Liberal, was first elected to the Legislative Assembly in a by-election held 29 November 1954 for 3rd Prince. He was re-elected in the general election of 1955. Gallant was defeated in the general election of 1951. Gallant served as Speaker from 21 February 1956 to 1958.

"Gus" Gallant attended Summerside High School and Prince of Wales College in Charlottetown. He also spent a summer studying at Mount Allison University in Sackville, New Brunswick, and received a first class teaching licence. Gallant returned to the province, where he taught for two years in Urbainville and was principal of the Dalton School in Tignish for three years. In the spring of 1940, he joined the Royal Canadian Air Force as a pilot, and saw action in France and England during the Second World War. In 1943 Gallant returned to Canada and trained pilots on the West Coast during the final years of the war. Following this he returned to Mount Allison University, before moving on to study at Dalhousie University in Halifax where he earned his law degree. In 1950 Gallant established a legal practice in Summerside. After retiring from politics, he and his family moved to Bagotville, Quebec, where Gallant worked as the principal of the high school. After 20 years in Quebec, he and his family returned to the Island, and in 1979 Gallant established a legal practice in Alberton where he worked until his retirement in 1990. On returning to the Island, he lived in Duvar until he retired. He then moved to Summerside. He was a member of the Prince Edward Island Law Society and the Royal Canadian Legion in Summerside. J. Augustin Gallant died 5 May 1994 at his home in Summerside.

Marcella Gallant was the daughter of Joseph Alphonse Bernard*, former MLA and Lieutenant-Governor, and Zoë Chiasson.

References
Blanchard *Acadians* pp. 90–91; Blanchard *Acadiens* pp. 91–92; *CPG* 1955, 1956, 1959; *Guardian* 4 June 1990, 6 May 1994; *Journal-Pioneer* 6 May 1994; *West Prince Graphic* 7 April 1987.

GALLANT, MARIN, teacher, farmer, and public school supervisor; b. 24 July 1873 in South Rustico, son of Arcade Gallant and Virginia Blanchard; m. 15 October 1907 Marie-Rose Arsenault, and they had four children, Virginia, Yvonne, Antonin, and Edmond; Roman Catholic; d. 25 October 1958.

Gallant, a Liberal, was first elected to the Legislative Assembly in the general election of 1935 for 3rd Prince. He was re-elected in the general elections of 1939 and 1943. He was defeated in the general election of 1927. On 15 August 1935, Gallant was appointed as a Minister without Portfolio, where he served until 1946. He also served as a President of the East Prince Liberal Association.

Gallant received his early education at St. Augustine School. Later he attended New Glasgow Grammar School and St. Dunstan's College. Gallant received a first class teacher's licence in 1899, and went on to teach in Rustico, Miscouche, and Egmont Bay from 1894 to 1910. From 1910 to 1922, and again from 1927 to 1932, he worked as a public school supervisor for the French schools in the province. Gallant served as president of the Acadian Teachers' Association of Prince Edward Island and was a member of the Artisans Canadiens Français of Montreal and the Société L'Assomption in Moncton. He had an interest in the early history of French settlement on the Island and studied the genealogy of the early settlers and their ancestors. Marin Gallant died on 25 October 1958.

Marie-Rose Gallant was the daughter of John Fidèle Arsenault of Abrams Village.

References
Blanchard *Acadiens* p. 92; *CPG* 1944; *CWW* 1936-1937 p. 401; PEI *Journal of the Legislative Assembly* 1946, p. 2; PARO: Leard Files.

GALLANT, PIUS AENEAS, farmer, merchant, and civil servant; b. 1 February 1882 in Rustico, son of Dr. Isidore Gallant and Marguerite Campbell; m. 27 November 1941 Lillian-Mae MacAusland of Bloomfield; they had one son, Pius; Roman Catholic; d. 10 November 1971 in Charlottetown.

Gallant, a Liberal, was first elected to the Legislative Assembly in the general election of 1935 for 1st Prince. He was re-elected in the general election of 1939.

Aeneas Gallant was a resident of Bloomfield Station, where he farmed and operated a store for a number of years. From 1943 to 1954, he held the position of accountant at the Falconwood Hospital in Charlottetown. Pius Aeneas Gallant died 10 November 1971.

References
Acadiens p. 93; *CPG* 1941; PARO: Bloomfield St. Anthony's Church Records.

GALLANT, SYLVAIN, farmer, lobster canner, and oyster shipper; b. 10 October 1866 in Bloomfield, son of Thomas Gallant and Marie Gallant; m. first 18 August 1891 Mary Gallant, and they had five children, Mary, Angeline, Edna, Thomas, and Andrew; m. secondly 3 November 1917, Sarah Ida Christopher, and they had two children, Everett and Christoper; Roman Catholic; d. 13 January 1960 in Charlottetown.

Gallant, a Conservative, was elected to the Legislative Assembly in the general election of 1912 for 1st Prince. He was defeated in the general elections of 1908 and 1915.

Gallant was educated in the local school at Piusville, and lived in Bloomfield and Piusville Station. Besides being a farmer, Gallant was involved in the fishery as a lobster canner and oyster shipper. He was chief provincial fisheries inspector from 1919 to 1936. Sylvain Gallant died 13 January 1960.

Mary Gallant, the daughter of Joseph Gallant of Bloomfield, died 5 April 1914 at the age of 44. Sarah Gallant was born 13 May 1880 and died 16 December 1974. She was the daughter of James Christopher and Sarah Ready. Sylvain Gallant's father, Thomas Gallant, a section hand on the Prince Edward Island Railway, was killed by a train.

References
Acadiens pp. 93–94; *CPG* 1910, 1915, 1916; *Patriot* 14 January 1960; PARO: Bloomfield St. Anthony's Church Records, Charlottetown Roman Catholic Cemetery Records.

GALLANT, WILLIAM MARSHALL, air force officer and credit union manager; b. 20 January 1915 in St. Charles, son of Leo and Judith Gallant; m. first 25 October 1941 Lucy Irene Long, and they had four children, Louise, Wilma, Mary, and Blair;

m. secondly Frances Griffen, and there were no children; Roman Catholic; d. 21 July 1988 in Fredericton, New Brunswick.

Gallant, a Liberal, was first elected to the Legislative Assembly in the general election of 1970 for 3rd Prince. He was re-elected in the general election of 1974. On 14 June 1973, he was appointed Minister of Community Services and Minister of the Environment and Tourism. Gallant served in these Ministries until 1974, and retired from provincial politics in October 1975.

Gallant was educated in New Acadia. He served in the Royal Canadian Air Force for 25 years. During this time, he held the position of recruiting officer. Upon retiring from the Canadian Air Force, Gallant became the civilian manager of the Credit Union on CFB Summerside. He also served as a director of the Prince County Family Services Bureau and the Prince Edward Island Alcoholic Foundation. He was a member of the Rotary Club, the Royal Canadian Legion, the Knights of Columbus, and the Summerside Chamber of Commerce. After ending his political career, Gallant and his family moved to Woodstock, New Brunswick. They spent their winters in Jensen Beach, Florida. William Gallant died 21 July 1988 at the Veterans Wing of the Victoria Health Centre in Fredericton.

References
COR p. 62; *CPG* 1974; *Patriot* 21 July 1988.

GAUDET, HUBERT J., fisher and building contractor; b. 12 September 1893 in Tignish, son of Peter U. Gaudet and Mary Harper; m. 13 April 1915 Mary Henrietta Arsenault, and they had three children, Marie, Melvin, and Gussie; Roman Catholic; d. 17 October 1972 in Tignish.

Gaudet, a Conservative, was first elected to the Legislative Assembly in the general election of 1951 for 1st Prince. He was re-elected in the general election of 1959. He was defeated in the general elections of 1955 and 1962.

Gaudet was educated in Tignish. He was a fisher and building contractor in the area. Gaudet built many homes in Tignish and supervised the building of the Tignish Regional High School, the Tignish Elementary School, the Legion Home, and the Parish Centre of St. Simon and St. Jude Church. He played an active role in the life of his community and in that of his church.

Gaudet was the director of Tignish Fisheries and was a charter member and early president of the Tignish Fisheries Co-operative. He was also a charter member of the Tignish Co-operative Association and the first president of the Tignish Credit Union. Hubert Gaudet died 17 October 1972 at his home.

Mary Gaudet died 29 January 1988.

References
Acadiens p. 94; *CPG* 1952, 1958, 1962, 1963; *Journal-Pioneer* 18 October 1972.

GAVIN, PETER, merchant and lobster factory owner; b. 15 October 1847 in Tignish, son of Michael Gavin and Catherine O'Neil, both of Wexford, Ireland; m. 19 June 1876 Anastasia Ryan, and they had five children, Mary E., Eugenie C., Francis J., Nellie (died at eight years and seven months in 1886 of smallpox), and George Frederick (died at one year and nine months in 1892 in Minnesota); Roman Catholic; d. 22 February 1931 in Duluth, Minnesota.

Gavin, a Conservative, was first elected to the House of Assembly in a by-election in September 1878 for 1st Prince. He was re-elected in the general election of 1879. He was defeated in the general election of 1882. During his time in the House of Assembly, Gavin served on Executive Council.

Gavin was educated at local schools in Tignish. He was a merchant with Gavin Brothers General Store and also owned a lobster factory. Peter Gavin died 22 February 1931.

Anastasia Gavin, the daughter of Edward Ryan and Ellen Flood, was born 13 November 1853 and died 3 November 1933.

References
CPG 1879, 1881, 1883; *Meacham's Atlas*; *Daily Examiner* 26 February 1892; *Maple Leaf Magazine* March 1931; *Summerside Journal* 7 January 1886; PARO: MNI-Census 1881.

GHIZ, Q.C., LL.D., D.C.L., LL.M., HONOURABLE JOSEPH ATALLAH, lawyer, Crown prosecutor, law school dean, and judge; b. 27 January 1945 in Charlottetown, son of Atallah Joseph Ghiz and Marguerite McKarris; m. 16 December 1972 Rose Ellen McGowan, and they had two children, Robert and Joanne; Anglican; d. 9 November 1996 in Charlottetown.

Ghiz, a Liberal, was first elected to the Legislative Assembly in the general election of 1982 for 6th Queens. He was re-elected in the general elections of 1986 and 1989. From 1982 to 1986, he was Leader of the Opposition, but in the 1986 general election he led the Liberals to victory, winning 21 of 32 seats. On 2 May 1986, Ghiz was sworn in as Premier and President of Executive Council. He was Minister of Agriculture from 26 October 1988 to 6 June 1989, and Minister of Health and Social Services 2 May 1986 to 12 June 1986. He was re-elected premier on 29 May 1989. Ghiz also served as Minister of Justice from 1989 to 1993. On 30 October 1992, he announced his resignation from provincial politics, but remained Premier and Minister of Justice until 25 January 1993, when the party elected a new leader.

Ghiz, the son of a Lebanese immigrant, grew up in the apartment above his parents' corner store in Charlottetown. The store was a neighbourhood hotbed of politics and debate, and it was there that Ghiz discovered his love of politics. Early in life, he became involved in the Liberal party. In 1977 he was elected its President and in 1981 its Leader. Ghiz's prime asset, in his legal and political careers, was a flair for rhetoric. His quick intellect and oratorical skills were significant, and his speeches were impassioned. The *Globe and Mail* described Ghiz's speaking ability: "For people who have never gone walking in a monsoon, listening to Liberal Joe Ghiz give a political speech would nicely simulate the experience."

When Ghiz led the Liberals to victory in 1986, he became Canada's first premier of non-European ancestry. During the election, a whisper campaign ensued regarding his racial heritage. When the issue began to be discussed by national and, finally, provincial media, he defused this argument by calling a news conference to address the issue. It was at this news conference that Ghiz made one of his most famous remarks: "I am Canadian and I am proud of it, I am an Islander and I am proud of it. I am a Canadian and an Islander of Lebanese extraction and I am proud of that as well."

Provincially, Ghiz's most significant accomplishment was his guidance of the process that led to the construction of the Confederation Bridge. In early 1988, with the fixed link debate in full swing on the Island, the Ghiz Administration held a plebiscite to determine Islanders' views on the issue. The population was debating whether or not to establish a fixed link with the Mainland to replace the Marine Atlantic ferry service. The plebiscite, the first in the province since 1948, was held

18 January 1988, and 59.1 per cent of Islanders voted in favour of the fixed link.

Premier Ghiz was very popular with Islanders, but it was on the national stage that he found his niche. He participated in the constitutional discussions of Meech Lake and the Charlottetown Accord, and became a leader in this process. Ghiz's pride in his country and his background in constitutional law combined to make him a passionate, articulate, and effective defender of Canadian nationalism.

The emphasis of Ghiz's economic policy was to add value to the products of the province's agriculture and fishing industry. Three large potato processing plants were constructed during his time in office. A major effort was made to expand tourism infrastructure, including golf course construction and the expansion of tourism accommodations.

The Ghiz government implemented a drug assistance program for seniors and a community hospital construction program. Significant renovations were made to schools in the Charlottetown area. His government had to cope with an escalating provincial debt, especially during the latter part of his second term when the national economy suffered a sharp recession. As a result, Ghiz instituted a government reform initiative.

Ghiz received his early education at West Kent School and Queen Charlotte High School. He subsequently attended Prince of Wales College in Charlottetown. Ghiz then studied at Dalhousie University in Halifax where he earned a Bachelor of Commerce and a Law degree in 1969. While at Dalhousie, Ghiz was awarded the Barristers' Society Scholarship for highest standing in his class. In 1981 he earned a Master of Laws from Harvard University. Ghiz was admitted to the provincial Bar in 1970 and appointed Queen's Counsel in 1984. From 1969 to 1972, he was a sessional lecturer in business law and, from 1974 to 1975, he was a lecturer in special courses in real estate law at the University of Prince Edward Island. Ghiz served as a federal narcotics drug prosecutor from 1970 to 1979 and as Crown prosecutor for Queens County from 1970 to 1972. He was a partner in the firm of Scales, Ghiz, Jenkins and McQuaid. In 1987 he was awarded an honourary Doctorate of Laws from the University of Prince Edward Island and in 1996 an honourary Doctorate of Civil Laws from Bishop's University in Lennoxville, Quebec.

Following his time in provincial politics, Ghiz assumed the position of Dean of Law at Dalhousie University Law School on 1 March 1993. He was appointed to the Trial Division of the Prince Edward Island Supreme Court on 5 April 1995 by federal Justice Minister Allan Rock and was officially sworn into the position on 28 April. Ghiz served on the Supreme Court until his death.

Ghiz was a member of the board of governors of Frontier College and served as regional chair for the Canadian Council on Multiculturalism. He helped found the Montague Boys and Girls Club and was a member of the Charlottetown Jaycees. Ghiz served as president of the provincial branch of the Canadian Bar Association and was a member of the Canadian Bar Association Committee on the Constitution. In 1977 Ghiz served as president of the Liberal Party. Joseph Ghiz died 9 November 1996 of cancer and is survived by his wife, their children, and his mother.

Three days before his death, he voted in the provincial election in an advance poll. Upon his death, Islanders and other Canadians poured out their emotions for the former premier. He was honoured by his province and country with a state funeral, attended by Prime Minister Jean Chrétien and sitting and former Canadian premiers.

Rose Ellen Ghiz, the daughter of Doug McGowan* and Elizabeth Margaret Watson, was born on 5 June 1953. Her father and uncle, Neil Murdock McGowan*, were members of the Legislative Assembly.

References
CPG 1993; *CWW* 1996 p. 443; ECO 617/88, ECO 295/89, ECO 255/86; MacDonald *If You're Stronghearted* pp. 352-5, 378-79; *WWPEI* p. ?; *Guardian* 5 February 1993, 8 January 1994, 6 June 1996, 11 November 1996, 29 August 2002; *Globe and Mail* 12 November 1996; *Journal-Pioneer* 29 April 1995.

GILLIS, M.D., C.M., DR. JOHN F., physician; b. 21 October ca. 1843 in Miscouche, son of John P. Gillis and Cecillia MacLellan; m. 26 September 1882 Regina Doyle, and they had five children, Patricia, Frank, Harold, Raymond, and Regina; Catholic; d. 23 January 1899 in Summerside.

Gillis, a Conservative, was first elected to the House of Assembly in the general election of 1882 for 5th Prince. He was re-elected in the general election of 1886.

For the majority of his adult life, Gillis lived in Summerside. While attending college, Gillis also lived in Charlottetown and Montreal. He went first to St. Dunstan's College, and later to McGill to study medicine. He graduated from McGill with honours in 1877. Census data indicates he boarded with John T. Linkletter of Summerside in 1881, shortly before his marriage.

According to his obituary, Gillis was a capable physician with significant surgical skill. His positive bedside manner was greatly appreciated by his patients. Later in his career, he concentrated solely on an office practice. John Gillis died 23 January 1899.

Regina Gillis, the daughter of Thomas Doyle, was born ca. 1846 and died 7 March 1904. The Gillis family immigrated to the Island from the western islands in Scotland, and settled on the north shore of Richmond Bay.

References
CPG 1889; *Maple Leaf Magazine* December 1930; *Summerside Journal* 1 February 1899; PARO: Marriage Register #13 1876–1887 p. 229; MNI-Census 1881, 1891; Summerside St. Paul's Roman Catholic Church Records.

GODKIN, GEORGE ALBERT, watchmaker and jeweller; b. 4 June 1860 in Charlottetown, son of James and Jane Turner; m. 5 November 1890 Sadie M. Brown, and there were no children; Methodist; d. April 1919, in Summerside.

Godkin, a Liberal, was first elected to the Legislative Assembly in the general election of 1893 for 5th Prince. He was re-elected in the general elections of 1900 and 1904. He was defeated in the general election of 1897. In January 1905 Godkin was appointed to Executive Council.

He was educated at local schools in Charlottetown, and was a watchmaker and jeweller. George Godkin died in April 1919.

Sadie Godkin was born in 1866 and died in 1929.

References
CPG 1905; *Daily Examiner* 14 November 1890; *Guardian* 23 April 1919; PARO: MNI-Census 1891; Summerside People's Protestant Cemetery Records.

GORDON, DANIEL, teacher, merchant, ship owner, shipbuilder, and officeholder; b. 2 June 1821 in Brudenell, son of Henry Gordon of Brudenell and Margaret McDonald of East Point; m. first 27 June 1854 Bridget E. Kearney, and they had three children, Ada, Fanny, and Henry; m. secondly 1893, Matilda Smith (née McGougan) of Prince Town, and there were no children; Presbyterian; d. 26 September 1907 in Georgetown.

Gordon, a Conservative, was first elected to the House of Assembly in 1876 for Georgetown Royalty. He was re-elected in the general elections of 1879, 1882, 1886, and 1890. He was elected to the Legislative Assembly in the general election of 1893 for 5th Kings. He was re-elected in the general elections of 1897 and 1900. Gordon was elected to the Legislative Council in 1866 and 1870 for 2nd Kings. He resigned his seat in Legislative Council in 1873. Gordon was a member of Executive Council from 1876 to 1878 in the L. H. Davies* Administration. Gordon joined the Free School Coalition organized by Davies for the 1876 election. Following the passing of the Public Schools Act, Gordon returned to the Conservative Party in the fall of 1878, after he and three other Conservative Free Schoolers resigned because they felt the coalition could not last. The resignations left the remaining Free-Schoolers in a minority. In early 1879, the Davies government fell on a vote of non-confidence. After the defeat of the William W. Sullivan* government in 1889, Gordon served as Leader of the Opposition until the election of John Mathieson* as Leader of the Conservatives. Gordon was a learned person, and many of his public addresses contained quotations from great writers and thinkers, often taken from the works in his large library.

Gordon, who had been educated in the local grammar school in Georgetown, taught from 1839 to 1840, before starting a business career in 1841. In Georgetown he operated a general retail business. Gordon was an importer-exporter, as well as a shipbuilder and ship owner. He was the sole owner of at least 15 vessels, most of which were built in Georgetown. Herbert Acorn* worked for him for some time starting in 1884. At his death on 26 September 1907, he was the oldest merchant in business in the province. Gordon was appointed a Justice of the Peace in 1851, served as the Commissioner under the Insolvent Debtors' Act, and was the Sheriff of Kings County beginning in 1863. He also served as chair of the Kings County Board of Agricultural and Exhibition Commissioners, as well as chair of the Georgetown Board of School Trustees.

Bridget Gordon was the daughter of John Kearney of Georgetown. She died 19 June 1884 at the age of 55. Matilda Gordon of Prince Town was born 8 October 1855. Gordon's father came originally from Perthshire, Scotland.

References

CPG 1879, 1901; *Centenary Celebration* pp. 30–31; *DCB* XIII pp. 75–76; Elections PEI; MacKinnon *Life of the Party* p. 61; *Meacham's Atlas*; *Examiner* 20 June 1884, 27 September 1907; *Islander* 30 June 1854; *Guardian* 28 September 1907; PARO: MNI-Hutchinson's pp. 123, 238, 248; MNI-Census 1881.

GORDON, ROBERT HUDSON, farmer; b. 8 August 1863, son of Henry and Sophia Gordon; m. Minnie A. Carruthers, and they had one daughter, Helen; Presbyterian; d. 1948.

Gordon, a Liberal, was elected to the Legislative Assembly in the general election of 1927 for 1st Prince.

Gordon was a farmer in Alberton. Robert Gordon died in 1948.

Minnie Gordon was born in 1869 and died in 1912.

References

CPG 1928; PARO: MNI-Census 1891; Census 1901; Montrose United Presbyterian Cemetery Records.

GRANT, M.D., C.M., HONOURABLE THOMAS VINCENT, physician and surgeon; b. 21 December 1876 in Peakes Station, son of Allan Grant and Mary Fisher; m. 27 October 1902 Minnie Donovan, and they had 13 children, Earl, Raymond, Vincent, Norbert, Byron, Roy, Anna Marie, Eileen, Cora, Mary, Jean, Beatrice, and Helen; Roman Catholic; d. 24 December 1966 in Charlottetown.

Grant, a Liberal, was elected to the Legislative Assembly in the general election of 1927 for 3rd Kings. On 12 August of that year, he was appointed to Executive Council as a Minister without Portfolio. He resigned his position on 30 May 1930 to contest the riding of King's in the federal election, but was defeated. However, in the 1935 federal election, Grant was elected to the House of Commons for King's, and was re-elected in 1940 and 1945. He was appointed to the Senate and served from 25 June 1949 to 19 August 1965.

Grant received his early education at the local schools in Peakes, Cardigan School, and at Prince of Wales College in Charlottetown. Following his time at Prince of Wales, he taught school in Morell from 1898 to 1901. Later he wrote the Civil Service exam and obtained a job at the Charlottetown Post Office. He served as both railway and post office clerk until 1907. In 1908 Grant sold insurance for Mutual Life of Canada. He then attended medical college in Boston, and upon completion of his medical training Grant returned to the Island. He set up his first practice in Cardigan, then in Vernon River, and finally in Montague. From 1920 to 1930, he served as the medical coroner for Kings County, and, from 1921 to 1930, he served as the secretary-treasurer for the Liberal Association of Kings County. He was a member of the executive of the PEI Liberal Association.

Grant did not belong to any fraternal organizations because he felt that they segregated rather than united society. Thomas Grant died 24 December 1966 in the Charlottetown Hospital.

Minnie Grant, the daughter of Patrick Donovan of Morell, was born 3 April 1880 and died 28 October 1968. Of the couple's thirteen children, the six sons were graduates of medical or dental colleges, four daughters were nurses, one daughter was a laboratory technician, and one joined a religious order and was also the pharmacist for many years at the Charlottetown Hospital. Anna Marie Grant died in Charlottetown several years before her parents.

References

CDP pp. 242–43; *Maritime Advocate and Busy East* October 1953; *Patriot* 27 December 1966; PARO: St. Theresa's Church Records, St. Cuthbert's Cemetery Records.

GRINDLAY, ROBERT ARTHUR, teacher; b. 5 January 1906 in London, England, son of John and Lavinia Anne Grindlay; m. 25 May 1933 Viola Mae Hiltz of Dayspring, Nova Scotia, and there were no children; Anglican; d. 28 December 1982 in Charlottetown.

Grindlay, a Conservative, was first elected to the Legislative Assembly in the general election of 1959 for 2nd Prince. He was re-elected in the general elections of 1962 and 1966. He was appointed Deputy Speaker of the Legislative Assembly on 18 February 1965.

Grindlay was educated in London, England. He moved to the Island where he taught school. Robert Grindlay died 28 December 1982 at Queen Elizabeth Hospital.

References

CPG 1970; *Guardian* 29 December 1982.

GUPTIL, NANCY EVELYN, radiotherapist and radiotherapy instructor; b. 28 April 1941 in Halifax, daughter of Lloyd and Evelyn Garrison; m. 23 May 1964 L. R. Gregg Guptil, and they had three children, Krista Evelyn, Nancy Elizabeth, and Peggy Elaine; Anglican.

Guptil, a Liberal, was first elected to the

Legislative Assembly in a by-election held 14 September 1987 for 5th Prince. She was re-elected in the general elections of 1989 and 1993. In 1996 she was elected for the new electoral district of St. Eleanors-Summerside. In 1999 Guptil resigned from the Legislature. From 1989 to 1991, Guptil was Minister of Tourism and Parks. On 14 November 1991, she was named Minister of Labour and Minister Responsible for the Status of Women and served in these positions until 15 April 1993. Following the 1993 general election, Guptil was elected Speaker and remained in that position until the 1996 general election. After the Liberals' defeat in 1996, Guptil became Opposition critic for health and social services. During her time in the Legislature, she served on several committees, including privileges, rules and private bills, social development, and the Special Committee on the Constitution of Canada.

Guptil served on the Summerside Town Council in 1982 and 1985, and chaired its Recreation Department. She was a member of the Summerside Area Regional Planning Board and of the Prince Edward Island Federation of Municipalities. Guptil served on the 1991 Canada Winter Games Task Force, in conjunction with her duties as a municipal politician.

Educated in Halifax, Guptil attended Queen Elizabeth High School and the Halifax Vocational School, before moving on to the Victoria General Hospital School of Radiotherapy, where she earned her designation as a radiotherapy technologist in 1961. Guptil was a radiotherapy technician at Victoria General Hospital and later a technologist and instructor in the radiotherapy department at St. John's General Hospital in St. John's, Newfoundland. In 1973 Guptil and her family moved to Bedeque, where she became active in the community, especially in the Kinette Club. It was at this time that she joined the Liberal party, first as a party worker and then as president of the 4th Prince Liberal Association. In 1977 the Guptil family moved to Summerside. Once again she became actively involved in the community. Guptil taught Sunday school, served as church superintendent, and was a member of the St. Mary's Church choir. Guptil was the coordinator of the Summerside Heart Fund, and a member of the Summerside Area Adult Development Centre and the Summerside Chamber of Commerce. She was a member of the host committee for the 1983 Canadian Junior and 1986 Canadian Senior Softball Tournaments. Nancy Guptil and her husband reside in Summerside.

References

Common Ground September 1987; *CPG* 1998–1999; *Eastern Graphic* 21 May 1997; *Guardian* 20 August 1987.

H

HACKETT, EDWARD, merchant and fish inspector; b. 6 July 1840 in Tignish, son of Thomas Hackett and Ellen Condon; m. 1860, Hannah Maria Fitzgibbon of Nova Scotia, and they had 11 children of whom 10 names are known, Thomas (died at 19 in a swimming accident), William, Augustin, John, Laura, Howard, Marcus, Bertha, Clara Lavinia (died in childhood), and Eveline Maude (died in infancy); Roman Catholic; d. 1916.

Hackett, a Conservative, was elected to the House of Assembly in the general election of 1876 for 1st Prince. He was elected to the Legislative Assembly for 1st Prince in the general election of 1904.

In 1878 Hackett resigned from the House of Assembly and was elected to the House of Commons in the federal election of the same year for Prince County. He was re-elected in the federal election of 1882. In the federal election of 1887, Hackett was defeated. Though re-elected for West Prince in the federal election of 1896, the riding results were declared void on 3 March 1897 due to a breach in the law. In the subsequent by-election held on 27 April 1897 for West Prince, S. F. Perry* defeated Hackett. In 1900 Hackett was elected in the federal election for West Prince.

Hackett received his education in Tignish schools. Throughout his life he resided in Tignish, where he owned a general store. For many years George Howlan*, Senator and Lieutenant-Governor, was a business associate. Hackett worked as an accountant and was Inspector of Fisheries for the province from July 1888 to June 1896. Edward Hackett died in 1916.

Hannah Hackett, daughter of James Fitzgibbon, was born ca. 1840 and was buried 13 June 1894.

References
CDP pp. 249–50; *CPG* 1879, 1899, 1903, 1905; *Daily Examiner* 2 August 1883, 29 April 29 1884, 14 November 1884; *Examiner* 15 October 1900; PARO: MNI-Mercantile Agency Reference Book 1876; MNI-Census 1881, 1891; Tignish St. Simon and St. Jude Roman Catholic Church Records.

HARRINGTON, KEITH STUART, teacher, farmer, and potato shipper; b. 6 August 1918 in Spring Valley, son of William John Harrington and Maude Lulu Ramsay; m. 28 August 1943 Irene Isabel MacAusland of Howlan, and they had five children, Myrna, Cordelia, Eleanor, Judy, William, and Alan; Anglican; d. 14 December 1987 in Halifax.

Harrington, a Conservative, was first elected in the general election of 1959. He was re-elected in the general elections of 1962 and 1966. He was defeated in the general election of 1970. While in Opposition, Harrington was Agriculture critic. Harrington served on the Public Buildings Committee and the Labour Management Committee. He also served as campaign manager for Angus MacLean*.

Harrington received his early education in Spring Valley and subsequently attended Prince of Wales College. When his studies were completed, he taught at schools in Clermont and Travellers Rest, before returning to the family farm where he began his farming career. Harrington would later become a major potato grower and shipper in Kensington. He was a member of the Kensington Board of Trade, the Board of the Prince County Hospital, and the Hospital and Health Services Commission. Harrington was a charter member of the Kensington Chamber of Commerce and a member of the Farmers Federation and the Masonic Lodge. He was an active member of St. Stephen's Anglican Church, and a member of the Anglican Laymen of the New London Parish. Keith Harrington died 14 December 1987 in the Halifax Infirmary.

References
CPG 1970, 1971; *Guardian* 20 January 1988; *Journal-Pioneer* 24 April 1974.

HASZARD, Q.C., HONOURABLE FRANCIS LONGWORTH, lawyer, city magistrate, city recorder, master of the rolls, judge, and farmer; b. 20 November 1849 in East Royalty, son of Charles Haszard and Margaret Longworth; m. 12 October 1876 Elizabeth DesBrisay, and they had seven children, Charles F., Louis G., Mary E., Hilda, Helen, Evelyn, and Ethel; Anglican; d. 25 July 1938 in Charlottetown.

Haszard, a Liberal, was first elected to the Legislative Assembly in the general election of 1904 for 4th Queens. He was re-elected in the general election of 1908. He was appointed to Executive

Council on 23 January 1905. Early in 1908, Haszard became Leader of the Liberal Party following the death of Premier Arthur Peters* on 31 January, and he led the Liberals to a narrow two-seat victory in that year's general election. Haszard served as Premier and Attorney-General from 1908 until, on 16 May 1911, he retired from politics, after having been appointed Master of the Rolls and Judge of the Supreme Court.

Premier Haszard was cautious with his legislative program as both parties were at almost equal strength in the Legislature. Following Haszard's appointment to the Supreme Court, new Premier H. J. Palmer* and fellow Liberal F. J. Nash* were both defeated in by-elections held in November 1911. As a result, the Conservative Party, led by John A. Mathieson*, assumed power.

Two major issues facing the Haszard Administration were the level of representation in the House of Commons and the level of federal subsidy to the province. At the time of Confederation, the Island had six federal seats. By 1904, its representation had been reduced to four. In response to the representation question, Premier Haszard stated that he would fight for more representation in Ottawa to the point of rebellion. In the spring of 1910, Haszard's government passed a resolution that called for a fixed number of representatives for each province. Furthermore, the resolution stated that the minimum representation for each province should be set at the number awarded at the entry into Confederation. In 1911, despite Haszard's efforts, the number of federal representatives for the Island was reduced from four to three, due to a decrease in the province's population.

The effort to increase the level of federal subsidy also frustrated Haszard, and the province received a much needed additional annual subsidy from the federal government of $100,000 only when Mathieson took office. Haszard was not entirely frustrated by the federal government as a new ferry, the *Earl Grey*, commenced service on 30 December 1909. He continued to make the case for increased federal support and represented the province at the Maritime and Inter-provincial Conferences in 1910.

Haszard, in tune with public opinion, strongly opposed the use of automobiles on Island roads. His reaction to the challenge of the automobile was to pass legislation banning them outright. It was 1913 before the ban was partially lifted.

Haszard received his early education at the local school in Charlottetown. He attended Prince of Wales College, and later studied law with his uncle, John Longworth. Haszard was called to the Bar in 1872, following which he became the junior partner in the firm of Longworth and Haszard. He remained in the firm until 1883 when Longworth retired, and subsequently practised law without a partner for a number of years. In November 1890 Haszard joined a law practice with L. H. Davies*. This partnership lasted until 1901 when Davies was appointed to the Supreme Court of Canada. In 1902 Haszard formed a partnership with Gilbert Gaudet. For a time Austin Fraser* studied with this firm. From 1893 to 1900, Haszard served as the magistrate and recorder for the City of Charlottetown. In 1911 he was appointed Master of the Rolls and Judge of the Supreme Court. He retired from the bench in 1930. Though the major pursuits of his career were law and politics, Haszard also had a deep interest in agriculture and maintained a farm in Bellevue.

Haszard was active at the community level. At the outbreak of the First World War, Haszard reorganized the local Red Cross society. He served as head of the Red Cross Society for a number of years, and later was named honourary president of the Red Cross Society. One Red Cross initiative spearheaded by Haszard and Dr. Ira Yeo was the establishment of a Child Welfare and Public Health Branch late in 1920. The Branch began medical inspections in Island schools. Haszard was a director of the Charlottetown Driving Park, and in 1907 and 1908 he was the president of the Prince Edward Island Exhibition Association. Francis Haszard died 25 July 1938.

Elizabeth Haszard, the daughter of Lestock P. W. DesBrisay, was born ca. 1852 and died in 1941. Haszard's ancestors had moved to the Island following the American Revolution. The Haszards were United Empire Loyalists and therefore left their home in Rhode Island for a grant of land on Prince Edward Island. Haszard's father was a Member of the Legislative Council.

References

CPG 1905, 1908, 1910; MacDonald *If You're Stronghearted* pp. 53, 56–57; *Past and Present* pp. 550–51; *Premier's Gallery*; *Charlottetown Guardian* 25 July 1938; PARO: MNI-Census 1881, 1891; St. Paul's Anglican Church Records; Sherwood Cemetery Records.

HAVILAND, Q.C., HONOURABLE THOMAS HEATH, lawyer and landowner; b. 13 November 1822 in Charlottetown, son of Thomas Heath Haviland and Jane Rebecca Brecken; m. 5 January 1847 Anne Elizabeth Grubbe, and they had seven children, Edith Constance Alice, Eustace Heath, Frances Rebecca (died at nine weeks), Robert Arthur, Madeline Elizabeth, Eleanor Blanche, and Mary Emily Dundas (died at four months); Anglican; d. 11 September 1895 in Charlottetown.

Haviland, a Conservative, was first elected to the House of Assembly in 1846 for Georgetown Royalty. He was re-elected in the general elections of 1850, 1854, 1858, and 1866. He was elected in the general election of 1870 for 3rd Queens, and in the general election of 1873 for Georgetown Royalty. During his political career he served in many capacities. He served on Executive Council and was Colonial Secretary from 1859 to 1862, 1866 to 1867, and 1870 to 1872. In 1859 he served as Solicitor-General, and, from 1863 to 1864, Speaker of the House of Assembly. He was Leader of the Opposition from 1867 to 1870 and Provincial Secretary from 1873 to 1876. Haviland, a Father of Confederation, was a delegate to the Quebec conference in 1864, and in 1873 travelled to Ottawa to arrange the final terms of union.

Haviland participated in debates on the land and school questions. As a proprietor and landlord, he was a spokesman for the landlords, proving a strong and able opponent of those seeking to purchase the properties of landowners at public expense in order to sell them to their tenants. Haviland was vocal in expressing opinions on the school issue, at one point arguing that denominational schools should be publicly funded, and insisting upon the importance of religion as an aspect of public education.

Haviland was one of the strongest advocates for Confederation. He was the first president of the Union Association of Prince Edward Island, established in January 1870. He was an active participant at the Quebec conference in 1867 and during the final negotiations on the terms of union in 1873. Haviland felt that the province's best opportunity for prosperity and for protection from the United States would be with Canada.

On 18 October 1873, Sir John A. Macdonald appointed Haviland to the Senate, where he remained until July 1879. He resigned to become the province's Lieutenant-Governor and served in that capacity from 19 July 1879 to 31 July 1884. Following the death of Charlottetown Mayor Henry Beer* in 1886, Haviland became mayor for the rest of Beer's term. In January 1887 Haviland was elected to the office, where he served until 1893, when he retired due to poor health.

His early years were marked with the prominence and privilege that came about due to the positions held by his father, a wealthy businessman and landowner, as well as a prominent provincial politician. Haviland was privately educated in Brussels, Belgium. Upon his return to the Island in the early 1840s, Haviland studied law in Charlottetown with James Horsefield Peters, and was called to the Bar in 1846 at the age of 24. He was designated Queen's Counsel in 1865. For 19 years, Haviland was a member of the firm Haviland & Brecken*. Thomas Haviland died 11 September 1895, predeceasing his wife and their five surviving children.

Anne Haviland was the daughter of John and Sarah Anne Grubbe of Horsenden House, Buckinghamshire, England.

References
CDP p. 262; *DCB* XII 1891–1900 pp. 415–18; *Daily Examiner* 12 September 1895.

HENDERSON, GEORGE ROLAND, electrician and shellfish technician; b. 10 November 1935 in Freeland, son of R. Edgar Henderson and Hazel Edna Hardy; m. 27 August 1960 Brenda Lue Matthews, and they had three children, Robert, Holly, and Jason; Presbyterian.

Henderson, a Liberal, was first elected to the Legislative Assembly in the general election of 1974 for 2nd Prince. He was re-elected in the general elections of 1978 and 1979. From 1974 to 1978, he served as Minister of Fisheries and Minister of Labour. Henderson was Minister of Highways and Minister of Public Works from 1978 to 1979. On 3 January 1980, he resigned his seat in the Legislature to run in the federal election of that year. Henderson was elected to the House of Commons for Egmont and was re-elected in 1984. He was appointed Parliamentary Secretary to the Minister of Fisheries and Oceans in March 1980 and remained in this position for two years. From 1982 to 1984, he served as the Parliamentary Secretary to the Minister of National Defence. While in Opposition, Henderson was the fisheries critic.

Henderson received his early education at

the Freeland Public School. From 1950 to 1953, he attended Prince of Wales College in Charlottetown. He was president and general manager of Malpeque Oyster Cultures Incorporated and also worked as a shellfish technician. In 1988 he was appointed to the Canadian Pension Commission, a board that adjudicates pension claims for death and disability from service in the Canadian Armed Forces. George Henderson is retired and lives with his wife in Freeland.

Brenda Henderson is the daughter of Lowell Matthews and Olive Keefe.

References
CPG 1979, 1988; *WWPEI* p. 56; *Guardian* 6 January 1988; *Journal-Pioneer* 12 August 1988; Questionnaire to Former MLAs.

HESSIAN, STEPHEN STANLEY, lawyer; b. 2 October 1891 in Georgetown, son of Thomas G. Hessian and Hannah Cummings; m. 15 January 1930 Blanche Wickham, and they had one son, Stephen; Roman Catholic; d. 5 November 1962 in Lagos, Nigeria.

Hessian, a Liberal, was first elected to the Legislative Assembly in the general election of 1919 for 5th Kings. He was re-elected in the general election of 1931 for 3rd Kings and re-elected in the general election of 1935. Hessian was elected in the general election of 1955 for 5th Queens, and was re-elected in the general election of 1959. He served as Speaker from 1935 to 1939, when the Liberals held every seat in the House under Premier Thane A. Campbell*. He served on the Montague Town Council and was chairman of its finance committee.

Hessian was educated at the Georgetown School and then at St. Dunstan's College in Charlottetown, where he received a Bachelor of Arts. In Montague he worked as a lawyer and Crown prosecutor. Hessian was a member of numerous community organizations. Hessian served as vice-president of the Kings County Boy Scouts and secretary of the Kings County Health Organization. He was a member of the Board of Trade and the chairman of the Building Committee for the Montague High School. Hessian was a member of the Montague Curling Club and the Holy Name Society. Stephen Hessian died 5 November 1962, while representing the province at a Commonwealth Parliamentary Association Conference in Lagos.

Blanche Hessian, the daughter of Mr. and Mrs. James F. Wickham of Montague, married Stephen Hessian in New York.

References
CPG 1921, 1962; *Patriot* 5 November 1962.

HICKEN, BARRY W., farmer and mechanic; b. 8 August 1946 in Pembroke, son of Harold M. Hicken and Reta Irving; m. 25 November 1972 Louise Alice McHerron, and they had two children, Charlene Dawn and Jason Barry; Presbyterian.

Hicken, a Liberal, was first elected to the Legislative Assembly in the general election of 1986 for 5th Kings. He was re-elected in the general elections of 1989 and 1993. He was defeated in the general election of 1982. He was defeated in the general election of 1996, in the new electoral district of Murray River-Gaspereaux. On 22 February 1988, Hicken was appointed Deputy Speaker. He held the positions of Minister of Energy and Forestry and Minister Responsible for the Energy Corporation from 1989 to 1991. On 14 November 1991, Hicken was appointed Minister of Community and Cultural Affairs and Minister of Fisheries and Aquaculture. In January 1993 he was appointed Minister responsible for Francophone Affairs. He served in these Ministries until April 1993. On 15 April 1993, he was named Minister of Environmental Resources. Hicken served on numerous legislative committees, including agriculture, energy and forestry, fisheries, industry, tourism, and labour. He also chaired several committees, including the Special Committee on Legislative Proposals, the Special Committee on the Meech Lake Accord, and the Special Committee on the Constitution of Canada.

Hicken received his early education at the Pembroke School. Later he attended Montague Regional High School and Holland College. Hicken worked as a mechanic at Wendell Graham Limited from 1980 to 1986. He is a farmer in the Gaspereaux area. Hicken is a member of St. Andrew's Masonic Lodge in Montague and the Murray Harbour North Presbyterian Church. Barry Hicken and his wife live in Gaspereaux.

Louise Hicken is the daughter of Lawrence and Cephenia McHerron.

References
CPG 1996, 1997; *WWPEI* p. 58; *Guardian* 18 October 1996; Questionnaire to Former MLAs.

HICKEY, THOMAS EARLE, chartered accountant and businessperson; b. 20 October 1907 in Summerside, son of Joseph Charles Hickey and Mary Evangeline Gaudet; m. first 3 August 1938

Elizabeth Margaret McCardle of Middleton, and they had five children, James Earle, Robert Joseph, Ronald Gerard, Helen Elizabeth, and T. Earle; m. secondly 1972, Beatrice Beauregard, and there were no children; m. thirdly April 1980 Marie Holden Gordon, and there were no children; Roman Catholic; d. 2 March 1994 in Charlottetown.

Hickey, a Liberal, was first elected to the Legislative Assembly in the general election of 1966 for 5th Prince. He was re-elected in the general elections of 1970 and 1974. In 1966 he was appointed Provincial Treasurer and served in this capacity until 1970. Hickey was also appointed Provincial Secretary on 28 July 1966 and continued in this position until 1972. Upon re-election in 1970, he was appointed Minister of Finance on 1 June and served until 1976. In 1973, the Island's Centennial year, Hickey was appointed Minister Responsible for Cultural Affairs and served in this position until 1976. He retired 30 June 1976.

T. Earle Hickey received his early education in Summerside schools and continued his studies at Queen's University in Kingston, Ontario, and at the Institute of Chartered Accountants in Toronto. In 1939 he was appointed to the provincial Auditor's Department and served there until 1942, when he opened his own business in Summerside, T. E. Hickey and Company Chartered Accountants. He was active within the business community, and served as chair of the Summerside Chamber of Commerce and was a member of the Board of Industrial Enterprises. He was a member of the Economic Council of Canada, the Summerside School Board, and a member of the Summerside Lobster Carnival Organizing Committee. While living in Queens County, Hickey contributed as a member of the Public Utilities Commission, the treasurer of the Queens County Literacy Council, and the treasurer and tutor for the Queens County Laubach Literacy Council.

Hickey was a member of the Queen Elizabeth Hospital Foundation and was a director of the Prince Edward Island Heritage Foundation. He was a member of the property and finance committee of St. Dunstan's Basilica. Hickey was active in the Knights of Columbus, acting as Grand Knight and State Deputy of the organization, and as a treasurer of the Knights of Columbus Mission Fund. T. Earle Hickey died 2 March 1994 at Whisperwood Villa.

Elizabeth Hickey, the daughter of James McArdle of Middleton, died in 1970. Beatrice Hickey died in 1978. Marie Hickey survives her husband.

References
CPG 1976; PEI ECO 600/76; PEI *Journal of the Legislative Assembly* 1971; *WWPEI* pp. 25, 58; *Evening Patriot* 2 September 1988; *Journal-Pioneer* 31 May 1976, 3 March 1994.

HIGGS, EDMUND TUCKER, businessperson, insurance company president, and ferry service board director; b. 24 November 1873 in Charlottetown, son of Benjamin Wilson Higgs and Amelia A Darby; m. ca. 1905 Anne Irving, and there were no children; Methodist; d. 9 December 1957 in Charlottetown.

Higgs, a Liberal, was elected to the Legislative Assembly in the general election of 1919 for 5th Queens. He was defeated in the general elections of 1915 and 1923.

Higgs received his education in the public schools in Charlottetown and later attended Charlottetown Business College. A successful business person, he began his career as a junior clerk in the office of Horace Haszard in 1889, and by 1892 became a chief clerk in the firm. In 1913 he began a business, Higgs & Company Limited, and held the dual roles of president and manager. He was also the vice-president of Goff Brothers Limited and became a director of Northumberland Ferries Limited upon its formation. Although occupied with his own business ventures, Higgs served the business community as president of both the Charlottetown Board of Trade and the Maritime Board of Trade. He was granted an honourary membership of the Charlottetown Board of Trade.

Higgs had other community involvements. He was a member of the board of directors of the Young Men's Christian Association and was the superintendent of the Kensington Hall Mission. He was a superintendent and secretary-treasurer of the Methodist Sunday School, as well as treasurer of the trustee board of the Methodist Church in Charlottetown. Higgs played a prominent role in the Victory Loan Campaign and, in 1921, was a member of the Navy League of Canada, Prince Edward Island Division. In addition to these activities and his business pursuits, Higgs was a member of the A.F. and A.M. and the International Order of Oddfellows. Edmund Higgs died 9 December 1957 at the Prince Edward Island Hospital.

Anne Higgs, the daughter of David P. Irving* and Anne Irving of Vernon, was born 12 April 1879 and died 15 September 1946. Her brother James Cephas Irving* also served in the Legislature.

References
CPG 1921; *PPMP* p. 84; *Patriot* 9 December 1957; PARO: Baptismal Record United Church Pownal Book 1 p. 63; Marriage License Book #16, 1882–1923, p. 112; Sherwood Cemetery Records.

HOLLAND, AUGUSTUS EDWARD CREVIER,

justice of the peace and farmer; b. 1824, in Tryon, son of Frederick B. Holland and Elizabeth Grathay; m. first 9 June 1858 Mary Conroy, and there were no children; m. secondly 1 October 1879 Emma Parker, and there were no children; m. thirdly 2 July 1898 Annie Page of Bedford, Nova Scotia, and there were no children; Presbyterian; d. 1919.

Holland, a Conservative, was first elected to the House of Assembly in the 1873 general election for 4th Prince. He was re-elected in the general elections of 1879 and 1883. He was defeated in the general election of 1879. In 1873 Holland was appointed a member of the Board of Works. He was best-known in the House of Assembly for supporting Cornelius Howatt* in April 1873 by seconding a motion to refuse the terms of admission into Union with the Dominion of Canada. The motion was defeated by a margin of 24 to 2. He testified as a landlord before the Land Commission in 1860, believing that under the landlord system in existence at the time, Islanders lived a life of plenty and prosperity, and that the landlords were benevolent.

A. E. C. Holland received his education in Tryon. For a time he lived in Searletown with his first wife, Mary, on a property called Holland Grove, named for the famous estate of the same name in Charlottetown where Holland's uncle, Carl John Frederick Holland, had lived. A. E. C. Holland died in 1919.

Holland's grandfather, the Major Honourable Samuel Holland, R.A., was for many years Surveyor General of the province, and he established the system of lots on Prince Edward Island. He also served as a member of the Legislative Council and the Executive Council. Major Holland was present with General Wolfe at the battles of Louisbourg and Quebec.

References
CPG 1876; Leard pp. 66, 68, 99; *Past and Present* pp. 689–92; *Examiner* 4 October 1879 p. 2; *Islander* 18 June 1858; PARO: RG 19

series 3 subseries 4 Marriage Licenses; MNI-Hutchinson's p. 251.

HOOPER, WILLIAM, farmer, tanner, innkeeper,

and officeholder; b. 23 July 1824 in Northleigh, England, son of Joseph Hooper; m. 1847, Luiza Maria Esperanza, and they had nine children, Mary Esperanza, William Charles, Samuel, Emma, Frederick, Percilla, George, Sophia, and Joseph; Methodist; d. 5 January 1899.

Hooper, a Liberal, was first elected to the House of Assembly in the general election of 1870 for 2nd Kings. He was re-elected in the general elections of 1872, 1879, and 1882. He was defeated in the general elections of 1876 and 1886.

Educated in Horiton, England, Hooper served as Her Majesty's Commissariat in Bermuda from 1847 to 1850, when he resigned to settle in Prince Edward Island. Hooper was the chairman of the Board of Railway Appraisers from 1872 to 1873. He was also a farmer, a tanner and an innkeeper, and lived in Marie Bridge. William Hooper died 5 January 1899.

References
CPG 1873, 1883, 1889; Elections PEI; *Meacham's Atlas*; PARO: MNI-Census 1881, 1891; MNI-Hutchinson's p. 158; Hooper Family File.

HOWATT, CORNELIUS, farmer, constable, jus-

tice of the peace, bank director, and teacher; b. 4 February ca. 1810 in Tryon, son of James Howatt, and Ellen Miller; m. 19 March 1840 Jane Bell, and they had nine or ten children, of whom seven are known, including Nelson, Arthur, Theodore, Pope, Montague, Helen, and Cornelius; Presbyterian; d. 7 May 1895 in North St. Eleanors.

Howatt, a Conservative, was first elected to the House of Assembly in 1859 for 4th Prince. He was re-elected in the general elections of 1863, 1867, 1870, 1872, and 1873. He was defeated in the general election of 1876. From 1874 to 1876, Howatt was Speaker of the House.

Howatt was best-known as a staunch opponent of Confederation. In April 1873 Howatt moved a resolution that read, in part, "that it is the opinion of the House that the best interests and future prosperity of Prince Edward Island would be secured by refusing terms of admission into Union with the Dominion of Canada." His resolution was seconded by his running mate Augustus Holland*. The resolution was defeated by a vote of 24 to 2. Howatt foresaw the role the railway debt would play in changing Islanders' opinion on the benefits of Confederation. His strong principles on issues such as Confederation, the building of the railway, and honest government often caused him to act independently of the Conservative party. He championed the interests of the farmer and the poor, and Howatt felt that government should be fiscally responsible, believing strongly in the Island's tradition of independence.

Howatt's historical significance became more profound almost 80 years after his death. Leading up to and during the Prince Edward Island Centennial Celebrations in 1973, the Brothers and Sisters of Cornelius Howatt was formed to provide satirical comment on the self-congratulatory tone of the celebrations. It also sought to publicize the province's past, and especially its tradition of self-reliance embodied in the life of the organization's namesake. As a result of the group's antics and the publicity generated, Howatt was rescued from relative obscurity, and became an Island political legend long after his time.

For a good portion of his life, Howatt lived in Tryon on his farm, where he was prosperous, perhaps due to the advanced methods he employed. In the 1860s he moved to North St. Eleanors, to a larger farm on the banks of Malpeque Bay. After leaving politics, at the age of 66, he continued farming for a few years. He then relocated to Summerside, where he resided for 10 years, until 1890. At that time, he suffered a partial paralysis, which forced him to move back to the North St. Eleanors farm until his death. Besides being a farmer, Howatt served as a constable, a Justice of the Peace, Commissioner for Affidavits in the Supreme Court, and as a director of the Summerside Bank. In an unusual turn, at the age of 83, he became a teacher for a few months at Springbrook School near French River. Cornelius Howatt died 7 May 1895.

Jane Howatt, born ca. 1818, was the daughter of John Bell of Cape Traverse and Elizabeth Little. Helen Howatt, daughter of Cornelius Howatt, married John Howatt Bell*, premier of the province from 1919 to 1923. William Hubert Howatt*, son of Nelson Howatt and grandson of Cornelius Howatt, also served in the Legislative Assembly.

References
The Bell History p. 31; *Challenged to Be; Cornelius Howatt Superstar* p. 30; *DCB* XII 1891-1900 pp. 452-53; MacDonald *If You're Stronghearted* pp. 318-19; *Royal Gazette* 1836; *Daily Examiner* 8 May 1895; *Island Farmer* 9 May 1895 p. 3; *Patriot* 7 May 1895; PARO: MNI-Census 1881; MNI-Hutchinson's pp. 238, 250.

HOWATT, WILLIAM HUBERT, farmer and businessperson; b. 7 September 1867 in New Village, son of Nelson Howatt and Catherine Platts; m. 2 July 1890 Mahala Bell, and they had three children, Pope, Marion, and Wilfred; Presbyterian; d. 9 January 1919 in St. Eleanors.

Howatt, a Liberal, was elected to the Legislative Assembly in the general election of 1915 for 5th Prince. He was defeated in the general election of 1912.

His grandfather, Cornelius Howatt*, had been the Island's most ardent opponent of Confederation.

Howatt studied at Summerside High School. Following school he became a farmer. Howatt was the director of Willow Hill and Radium & Pavilion Silver Black Fox Companies. He was a member of the Knights of Pythias, the Masons, and the Oddfellows. William Howatt died 9 January 1919 at his home, while a Member of the Legislative Assembly.

Mahala Howatt, the daughter of Andrew Bell of Bloomfield, was born in 1866 and died 17 November 1953.

References
CPG 1916; *Patriot* 9 January 1919; PARO: Summerside People's Protestant Church Records.

HOWLAN, HONOURABLE GEORGE WILLIAM,

merchant, ship owner, ship builder, and customs officer; b. 19 May 1835 in Waterford, Ireland, son of William Howlan and Ann Carroll Lomasmagh; m. first 1 October 1866 Elizabeth Olson, and there were no children; m. secondly 22 February 1881 Mary Doran of Kingston, Ontario, and there were no children; Roman Catholic; d. 11 May 1901 in Charlottetown.

Howlan, a Liberal, was first elected to the House of Assembly in the 1862 general election for 1st Prince. He was re-elected in the general elections of 1867, 1870, 1872, and 1873. Howlan was appointed to Executive Council in 1867, when the Liberals were returned to power under George Coles. In 1868 he was a leading participant in the effort to have the Liberals fund Catholic schools. Following the election in 1870, Howlan demanded an endorsement of denominational schools in return for his support. The Protestant Liberals, led by Premier Haythorne, refused. Howlan then approached Conservative opposition leader J. C. Pope* with an offer to form an alliance. As a result, the balance of power shifted when Howlan and other Catholic Liberals joined Pope's Conservatives. Government accounts reveal that Howlan was not successful in his quest for funding for denominational schools. During the Pope administration, Howlan served in Executive Council from 1870 to 1872. In 1871, despite previously being opposed to a railway for Prince Edward Island, Howlan engineered the passage of the railway bill of 1871. During this time, he was involved in the settlement of the Island's land question and in the Prince Edward Island Railway. In 1873 Howlan was sent to Washington to settle a dispute over the fishery on behalf of the Island, and also served as a delegate to Ottawa to arrange the terms under which Prince Edward Island should enter Confederation. He resigned his seat in the Assembly to accept the appointment as Collector of Customs for Charlottetown in June 1873.

After a few months, Howlan resigned to contest Prince County for the House of Commons in the special federal election on 29 September 1873. Though unsuccessful in this attempt, he was appointed to the Senate on 18 October 1873. Howlan resigned his Senate seat on 27 December 1880 and was reappointed to the Senate on 5 January 1881. In February 1891 he again resigned, offering himself as a candidate in the federal general election for Prince County. Once more he was defeated. He was reappointed that same year to the Senate, resigning for the third time in 1894, when he accepted the position of Lieutenant-Governor of the province. Howlan served in this office from 24 February 1894 until 31 May 1899.

Howlan was perhaps best-known for his advocacy of a tunnel from the Island to the Mainland, helping to promote the idea to such a degree that it became a serious topic of debate within the province. He is also credited with coining the phrase "million acre farm" to describe Prince Edward Island.

Howlan came to the province with his family in 1839 at the age of four, settling in Charlottetown, where he was educated at the local school and at Central Academy. In his early career as a merchant, Howlan clerked in Charlottetown at Henry Haszard's general store on Great George Street, following which he occupied a similar position for Captain Ryder in Alberton. When Howlan returned to Charlottetown, he went into business with Charles McNutt for several years. Later he returned to Alberton to operate his own business, which included shipbuilding and fishing. He was vice president of the Dominion Board of Trade and served as a governor of Prince of Wales College. George Howlan died 11 May 1901.

Elizabeth Howlan of Saint John, New Brunswick, was the daughter of James Olson of Norway. She died on 10 April 1876.

References

CDP 1968; *DCB* XIII, pp. 481-83; *Eminent Men,* pp. 714-15; *Charlottetown Herald* 15 May 1901; *Daily Patriot* 13 May 1901; *Examiner* 5 November 1866, 25 September 1873; *Guardian* 13 May 1901, 14 May 1901; PARO: MNI-Hutchinson's pp. 135, 229.

HUBLEY, HONOURABLE ELIZABETH M., choreographer, dance instructor, artist, and secretary; b. 8 September 1942 in Howlan, daughter of Bennett Haywood and Florence Brown; m. 12 November 1966 Richard Beck Hubley, and they had six children, Brendan, Susan, Allan, Amos, Jennifer, and Florence; United.

Hubley, a Liberal, was first elected to the Legislative Assembly in the general election of 1989 for 4th Prince. She was re-elected in the general election of 1993. Hubley served as Deputy Speaker from 1991 to 1995. During her time in the Legislature, she served on several legislative committees, including economic development and tourism, health and social services, the Special Committee on the Constitution of Canada, and the Election Act and Electoral Boundaries Commission. On 8 March 2001, Hubley was appointed to the Senate by Prime Minister Jean Chrétien.

"Libbe" Hubley received her early education in local schools and Prince of Wales College in Charlottetown. She then attended the Nova Scotia College of Art and Design in Halifax. In her early career, Hubley worked as a secretary at Trans Canada Credit in Charlottetown and held various positions with companies and organizations in Calgary, Montreal, and Halifax. For many years, she has been actively involved in choreography, dance, and dance instruction, and is the founder of Stepping Out, a studio of traditional Island dancing in Kensington, and home of the Lady Slipper Step Dancers. Following her time in the provincial Legislature, Hubley was appointed to the Veterans Review and Appeal Board at the Department of Veterans Affairs in Charlottetown. Senator Elizabeth Hubley and her husband live in Kensington.

Richard Hubley is the son of Amos H.

Hubley and Helen W. Peters of Summerside. He worked as a lawyer and Crown Prosecutor.

References
CPG 1996; *Guardian* 18 April 1989, 15 May 1996, 23 May 1996, 9 March 2001; Questionnaire to Former MLAs.

HUBLEY, ROBERTA MILDRED, teacher and school principal; b. 27 May 1941 in Hopefield, daughter of Leon MacPhee and Gladys Brown; m. 26 December 1964 Alan Hubley, and they had two children, Tracey Joan and Tamara Alane; Presbyterian.

Hubley, a Liberal, was first elected to the Legislative Assembly in the general election of 1989 for 3rd Kings. She was re-elected in the general election of 1993. Hubley served as Minister of Labour and as Minister Responsible for the Prince Edward Island Housing Corporation, Workers Compensation, the Status of Women, and the Human Rights Commission from 1989 to 1991. From 14 November 1991 to 15 April 1993, she was Minister of Energy and Forestry. Hubley chaired the Standing Committee on Education and Human Resources and was a member of the Select Standing Committee on Provincial Affairs and the Environment. She was a member of Policy Board.

Hubley received her early education at the Hopefield School. She later attended Prince of Wales College, where she completed her teacher training, and the University of Prince Edward Island, where she earned a Bachelor of Arts. For many years, she taught in a number of Island schools. In 1985 Hubley became principal of Cardigan Consolidated Elementary School. She has served as president of the Prince Edward Island Teacher's Federation and as a member of the board of governors of the University of Prince Edward Island. Hubley has also been a director of the Canadian Teacher's Federation and a member of the Hospital and Health Services Commission. She is a member of the Retired Teachers' Association and the Hospice Association of Southern Kings. Roberta Hubley and her husband reside in Montague.

Alan Hubley is the son of Amos H. Hubley and Helen W. Peters of Summerside. He was a teacher and school principal at the Montague Regional High School.

References
CPG 1996; *Guardian* 12 April 1989, 13 March 1993, 17 May 1996.

HUESTIS, STAVERT, farmer; b. 20 June 1938 in Wilmot Valley, son of Ira W. Huestis of Wilmot Valley and Etta Jean Stavert of Kelvin Grove; m. 4 July 1964 Edith MacGregor, and they had four children, Janalee, Jeanne, Lynne, and Dianne; Presbyterian.

Huestis, a Liberal, was first elected to the Legislative Assembly in a by-election held 2 December 1985 for 4th Prince. He was re-elected in the general elections of 1986, 1989, and 1993. He was defeated in the general election of 1978, and again in 1996 in the new electoral district of Borden-Kinkora. Huestis served as Deputy Speaker from 15 June 1989 to 1993. While in the Legislature, he served on numerous legislative committees, including public works, fisheries, industry, tourism and labour, education and community affairs, labour and industry, the Special Committee on Lands Protection, and the Justice Committee. He chaired the Standing Committee on Agriculture.

Huestis received his education in Wilmot Valley. Following school, he started a potato and grain farming operation, which he operated with his brother Layton. Huestis is a well-established potato producer on the Island and has always been active in farm and community organizations. He was involved in the International Family Farm Exchange Association, the Prince Edward Island Federation of Agriculture and Partnership Africa-Canada, and was a member of the Co-op Board. Stavert Huestis is a member of the Kensington Lions Club, the Masonic Lodge, the Junior Farmers of Kensington, and the Kensington Presbyterian Church.

References
CPG 1979, 1986, 1996, 1997; *WWPEI* p. 62; *Guardian* 29 October 1985, 7 March 1986, 2 April 1986, 13 November 1996.

HUGHES, GEORGE EDWARD, pharmacist, businessperson, and farmer; b. 15 April 1854 in Charlottetown, son of Frederick William Hughes and Margaret Binns; m. 13 January 1878 Anna Gordon Boyle, and they had seven children, Gordon, Frank M., Mamie, Hazel, Helen, Laura, and Mary E.; Methodist; d. 4 November 1937 in Charlottetown.

Hughes, a Liberal, was first elected to the Legislative Assembly in the general election of 1900 for 2nd Queens. He was re-elected in the general elections of 1904, 1908, 1915, and 1919. He was defeated in the general elections of 1912 and 1923. On 19 September 1919, Hughes was appointed to

Executive Council as a Minister without Portfolio.

Before entering provincial politics, Hughes was a member of Charlottetown City Council for 12 years, during which time he advocated permanent sidewalks in the city, as well as the Victoria Park roadway.

He received his early education in private schools and then went on to Prince of Wales College and St. Dunstan's College. At the age of 15, he studied medicine under Dr. Frank D. Beer, and from him learned to dispense medicine and prepare prescriptions.

Hughes opened a drugstore with Samuel W. Dodd at Medicine Hall on the corner of Queen and Grafton Streets in Charlottetown in 1872. In 1874, at the age of 21, he moved to the opposite corner, where he leased space in Apothecaries Hall, owned by the DesBrisay family. Hughes later purchased this property and carried on a business there for the rest of his life. In 1900 he erected a new building on the site, which continues to be used as a retail outlet. Hughes was a well-respected pharmacist in the province, and carried on an extensive business with branch stores in Souris, Montague, Victoria, and Crapaud.

Apart from his business and political concerns, Hughes served as honourary president of the Provincial Pharmaceutical Association, and on the executive of the Canadian Pharmaceutical Association. He was a president of the Charlottetown Fire Insurance Company and President of the Board of Trade. Hughes was also a director of the Provincial Exhibition Association, and, as president, he proved instrumental in the establishment of the Prince Edward Island Development and Tourist Association, whose objective was to increase visitors to the province, especially to Charlottetown.

Hughes owned a farm in Brookfield, which was well-stocked with cattle, as well as horses, of which he was especially fond. He bred harness racehorses. Hughes was a member of the Free and Accepted Masons, the Independent Order of Oddfellows, and the Independent Order of Forresters. He published a calendar and cookbook called *1909 Household Calendar Cook Book*. George Hughes died 4 November 1937.

Anna Hughes of Charlottetown, the daughter of William Boyle, was born 24 December 1853 and died 22 November 1931.

References
CPG 1917, 1922; *Past and Present* pp. 574–75; *Patriot* 4 November 1937 p. 1; PARO: Census 1901; Charlottetown People's Cemetery Records.

HUGHES, WILLIAM "WADE", merchant; b. 3 July 1888 in Souris, son of James Joseph Hughes and Annie R. McWade; m. 27 September 1927 Ellen Keays, and they had nine children, Mary Doris, Eileen Gertrude, Helen Geraldine, James Joseph, Elizabeth Doreen, William Wade, Thomas Francis, Catherine Elizabeth, and John George; Roman Catholic; d. 11 November 1964.

Hughes, a Liberal, was first elected to the Legislative Assembly in the general election of 1935 for 5th Kings. He was re-elected in the general elections of 1939, 1943, 1947, and 1951. Hughes served as Provincial Treasurer from 1943 to 1948 and as Minister of Public Welfare from 1944 to 1948. On 25 May 1953, he was appointed Provincial Secretary.

His father represented the riding of King's in the House of Commons from 1900 to 1908, 1911 to 1917, and 1921 to 1925, and was appointed to the Senate on 5 September 1925. Wade Hughes' daughter, Senator Eileen Rossiter, was appointed to the Senate on 17 November 1986.

Wade Hughes was educated at the local school in Souris and at St. Dunstan's College. Later he worked for his father's large mercantile business, J. J. Hughes, in Souris, and became vice-president of the company. William "Wade" Hughes died in 1964.

Ellen Hughes, the daughter of James Keays of Souris, died on 16 December 1961.

References
CDP p. 282; *CPG* 1944, 1948, 1955; *CWW* 1948 p. 460; *Maritime Advocate and Busy East* May 1943.

HUNTER, LESLIE STEWART, farmer and business person; b. 3 October 1889 in Dundas, son of Stewart Hunter and Christina Catherine Hunter; United; d. 1970.

Hunter, a Conservative, was first elected to the Legislative Assembly in the general election of 1923 for 3rd Kings. He was re-elected in the general elections of 1931 and 1943. He was defeated in the general elections of 1927, 1935, 1939, 1947, and 1951.

Hunter, a farmer in the Dundas area, was also the manager of Matthew and McLean Limited and the secretary-treasurer of the Dundas Dairying Association. He was associated with the Central Kings Carry-on Canada Corporation. During the First World War, he served overseas. Leslie Hunter died in 1970.

References
CPG 1932, 1936, 1944, 1948; PARO: 1901 Census.

I

phy, singing, fiddling, gardening, and for rebuilding Volkswagen cars. Bud Ings and his wife live in Montague.

References
CPG 1981; ECO 290/78; *WWPEI* p. 63; *Eastern Graphic* 16 June1982, 19 November1982, 27 August 1983, 19 September 1983, 31 July 1991; *Guardian* 12 June 1982.

INGS, D.V.M., ALBERT EARLE "BUD," veterinarian; b. 5 February 1926 in Mount Herbert, son of Henry Earl Ings and Evelyn Racham; m. 25 May 1949 Constance Margaret Mair, and they had three children, Jeanne, Joanne, and Jayne; United.

Ings, a Liberal, was first elected to the Legislative Assembly in the general election of 1970 for 3rd Kings. He was re-elected in the general elections of 1974, 1978, and 1979. Ings served as Minister of Agriculture and Forestry from 1974 to 1978, and held the positions of Minister of Health and Minister of Social Services from 27 April 1978 to 3 May 1979. He was instrumental in launching the construction of the Queen Elizabeth Hospital in Charlottetown. Ings was President of the 3rd Kings Liberal Association and was elected president of the provincial Liberal party on 17 September 1983. He served on the Montague Town Council.

"Bud" Ings, as he is known, received his elementary education in Mount Herbert and attended West Kent School and Prince of Wales College, before graduating from the University of Guelph in 1952 with a degree in veterinary medicine. He began a veterinary practice in Souris in 1952, but moved to Montague in 1954. Ings opened the Montague Veterinary Clinic in 1967 and served as its president. He served in the Canadian Army as a private from 1944 to 1946.

Ings was a trustee of the Kings County Memorial Hospital and was a member of the Montague School Board. He was a member of the Prince Edward Island Centennial Commission and the Holland College Board of Governors. Ings served as president of the Queens County Chapter of the Prince Edward Island Fiddlers Association. He has been a member of the Canadian Club, the Brudenell Golf Club, the Montague Curling Club, the Junior Chamber of Commerce, and the Royal Canadian Legion. Ings chaired a fundraising campaign for the Friends of the Farm Centre in 1991. He also is a former president of the Montague Rotary Club. He is known for his fine photogra-

INMAN, GEORGE STRONG, lawyer and judge; b. 25 June 1870 in Bedeque, son of Nelson Inman and Martha B. Doull; m. 26 September 1910 Florence "Elsie" MacDonald, and they had four children, William Robert, George Strong, Wilfred Nelson, and Roland Victor; United; d. 30 November 1937 in Summerside.

Inman, a Liberal, was elected to the Legislative Assembly in the general election of 1927 for 4th Kings. He was defeated in the general elections of 1904, 1908, 1912, and 1915. He was appointed as a Minister without Portfolio in the government of Albert C. Saunders*. During the visit of British Prime Minister Stanley Baldwin to Charlottetown, Inman served as acting Premier. He resigned his seat in 1928 to accept a position on the Prince County Court Bench.

Inman was educated at the Bedeque school and at Prince of Wales College. He taught school in Clinton and York, before attending Dalhousie University in Halifax where he obtained a law degree in 1896. Inman also studied law in Charlottetown with Judge Hector McDonald*. He was admitted to the Bar in 1897, and in 1898 moved to Montague to practise law. From 1900 to 1904, Inman served as Law Clerk of the Legislative Assembly. In 1911 Inman returned to Charlottetown to practise in partnership with James J. Johnston". He was appointed to the position of Judge of the Prince County Court in 1928. He was a member of the Masonic Order, Rotary, and the Charlottetown Club. George Inman died 30 November 1937.

Florence "Elsie" Inman, a champion of women's suffrage, was appointed to the Senate in 1955. The daughter of Alexander MacDonald of Montague, she was born 5 December 1890 and died 31 May 1986.

References
CPG 1927, 1928; *CWW* 1936-1937 pp. 547-48; *Past and Present* p. 365; *Patriot* 30 November 1937.

IRVING, DAVID PURDY, farmer; b. 6 April 1841 in Cherry Valley, son of James Irving and Anne MacKenzie; m. 11 September 1867 Anne Tweedy, and they had 12 children, Sarah A., James Cephas*, Margaret, Thomas, Elizabeth, George, Anne, Alexander, John, William, Pansey, and Edith; Presbyterian; d. 1922.

Irving, a Liberal, was first elected to the Legislative Assembly in the general election of 1900 for 4th Queens. He was re-elected in the general elections of 1904 and 1908. Irving was defeated in a by-election held in 1900.

Irving was educated at Prince of Wales College in Charlottetown, where he received a teachers' diploma. David Irving died in 1922.

Anne Irving was born in 1849 and died in 1917. James Cephas Irving* served in the Legislative Assembly, and another child, Anne, married Edmund T. Higgs*, also a politician.

References
CPG 1910; *Islander* 13 September 1867; PARO: MNI-Census 1881, 1891.

IRVING, JAMES CEPHAS, farmer; b. 9 May 1870, son of David Purdy Irving* and Anne Tweedy; m. 2 September 1898 Eva Nicholson of Eldon, and there were no children; Presbyterian; d. 14 October 1939.

Irving, a Liberal, was first elected to the Legislative Assembly in the general election of 1919 for 4th Queens. He was re-elected in the general election of 1923.

Irving's father had served as a Member of the Legislative Assembly for 4th Queens. James Irving died 14 October 1939.

Eva Irving was born 5 December 1869 and died 8 January 1940. Irving's sister Anne was married to Edmund Higgs*, who served in the Legislative Assembly.

References
CPG 1903, 1921, 1924; *Patriot* 18 October 1939; PARO: United Church of Pownal Book 1 p. 55; MNI-Census 1891; Census 1901.

J

JARDINE, FRANK, farmer; b. 18 November 1905 in Wilmot Valley, son of Benjamin Jardine and Jessie Cairns; m. Jennie Adelaide Muttart, and they had one child, Beulah Joan; United; d. 19 August 1981 in Summerside.

Jardine, a Liberal, was first elected to the Legislative Assembly in the general election of 1962 for 4th Prince. He was re-elected in the general elections of 1966, 1970, and 1974.

Jardine received his education at Wilmot Valley Rural School. He was a farmer and a director of Amalgamated Dairies Limited. He served as president of the Prince Edward Island Federation of Agriculture and president of the Prince Edward Island Dairymen's Association. Jardine served as a member of both the Board of Trade and the Potato Producers Association. He took an active part in community organizations and was a member of the Prince Edward Island Sons of Temperance and the Orange Lodge. Jardine was an elder at North Bedeque United Church and a member of the Church Men's Association. Frank Jardine died 19 August 1981 at Summerside Manor.

Jenny Jardine was the daughter of Hedley Muttart.

References
CPG 1978; Jardine p. 129; *Guardian* 21 August 1981.

JENKINS, M.D., JOHN THEOPHILUS, physician, surgeon, coroner, and druggist; b. 12 October 1829 in Charlottetown, son of Reverend L. C. Jenkins and Penelope Desbrisay; m. 14 August 1856 Jesse Esther Carson Rice, and they had six children, Stephen Rice*, Louis Leoline*, Alice Penelope, Henry Herbert, Mary Johnstone, and Francis; Anglican; d. 17 January 1919 in Charlottetown.

Jenkins, a Conservative, was first elected to the House of Assembly in the general election of 1867 for Charlottetown Royalty. Though defeated in the federal election of 1873 for Queen's County, he was re-elected to the House of Assembly in a by-election held in September of the same year. In the 1882 federal election, Jenkins was elected to the House of Commons for Queen's County by two votes over Frederick Brecken*. On a later recount, Jenkins' victory was confirmed. This decision was overturned by the Supreme Court of Prince Edward Island, which awarded the seat to Brecken. When Brecken resigned in 1884, Jenkins was re-elected to the House of Commons in a by-election. In 1891 Jenkins returned to provincial politics, but was defeated in a bid to represent the Charlottetown riding as an independent.

Jenkins was educated at local schools, at Central Academy in Charlottetown, and then at St. Bartholomew's Hospital in London, England. In his early medical career, Jenkins served in the Crimean War as a surgeon for the British and Turkish armies. After the war, he returned to the Island and settled in Upton, just outside Charlottetown. Along with his medical practice, Jenkins was a breeder of horses. He was also engaged in ranching in Western Canada. John Jenkins died 17 January 1919.

Jesse Jenkins of Newfoundland was the daughter of a Captain Rice. Stephen* and Louis Jenkins* both served in the Legislative Assembly.

References
CPG 1874, 1877; *DCB XIII*, p. 110; *Islander* 15 August 1856 p. 7; *Patriot* 17 January 1919 pp. 1-2; *Guardian* 12 April 1919 p. 14; MNI-Hutchinson's p. 98; MNI-Mercantile Agency Reference Book 1876; MNI-Census 1881, 1891.

JENKINS, LOUIS LEOLINE, farmer; b. 3 September 1860 in Charlottetown, son of John Theophilus Jenkins* and Jessie Esther Carson Rice; m. 7 September 1892 Hannah Sarah Holroyd, and there were no children; Anglican; d. 24 August 1939 in Charlottetown.

Jenkins, a Conservative, was first elected to the Legislative Assembly in the general election of 1912 for 2nd Queens. He was re-elected in the general election of 1923. He was defeated in the general elections of 1915, 1919, 1927, and 1931. Jenkins was a Minister without Portfolio from 1912 to 1915 in the John Mathieson* Administration, and was Speaker from 1923 until 1927.

Jenkins' brother Stephen*, and their father John Theophilus*, were Members of the Legislative Assembly.

Jenkins was educated at local schools in Charlottetown and then at Guelph Agricultural

College in Ontario. After completing Agricultural College, he went to Pincher Creek, Alberta, for a year to manage his father's ranch. When he returned to the Island, he established a farm in North Wiltshire. Louis Jenkins died 24 August 1939 in the Charlottetown Hospital.

Hannah Jenkins was the daughter of Joseph Holroyd of Yorkshire, England.

References
CPG 1916, 1921, 1927, 1928, 1932; Elections PEI; *Patriot* 24 August 1939; PARO: Milton Anglican Church Records.

JENKINS, M.D., STEPHEN RICE, physician and surgeon; b. 12 November 1858 in Charlottetown, son of John Theophilus Jenkins* and Jessie Esther Carson Rice; m. 7 October 1886 Ellen Josephine Sweeney, and they had nine children, John Stephen, Mary E., Frances, Harry, Helen, Nora I., Margaret, Hilda, and Joseph; Roman Catholic; d. 15 September 1929 in Charlottetown.

Jenkins, a Conservative, was first elected to the Legislative Assembly in the general election of 1912 for 5th Queens. He was re-elected in the general election of 1915. He was defeated in the general election of 1900. Jenkins was appointed as a Minister without Portfolio in 1915. He also served as Chief Aide-de-Camp to three Lieutenant-Governors.

Jenkins' brother Louis Leoline* and their father John Theophilus* were Members of the Legislative Assembly.

Jenkins was educated at St. Peter's School in Charlottetown and at King's College in Windsor, Nova Scotia. He received his preliminary medical training with his father, who was a successful doctor. Later Jenkins attended the University of Pennsylvania, from which he graduated in 1884. After that he served as the house surgeon at Brockley Hospital in Philadelphia. Jenkins returned to the province in 1885 and established a practice, first in Cardigan and then in Charlottetown. During the 1885 smallpox epidemic, he was in charge of the Emergency Hospital, where he rendered valuable service in fighting the disease.

In February 1886, Jenkins, a surgeon, was commissioned to the 4th Prince Edward Island Regiment of Artillery, and was eventually promoted to the rank of Lieutenant-Colonel. He also served as registrar of the Medical Council of Prince Edward Island and as a president of the Maritime Medical Association and the Canadian Medical Association.

He was a member of the first Dominion Medical Council and a Fellow of the American College of Surgeons. Jenkins served on numerous medical committees such as Cancer Research and Social Hygiene. He was the secretary of the Prince Edward Island Branch of the Red Cross and president of the Anti-tuberculosis Association. He founded the Free Dispensary for the Poor in Charlottetown. Stephen Jenkins died 15 September 1929 at his home.

Ellen Jenkins, the daughter of Patrick and Joanna Sweeney of Ireland, was born 3 September 1862 and died 23 September 1949.

References
CPG 1917; *Past and Present* pp. 478-79; *Maple Leaf Magazine* December 1929; *Patriot* 16 September 1929; PARO: Census 1901.

JOHNSTON, K.C., JAMES J., lawyer; b. 2 May 1868 in Charlottetown, son of John Johnston and Catherine Connolly; m. 9 July 1894 Mary Elizabeth Dorsey, and they had nine children, Raymond, James Blaise, Richard B., John, Gerald, Eileen, Mary E., Olive, and Helen; Roman Catholic; d. 8 September 1948 in Charlottetown.

Johnston, a Liberal, was first elected to the Legislative Assembly in the general election of 1915 for 3rd Kings. He was re-elected in the general election of 1919. He was defeated in the general election of 1908. From 1919 to 1923, he served as Attorney-General in the John H. Bell* Administration. He was defeated in the federal elections of 1925 and 1926 for King's.

Johnston's dislike of Bell was well-known. While Attorney-General, Johnston went to Ottawa without the premier's knowledge to authorize the appointment of an extra judge to the province's Supreme Court. He also reduced the three county judges to two. Premier Bell moved a motion in Cabinet to censure Johnston for this action.

Johnston was educated in Charlottetown, at St. Patrick's School and St. Dunstan's College. After graduating from St. Dunstan's in 1887, he entered law studies with W. W. Sullivan*, and with Sullivan's elevation to the position of Chief Justice, Johnston practised law with Malcolm MacLeod. He was admitted to the Bar in 1892 and designated King's Counsel in 1908. In 1911 George Inman* partnered with Johnston, who carried on his law career continuously until just before his death, when he was forced to retire due to illness. He was regarded as one of the most capable lawyers in the province. Along with his legal and political obligations, Johnston was a member of many community organizations, including the Knights of Columbus and the International Order of Foresters. He also served on the Charlottetown School Board. James Johnston died 8 September 1948.

Mary Johnston, the daughter of James Dorsey and Annie Murphy of Charlottetown, was born 6 August 1869 and died in 1950.

References

CPG 1916, 1923; *Past and Present* p. 259; *Guardian* 9 September 1948; PARO: St. Dunstan's Basilica Book 3 p. 232; Census 1901; Charlottetown Roman Catholic Cemetery Records.

JOHNSTON, LOWELL STERLING, farmer, fisher, carpenter, salesperson, and merchant; b. 3 July 1926 in Murray Harbour North, son of Frederick George Johnston of Peters Road and Elsie Mayburne MacKinnon of Sturgeon; m. 3 January 1948 Mary Eileen VanIderstine, and they had four children, Paulette Jean, Frederick Edgar, Judith Alma, and Roger Lowell; Presbyterian.

Johnston, a Conservative, was first elected to the Legislative Assembly in the general election of 1978 for 5th Kings. He was re-elected in the general elections of 1979 and 1982. He was defeated in the general election of 1974.

Johnston received his education at the Murray Harbour North Community School. In the early 1950s, and for most of the 1960s, he fished and was co-owner of a lobster-packing operation. He then travelled throughout the province selling farm equipment. Johnston also operated a cattle and grain operation on the family farm in his home community, and was a carpenter. In 1965 he purchased a small country store, which he operated with his wife and children, and two years later he opened Johnston's Centennial Tent and Trailer park. Johnston was a member of the Southern Kings Tourist Association and an elected member of the Southern Kings Regional Advisory Board. He was chair of the property committee of the Murray Harbour North Presbyterian Church and a member of the board of managers for the church and the cemetery committees. Lowell Johnston was a board member of the Hillsborough Home for Special Care.

Eileen Johnston is the daughter of Edgar and Alma VanIderstine.

References

CPG 1986; WWPEI p. 66.

JOHNSTONE, RALPH WARREN, farmer and fox rancher; b. 5 May 1914 in Long River, son of Oscar Johnstone and Annie G. Warren; m. 14 February 1945 Marion Hazel Howard of Margate, and they had two children, Ronald Dale and Barry Gordon; United.

Johnstone, a Liberal, was first elected to the Legislative Assembly in the general election of 1970 for 1st Queens. He was re-elected in the general elections of 1974 and 1978. He was defeated in the general election of 1979. Johnstone served on the Agriculture Committee, chaired the Rules, Orders and Privileges Committee, and served on the Special Committee on Government Regulations.

Johnstone received his early education in Long River. As a farmer, he operated Loch View Farm and Western Silver Fox Ranch. He was an active member of the Federation of Agriculture, and served as a director of the Kensington Co-operative. From 1956 until his retirement in 1984, he served as president, director, and Claims Adjustor of the Prince Edward Island Mutual Fire Insurance Company. Johnstone is a charter member of the New London Lions Club and a member of the Masonic Lodge and Scottish Rite Lodge and a 32nd Degree Mason. He served for several terms as a trustee of the Long River School and has served as an elder, and as a member of the boards of Trustees and Stewards of Long River United Church.

Marion Johnstone was born 28 September 1922. She is the daughter of Chester Howard and Elsie (née Mayhew) Howard of Margate.

References

CPG 1978, 1980; Elections PEI; *Guardian* 16 April 1979.

JONES, LL.D., D.C.L., M.A., HONOURABLE JOHN WALTER, farmer, scientist, and teacher; b. 14 April 1878 in Pownal, son of James Benjamin Jones and Maria Isabel Stewart; m. 23 December 1909 Katherine Francis Bovyer of Bunbury, and they had five children, Lois, Vimy, Helen, Bovyer, Bernard ("Bus"), and another son who died in infancy; Baptist; d. 31 March 1954 in Ottawa.

Jones, first a Farmer-Progressive, and later a Liberal, was first elected to the Legislative Assembly in the general election of 1935 for 4th Queens. He was re-elected in the general elections of 1939, 1943, 1947, and 1951. On 11 May 1943, he became premier, when Thane A. Campbell* resigned to become Chief Justice of Prince Edward Island. He continued in the position until 25 May 1953. In 1943 Jones served as Minister of Public Welfare and Minister in Charge of Air Raid Precautions. On 31 January 1944, he assumed the portfolio of Minister of Agriculture, which he held until 28 February 1945. He was also Minister of Education until February 1950. At that time, Jones served in the capacity of Minister of Reconstruction from 28 February 1945 to January 1949, at which time he became Provincial Secretary-Treasurer. He served in this office until February 1950. From February to December of that year, he held the Ministry of Public Works and Highways. In December 1951 he commenced his second term as Minister of Education and continued in the office until his appointment to the Senate on 19 May 1953. In 1920, before joining the Liberals, he was elected secretary-treasurer of the United Farmers of Prince Edward Island. He was nominated as a Farmer-Progressive candidate for Queen's for the 1921 federal election, but was defeated.

Jones was only the second farmer to become premier, and his unceasing commitment to the value of agriculture and rural life in the province made him popular with rural voters. He was known for his flamboyant style, snap decisions, and sometimes autocratic manner. In 1948 Jones, who opposed Prohibition, shifted control of the Island's liquor supplies into the hands of government.

Although Jones became premier when North America was enjoying the post-war economic boom based on industrialization and modernization, he did not get elected expounding the virtues of industrial development in the province. He was a champion of the agricultural community and this was best demonstrated in his determined tactics during the 1947 packinghouse strike at Davis and Fraser, which later became Canada Packers. When workers walked off the job in a dispute, it left farmers without means to market their hogs. Jones took over the plant and hired non-union workers to get production going again. He even had his government approve a short-lived anti-union bill. He felt that the heart of the province was in its agricultural areas and he was capable of diminishing the importance of urban areas. In one of his most often quoted statements on the important role rural Islanders played, he stated that "...If the farmers all go foolish like the people in the towns, good-bye Prince Edward Island." Jones' commitment to dairy farmers was best demonstrated when he banned the sale of margarine, despite the fact that it was cheaper for the consumer than butter.

Jones realized the importance of modern improvements and believed that some modern conveniences would be beneficial to agriculture in the province. Through increased funding from the federal government brought on by the new interventionist economy spawned by the Second World War, he was able to make improvements in the province. Jones instituted rural electrification programs, provincial soil analysis and veterinary services were improved, and a forestry program was established. Under Jones, the Beach Grove Inn was converted into a senior citizens' home. The Trans-Canada Highway was paved from "ferry to ferry," and was paid for largely by the federal government.

"Farmer" Jones received his primary education in Pownal. In 1897 he entered Prince of Wales College and obtained a teaching certificate. Following graduation, Jones taught school for three years. He obtained a Bachelor of Arts at Acadia University in 1904. From 1905 to 1907, he was the first principal of MacDonald Consolidated School. In 1909 he graduated from the University of Toronto with a Bachelor of Science in agriculture. Later, as a result of being awarded a fellowship, Jones studied at Chicago, Clark, Columbia, and Cornell Universities. In 1910 he taught agriculture at the Hampton Agriculture Institute in Hampton, Virginia. From 1911 to 1912, he worked for the United States government in the Department of Agriculture as associate superintendent and, soon after, as superintendent of an experimental farm in Arlington. At this time, the facility was the largest of its kind in the world. Jones specialized in experimental technology.

While in the United States, Jones remained in contact with Island farmers and convinced many that the seed potato market was expanding and that the Island should jump on the bandwagon. He also extolled the virtues of the Island seed potato to American farmers, and as a result was instrumental in the formation of the Island seed potato industry. From 1912 to 1913, Jones was employed by the Federal Commission of Conservation in Canada. While working for the Commission, he wrote a report entitled *Fur Farming in Canada*. Published in 1913, it became a world-wide reference book on fur farming. A year previous, Jones had published another work on fur farming in cooperation with Island fox rancher B. I. Rayner. This was an educational pamphlet titled *The Domestication of the Fox*. In 1914 Jones graduated from Acadia University with a Master of Arts degree.

Ca. 1914 Jones took over his father-in-law's farm in Bunbury and began mixed farming and fox ranching. He imported cattle and developed the famous Abegweit herd. His dairy cows won many awards and one cow set a world record for butter fat production. In 1931 Jones won the coveted Master Breeder's Award from the Holstein-Friesian Association. He was the first individual ever to win, as previously the award had gone to large companies that specialized in breeding. In 1932 Jones was the highest winner at the Royal Winter Fair in Toronto and second-highest winner at the Canadian National Exhibition. Three years later, he was awarded the King George V Medal for being the best farmer in Prince Edward Island, and the King's Jubilee Medal for his outstanding contribution to farming. Jones received an honourary Doctor of Civil Law degree from Acadia in 1951. In 1962 he was posthumously inducted into the Canadian Agriculture Hall of Fame. He was dubbed the first "Master Breeder of Holsteins in Canada." Jones also played a key role in the fur farming industry in the Province. In 1929 he became the first president and a charter member of the Silver Fox Exhibitor's Association of Prince Edward Island. From 1937 to 1938, he worked for the Dominion Department of Agriculture to ascertain what the department might do to improve the fox industry.

In 1898 Jones joined the Abegweit Amateur Athletic Association and participated in many track and field events. He set a Maritime record for the hammer throw. While at the University of Toronto he tied for the all-round track and field championship and set Canadian college records in the 16-pound hammer throw and the 16-pound shot. At Acadia, Jones was captain of the rugby and track-and-field teams. He became the first Islander picked for a national team when he was selected to an All-Canadian rugby team that was to tour Europe, but he declined the invitation. Jones served on the executive of the Abegweit Club after he retired from competition. He was elected to the Prince Edward Island Sports Hall of Fame in 1986. J. Walter Jones died 31 March 1954 in his office at the Parliament Buildings in Ottawa.

Katherine Jones was the daughter of Franklin Bovyer and Theresa Jane Baker.

References
CDP p. 297; *CPG* 1944, 1945, 1946, 1947, 1948, 1949, 1950, 1951, 1952; Forester pp. 115-16; MacKinnon *J. Walter Jones: The Farmer Premier* pp. 4, 7-8, 13-14, 18-19, 24; MacKinnon *Life of the Party* pp. 110-16; *Provincial Premiers Birthday Series 1873-1973*; *Who's Who in the Agricultural Institute of Canada* p. 102; *Guardian* 24 December 1909, 1 April 1954, 14 April 1973, 14 May 1986; *Island Magazine* No. 35 Spring/Summer 1994.

KELLY, FRANCIS, teacher, law clerk, land surveyor and agent, farmer, postmaster, justice of the peace, and commissioner for affidavits; b. ca. May 1806, in Mulloloughan, Monaghan County, Ireland, son of Donagh O'Kelly; m. first May 1835 Catherine Lennon of Tullycorbet in Ireland, and they had seven children, Elizabeth, James Edmond, John, Thomas, Ann, Margaret, and Francis; m. secondly Sarah McCarron, and they also had seven children, Edwin, Peter, Charles, Mary, Sarah, Lucius Owen*, and Susan; Roman Catholic; d. 19 April 1879 in Fort Augustus.

Kelly, at various times a Liberal and a Conservative, was first elected to the House of Assembly in 1858 for 3rd Queens. He was re-elected in the general elections of 1863, 1867, 1870, 1873, and 1876. He was defeated twice in the 1840s and in the general election of 1872. Kelly held the seat almost uninterrupted until his death. He was a member of Executive Council and Chief Commissioner of Crown Lands.

Kelly's son, Lucius Owen*, also served as a member of the House of Assembly for 3rd Queens.

In 1870 an internal crisis within the Liberal government over the granting of public funds to St. Dunstan's College caused Kelly and six other Catholic Assemblymen to leave the Liberal party and join the Conservatives. He was in the forefront of attempts by the Church to gain educational concessions. The crisis brought the Conservatives to power, and as a reward for his efforts Kelly was made Chief Commissioner of Crown Lands. He was opposed to Confederation, but eventually joined Premier J. C. Pope* to seek better terms from Canada, given the financial state of the railway. Kelly also sought easier conditions for tenants seeking to become owners of the land upon which they were tenants.

Kelly was educated in Mulloloughan and Dublin, Ireland. In Dublin he worked as a teacher and a law clerk. Francis Kelly came to PEI in May 1835 and settled in Fort Augustus. Upon his arrival in PEI, he became a land surveyor and land agent for Reverend John McDonald until 1846. Kelly was a farmer, served as postmaster, justice of the peace and commissioner for affidavits, and as commissioner for establishing the boundaries of counties and townships. He was a member of the Board of Works and the Board of Education. Kelly served as a governor of Prince of Wales College, as a governor of St. Andrew's Roman Catholic College, and as a church trustee. In support of his agricultural interests, Kelly was a member of the Royal Agricultural Society. He was also involved in the military, and served as captain of 2nd Queens County Regiment of the militia.

Catherine Kelly was born ca. 1820 and died in 1842. Sarah Kelly died ca. 7 August 1901.

References
CPG 1876; DCB X 1871–1880 pp. 397-98; *Charlottetown Herald* 14 August 1901, 19 August 1901; *Colonial Herald* 11 July 1840, 24 October 1840; *Daily Examiner* 19 April 1879; *Examiner* 22 February 1882; *Islander* 1 January 1847; *Royal Gazette* 24 May 1836; PARO: MNI-Hutchinson's pp. 234, 238; Personal Collection of Danny Keoughan.

KELLY, LUCIUS OWEN, farmer and commissioner of the peace; b. 18 June 1858 in Fort Augustus, son of Francis Kelly* and Sarah McCarron; Roman Catholic; d. 11 July 1932 in Boston.

Kelly, a Conservative, was elected to the House of Assembly in the general election of 1886 for 3rd Queens. He was defeated in the general election of 1890 and in a by-election in 1891.

Kelly's father, Francis Owen*, was also a member of the House of Assembly for 3rd Queens.

Kelly was first educated at grammar school in Fort Augustus. Later he attended both Prince of Wales College and Business College in Charlottetown. In his early life, he resided in Fort Augustus, then in Charlottetown, and after that returned to his native community. During his political career, he was a farmer in Fort Augustus. He also served as a Commissioner of the Peace. Later in life he moved to Boston. Lucius Kelly died 11 July 1932.

References
CPG 1876, 1889, 1891; Elections PEI; *Maple Leaf Magazine* September 1932; PARO: MNI-Census 1881; Personal Collection of Danny Keoughan.

KELLY, PATRICK, merchant, dealer of spirits, and farmer; b. 17 March 1846, son of John Kelly and

Sally Woods, both of Ireland; m. 22 August 1876 Mary Jane Hynes, and they had two children, Margaret (Margory) and Florence; Roman Catholic; d. 2 August 1916.

Kelly, a Conservative, was elected to the Legislative Assembly in a by-election held 29 March 1904 for 3rd Kings. He was defeated in the general election of 1904.

A farmer and a merchant, Kelly resided in Montague. He may also have lived for a time in Charlottetown, as a Patrick Kelly was listed in the 1881 Census. There was a Patrick Kelly listed as a farmer in the Montague area in *Meacham's Atlas* and in the 1891 Census. Patrick Kelly died 2 August 1916.

Mary Kelly was born 2 May 1856 and died 4 January 1932.

References

CPG 1908; Elections PEI; *Meacham's Atlas*; PARO: St. Joachim's Roman Catholic Church, Book 1 p. 39; Marriage Register 1871-78; MNI-Census 1881, 1891; Census 1901; Vernon River St. Joachim's Roman Catholic Church Records.

KELLY, THOMAS, lawyer and judge; b. October 1833 in Covehead, son of Thomas Kelly and Mary Grace, both of County Kilkenny, Ireland; m. first 4 September 1867 Mary Emmeline Eskildson, and there were no children; m. secondly 15 November 1871 Marianne H. Campbell, and they had four children, Florence M., Thomas B., Constance M., and one boy unnamed; Roman Catholic; d. 1893.

Kelly, a Conservative, was elected to the House of Assembly in the general election of 1873 for 5th Prince. He was defeated in the general election of 1879. In 1870 he was defeated in the Legislative Council election. He was offered the chairmanship of the Railway Board in 1873, and the office of Speaker of the House in 1874. He declined these positions due to a misunderstanding on the question of public education. Kelly resigned his seat in January 1875.

Kelly was educated at Central Academy and St. Dunstan's College. He studied law in New Brunswick and with Judge Watters in Saint John. In 1865 he was called first to the New Brunswick Bar and then to the Prince Edward Island Bar. Kelly spent most of his life in Summerside, beginning work there in 1865 while maintaining an office in Charlottetown. In 1879 he became County Court Judge, and served as Commissioner for taking affidavits for Quebec, Nova Scotia, New Brunswick, and the Island, as well as Commissioner for administering oaths for Dominion appointees.

In 1870 Kelly was Master in Chancery and in 1871–72 Railway Commissioner. He was a director of the Summerside Bank, License Commissioner in 1877, and the Recorder for the Town of Summerside. In October 1886 Kelly was Revising Officer. Thomas Kelly died in 1893.

Mary Kelly, the daughter of Henry W. Eskildson of Saint John, New Brunswick, and formerly of New York, was born ca. 1847 and died 19 October 1868. Marianne Kelly was born ca. 1846 and was the daughter of William A. Campbell of Toronto.

References

CPG 1874, 1875, 1880; *ECB* 1888 pp. 84–85; Elections PEI; Polland p. 27; *Islander* 13 September 1867, 24 November 1871; *Royal Gazette* 14 December 1865; *Summerside Journal* 14 December 1865; PARO: MNI-Census 1881.

KENNEDY, JAMES, merchant, telegraph operator, and exporter; b. 14 May 1869 in Breadalbane, son of Samuel Kennedy and Christy MacKinnon; m. 27 August 1890 Mary Jane Gillis, and they had six children, Rachel, Marion, Earl, Preston, Charles, and Roy; Methodist/Presbyterian; d. 23 April 1915 in Kensington.

Kennedy, a Conservative, was first elected to the Legislative Assembly in the general election of 1908 for 4th Prince. He was re-elected in the general election of 1912. Kennedy died while in office.

Kennedy's brother Murdoch* was also a member of the Legislative Assembly. The two brothers served concurrently from 1908 to 1915.

Kennedy operated a general store and was a large exporter of farm produce. He was a member of both the Oddfellows and the L.O.L. James Kennedy died 23 April 1915.

Mary Kennedy was born 15 January 1867 and died 3 December 1933.

References

CPG 1915; Elections PEI; *Guardian* 24 April 1915; *Patriot* 24 April 1915; PARO: MNI-Census 1881; Census 1901.

KENNEDY, MURDOCH, merchant; b. 25 March 1873 in Breadalbane, son of Samuel Kennedy and Christy MacKinnon; m. 4 December 1894 Margaret Davison Biggar, and they had one child, Maude; Presbyterian; d. 1950.

Kennedy, a Conservative, was first elected

to the Legislative Assembly in a by-election on 19 December 1906 for 1st Queens. He was re-elected in the general elections of 1908, 1912, 1915, 1919, and 1923. Kennedy was appointed Provincial Secretary-Treasurer and Commissioner of Agriculture in the Mathieson* Administration. In 1913 he resigned his Cabinet position because he disagreed with government's support for the use of automobiles on public roads.

Kennedy was a general merchant in the Breadalbane area. His brother James Kennedy* was also a Member of the Legislative Assembly. The two men served concurrently in the Assembly from 1908 to 1915. Murdoch Kennedy died in 1950.

Margaret Kennedy, the daughter of James and Elizabeth Biggar, was born 28 March 1873. She died in 1936.

References
CPG 1908, 1922; Elections PEI; *Past and Present* pp. 472–73; PARO: Census 1901; St. Elizabeth's Anglican Church Records.

KICKHAM, JOHN, blacksmith, farmer, and trader; b. 1847 in Souris, son of John Kickham and Mary Cahill; m. 27 September 1870 Catherine McLean, and they had five children, Annie, Flora A., Mary Maud, Alphonsus C., and Francis; Roman Catholic; d. 2 January 1917.

Kickham, a Conservative, was first elected to the Legislative Assembly in the general election of 1897 for 1st Kings. He was re-elected in the general elections of 1900, 1904, and 1912. He was defeated in the general election of 1908.

Educated at local schools in Souris, Kickham was a blacksmith and trader in that area, where he lived throughout his life. John Kickham died 2 January 1917.

Catherine Kickham, of East Point, the daughter of Alexander McLean and Mary McDonald, was born ca. 1841. She died 16 October 1892.

References
CPG 1908, 1909; Elections PEI; PARO: Kickham Genealogy; MNI-Mercantile Agency Reference Book 1876; MNI-Census 1881, 1891; Rollo Bay St. Alexis Roman Catholic Church Records.

KICKHAM, HONOURABLE THOMAS JOSEPH, farmer, livestock and produce dealer, shipper, and importer-exporter; b. 11 March 1901 in Souris West, son of Richard Kickham and Alice Landrigan; m. 30 June 1943 Mabel MacDonald, and they had five children, Charles (deceased), Eileen, Josephine, Eleanor, and Thomas; Roman Catholic; d. 1 December 1974 in Souris West.

Kickham, a Liberal, was first elected to the Legislative Assembly in the general election of 1943 for 1st Kings. He was re-elected in the general election of 1947. He resigned in 1949 to contest, successfully, the federal riding of King's. He was re-elected to the House of Commons in 1953. He was defeated in 1957, 1958, 1961, and 1962. On 8 July 1966, Kickham was appointed to the Senate. Early in his political career, he was a candidate in a provincial by-election in 1940 and was defeated by one vote.

Kickham received his early education at the local school in Souris West. Later he attended St. Dunstan's College, and worked in farming and the shipping business. He was active within the Island's agriculture industry and served as the president of the Kings County Livestock Exhibition, as well as a director of the Prince Edward Island Potato Growers Association. Kickham was a supporter of the credit unions within the Province, acting as secretary-treasurer of the Rollo Bay Credit Union and as a director of the Credit Union League. In addition to these leadership roles, Kickham served his home county of Kings as the director of the Kings County Hospital. Thomas Kickham died 1 December 1974 at his home.

Mabel Kickham was the daughter of Charles B. MacDonald and Irene (MacDonald) MacDonald of North Lake.

References
CPG 1941, 1947, 1957, 1974; *HFER* King's pp. 3–4; *Guardian* 17 January 1975; PARO: Kickham Genealogy.

KITSON, GEORGE CLARK, farmer, livestock exhibitor, and produce dealer; b. 29 July 1893 in Hampshire, son of Frederick Kitson and Angelina Newson; m. 22 November 1917 Emma Pearl Cruwys, and they had seven children, Norris H., Verna M., Fulton G., Calvin L. (died at nine months), Lona I., Frederick F. and Audrey I.; Protestant; d. 23 February 1984 in Charlottetown.

Kitson, a Liberal, was first elected to the Legislative Assembly in a by-election held 7 November 1940 for 2nd Queens. He was re-elected in the general elections of 1951 and 1955. He was defeated in the general elections of 1943 and 1959.

Kitson received his education in Hampshire. He was a successful exhibitor of livestock, specializing in Clydesdale stallions, and was a progressive farmer and a well-known dealer of farm produce. George Kitson died 23 February 1984 at the Queen Elizabeth Hospital in Charlottetown.

Emma Kitson, the daughter of George and Hannah Cruwys, was born 11 April 1896 and died 13 August 1983 at the Garden of the Gulf Nursing Home in Charlottetown.

References
CPG 1941, 1943, 1944, 1958, 1960; *Maritime Advocate and Busy East* March 1943; *Patriot* 24 February 1984.

L

LAIRD, ALEXANDER, farmer; b. 1830 in New Glasgow, son of Alexander Laird, Sr., and Janet Orr; m. first 5 January 1864 Rebecca Read, and they had eight daughters and four sons, of whom the following names are known, Dora, Albert, Alwin, William, Emma, Edna, Mary, Rosara, and Amy; m. secondly 30 September 1886 Ann Carruthers, and they had one daughter and three sons, of whom the following names are known, Sarah and David; Presbyterian; d. 9 August 1896 in North Bedeque.

Laird, a Liberal, was first elected to the House of Assembly in the general election of 1867 for 4th Prince. He was elected to the Legislative Assembly in the general election of 1893. He was defeated in the general election of 1882. He was elected to the Legislative Council in 1874, 1886, and 1890 for 2nd Prince. Between 1867 and 1870, Laird served in the Liberal governments of George Coles, Joseph Hensley, and Robert Poore Haythorne. From 1876 to 1878, Laird served in the administration of Louis Henry Davies*. Laird was appointed to Executive Council in 1891 by Premier Frederick Peters*. He remained in Executive Council until his death in 1896.

Laird was regarded as a man of consistent political stance. He was committed to the settlement of the land question and was in opposition to the establishment of denominational schools. Laird was one of the strongest allies of Premier L. H. Davies on the school question, and campaigned for public funding for an improved non-denominational school system.

Like his younger brothers David* and William*, who both became politicians, Laird received his education in New Glasgow. Throughout his life, he worked on and later maintained the family farm there, which was reputed to be one of the finest in the province. Laird was very involved in farming organizations, as founder and president of the Agricultural Mutual Fire Insurance Company and as a president of the Farmers' Association and Dairymen's Association. He served as a director of

the Prince County Exhibition and was a supporter of the Government Stock Farm. Laird also exhibited an interest in journalism, much like his brother David, who was the founder of the Charlottetown *Patriot*. At the time of his death, he was president of the *Pioneer*, a Summerside newspaper. In 1894 Laird was involved in an accident with an enraged bull that attacked him, leaving him crippled mentally and physically. Alexander Laird died 9 August 1896.

Alexander Laird, Sr., his father, of Sterling, Renfrewshire, Scotland, was a member of the House of Assembly. Laird Sr. served from 1850 to 1853 and 1854 to 1866, and was a member of Executive Council from 1859 to 1863.

Rebecca Laird was the daughter of Ephraim Read. She died in 1882 at the age of 40. Ann Laird was the daughter of Samuel Carruthers of North Bedeque.

References
CPG 1891; *DCB* X pp. 419–20; *DCB* XII 1891–1900 pp. 512–13; PARO: Marriage Book 8 1862–1867 p. 94; Marriage Register 13 1870–1877 p. 476; MNI-Census 1881, 1891.

LAIRD, P.C., HONOURABLE DAVID, journalist and public servant; b. 12 March 1833 in New Glasgow, son of Alexander Laird and Janet Orr; m. 30 June 1864 Mary Louisa Owen, and they had six children: David Rennie, Mary Alice, Arthur Gordon, William Charles, James Harold, and Fanny Louisa; Presbyterian; d. 12 January 1914 in Ottawa.

Laird, a Liberal, was first elected to the House of Assembly in the general election of 1872 for 4th Queens. He was re-elected in the general election of 1873. He was defeated in the general elections of 1867 and 1870. He was a member of Executive Council in the Haythorne Administration from 1872 to 1873, and was a delegate to Ottawa to negotiate the terms of union in 1873.

In the special federal election of 29 September 1873, Laird was elected to the House of Commons for Queen's. He was re-elected in a by-election on 3 December 1873, after accepting a position as a Member of the Privy Council on 7 November. Laird's early days in Ottawa were significant in that his vote helped bring down the Conservative government of Sir John. A. Macdonald, as a result of the Pacific scandal in the fall of 1873. Laird served as Minister of the Interior and Superintendent General of Indian Affairs from 7 November 1873 until 6 October 1876, when he resigned. At this time, he accepted the position of Lieutenant-Governor of the North West Territories, holding that office from 7 October 1876 until 2 December 1881. In 1882 Laird returned to the Island and was defeated as a candidate for Queen's in that year's federal election. He offered as a candidate in the newly created riding of Saskatchewan (Provisional District) in the 1887 federal election, but was defeated. He was then appointed Indian Commissioner for the North West Territories, Manitoba, and Keewatin on 4 October 1898. In 1909 he returned to Ottawa as an advisor to the government on aboriginal issues.

Laird, like his older brother Alexander* and his younger brother William*, was first educated at the local school in New Glasgow and later at Charlottetown's Central Academy. He attended Presbyterian Theological Seminary in Truro, Nova Scotia. After graduation in 1859, Laird returned to Prince Edward Island and entered the same field as Alexander, becoming a journalist and editor of the Charlottetown *Patriot*, originally known as the *Protestant and Evangelical Witness*. In the 1860s he was a trustee and elder in the Presbyterian Church, a member of the Auxiliary Bible Society, and vice-president of the Young Men's Christian Association and Literary Institute. He served as a member of Charlottetown City Council. Laird was a member of the Charlottetown Board of Education and Board of Governors for Prince of Wales College.

Laird was considered a successful negotiator. He was trusted and respected by the Aboriginal populations in the west and north of Canada. While serving in federal office, Laird concluded several land treaties with the aboriginal populations and was known among them as "The Big Chief." He wrote a book about these experiences entitled *Our Indian Treaties*. In 1909 *The Globe & Mail* described him as one of Canada's nation builders. Laird, a significant contributor to the Confederation debate, was opposed to Confederation until the reality of the railway debt convinced him to change his position. David Laird died 2 January 1914.

Mary Laird was the daughter of Thomas Owen and Ann Campbell. She was a sister of Lemuel Cambridge Owen*, premier from 1873 to 1876.

References
CDP p. 315; *DCB* XIV 1911–1920 pp. 578–81; *MWOT* p. 628; PARO: Hon. David Laird Family File.

LAIRD, WILLIAM, farmer; b. 5 June 1835 in New Glasgow, son of Alexander Laird, Sr., and Janet Orr; m. 22 February 1866 Eliza Jane Bradshaw, and there were no children; Presbyterian; d. 13 February 1911 in New Glasgow.

Laird, a Liberal, was elected to the Legislative Assembly in the general election of 1908 for 2nd Queens. He was defeated in the general election of 1882. In 1911, due to failing health, Laird resigned his seat.

His brother Alexander* served in the House of Assembly, the Legislative Council, and on Executive Council, under various premiers. Another brother, David*, served as a Member of the House of Assembly and as a Member of Parliament. David was also Lieutenant-Governor of the North West Territories and an advisor to the federal government on aboriginal matters.

Laird received his education in the public schools in New Glasgow, after which he took up farming in the area. He spent some time in the militia, where he achieved the position of Captain, and continued to serve at that rank until the company was disbanded. He was a longtime member and elder of the Presbyterian Church. William Laird died 13 February 1911.

Eliza Laird died 20 February 1907.

References
CPG 1883, 1910; Elections PEI; *Patriot* 14 February 1911; PARO: MNI-Census 1881, 1891; New Glasgow Community Cemetery Records.

LANK, GORDON, farmer; b. 17 November 1941 in Charlottetown, son of Willard Albert Edward Lank of Covehead and Millicent Jean Dunsford of South Melville; m. 14 September 1960 Shirley Grace Diamond, and they had six children, Norma Jean, Isabel Darlene, Shirley Susan, Donna Lillian, Gordon David, and Daniel Trevor; United.

Lank, a Conservative, was first elected to the Legislative Assembly in the general election of 1979 for 2nd Queens. He was re-elected in the general election of 1982. He was defeated in the general elections of 1978 and 1986. From 28 October 1982 to 3 November 1983, Lank held the position of Minister of Community and Cultural Affairs. On 3 November 1983, he became Minister of Transportation and Public Works. He was appointed Minister of Finance and Tourism on 13 August 1985. From 1979 to 1982, Lank chaired the Select Standing Committee on Agriculture and, from 1984 to

1985, he was a member of Treasury Board. Lank was defeated in the federal election of 1988.

Lank received his early education at the West Royalty School and later attended Prince of Wales College in Charlottetown. A farmer by trade, he farms in Hampshire and Ebenezer, specializing in cattle and hogs, in partnership with a number of his children. He has worked as an artificial insemination technician. Lank was a member of the Central Queens Home and School Association and a charter member of the North River Fire Department. He chaired the Hampshire Community Council and served as president of the Cornwall Curling Club. He has served as chair of the Marine Atlantic Pension Management committee and was a member of the Board of Directors of the Queen Elizabeth Hospital. Gordon Lank is a member of the Prince Edward Island Cattlemen's Association and the Federation of Agriculture.

Shirley Lank is the daughter of Harold Diamond and Jean Houston of Winsloe.

References
CPG 1979, 1986, 1987; *WWPEI* p. 71; *Guardian* 17 November 1988; Questionnaire to Former MLAs.

LARABEE, JOHN JAMES, fisheries supervisor, blacksmith, and produce shipper; b. 10 April 1885 in Eldon, son of Nathaniel Spaldin Larabee and Katie Ann Murchieson; m. 8 January 1910 Ethel M. Wadman, and they had five children, James, Austin Brockton, Catherine, Jack, and Nathaniel; Presbyterian; d. 28 November 1954 in Charlottetown.

Larabee, a Liberal, was first elected to the Legislative Assembly in the general election of 1927 for 4th Queens. He was re-elected in the general election of 1931. In the 1935 federal election, Larabee was elected to the House of Commons for Queen's, but he did not serve in Parliament, and resigned to allow Charles A. Dunning to contest the seat.

In his early years, Larabee became associated with his father in the blacksmith trade, and only later did he go into the shipping business. He eventually became one of the largest produce shippers on the Island. In 1935 Larabee accepted the position of Chief Supervisor of Fisheries for the province. During his time in this position, the staff of the Prince Edward Island Fisheries Office increased from 5 to 20, and the Office increased its number of boats. Larabee was an avid curler and a member of the Charlottetown Curling Club. He was a member of the Masonic Lodge in Eldon. John Larabee died 28 November 1954 in the Prince Edward Island Hospital.

Ethel Larabee was born in 1889 and died 16 September 1939.

References
CPG 1931; *Patriot* 29 November 1954; PARO: Marriage License Book #16 1882-1923 p. 131; MNI-Census 1891; Census 1901; Belfast St. John's Presbyterian Cemetery Records.

LARGE, K.C., HONOURABLE FREDERIC ALFRED, lawyer and judge; b. 7 December 1913 in Breadalbane, son of Ernest Alfred Large and Georgie Leard; m. 7 November 1939 Mildred Grace Cox, and they had three children, David, Susan, and Donald; United; d. 5 April 1998 in Charlottetown.

Large, a Liberal, was first elected to the Legislative Assembly in the general election of 1947 for 1st Queens. He was re-elected in the general election of 1955. He was defeated in the general election of 1951 by a margin of four votes. In 1948 Large was appointed Attorney-General and Advocate General. He was appointed Minister of Education in 1949. Large was president of the Prince Edward Island Liberal Association and also president of the 20th Century Liberal Club in Charlottetown.

Large attended Summerside High School and Mount Allison Academy, and later studied at Prince of Wales College where he enrolled in a two-year arts course. He articled with various lawyers and in 1937 was admitted to the Bar. For the two years prior to the outbreak of the Second World War, Large practised as a lawyer and served as Crown prosecutor. From 1937 to 1939, he held the rank of Lieutenant with the Royal Canadian Navy volunteers, and, from 1939 to 1944, he was Lieutenant-Commander of HMCS *Niagara*. Large's tour of duty included service in Canada, England, and at sea. He retired from the Navy in May 1944 in order to return to the Island, at the request of Premier J. Walter Jones*. Large became Attorney-General in the Jones Administration and continued to practise law while on Executive Council. In 1945 he was designated King's Counsel. He was a partner with Donald P. Large in the firm of Large and Large from 1973 to 1975. In 1975 he was appointed Justice of the Kings County Court, and later became a Justice of the Supreme Court of Prince Edward Island. Large retired from the Supreme

Court in 1985 to become Supernumary Judge. He served as president of the Prince Edward Island Law Society and as provincial vice-president of the Canadian Bar Association.

Large was president of the Prince Edward Island Hospice Association, and was a member of the Rotary Club, the Little Theatre Guild, the Royal Commonwealth Society, the Charlottetown Yacht Club, and the Port La Joye French Club. He was also a Friend of the Confederation Centre. Frederic Large died 5 April 1998 at his home.

Mildred Large was the daughter of Chester M. Cox of Charlottetown.

References
CPG 1953, 1958; WWPEI p. 72; Guardian 20 June 1975, 20 March 1985, 8 April 1998; Maritime Advocate and Busy East February 1946, December 1949.

LARKIN, ALEXANDER JAMES, businessperson; b. 13 September 1946 in St. Peters Bay, son of Alexander James Larkin and Mary Gertrude MacDonald; m. 27 August 1971 Helen Elizabeth MacDonald, and they had three children, Steven James, Kelly Marie, and Corinne Elizabeth; Roman Catholic.

Larkin, a Conservative, was elected to the Legislative Assembly in the general election of 1979 for 6th Queens. He was defeated in the general elections of 1978 and 1982. While in the Legislature, Larkin chaired the Conservative caucus.

"Jim" Larkin received his early education at the Cable Head East School, and later attended the school in St. Peters Bay and Morell Regional High. In 1972 he earned a Bachelor of Science degree from the University of Prince Edward Island. Larkin was the coordinator of the Prince Edward Island Federation of Municipalities. He also worked as the general manager of the Tourism Industry Association of Prince Edward Island and served on the executive of the Tourism Industry Association of Canada. Larkin has been a member of the University of Prince Edward Island Alumni Association and the Board of Governors. In 1977 he chaired the search committee for a new University president. Jim Larkin and his wife currently own and operate Lobster on the Wharf Restaurant and Seafood Market in Charlottetown. Jim Larkin and his wife reside in Charlottetown.

Helen Larkin is the daughter of Michael MacDonald and Marguerite (Sharkey) MacDonald of Newport.

References
CPG 1981, 1982-1983; Evening Patriot 17 April 1984; Guardian 12 June 1982, 8 December 1993; Monitor 12 January 1977.

LAVERS, JAMES WALDRON, judicial clerk; b. 1 February 1911 in Georgetown, son of William Wallace Lavers and Laura Skinner; m. 22 August 1936 Lillian Blanche Walker, and they had two children, John William and Corinne Merilyn; Anglican; d. 4 July 1979 in Charlottetown.

Lavers, a Liberal, was elected to the Legislative Assembly in the general election of 1974 for 5th Kings. He was defeated in the general election of 1978.

Lavers received his primary education at the local school in Georgetown, and later attended St. Dunstan's College. During the Second World War, he served with the Nova Scotia Highlanders. From 1947 to 1974, Lavers worked as a Judicial Clerk in the Magistrate, County, and Supreme Courts. He also worked as a reporter for The Guardian. Lavers served on the Georgetown Town Council and also as Deputy Mayor. He was a member of the Health and Social Services Commission. Lavers served as president of the Georgetown Royal Canadian Legion, and he was a member of the Lions Club and the Community Welfare League. Waldron Lavers died 4 July 1979 at the Prince Edward Island Hospital.

Lillian Lavers was the daughter of John Walker of Georgetown.

References
CPG 1978, 1979; Guardian 5 July 1979.

LEA, SARAH JEAN "JEANNIE," teacher, craftsperson, and educational administrator; b. 16 October 1950 in Moncton, daughter of Maurice D. Robidoux and Dorothy E. Fraser; m. 21 April 1973 James A. Lea, and they had two children, Andrew and Sarah; Presbyterian.

Lea, a Liberal, was elected to the Legislative Assembly in the general election of 1993 for 6th Queens. Lea served as Minister without Portfolio and Minister Responsible for Government Reform and the Status of Women from 1993 to 1994 and, from 1994 to 1996, was Minister without Portfolio and Minister Responsible for Higher Education, Adult Training and Literacy and the Status of Women. She chaired the Community Consultative Committee and the Cabinet Committee on Social Policy Reform.

"Jeannie" Lea received her early education in Moncton area schools, and received a Bachelor of Science with Honours in Biology from Mount Allison. Following university Lea attended Holland College in Charlottetown, where she earned a diploma in weaving in 1975. From 1973 to 1976, she worked as a substitute teacher in Charlottetown and as a craftsperson. In 1987 Lea was elected to the Unit Three School Board and served in that position continuously until 1992, when she was elected chair of the Unit Three School Board. In 1997 Lea became Liaison Officer with the Centre for International Education at the University of Prince Edward Island, and was a director of the Canadian Bureau of International Education. In 2002 she became a consultant in strategic planning and research.

Lea is a member of a number of associations and boards. She is a director of the Canadian Millennium Scholarship Foundation, a member of the National Statistics Council, a member of the Advisory Board of the Institute of Island Studies, and a member of the Eastern School Board Education Foundation. Lea has served as a director of the Canadian School Boards Association, as president of the Prince Edward Island School Boards Association, as a member of the Prince Edward Island Industrial Relations Committee, as a member of the Human Resource Development Committee, and as a member of the Provincial Task Force on Education. She has been president of the Prince Edward Island Spinners and Weavers Guild and secretary of the Prince Edward Island Crafts Council. She has been president of the Heart and Stroke Foundation of PEI and served as a director on the Heart and Stroke Foundation of Canada. Jeannie Lea and her husband reside in Charlottetown.

James Lea is the son of Dr. R. Gordon Lea and Mary Armstrong of Charlottetown, and grandson of Premier Walter Maxfield Lea*.

References

CPG 1996; *Guardian* 23 March 1993, 23 April 1996; Questionnaire to Former MLAs.

LEA, WALTER MAXFIELD, farmer; b. 10 February 1874 in Tryon, son of William Charles Lea* and Anna Lea; m. ca. 2 October 1899, Helena Esma Maude Mary Rogerson, and they had five children, Marion, Edith, Gordon, Chester, and Clifford; Methodist; d. 10 January 1936 in Charlottetown.

Lea, a Liberal, was first elected to the Legislative Assembly in the general election of 1915 for 4th Prince. He was re-elected in the general elections of 1919, 1927, 1931, and 1935. He was defeated in the general election of 1923. Under Premier John H. Bell*, Lea was Minister of Agriculture, and he established the Agricultural and Technical School. In the Albert C. Saunders* Administration he was appointed Commissioner of Agriculture and Provincial Secretary-General. Premier Saunders was appointed to the Supreme Court and Lea was called on to form a government, which he did on 20 May 1930. The Lea Administration was defeated at the polls in August of 1931, but Lea was re-elected in his district and served as Leader of the Opposition.

Lea was the first farmer to become premier in the province's history. During his first term as premier, the Island was the only province to reduce its bonded debt in the midst of the Great Depression. Lea's platform for the 1931 general election was based largely on fiscal stewardship. However, the effects of the Depression were just beginning to be felt and the electorate desired more services from government. Conservative Leader James D. Stewart* argued that he would be in a more favourable position to increase financial support from fellow Conservatives in the federal government of R. B. Bennett. In the general election of 1935, in contrast to the 1931 defeat, Lea and his Liberals took all 30 seats in the Legislative Assembly, marking the first time in the history of the British Commonwealth that a government faced no opposition in the Legislature. Some Liberal Members served as an unofficial opposition and criticized the actions of their own government. Premier Lea became Minister of Agriculture and Secretary-General. Lea, who had been in ill health for some time, died as a result of pneumonia less than five months into his second term as premier.

Lea's father, William Charles*, had been a Member of the Island's government. He was first elected to the House of Assembly in 1872 for 1st Queens and was re-elected in the general election of 1876 for 4th Prince.

Lea was born in Tryon but resided in Victoria where he attended public school. He farmed extensively in Victoria and was interested in the improvement of his stock through breeding. He served as president, director, and vice-president of the Holstein Breeders Association. Lea was a promoter of the Co-operative Cream System and supplied milk and cream to the creamery for over 30 years. He was interested in the farming practices of other countries and represented the province as a member of the Canadian Farmers Party, where he inspected the breeding establishments and the marketing systems of European countries. Walter Lea died 10 January 1936, while in office, at the Prince Edward Island Hospital.

Helena Lea, the daughter of Thomas Rogerson and Ellen Howatt of Crapaud, was born 17 March 1875 and died in 1962. Marion married Walter Fitz-Alan Stewart* who represented 1st Queens.

References

CPG 1936; MacDonald *If You're Stronghearted* pp. 156, 159, 169, 170; *Patriot* 10 January 1936; *Provincial Premiers Birthday Series*; PARO: Baptismal Record, St. John's Anglican Church Crapaud p. 55; Marriage Record: Marriage License RG Vital Statistics Box M; MNI-Census 1881; Census 1901; Tryon People's Cemetery Records.

LEA, WILLIAM CHARLES, farmer; b. 22 March 1833 in Tryon, son of John Lea and Hannah Maxfield; m. first 23 November 1858 Rebecca E. Reid, and they had three children, Herbert, John J. and Artemas; m. secondly 30 December 1865 Annie Murphy, and they had six children, Richard L., Mary R., Henry A. (Harry), Eliza B., Walter Maxfield*, and William L.; Methodist; d. March 1911.

Lea, a Liberal, was first elected to the House of Assembly in 1872 for 1st Queens. He was re-elected in the general election of 1876 for 4th Prince.

Lea lived in Tryon for a number of years, but, in 1866 and later, he resided in Victoria where he owned some agricultural land known as Riverside Farm. William Lea died March 1911.

Rebecca Lea, the daughter of William Reid and Sophia Rozander, was born in 1835 and died 2 April 1863 when Herbert, John, and Artemas were very young. Annie Lea, the daughter of Edward Murphy of Cape Clear Lighthouse, Wexford, Ireland, was born in 1842 and died in 1924. William Lea's son Walter Mayfield Lea* was premier from 1930 to 1931, and again from 1935 to 1936.

References

Boswell pp. 20–22; *CPG* 1877, 1879; Elections PEI; Meacham's Atlas; PEI *Journal of the House of Assembly* 1872 p. 2; *Remember Yesterday* pp. 179–80; *Examiner* 6 April 1863; PARO: MNI-Census 1881; Hampton United Church Records Book 2 p. 5; Tryon People's Cemetery Records.

LEE, P.C., HONOURABLE JAMES MATTHEW, real estate broker, tourist operator, and businessperson; b. 29 March 1937 in Charlottetown, son of James Matthew Lee and Catherine Blanchard; m. 2 July 1960 Patricia Laurie, and they had three children, Laurie Anne, Patricia Susan, and Jason; Roman Catholic.

Lee, a Conservative, was first elected to the Legislative Assembly in a by-election held 17 February 1975 for 5th Queens. He was re-elected in the general elections of 1978, 1979, and 1982. He was defeated in the general elections of 1974 and 1986. Lee was a candidate for the party leadership in 1976, which was won by J. Angus MacLean*. On 3 May 1979, he became Minister of Tourism, Parks and Conservation. In 1980 Lee was appointed Minister of Health and Social Services. Lee was elected Leader of the provincial Conservatives upon the retirement of MacLean on 9 November 1981. On 17 November of that year, Lee was sworn in as Premier. He and the Conservative party were returned to power in the 1982 general election, winning 21 of 32 seats in the Legislature. Later that year, he was sworn into the Privy Council of Canada by Queen Elizabeth II.

Lee's time as Premier was marked by difficult economic conditions. The North American economy was in its most marked recession in 30 years. Furthermore, the Comprehensive Development Plan ended during his time in office. The focus of Lee's government was to manage the finances wisely given the poor economic climate. Lee was a prudent, common-sense leader with a reserved style. He championed smaller government and less restriction for private enterprise. One of the most significant accomplishments of Lee's government was the successful negotiation process that resulted in the Atlantic Veterinary College being located at the University of Prince Edward Island. Lee was also successful in reducing energy costs for Islanders.

Although Lee's Conservatives went into the 1986 election ahead in the polls, they lost support as the contest went on. Lee had staked his campaign in part on the attraction to the Island of Litton Enterprises and the high-tech jobs that came with it. Opposition leader Joseph Ghiz opposed this on the grounds that the government's financial arrangement with Litton was too generous. Lee resigned as Conservative Leader on 13 November 1986.

Lee began his association with the Conservative party in 1957 as a member of the Queens County Young Conservatives. He served in several offices on the executive of the Young Progressive Conservatives and became Provincial Director of the Conservative Party in 1965. Lee was a party organizer for many years and also served as its Executive Director.

"Jim" Lee received his early education at Queen Square School in Charlottetown. He then attended St. Dunstan's University and also trained as an architectural draughtsman at the Provincial Vocational School. Lee owned and operated Island Real Estate Limited. He was a real estate broker and developer until 1979, when he sold his business interests. Lee also operated a tourist business in Stanhope. Following his retirement from provincial politics, Lee served as Commissioner of the Canadian Pension Commission in Charlottetown. He is presently Chair of the Workers Compensation Board. Lee served as vice-president of the Charlottetown Jaycees and as director of the United Commercial Travellers, and is a member of the Royal Canadian Legion, the United Services Officers Club, and the Royal Canadian Air Force Association. For the past 10 years, Lee has been involved with the Council for Canadian Unity and presently serves as National President. Lee has served as chairperson on the North Shore Community Council for the past five years. He also served as a director of the Stanhope Historical Society and as a 4-H leader. Jim Lee and his wife currently reside in Stanhope.

Patricia Lee is the daughter of Ivan A. Laurie and Anne Gillan of Charlottetown.

References

CPG 1975, 1976, 1986, 1987; MacDonald *If You're Stronghearted* pp. 351-54; *WWPEI* p. 75; *Guardian* 31 March 1978, 16 April 1979, 13 November 1986, 14 November 1986, *Journal-Pioneer* 23 September 1982.

LEFURGEY, ALFRED ALEXANDER, lawyer, businessperson, real estate agent, and stock broker; b. 22 April 1871 in Summerside, son of John Lefurgey* and Dorothea Read; m. Eva Weist of Vancouver, and they had two children, John and Virginia; Presbyterian/Universal; d. 1 November 1934 in Vancouver.

Lefurgey, a Conservative, was elected to the Legislative Assembly in the general election of 1897 for 5th Prince. In 1898 he resigned this seat to contest a by-election for East Prince for the House of Commons. Lefurgey was defeated. Lefurgey was elected to the House of Commons in 1900 for East Prince. He was re-elected in the general election of 1904. He was defeated in the general election of 1908. During his time in the Commons, Lefurgey served as Conservative Whip for the Maritime provinces.

Lefurgey's father John was a member of the House of Assembly.

Lefurgey received his early education in Summerside schools, after which he attended St. Dunstan's College in Charlottetown and Mount Allison University where he earned a Bachelor of Arts in 1891. Lefurgey graduated from Harvard University law school in 1894, returning to Summerside where he practised law with J. E. Wyatt and J. E. Lefurgey. He also had a commercial career with interests in the province and Cape Breton. In 1909 he moved to Vancouver where he became a real estate agent and a stock broker. He died on 1 November 1934.

References

CDP pp. 331–32; *Past and Present* pp. 633–34; *Examiner* 17 October 1900; *Maple Leaf Magazine* November 1934; *Pioneer* 3 November 1934.

LEFURGEY, JOHN, merchant, shipowner, bondsman, justice of the peace, and shipbuilder; b. 17 March 1825 in Bedeque, son of William Lefurgey and Catherine Monroe; m. 18 July 1855 Dorthea Reid, and they had 10 children: Rowena Catherine (died c. three months), Rosara, Beatrice, Charles Emmanuel, Cecilia, William Allen, John Ephraim, Alfred Alexander*, Dorthea, and Raymond David (died age two); Presbyterian/Universal; d. 5 May 1891 in Boston.

Lefurgey, a Conservative, was first elected to the House of Assembly in the general election of 1870 for 5th Prince. He was re-elected in the general elections of 1873, 1876, 1879, 1883, and 1886. He was also re-elected by acclamation in a by-election held 5 March 1887. Previous to his by-election win, he resigned from the House of Assembly to contest the Prince County riding in the federal election held 22 February 1887. Lefurgey was defeated. Lefurgey served on Executive Council from 1873 until 1890. In 1886 he was appointed to the government board that examined candidates for the position of Fish Inspector in Prince County. Lefurgey advocated the Island joining Confederation. During his time in the Assembly, he supported the Railway bill, the Purification of Parliament Bill, and the Election Bill. He differed with J. C. Pope* over the question of free schools and for a short time was a member of the L. H. Davies* coalition of 1876.

Lefurgey was born in Bedeque where he was educated at the local schools. Later he moved to Summerside, where he operated a general store and a shipyard on Water Street. Lefurgey owned the Golden Shipyard below present-day Water Street. He also held mortgages throughout Summerside. His house and the house of his daughter Cecilia still exist and are part of the Heritage Centre at Wyatt Heritage Properties. John Lefurgey died suddenly on 5 May 1891 while on a business trip to Boston.

Dorthea Lefurgey was the daughter of Ephraim Reid of Wilmot Creek.

References
A Bridge to the Past pp. 153, 154, 157, 158; *Meacham's Atlas*; *Islander* 27 July 1855 p. 3; *Daily Examiner* 6 May 1891; *Century on Spring Street*; *Summerside Journal* 1904-1928; PARO: ACC. 2810; MNI-Census 1861, 1881, 1891; Lefurgey Family Genealogy; MNI-Hutchinson's p. 251; MNI-Mercantile Agency Reference book 1876.

LEPAGE, HONOURABLE BRADFORD WILLIAM,

merchant and lobster packer; b. 19 February 1876 in Anglo Rustico, son of Elisha Christopher LePage and Millicent Woolner LePage; m. 24 February 1897 Harriet Edna Christie, and they had two children, William Reuel and Hilda Ruth; United; d. 4 December 1958 in Charlottetown.

LePage, a Liberal, was elected to the Legislative Assembly in the general election of 1919 for 2nd Queens. He was re-elected in the general elections of 1927, 1931, and 1935. He was defeated in the general election of 1923. He was a Minister without Portfolio in the Albert Saunders* Administration from 1927 to 1930, in the Walter Lea* Administration from 1930 until 1931, and then again under Lea in 1935. LePage served as President of Executive Council in the government of Thane A. Campbell*. For a brief period, he was acting Premier and acting Minister of Agriculture. LePage represented the province at the coronation of King George VI in 1937.

In the general election of 1939, in the district of 2nd Queens, the unofficial count on election night declared R. Reginald Bell the winner by one vote over LePage. However, the official numbers announced on Declaration Day declared LePage the winner. A recount and appeals by both candidates followed, until the case was finally settled in Supreme Court. Finally, the Legislature passed a bill in 1940, declaring the seat vacant. A by-election was to be held, but before that occurred LePage was named Lieutenant-Governor on 11 September 1939. Bell ultimately lost the by-election to Alexander W. Matheson*.

LePage served as Lieutenant-Governor from 1939 until 1945. Near the end of his term, on 9 April 1945, he refused to give Royal Assent to a bill, known locally as the Cullen Amendment, designed to loosen the more stringent clauses of the Prohibition Act. Premier J. Walter Jones* waited for LePage's term to expire and presented the bill to his successor, Joseph A. Bernard*. The bill was signed into law in September of that year. This action was eventually declared invalid by the province's Supreme Court, but by 1948 the original Prohibition Act had been further amended.

LePage was educated at the Anglo Rustico School. He became a general merchant in his father's business, where he built one of the largest mercantile firms in the province by exporting agricultural and fishery products. LePage was manager of the first Fishermen's Co-operative Lobster Packing Association in North America. He was also involved in the silver fox industry as a director of the Magic Silver Black Fox Company. After 26 years, LePage sold his business interests in Rustico and in 1920 began the LePage Shoe Company Ltd. in Charlottetown with his son Reuel. In addition to his business pursuits, LePage served the Island community as a member of the Board of Education, as a director of the Young Men's Christian Association, and as a trustee of the Falconwood Hospital. He was a member of the Rotary Club and was active as a senior presiding elder of Trinity United Church in Charlottetown. Bradford LePage died 4 December 1958 at the Prince Edward Island Hospital.

Harriet LePage, the daughter of James A. Christie of Mayfield, was born 24 October 1875 and died 19 July 1961. She, too, was very active in Trinity United Church in Charlottetown.

References
CPG 1921; MacDonald *If You're Stronghearted* p. 237; Zonta Club p. 117; *Guardian* 5 December 1958; *Maritime Advocate and Busy East* August 1953; *Patriot* 4 December 1958; PARO: Sherwood Cemetery Records.

LINKLETTER, THOMAS MAXFIELD, farmer and shipper; b. 14 April 1868 in St. Eleanors, son of Thomas Linkletter and Mary Ann Ramsay; m. 10 April 1895, Clara Craswell, and they had seven children, Amy W., W. Maxfield, G. Bradford, Harold C., T. Leland, Irene, and Zilpha; United; d. 15 February 1954 in Summerside.

Linkletter, a Liberal, was first elected to the Legislative Assembly in the general election of 1935 for 3rd Prince. He was re-elected in the general elections of 1939, 1943, and 1947. He was defeated in the general elections of 1919 and 1923.

Linkletter was a farmer and also engaged in the lobster-packing business. He was one of the larger shippers of Island oysters to Montreal. Thomas Linkletter died 15 February 1954 in Prince County Hospital.

Clara Linkletter, the daughter of William Craswell of St. Eleanors, was born 5 April 1874 and died 9 February 1944.

References
CPG 1944; *Patriot* 16 February 1954; PARO: Summerside People's Cemetery Records.

M

MACARTHUR, HONOURABLE CREELMAN, merchant and business person; b. 12 June 1874 in Summerside, son of Jeremiah MacArthur and Ellen Donald; m. first 5 July 1899 Hannah Lois Beattie, and they had four children, Katherine Adele, Dorothy Grace, Constance Creelman, and Marion Beattie; m. secondly 10 February 1937 Muriel Mabel Lee, and they had one son, Creelman Lee; Presbyterian; d. 27 December 1943 in Summerside.

MacArthur, a Liberal, was first elected to the Legislative Assembly in the general election of 1919 for 5th Prince. He was re-elected in the general election of 1923. He resigned his seat to accept an appointment to the Senate on 5 September 1925, where he served until his death.

MacArthur was educated at the local school in Summerside and at Summerside High School. He worked in Summerside with R. T. Holman Limited and later as president of Brace MacKay and Company and of Harding Motors Limited. MacArthur was vice-president of the Mount Sherman Company and a director of Central Trust Company of Canada. He served on the Summerside Town Council from 1912 to 1913. Creelman MacArthur died 27 December 1943.

Hannah MacArthur died 11 May 1932. Constance MacArthur married John David Stewart* who represented 5th Queens from 1959 to 1970. He was the son of Premier James D. Stewart*.

References
CDP pp. 385–86; CPG 1921, 1924, 1929; *Maple Leaf Magazine* January/ February 1944; *Patriot* 27 December 1943, 29 December 1943.

MACARTHUR, JOSHUA GORDON, carpenter and farmer; b. 19 October 1911 in Poplar Grove, son of George Percy MacArthur and Caroline Alice Adams; m. first 29 May 1933 Edna Noye, and they had 10 children, George (d. 30 January 1973), Joyce, Arnold, Nita, Wilfred (d. 2 June 1987), Wyman, Verna, Audrey, Eric, and Ivan; m. secondly 30 August 1969 Vera Janette Smallman (*née* Phillips), and she had one child, Herman Smallman; Presbyterian; d. 23 July 1980 in Tyne Valley.

MacArthur, a Liberal, was first elected to the Legislative Assembly in the general election of 1970 for 2nd Prince. He was re-elected in the general election of 1974. He resigned due to ill health in 1976. On 13 April 1970, he won the Liberal nomination for the councillor position in 2nd Prince on the second ballot over three other competitors. In an unusual twist, MacArthur moved the nomination of the candidate who proved to be his main competitor for the nomination. A few weeks later, MacArthur won the councillor's seat in the 1970 general election by a mere eight votes over his cousin and then-Leader of the Conservatives, George Key.

MacArthur worked as a farmer and a carpenter. Prior to being elected to the Legislative Assembly, MacArthur was employed as a carpenter by the Lennox Island Band Council. He served as a school trustee and was a member of the hospital board of the Stewart Memorial Health Centre in Tyne Valley. He contributed to the establishment of the Ellerslie area senior citizens club. MacArthur was a member of the Freeland Presbyterian Church, where he served as an elder and Sunday School superintendent. Joshua MacArthur died 23 July 1980 at the Stewart Memorial Health Centre.

Edna MacArthur, the daughter of Wallace and Ella May Noye of Enmore, died 23 October 1967. Vera MacArthur, who now resides in O'Leary, is the daughter of Forrest W. Phillips*, a Member of the Legislative Assembly, and Gertrude MacArthur of Mount Royal.

References
CPG 1976, 1977; Elections PEI; *Guardian* 11 July 1972, 25 July 1980; *Journal-Pioneer* 13 April 1970, 14 April 1970; Personal Interview: Ivan MacArthur.

MACDONALD, AENEAS A., lawyer and judge; b. 30 November 1864 in Georgetown, son of Andrew A. MacDonald and Elizabeth L. Owen; m. 30 August 1904 Margaret J. MacDonald, and they had four children, Reginald A. C., Margaret E., Anna M. O., and Marjorie; Roman Catholic; d. 30 June 1920 in Charlottetown.

Aeneas MacDonald, a Conservative, was first elected to the Legislative Assembly in the general election of 1912 for 2nd Kings. He was defeated in the general election of 1915.

His father, Andrew A. MacDonald, was a Lieutenant-Governor, a senator, a member of the

House of Assembly, and a Father of Confederation.

Aeneas MacDonald was educated at St. Dunstan's College and Prince of Wales College in Charlottetown. He studied law in the office of Peters and Peters, and was admitted to the Bar in 1890. In his early career, he was a law partner of C. B. MacNeill, and subsequently with P. J. Trainor. In 1905 MacDonald entered into partnership with John A. Mathieson* until Mathieson's appointment as Chief Justice of the province in 1917. A partnership he formed with James D. Stewart* ended when MacDonald was appointed as Judge of Probate in April 1916. He also served as Private Secretary to the Lieutenant-Governor, his uncle, Augustine Colin Macdonald*, who held that office from 1915 to 1919.

At the time of his death, MacDonald was chairman of the Relief Committee of the Canadian Patriotic Fund. He was also a charter member of the Charlottetown Club and served as its Secretary. Aeneas MacDonald died suddenly on 30 June 1920.

Margaret MacDonald of Glenaladale, the daughter of John Archibald MacDonald, was born in 1873 and died in 1950.

References
CPG 1915, 1916; Elections PEI; Patriot 30 June 1920; PARO: MNI-Census 1881; MNI-Charlottetown Roman Catholic Cemetery Records.

MACDONALD, ARCHIBALD JOHN, merchant,
comptroller of navigation laws, consular agent, and controller of customs; b. 10 October 1834 in Panmure, son of Hugh Macdonald of Panmure and Catherine McDonald; m. 1 July 1873 Marian Murphy, and they had nine children, Marian, Alice, Catherine, Maude, Gladys, Temple*, Glen, Allister, and Howard; Roman Catholic; d. 18 August 1917 in Georgetown.

Macdonald, a Conservative, was first elected to the House of Assembly for Georgetown Royalty in March 1872. He was re-elected by acclamation in the general election of 1873. He was re-elected in the general elections of 1879, 1883, 1886, 1890. Macdonald was elected to the Legislative Assembly in the general election of 1893 for 5th Kings. He was re-elected in the general elections of 1897, 1900, 1904, and 1908. He was defeated in the general election of 1876. Macdonald served on Executive Council as a Minister without Portfolio from 1873 to 1876, and again from 1883 to 1891.

Macdonald continues to be the longest-serving Member of the House of Assembly and Legislative Assembly, since PEI became a Province of Canada.

Macdonald came from a family of merchants and politicians. They were considered to be a Prince Edward Island Scots Catholic aristocracy due to their relative affluence, political involvement, and ancestry. Their status was due to their dominance of the political and economic life of central Kings County for over a century. His father Hugh Macdonald and uncle Angus Macdonald were first elected to the House of Assembly in 1830. The brothers were among the first Catholic members of the Island Legislature. Macdonald's brother Andrew Archibald was a Father of Confederation, a member of Executive Council and Lieutenant-Governor, as well as a member of the Legislative Council and a Member of the House of Assembly. Another brother, Augustine Colin*, was a Member of the House of Assembly, a Member of the House of Commons for King's County, and Lieutenant-Governor of the province. Macdonald's son Temple was elected in 1912 for 5th Kings by acclamation as a Conservative.

Macdonald studied at the Central Academy in Charlottetown. He was a merchant with A. A. Macdonald and Brothers. The firm, originally owned by his brother Andrew, shipped grain, potatoes, and lumber to New England, Newfoundland, and Great Britain, as well as imported manufactured goods for sale in their Georgetown and Montague Bridge stores. Shipbuilding was another interest. In the 1860s and 1870s the firm became involved in the Gulf of St. Lawrence mackerel fishery.

Beyond his mercantile affairs, Macdonald served as Comptroller of Navigation Laws, as the Sheriff of Kings County, as the Consular Agent of the United States Controller of Customs, and as the Collector of Imposts at Three Rivers. He also served as the chief executive of the Kings County Industrial Exhibition.

Macdonald died 18 August 1917 in Georgetown, which he represented for a great part of his life.

Marian Macdonald, the daughter of Dennis Murphy of London, England, and the niece of William Murphy of Charlottetown, was born ca. 1848.

References
CPG 1874, 1876, 1877, 1915; DCB XIV 1911-1920 pp. 682-85;

Elections PEI; *Guardian* 20 August 1917; *Islander* 11 July 1873; PARO: MNI-Census 1891; Hutchinson's p. 124; Montague Funeral Home Records 1889-1903.

MACDONALD, ARTHUR JOSEPH, farmer; b. 24 August 1931 in Little Pond, son of Vincent A. MacDonald and Jessie Anne Nickerson; m. 15 January 1958 Mary Ellen Walker, and they had seven children, Wendy Anne, Mary Delores, Paul Angus, Joan Marie, Verna Claire, Kimberley Ellen, and Janine Teresa; Roman Catholic.

MacDonald, a Liberal, was first elected to the Legislative Assembly in the general election of 1962 for 5th Kings. He was re-elected in the general elections of 1970, 1974, 1978, 1979, 1982, and 1986. He was defeated in the general election of 1966. Appointed Deputy Speaker on 24 January 1973, he served in this capacity until 18 September 1978. On 9 June 1986, MacDonald was again appointed Deputy Speaker. He held the positions of Minister of Tourism, Parks and Conservation, and Minister of Environment from 18 September 1978 to 3 May 1979. During his lengthy political career, MacDonald served as Provincial Secretary and acting Minister of Highways. He resigned on 7 January 1988 to become Chair of the Workers Compensation Board where he remained for approximately 10 years.

MacDonald resides in Little Pond where he farmed for a living. He attended school in Little Pond and St. Peters. From 1947 to 1951, MacDonald studied at St. Dunstan's University. He was a volunteer within his community, and was a member of the Dundas Lions Club, where he served as King Lion, and the Knights of Columbus, where he served as Grand Knight from 1972 to 1974, and again from 1984 to 1985. Arthur Macdonald is currently retired and lives with his wife in Little Pond.

"Ellie" MacDonald was the daughter of Peter Walker and Margaret Morrison of St. Georges.

References
CPG 1967, 1988, 1989; *WWPEI* p. 78; Questionnaire to Former MLAs.

MACDONALD, O.C., M.D., (C.M.), LL.D., AUGUSTINE A., physician; b. 7 February 1876 in St. Andrew's, son of Joseph MacDonald and Catherine MacDonald; m. first 3 February 1904 Estelle Lachance of Ganonoque, Quebec, and there were no children; m. secondly Laura Adeline Curly, and there were no children; Roman Catholic; d. 14 January 1970 in Souris.

MacDonald, a Conservative, was first elected to the Legislative Assembly in the general election of 1915 for 1st Kings. He was re-elected in the general elections of 1923, 1927, and 1931. He was defeated in the general election of 1919. MacDonald served as Speaker from 1931 to 1935. In 1939 he was defeated in the federal election for the riding of King's.

As a boy, "Gus" MacDonald lived with his uncle, Father Donald MacDonald, the local parish priest in Souris. He attended Agriculture Hall, a school attached to St. Mary's Convent. MacDonald graduated from St. Dunstan's College in 1895 and worked as a school teacher for several years before entering medical school. He received his medical degree from McGill in 1902. After spending a year in Boston and another year in Mount Stewart, he returned to Souris where he set up a medical practice in 1904.

Dr. "Gus", as he was affectionately known to his patients, is sometimes credited with the introduction of sulfa drugs to the province in 1939. He delivered most of the babies in his district and performed kitchen table surgery. His pay would often be a bag of potatoes or a chicken. In the Legislature he spoke out against the ban on automobiles and in favour of voting rights for women.

MacDonald served as president of the Souris St. Andrew's Society. In 1968 Governor General Roland Michener made a special trip to Souris to invest him into the Order of Canada, the first Islander given this honour. MacDonald loved music and singing, and for many years directed the St. Mary's Church choir. He was made an honourary member of the Canadian College of General Practitioners the year it was created. Augustine MacDonald died 14 January 1970 at the Souris Hospital.

Estelle MacDonald, the daughter of F. X. Lachance, died of rheumatic fever a few years into the marriage. Laura MacDonald, the daughter of Selvanus Campbell and Jessie Steel, was born 29 December 1878 and died in 1955 in Souris.

References
Arrival of the First Scottish Catholic Emigrants; CPG 1916, 1921, 1928, 1932; *Past and Present* p. 604; *Island Magazine*, Fall/Winter 1997; PARO: Baptism, St. Mary's Roman Catholic Church book 1, p. 281; Census 1901; MNI-Cemetery Transcripts.

MACDONALD, HONOURABLE AUGUSTINE COLIN, merchant; b. 30 June 1837 at Panmure, son of Hugh Macdonald and Catherine Macdonald; m. 27 June 1865 Mary Elizabeth MacDonald, and they had six children, M. Josephine, W. Jane, S. Francis, C. Helena, A. Florence, and A. J. Louis; Roman Catholic; d. 16 July 1919 in Charlottetown.

Macdonald, a Conservative, was first elected to the House of Assembly in the 1870 general election for 3rd Kings. He was re-elected in the general election of 1873. In September of that year he resigned from the Assembly to run successfully in the special federal election in the riding of King's. He was re-elected in the federal elections of 1878, 1882, 1891, and 1896, and defeated in the federal elections of 1874, 1887, and 1900. On 2 June 1915, Macdonald was appointed Lieutenant-Governor for the province. His nephew, Aeneas MacDonald*, served as his Private Secretary.

Macdonald came from a family of merchants and politicians. They were considered to be a Prince Edward Island Scots Catholic aristocracy due to their relative affluence, political involvement, and ancestry. Their status was due to their dominance of the political and economic life of central Kings County for over a century. In 1830 Macdonald's father Hugh Macdonald and uncle Angus Macdonald were elected to the House of Assembly. The brothers were among the first Catholic members of the Island Legislature. Macdonald's brother Andrew Archibald was a Father of Confederation, a member of Executive Council, and Lieutenant-Governor, as well as a member of the Legislative Council and a Member of the House of Assembly. Another brother, Archibald John*, was also a Member of the House of Assembly, later of the Legislative Assembly, and a member of Executive Council.

Macdonald's early education was at Georgetown Grammar School and Central Academy, following which he became a merchant at Montague Bridge, and a partner in the firm of A. A. Macdonald and Brothers shortly after its founding in 1851. The firm, originally owned by his brother Andrew, shipped grain, potatoes, and lumber to New England, Newfoundland, and Great Britain, and imported manufactured goods for sale in their Georgetown and Montague Bridge stores. A. A. Macdonald and Brothers was also involved in the shipbuilding industry. In the 1860s and 1870s,

the firm became involved in the Gulf of St. Lawrence mackerel fishery.

Beyond his political and professional life, Macdonald served as a local commissioner of the Exhibition of Local Industry for Prince Edward Island, and was a captain in a local militia.

For a large part of his life Macdonald lived in Panmure Island and Montague Bridge before moving to Charlottetown in 1915 to serve as Lieutenant-Governor. He died 16 July 1919 while still in office.

Mary Macdonald was born ca. 1844 to John Small MacDonald and Isabella MacDonald. Her father served in the provincial Legislature and on Executive Council.

References
CCB p. 354; *CDP* p. 396; *CPG* 1878, 1916; *DCB* XIV 1911–1920 pp. 682–85; *Daily Examiner* 17 December 1902; *Examiner* 22 January 1849; *Islander* 8 January 1847; PARO: RG 19 Vital Statistics series 3 subseries 1, Marriage Records, vol. 2 1855–1865; RG 19 Vital Statistics series 3 subseries 3, Marriage Register, vol. 6 1862–1867; Accession 3043; MNI-Census 1861, 1891; MNI-Hutchinson's p. 102.

MACDONALD, BENJAMIN EARLE, accountant and grocer; b. 27 January 1907 in Covehead, son of Peter J. MacDonald and Ethel Birt; m. 31 July 1928 Jean Bell MacLean, and they had one child, Jean Beryl; Presbyterian; d. 17 July 1965 in Charlottetown.

MacDonald, a Liberal, was first elected to the Legislative Assembly in the general election of 1951 for 5th Queens. He was re-elected in the general election of 1955. He was defeated in the general election of 1959. MacDonald was appointed Minister of Health and Welfare in the government of Alexander W. Matheson* in 1953. On 16 June 1955, he was appointed Provincial Secretary and Treasurer.

Before entering provincial politics, MacDonald served on the Charlottetown City Council from 1940 to 1946, and during this time chaired both the fire and finance committees. In 1946, at the age of 33, MacDonald was elected Mayor. At that time, he was the second-youngest person to hold the office of Mayor of Charlottetown. MacDonald held the position of Mayor until 1951 when he offered himself as a candidate in that year's provincial general election.

B. Earle MacDonald moved with his family to Charlottetown at the age of 12. He attended city schools and also completed courses at the Charlottetown Business College. He then became employed in the accountant's office of the Canadian National Railway. Later MacDonald was transferred to the superintendent's office where he worked as the paymaster. After 16 years of service with the railway, he resigned to take over the family grocery business with his brother Elmer. Earle MacDonald died 17 July 1965 at the Prince Edward Island Hospital.

Jean MacDonald was the daughter of Reverend Daniel MacLean.

References
CPG 1959, 1960; *Evening Patriot* 19 July 1965; *Guardian* 19 July 1965; *Maritime Advocate and Busy East* February 1956.

MACDONALD, DANIEL CHARLES, farmer and teacher;

born ca. 1882 in Greenvale, son of Ronald MacDonald; m. Sara MacDonald and had three children, one of whom was named Bernard; Roman Catholic; d. in Boston, Massachusetts.

MacDonald, a Liberal, was elected to the Legislative Assembly in the general election of 1919 for 1st Kings. He was defeated in the general election of 1923.

He resided in Greenvale and lived there until after he was defeated in 1923. While living in Prince Edward Island, he was the president of the local chapter of the St. Andrew's Society. It is known that he resided in Massachusetts after leaving Prince Edward Island prior to 1927. He died in Boston in old age and is buried in Massachusetts.

Sara MacDonald was born in Rockbarra. She was the daughter of Angus B. MacDonald of Rockbarra and Ellen MacPhee of Bayfield.

References
CPG 1921, 1923; *Arrival of the First Scottish Catholic Emigrants*; *Guardian* 12 January 1929; PARO: 1840 Roman Catholic Census, MNI-Census 1891; Leard Files.

MACDONALD, P.C., HONOURABLE SERGEANT AND HONOURARY LIEUTENANT-COLONEL DANIEL JOSEPH, farmer;

b. 23 July 1918 in Bothwell, son of Daniel L. MacDonald and Elizabeth Fisher; m. 13 November 1946 Pauline Peters, and they had seven children, Blair, Heather, Gail, Daniel, Leo, Gloria, and Walter; Roman Catholic; d. 30 September 1980 in Charlottetown.

MacDonald, a Liberal, was first elected to the Legislative Assembly in the general election of 1962 for 1st Kings. He was re-elected in the general elections of 1966 and 1970. On 28 July 1966, he was appointed Minister of Agriculture and Forestry, and held this Ministry until summer 1972, when he resigned to run federally. On 30 October of that year, MacDonald became a Member of the House of Commons for Cardigan. He was re-elected in 1974, was defeated in 1979, and was re-elected in 1980. Prime Minister Pierre Trudeau appointed MacDonald Minister of Veterans Affairs in 1972 and he served in this position until 1979. He was reappointed to Privy Council in 1980 where he served only a short time due to the illness that ended his life. In his federal career, MacDonald was Minister Responsible for the Pension Review Board, the Canadian Pension Commission, the War Veterans Allowance Board, and the Bureau of Pension Advocates. During his Ministry, the head office of the Department of Veterans Affairs moved to the Island. He turned the sod to begin construction. After MacDonald passed away, and the building was finished, Prime Minister Trudeau named the building that housed the Department after the war hero.

"Dan" MacDonald received his education in Bothwell. He became a farmer and eventually purchased his own farmland above Bothwell beach, where he also helped out on his father's farm. In August 1940, MacDonald enlisted in the Canadian Army and served with the Prince Edward Island Highlanders. He remained with this regiment until 1943 when he was transferred to the Cape Breton Highlanders. By October of that year, he was made Sergeant of the front line in the Allied Campaign of Italy. In an assault on the Gothic Line, MacDonald was injured, but returned to the front shortly after recovering. However, on 21 December 1944, a shell exploded 20 feet from him, causing severe injuries. MacDonald's left arm and leg had to be amputated. He retired from the military in 1945 and returned to the province to receive a hero's welcome from his community. At the homecoming celebration he met his future wife.

MacDonald farmed and raised a family in Bothwell. He served as the provincial director of the Artificial Breeding Unit Board and the president of the Souris Co-operative Association. He was a member of the school board and the Home and School Association. MacDonald served fellow veterans as the branch president of the Royal Canadian Legion and with the War Amputees of Canada. He was honoured by the Prince Edward Island Regiment in 1977 with the title of Honourary Lieutenant-Colonel.

Daniel J. MacDonald predeceased his wife when he died of a heart attack on 30 September 1980. His state funeral was attended by many dignitaries, and wreaths were sent from as far away as Buckingham Palace. In his eulogy, Prime Minister Trudeau described MacDonald in these words: "He was a politician with a long list of achievements but I always sensed that he himself felt happier when he was described in ways which to him were more important: a devoted husband, father and grandfather, a good soldier, a good farmer, a good man, a public servant, a true and loyal friend. He was all of these things, and for that reason I have come today not so much to honour his death as to celebrate his life."

Pauline MacDonald is the daughter of Augustus Peters of St. Charles.

References

Capital List p. 287; *CPG* 1963, 1968, 1972; *CWW* 1973–1975 p. 619; Mahar; *Guardian* 1 March 1980; *Patriot* 4 November 1977.

MACDONALD, DONALD A., farmer; m. September 1880, Margaret McDonald, and there were no children; Roman Catholic.

MacDonald, a Conservative, was elected to the House of Assembly in a by-election held in May 1879 for 3rd Queens. He was defeated in the general election of 1882.

Donald MacDonald was a farmer who resided in French Village.

Margaret MacDonald of Tracadie, the daughter of Hugh McDonald, was born ca. 1849 and died 9 May 1884.

References

CPG 1881, 1883; Elections PEI; *Meacham's Atlas* 1880; *Daily Examiner* 27 May 1884; *Examiner* 30 September 1880.

MACDONALD, DONALD DAVID, farmer; b. 13 March 1862 in Glenfinnan, son of Donald A. and Isabel MacDonald; m. 13 November 1894 Mary J. McIntyre, and there were no children; Roman Catholic; d. June 1939, in Glenfinnan.

MacDonald, a Liberal, was first elected to the Legislative Assembly in the general election of 1915 for 3rd Queens. He was re-elected in the general election of 1919. He was defeated in the general elections of 1912 and 1923. On 9 September 1919, MacDonald was sworn in as a Minister without Portfolio in the government of Albert C. Saunders*.

Donald MacDonald was educated at the Glenfinnan school. He then became a farmer. From 1901 to 1911, he served as the Census Commissioner for the province and was also a Justice of the Peace. He was a member of the Knights of Columbus and was president of the Glenfinnan Branch of the St. Andrew's Society. David MacDonald died 7 March 1939.

Mary MacDonald, the daughter of Hugh McIntyre of Clermont, was born 13 April 1873.

References

CPG 1917, 1924; Elections PEI; *Maple Leaf* June 1939; PARO: MNI-Census 1881; Census 1901; St. Patrick's Roman Catholic Church Cemetery Records.

MACDONALD, GEORGE ALLISON, salesperson, manufacturer's agent, and wholesaler; b. 29 August 1918 in West Covehead, son of Peter MacDonald and Margaret Ethelbert; m. 9 February 1939 Olave Partridge, and they had six children, Marilyn, Judith, Susan, Linda, Kim, and Peter J.; Presbyterian; d. 11 February 2000 in Halifax.

MacDonald, a Liberal, was first elected to the Legislative Assembly in the general election of 1970 for 6th Queens. He was re-elected in the general election of 1974. He was defeated in the general elections of 1978 and 1979. In 1970 MacDonald was named Liberal Whip and held that position throughout his term in the Legislative Assembly. He served as president of the 5th Queens, Queens County, and Prince Edward Island Liberal Executives respectively. While a Member of the Legislature, his major areas of interest were seniors' housing, social services, and attracting jobs to his constituency. MacDonald was elected as councillor of the City of Charlottetown from 1966 to 1969. His brother B. Earle* was a Member of the Legislative Assembly from 1951 to 1959, and served as Minister of Health and Welfare and Provincial Secretary and Treasurer.

"Addie" MacDonald, as he was known, and his family moved to Charlottetown at an early age. When he was two years old, his father opened P. J.'s grocery store in Charlottetown and continued the business until his death in 1948. MacDonald was educated at West Kent School and Prince of Wales College. Following service in the military, he worked as a travelling salesperson on the Island, and was employed by Purity Flour, DeBlois Brothers, and Cody's Limited. In 1968 MacDonald established his own business as a manufacturer's agent and marketed a number of sanitation products to hotels, businesses, and institutions. In the early 1970s, he started his own company, Isan Limited, and sold sanitation products until shortly before his death. MacDonald was the provincial commissioner for the National Centennial Commission in 1967. He served as an elder and a member of the board of trustees at Zion Presbyterian Church, and took part in a number of outreach ministries. Addie MacDonald died 11 February 2000.

Olave MacDonald is the daughter of Cyrus L. Partridge of Mount Stewart and Annabelle MacKenzie of Murray River. She was born on 30 June 1918.

References
CPG 1959, 1978, 1979; *Guardian* 10 February 2001, 14 February 2000; *Monitor* 2 March 1977.

MACDONALD, JAMES B., b. 6 December 1862, son of James and Mary Helen MacDonald; m. Lousenina (surname unknown), and they had two children, Eaneas C. and Reginald; Roman Catholic; d. 19 December 1942 in Charlottetown.

MacDonald, a Conservative, was elected to the Legislative Assembly in the general election of 1923 for 2nd Kings. He was defeated in the general election of 1927.

James MacDonald died 19 December 1942.

References
CPG 1924, 1928; *Guardian* 21 December 1942; *Maple Leaf Magazine* January/February 1943; PARO: MNI-Census 1881; Census 1901.

MACDONALD, JAMES EMMANUEL, shipbuilder and merchant; b. 5 January 1842 in Georgetown, son of Angus and Mary MacDonald of Seal River; m. 4 July 1877 Georgina Stephens, and there were no children; Roman Catholic; d. 1 October 1903 in Boston.

MacDonald, a Conservative, was first elected to the House of Assembly in a by-election in 1873 for 3rd Kings. He was re-elected in the general elections of 1876 and 1879 and in a by-election held in November 1890, which he won by acclamation. MacDonald was elected to the Legislative Assembly in the general election of 1893 for 3rd Kings. He was re-elected in the general elections of 1897 and 1900. He died while sitting as a Member of the House of Assembly.

MacDonald was a shipbuilder and merchant in Cardigan. He served on the Dairymen's Board of Trade and on the provincial Dairymen's Association. For a short time, he was Commissioner of Public Works. He died on 1 October 1903, while on a trip to Boston. On the day of his death, the flag at the Provincial Building flew at half-mast in his honour.

Georgina MacDonald, the daughter of Patrick Stephens of Orwell, was born in 1851 and died 23 September 1929.

References
CPG 1880, 1901; Elections PEI; *Maple Leaf Magazine* November 1929; *Patriot* 1 October 1903, 12 October 1903; PARO: MNI-Census 1881; Mercantile Agency Reference Book 1876.

MACDONALD, JOHN ALEXANDER, farmer and justice of the peace; b. 21 October 1838, son of Angus MacDonald of North Bedeque, and nephew of Bishop Bernard Donald MacDonald of Charlottetown: m. June 1874, Annie C. McKelvie, and there was at least one child, Bernice (died in 1935); Roman Catholic; d. 1905.

MacDonald, a Conservative, was first elected to the House of Assembly in the general election of 1867 for 3rd Prince. He was re-elected in the general elections of 1870, 1872, 1873, 1876, 1879, 1883, 1882, and 1886. He was elected to the Legislative Assembly in the general election of 1893 for 3rd Prince. He was re-elected in the general election of 1897. MacDonald was defeated in the general election of 1900. From 1879 to 1887, he held the position of Speaker of the House of Assembly. His nephew Bernard McLellan* served as Speaker of the House of Assembly from 1891 to 1893.

MacDonald was educated in North Bedeque. He was a farmer and, for a time, a justice of the peace. He served as chairman of the Board of Railway Appraisers from 1873 until 1876. He was also a governor and trustee of Prince of Wales College. John MacDonald died in 1905.

Annie MacDonald of Indian River was born in 1844 and died in 1925. Her parents were Robert McKelvie of Indian River and Johanna McIntyre, who emigrated from Sutherlandshire, Scotland. Bernice MacDonald, the daughter of John Alexander MacDonald, was the first wife of Adrien F. Arsenault*.

References
CPG 1878, 1899; *Journal of the House of Assembly* 1871 p. 2; *Summerside Journal* 25 November 1886; PARO: St. Mary's Roman Catholic Church Records; St. Paul's Roman Catholic Church Records.

MACDONALD, HONOURABLE JOHN ALEXANDER "JOHN A.," merchant, produce exporter, business person, and shipbuilder; b. 12 April 1874 in Tracadie, son of John Charles and Elizabeth Mary MacDonald; m. 18 September 1905 Marie Josephine MacDonald, and they had nine children, Barbara Eleanor, Anna Elizabeth, George Albert (died in infancy), Margaret Isabella, Charles Joseph, John Augustine*, Mary Burke (d. 1929), Gertrude Frances, and David Bernard; Roman Catholic; d. 15 November 1948 in Cardigan.

MacDonald, a Conservative, was first elected to the Legislative Assembly in the general election of 1908 for 3rd Kings. He re-elected in the general elections of 1912 and 1923. He was defeated in the general elections of 1915 and 1919. He served as a Minister without Portfolio from 5 December 1911 to September 1915 in the Mathieson* Administration, and was a member of Executive Council as Minister of Public Works and Highways from 5 September 1923 to October 1925 in the Stewart* Administration. MacDonald was elected to the House of Commons in 1925 for King's. He was re-elected in 1926 and 1930. He was appointed as a Member of the Privy Council as a Minister without Portfolio on 13 July 1926. MacDonald served in this capacity until 25 September of that year, and again from 7 August 1930 to 13 August 1935. He was appointed to the Senate on 20 July 1935, where he served until his death.

MacDonald received his early education at public schools in Tracadie, and his education continued throughout his life, as he was an avid reader and a well-informed man. He was a merchant and produce exporter in Cardigan, and was also president of J. A. MacDonald and Company Limited and of the Prince Edward Island Associated Shippers Incorporated. Between 1918 and 1920, he built the last three large wooden sailing vessels constructed on PEI. MacDonald served as a director of the Cardigan Electric Company, the Cardigan Silver Fox Company Limited, and the Georgetown Fish Company. He was a director of National Service and Honourary Fuel and Food Control Administration for the province during the First World War. Senator John MacDonald died 15 November 1948.

Marie MacDonald of Cardigan was the daughter of Captain Joseph MacDonald. The couple married in Boston. Mary Burke predeceased both parents. John Augustine Macdonald* served in the Legislative Assembly and the House of Commons.

References
CDP pp. 400–01; *CPG* 1924; *Past and Present* pp. 453–54; *Patriot* 15 November 1948.

MACDONALD, MAJOR JOHN AUGUSTINE,

soldier and business person; b. 4 February 1913 in Cardigan, son of John Alexander MacDonald* and Marie Josephine MacDonald; m. 1 October 1941 Margaret Mary Smith, and they had four children, Judy, Ian, Heather, and John; Roman Catholic; d. 4 January 1961 in Cardigan.

Macdonald, a Conservative, was first elected to the Legislative Assembly in a by-election held 4 June 1945 for 3rd Kings. At the time of the election, he was convalescing in hospital from war injuries. He was re-elected in the general election of 1951. He was defeated in the general elections of 1947 and 1955.

In 1949 and 1953, Macdonald was unsuccessful as a candidate in the federal elections for King's. He was elected to the House of Commons for King's in the federal election of 1957 and was re-elected in 1958.

Following Macdonald's death, his wife, Margaret Mary, was elected to the House of Commons for the riding of King's in a by-election held 29 May 1961. She was re-elected in the federal election of 1962. She was PEI's first female Member of Parliament. Macdonald's father, John Alexander MacDonald*, served in the Legislative Assembly, the House of Commons, and in the Senate.

Macdonald received his early education at the Cardigan School. He then attended St. Dunstan's High School and St. Dunstan's College, where he received a Bachelor of Arts and a Commerce Certificate in 1938. Macdonald enlisted in the Canadian armed forces as a Private in 1939, and in his military career worked up through the ranks to Lieutenant. He served as a Commanding Officer of the "B" Squadron, 17th Reconnaissance Regiment, and as Commander of the North Nova Scotia Highlanders. Wounded on 25 July 1944, while leading his company through heavy fighting at Caen, Macdonald returned to Canada where he remained hospitalized until April of 1946.

In his private career, Macdonald participated in the family business of J. A. MacDonald and Company Limited, serving as the firm's secretary and president. He was a merchant specializing in the dealing of produce. Macdonald was a member of the Kings County Board of Trade, the Kings County Hospital Board, the Prince Edward Island Federation of Agriculture, and the Prince Edward Island Plowing Match and Agricultural Association. He was also a member of the Island Historical

Society, the Red Cross, and Children's Aid Societies. John A. Macdonald died 4 January 1961, at his home, while serving as a Member of the House of Commons.

Margaret Macdonald was the daughter of Richard C. Smith and Alice Smith of East Chezzetcook, Nova Scotia. Margaret Macdonald died 3 February 1968 in Halifax.

References
CDP p. 401; *CPG* 1947; *Guardian* 5 January 1961, January 1961; *Patriot* 4 January 1961.

MACDONALD, JOHN HOWARD, b. 13 July 1880, son of Archie and Marion MacDonald; m. Janette King, and they had one child, Donald; Roman Catholic; d. 19 February 1965.

MacDonald, a Conservative, was first elected to the Legislative Assembly in the general election of 1923 for 5th Kings. He was re-elected in the general election of 1931. He was defeated in the general elections of 1927 and 1935.

John Howard MacDonald died 19 February 1965.

References
CPG 1924, 1928, 1932, 1936; PARO: MNI-Census 1891; Census 1901; UPEI: Robertson Library: PEI Collection.

MACDONALD, HUGH LORD, contractor, trader, merchant, and farmer; b. ca. 25 March 1841 in Cardigan River, son of Angus McDonald and Jenny McDonald; m. 20 July 1875 Anna Louise Owen, and they had four children, Clarence, Jenevive, Edith G., and Hugh A.; Roman Catholic; d. 27 January 1891.

MacDonald, a Conservative, was first elected to the House of Assembly in the general election of 1886 for 3rd Kings. He was re-elected in the general election of 1890. He served as Commissioner of Public Works.

MacDonald worked as a farmer, contractor, and trader. He was also a merchant and owned a general store. He exported produce to a number of destinations, principally Halifax and Cape Breton, but also Newfoundland and St. Pierre Island. Hugh Lord MacDonald died 27 January 1891, while a member of the House of Assembly.

Anna Louise MacDonald, born ca. 1852, was the daughter of Thomas Owen, Postmaster-General of Prince Edward Island, and a sister of Lemuel Cambridge Owen, Sr.*, premier from 1873 to 1876. MacDonald's father was a native of the island of Uist, Scotland.

References
CPG 1889; Elections PEI; *Highlights of Cardigan Area* pp. 84-86; *Daily Patriot* 27 January 1891; *Island Argus* 10 August 1875; PARO: MNI-Mercantile Agency Reference Book 1876; MNI-Census 1881, 1891; St. Joachim's Roman Catholic Church Records; All Saints Roman Catholic Church Records.

MACDONALD, LAUCHLIN, farmer, merchant, lighthouse keeper, and teacher; b. 25 March 1844 in East Point, son of "Big" Ronald MacDonald and Catherine MacDonald; m. 21 November 1876 Teresa MacLean of East Point, and they had two children, Ronald and Mary Ann (died in 1914); Roman Catholic; d. 27 October 1928 in Charlottetown.

MacDonald, a Liberal, was first elected to the House of Assembly in a by-election held 5 November 1875 for 1st Kings. He was re-elected in the general elections of 1876 and 1879. He was defeated in the general election of 1873.

MacDonald's early education was at the district schools, and later he attended St. Dunstan's College in Charlottetown from 1865 to 1871. Following this, he opened a general store, which he operated for 13 years near his home. According to another source, he taught school shortly after attending St. Dunstan's, and prior to operating the store. After giving up the business, MacDonald began farming at his family's homestead on Prospect Hill in East Point. He was known as a successful and progressive farmer. He also operated a mill on East Lake Creek. In 1897 he was appointed lighthouse keeper at East Point.

MacDonald was a director of the Prince Edward Island Dairy Association, president of the Cheese Board of Trade, president of the East Point Farmer's Institute, as well as secretary, cashier, and managing director of East Point Dairy Association, which operated the East Point Cheese Factory at Lakeville. Due to his experience in agriculture, MacDonald accomplished a great deal in developing the dairy and cheese industry. He served as a school trustee for the local school district. In celebration of his Scottish heritage, he served as president of East Point Branch of St. Andrew's Society. Lauchlin MacDonald died 27 October 1928.

Teresa MacDonald, the daughter of Allan MacLean of East Point and Flora McDonald of St. Peters, died 19 March 1916.

References
CPG 1876, 1880; Elections PEI; *Past and Present* pp. 458-59; *Maple Leaf Magazine* December 1928; *Patriot* 27 October 1928; PARO: Royal Gazette 19 Marriage Register Vital Statistics series 3 subseries 3 Vol. 9 1871-1878; MNI-Census 1891; UPEI: Robertson Library PEI Collection: Cheverie.

MACDONALD, K.C.S.G., M.D. (C.M.), RODERICK JOSEPH,

teacher and physician; b. 16 May 1858 in Maple Hill, son of Ronald Macdonald and Jean Macdonald; m. 19 July 1894 M. Josephine Macdonald, and they had nine children, Marie Alycia, R. Colin, Jean, Somerled, George, Cyril, Roderick E., Jean, and Cyril; Roman Catholic; d. 4 June 1961 in St. Peters.

Macdonald, a Conservative, was elected to the Legislative Assembly in a by-election held 7 November 1917 for 2nd Kings. He was defeated in the general election of 1919. In the by-election he admittedly did not campaign enthusiastically, and was elected by a five-vote majority. Macdonald later confessed that he never had any love for politics. According to the *Atlantic Advocate*, he was defeated because his constituents wanted him to have more time to practise medicine.

"Doctor Roddie," as he was known, received his primary education in Maple Hill, and later attended Prince of Wales College and St. Dunstan's College. After teaching school for several years, and working in the evening as a bookkeeper for a local merchant, Macdonald had saved sufficient money to enroll in medical school in Trinity College, Toronto. He graduated with a medical degree in 1888 and began practising medicine in St Peters. Macdonald continued his practice for 69 years. In 1952 Pope Pius XII conferred upon him the title Knight of St. Gregory the Great. In 1958 he was dubbed "the doctor of the century" and "the dean of Canadian physicians" at a dinner held in his honour by the executive committee of the Canadian Medical Association in Charlottetown. Macdonald was a life member of this organization. As a result of such commitment to the medical needs of his community, Roderick Macdonald was greatly admired, and in testament to the respect he received from the community, after his death on 4 July 1961, the procession at his funeral was three miles long.

M. Josephine Macdonald died October 1947. She was the daughter of Augustine Colin Macdonald* and Mary Elizabeth Macdonald.

References
CPG 1918, 1919, 1921; *Past and Present* p. 451; *Atlantic Advocate* October 1985; *Island Magazine* Fall/Winter 1997 vol. 42; *Patriot* 5 June 1981.

MACDONALD, ROSE MARIE,

cook, farmer, realtor, and civil servant; b. 3 July 1941 in Woodville Mills, daughter of Andrew and Mary MacLean; m. 27 February 1960, Ronald D. MacDonald, and they had seven children, David, Robbie, Nancy, Kent, Gary, Mark, and Michael; Roman Catholic.

MacDonald, a Liberal, was first elected to the Legislative Assembly in a by-election held 11 July 1988 for 5th Kings. She was re-elected in the general elections of 1989 and 1993. She was defeated in the general election of 1996 in the new electoral district of Georgetown-Baldwin's Road. From 1989 to 1993, MacDonald served as government Whip. She chaired the Standing Committee on Education and Community and Cultural Affairs, and the Standing Committee on Natural Resources and the Environment. MacDonald was a member of the Committee on Health and Social Services, and of the Special Intersessional Committee on Rules, Privileges and Private Bills. She also served on the Standing Committee on Justice, Health and Social Services, and chaired the Special Committee on the Legislative Reform Act in 1995.

MacDonald received her education at the Cardigan North School. In her career, she has worked as a professional cook, as an employee of the Bank of Montreal, and as an office clerk at Georgetown Seafood. MacDonald has also been a project manager in the Department of Consumer and Corporate Affairs, and has been employed at the Colville Manor in Souris. MacDonald and her husband have recently retired from the management of the family farm. She has recently retired from the realty firm Coldwell Banker Parker Realty. MacDonald has been a member of the Eastern Kings Advisory Board, the board of trustees of the Souris Hospital, and the Hospital Consultation Committee. She has served on the consultative committees of the Dundas and Souris schools and was a member of the Prince Edward Island 4-H Council and of the Island Community Theatre. MacDonald was recently appointed to the Board of Canada Mortgage and Housing Corporation. She is also a member of the Souris Hospital Foundation. Rose Marie MacDonald and her husband live in Little Pond, and enjoy breeding and racing harness race horses.

Ronald D. MacDonald was born on 1 May 1941 and is the son of Alex and Cecilia MacDonald.

References
CPG 1989, 1996, 1998-1999; *Guardian* 23 March 1996, 1 November 1996.

MACDONALD, TEMPLE WILLIAM FABER, merchant, business person, and military officer; b. 27 January 1875 in Georgetown, son of Archibald J. Macdonald* and Marion Murphy; m. a MacInnis from the United States of America and they had one son; Roman Catholic; d. 2 April 1918 in France.

Macdonald, a Conservative, was elected to the Legislative Assembly in the general election of 1912 for 5th Kings, the seat that had been held for many years by his father.

Macdonald was educated in Georgetown, St. Mary's College, and St. Ignatius College in Montreal. He was a merchant engaged in business in Georgetown as a partner with A. A. Macdonald and Brothers.

Upon the outbreak of the First World War, Macdonald left the province for Quebec in 1914, where he was named a Lieutenant in artillery. Eventually he served with the 98th Battery, which subsequently became the Second Siege Battery. Macdonald returned home briefly in 1915, before leaving for Europe in November of that year. He was named Captain in February 1916, after service in France. Later Macdonald was appointed to command the Fifth Siege Battery as a Major. He was killed in action in France on 2 April 1918, and was buried at Aubigny Communal Cemetery, Pas de Calais, France.

References
Canada: Veterans Affairs; *CPG* 1915; Elections PEI; *Guardian* 6 April 1918; *Patriot* 5 April 1918; PARO: St. James Roman Catholic Cemetery Records; MacDonald family research of Daryl MacDonald.

MACDONALD, WILBUR BERNARD, farmer, racehorse owner and breeder, and chair of land use commission; b. 13 September 1933 in Orwell, son of Leo R. MacDonald and Helen Morrissey; m. 4 August 1958 Pauline Murphy, and they had nine children, Dana, Helena, Laurena, Ronald, Bernard, Juanita, Timothy, Andrew, and Faber; Roman Catholic.

MacDonald, a Conservative, was first elected in the general election of 1982 for 4th Queens. He was re-elected in the general election of 1986 for 4th Queens. He was elected in the general election of 1996 and re-elected in the general election of 2000 for the electoral district of Belfast-Pownal Bay. He was defeated in the general elections of 1989 and 1993 in 4th Queens. In 1982 MacDonald was chair of the Conservative caucus, and, in 1983 and 1984, chair of the Legislative Committees on agriculture, fisheries, tourism, and industry. From 1984 to 1986, he served as Minister of Industry. MacDonald held the position of Speaker from 1996 to 2000. He was also a chair of the Standing Committee on Legislative Management. From 1979 to 1980, MacDonald served as a Member of Parliament for Cardigan. He was a member of the House of Commons' committees on agriculture, fisheries, and regional industrial expansion. He was defeated in the federal elections of 1980 and 1993, and in a by-election in 1981 for Cardigan.

MacDonald received his primary education at the Orwell Public School and later attended St. Dunstan's High School. He is a dairy, beef, and potato farmer. MacDonald was an owner and breeder of standardbred race horses. In 1979 he was a member of the National Beef Import Committee and in 1980 served as chairman of the Prince Edward Island Land Use Commission. MacDonald was a president of the Sir Andrew Macphail Foundation and a vice-president of the Prince Edward Island Right to Life Association. He was a member of the 4-H Movement, Vernon River Lions Club, and the Vernon River Council of the Knights of Columbus. Wilbur MacDonald lives in Orwell Corner with his family.

References
CPG 1998-1999; *HFER Cardigan* pp. 1-2; *WWPEI* p. 82; *Guardian* 17 April 1986, 12 March 1993, 23 June 1993, 14 September 1993, 27 May 1996.

MACDONALD, WILFRED, merchant; b. 2 May 1917 in Vernon River, son of Benjamin B. MacDonald of Glencoe and Mary A. Johnson of St. Georges; m. 15 August 1946 Stella Horgan, and they had eight children, Cecil, Michael, Wilfred, Paul, Regina, Maureen, John, and Claudia; Roman Catholic; d. 4 April 1992 in Halifax.

MacDonald, a Conservative, was first elected to the Legislative Assembly in the general election of 1979 for 5th Queens. He was re-elected in the general election of 1982. He was defeated in the general election of 1986. While in the Legislature, MacDonald was a member of several Legislative Committees. He also served as Conservative Whip and as chair of the Conservative caucus.

MacDonald received his education at the Vernon River Public School. In the Second World War he saw action in England, France, Belgium, Holland, and Germany. On returning to the province, he settled in Parkdale. MacDonald spent 35 years working in the construction industry and retail business. He was the store manager at M. F. Schurman.

MacDonald was a school trustee in Parkdale for 10 years and chaired the community's recreation committee for five years. He also coached minor hockey and baseball and was a member of the building committee for the Sherwood-Parkdale Sportsplex. MacDonald was a member of St. Pius X Church and served on its building committee, and also was a member of the Catholic Social Welfare Bureau. Wilfred MacDonald died 4 April 1992 at the Victoria General Hospital.

Stella MacDonald is the daughter of Thomas Horgan of Stanhope.

References
CPG 1986, 1987; *WWPEI* p. 83; *Guardian* 16 April 1979, 3 February 1986, 6 April 1992 p. 3.

MACDONALD, K.C., JAMES AUGUSTINE, lawyer; b. 4 April 1888 in Emerald, son of James Macdonald and Catherine Croken; m. 25 July 1920 Nellie Morgan and they had two children, Mary Catherine and Anna Pauline; Roman Catholic; d. 10 February 1965 in Charlottetown.

Macdonald, a Conservative, was elected to the Legislative Assembly in the general election of 1923 for 3rd Queens. He was re-elected in the general election of 1931. He was defeated in the general election of 1927.

Macdonald received his post-secondary education at Prince of Wales College and St. Dunstan's College in Charlottetown, where he earned a Bachelor of Science degree. Following college, Macdonald read law with James D. Stewart* and was called to the Bar in 1919. He was appointed King's Counsel in 1926. Macdonald became acting Attorney-General of the Summerside Court in 1933, where he successfully prosecuted five criminal cases. He served as solicitor for the Canadian Farm Loan Board of Prince Edward Island and the Board of Public Utilities. In addition to his public legal endeavours, he was associated with the firm of Macdonald and MacPhee, and, when this partnership terminated, began his own practice, specializing as a defence lawyer. In later years, he served as secretary of the Liquor Control Commission. He was a member of the Knights of Columbus and the Caledonia Club. James Macdonald died 10 February 1965 at the Charlottetown Hospital.

Nellie Macdonald, the daughter of James Morgan, died in 1944.

References
CPG 1931, 1932; *CWW* 1936-1937 p. 661; *Guardian* 11 February 1965.

MACDOUGALL, PH.D., REVEREND WILLIAM JAMES, clergyman and professor; b. 8 May 1944 in Kentville, Nova Scotia, son of James Lorn MacDougall and Gertrude Isabel MacLean; m. 22 July 1966 Patricia Ann Campbell, and they had three children, Shane William Lorn, Christiana Kate, and Charity Jill.

MacDougall, a Conservative, was first elected to the Legislative Assembly in the general election of 1978 for 4th Prince. He was re-elected in the general elections of 1979 and 1982. He was appointed Deputy Speaker on 18 May 1983. In 1985 MacDougall resigned and left the province, with his family, in order to become minister at a United Church pastoral charge in Middleton, Nova Scotia.

"Bill" MacDougall received his secondary education at the Summerside High School and later attended Prince of Wales College in Charlottetown, where he earned a Bachelor of Arts. He then attended the Pine Hill Divinity Hall — now the Atlantic School of Theology — in Halifax where he earned a Master of Divinity. MacDougall did further study at New College, University of Edinburgh, where he earned a Doctor of Philosophy. While in Scotland, he served a congregation for one year. In 1973 MacDougall returned to the province, where he was a minister in Freetown, Lot 16, and North Bedeque. He also taught a course at the University of Prince Edward Island in the Department of Religious Studies. Bill MacDougall was a member of the Summerside Christian Council and several community groups.

Rev. Dr. William MacDougall and his wife Patricia live in Middleton, Nova Scotia.

References
CPG 1985; *Guardian* 25 January 1978, 3 April 1985; *Journal-Pioneer* 25 January 1978.

MACEWEN, HARVEY DAVID, teacher, merchant, and business person; b. February 1860, in West St. Peters, son of John MacEwen and Jane Coffin; m. 14 September 1882 Bessie Clark, and they had three children, Heber R. (predeceased both parents in 1912), Bruce W., and Claude; Presbyterian; d. 1938.

MacEwen, a Conservative, was first elected to the Legislative Assembly in the general election of 1915 for 2nd Kings. He was re-elected in the general election of 1923. He was defeated in the general elections of 1904, 1908, 1919, and 1927.

MacEwen was educated at local schools and at the Normal School in Charlottetown. Following the completion of his education, he taught for seven years. MacEwen was a general merchant and dealer in fish, and he canned lobster for many years. He then began making potato starch and acted as an agent for six mills in the province. MacEwen was half-owner and manager of the Morell Starch Company's mill. He operated a farm of over 100 acres and was president of the Morell Dairy Company. With his partner Robert N. Cox*, he operated two factories, one in St. Peters and another in Lot 40. McEwen was a member of the Masons and the Oddfellows. Harvey McEwen died in 1938.

Bessie MacEwen was the daughter of George Clark and Margaret Crosby of Wilmont Valley.

References
CPG 1916, 1921, 1925, 1930; *Past and Present* pp. 455–56; PARO: Mount Stewart People's Cemetery Records; Midgell Cemetery Records.

MACFARLANE, LORNE HERBERT, farmer, produce dealer, and company vice-president; b. 28 April 1904 in Bedeque, son of Neil Howard MacFarlane and Helen Leard; m. 27 August 1927 Pearl H. Vaughan, and they had four children, Nancy, John Alan, Malcolm, and Howard Vaughan (died 18 January 1951); Presbyterian; d. 11 January 1971.

MacFarlane, a Liberal, was first elected to the Legislative Assembly in the general election of 1947 for 5th Prince. He was re-elected in the general election of 1951.

MacFarlane, though born in Bedeque, also lived in Summerside. He received his early education in Bedeque. MacFarlane was a farmer and a produce dealer. He was the founder and vice-president of MacFarlane Produce for 25 years. MacFarlane was the Captain Commission of the New Reserve Club in Summerside, and a member of the United Services Officers Club in Charlottetown. Lorne MacFarlane died 11 January 1971.

Pearl MacFarlane was the daughter of George C. Vaughan of Charlottetown.

References
CPG 1955; PARO: Summerside People's Protestant Cemetery Records.

MACGUIGAN, K.C., HONOURABLE MARK RUDOLPH, teacher, lawyer, and judge; b. 5 November 1894 in Hope River, son of Peter P. MacGuigan and Annie M. Hughes; m. 17 September 1923 Agnes Violet Trainor, and they had two children, Mark Rudolph and Roberta Ann; Roman Catholic; d. 4 April 1972 in St. Petersburg, Florida.

MacGuigan, a Liberal, was first elected to the Legislative Assembly in the general election of 1935 for 3rd Queens. He was re-elected in the general elections of 1939 and 1943. He was defeated in the general election of 1931. On 14 January 1936, MacGuigan was sworn in as Minister of Education and Health, and served until 11 May 1943, when he became Attorney-General. In 1944 MacGuigan resigned his seat to accept an appointment to the provincial Supreme Court.

MacGuigan received his early education at St. Anne's School. He taught from 1910 to 1912, then attended St. Dunstan's College, where he graduated with a Bachelor of Arts in June of 1914. MacGuigan studied law in the offices of MacKinnon and MacNeill and was called to the Bar on 5 November 1918. He opened his own practice, but later took in a partner, Charles St. Clair Trainor*, and both men practised under the name MacGuigan and Trainor. MacGuigan was appointed to the Supreme Court of Prince Edward Island in 1944 and he served on the bench until his retirement in 1967. Mark MacGuigan died 4 April 1972 in St. Petersburg, Florida, while vacationing with his wife.

Agnes MacGuigan, the daughter of John J. Trainor and Katherine Kelly, was born 27 January 1895. Mark MacGuigan, Jr., the son of Mark MacGuigan, Sr., served as a Member of the House of Commons, a federal cabinet minister, and on the Supreme Court of Canada.

References
CPG 1932, 1938, 1940, 1944, 1945; *CWW* 1967–1969 p. 676; *PPMP* p. 130; *Patriot* 5 April 1972.

MACINNIS, GORDON, teacher, school principal, and business person; b. 13 July 1945 in Charlottetown, son of Ernest MacInnis and Celia Stevenson, stepson of Leslie MacDowell; m. 12 October 1968 Winnifred Anne Lowther, and they had three children, Roxanne, Tyson, and Blythe; Protestant.

MacInnis, a Liberal, was first elected to the Legislative Assembly in the general election of 1986 for 2nd Queens. He was re-elected in the general elections of 1989 and 1993. He was defeated in the general election of 1996 in the new electoral district of Park Corner-Oyster Bed. On 2 May 1986, MacInnis was appointed Minister of Tourism. He served as Minister of Transportation and Public Works from 1989 to 1991. From 14 November 1991 to 1993, MacInnis was the Minister of Tourism and Parks and Recreation. On 15 April 1993, he was appointed Minister of Transportation and Public Works and, on 9 June 1994, was appointed Minister of Education. In 1995 the Human Resources Ministry was added to his responsibilities.

MacInnis received his early education in the Pleasant Valley School, Kensington High School, and Central Queens High School. MacInnis studied at Prince of Wales College and the University of Prince Edward Island, from which he received a Bachelor of Arts degree. Following the completion of his education, he taught in the North Granville, Ebenezer, and Cornwall schools before serving as vice-principal of Cornwall Elementary and Eliot River Elementary. From 1975 to 1986, MacInnis was principal of Eliot River Elementary School. He is the former owner of the Cavendish Esso and is the owner of Cavendish Maples Cottages. He currently works as a consultant in Charlottetown. MacInnis is a member of the Rotary Club. He has served in various capacities on the North River Minor Hockey Association, has been a member of the executive board of the Tourism Association of Prince Edward Island, and president of the Retail Gasoline Dealers' Association. He is a member of the Cavendish Area Resort Association, serves on the Executive of the Tourism Industry Association of Prince Edward Island, and is a member of the Charlottetown Airport Authority. Gordon MacInnis and his wife live in Charlottetown.

Winnifred MacInnis is the daughter of Edward and Mary Lowther of Cavendish.

References
CPG 1996, 1998-1999; *WWPEI* p. 84; *Guardian* 27 February 1993; Questionnaire to Former MLAs.

MACINTYRE, HONOURABLE JAMES PETER,

farmer, business person, fisher, and lobster packer; b. 19 July 1882 in Mt. Stewart, son of William D. MacIntyre and Elizabeth MacKinnon; m. 28 April 1908 Marion Amelia Story, and they had eight children: Margaret, Eileen, Winnifred, Rita, Russell, Elmer, Audrey, and Freda; Roman Catholic; d. 8 April 1957.

MacIntyre, a Liberal, was first elected to the Legislative Assembly in the general election of 1919 for 2nd Kings. He was re-elected in the general elections of 1927, 1931, 1935, and 1939. He was defeated in a 1917 by-election as well as in the general election of 1923. MacIntyre held the portfolio of Minister of Public Works and Highways. As Minister of Public Works and Highways, he was responsible for paving the first road in the province. The road extended from St. Dunstan's College toward the Malpeque Road and was dubbed the MacIntyre Highway. On 19 February 1943, MacIntyre was appointed to the Senate, where he served until his death.

MacIntyre, or "Big Jim Bill," as he was known, was born in the Mt. Stewart area. He received his education at the local school. He began his career as a farmer when his father died. MacIntyre then started a lobster packing business in Savage Harbour. Later he became director of the French Village and Savage Harbour Telephone Companies. He also served as president of the Canadian Good Roads Association. MacIntyre was a member of the Knights of Columbus and the C.M.B.A. James MacIntyre died 8 April 1957, while visiting a daughter in Massachusetts.

Marion MacIntyre, the daughter of Mr. and Mrs. John Story of Chicago, was born in 1888 and died in 1968.

References
CPG 1921; MacDonald *If You're Stronghearted* p. 118; *Maritime Advocate and Busy East* vol. 32 no. 4 November 1941; *Patriot* 19 April 1957; PARO: St. Andrews Roman Catholic Church Baptism Records.

MACINTYRE, VERNON J., farmer and funeral

director; b. 21 August 1928 in Millcove, son of Alphonsus Joseph MacIntyre and Margaret Alice Coady; m. 19 September 1950 Sarah Ann Lauretta MacDonald, and they had five children, Daphne, Dolores, David, Jeanie, and Mary; Roman Catholic; d. 21 May 1976 in Millview.

MacIntyre, a Conservative, was elected to the Legislative Assembly in the general election of 1974 for 4th Queens. He was defeated in the general election of 1970. MacIntyre served as Party Whip during his time in office. He died while serving as a Member of the Legislative Assembly.

MacIntyre's family moved from Millcove to Millview in 1937. He was a farmer in Millview all his adult life. In 1956 MacIntyre joined the

Jenkins Funeral Home in Millview, where he worked in partnership until 1965, when he assumed ownership of the business. He was a member of the Prince Edward Island Funeral Directors and Embalmers Association, and was a director of the Prince Edward Island United Way Fund, the president of the Prince Edward Island Ambulance Operators' Association, and a member of the Advisory Board of the Kings County Hospital. MacIntyre was a charter member of the Vernon River Lions Club and a member of the Knights of Columbus. He and his family were parishioners of St. Joachim's, where MacIntyre served as a member of the Diocesan Budget Committee, the Parish Council, and the choir. Vernon MacIntyre died 21 May 1976, while working on his farm.

Sarah MacIntyre was the daughter of Angus MacDonald of St. Margarets.

References
CPG 1971, 1976; *Guardian* 4 August 1976; *Journal-Pioneer* 25 April 1974.

MACISAAC, ALEXANDER ANDREW, business person; b. 10 December 1907 in Inverness, Cape Breton, Nova Scotia, son of Mr. and Mrs. D. A. MacIsaac; m. 15 August 1931 Lillian Griffis of Sault Ste. Marie, Michigan, and they had six children, Jeana, Maitland, Lynn, Scott, Bruce, and Neil; Roman Catholic; d. 27 November 1988 in Charlottetown.

MacIsaac, a Liberal, was elected to the Legislative Assembly in the general election of 1955 for 5th Queens. He was defeated in the general election of 1959. MacIsaac served as Minister of Welfare and Labour from 1958 to 1959, and was the province's first Minister of Labour.

MacIsaac was educated at Inverness Public School. He moved to the Island in the mid-1930s, where he worked as a salesperson for DeBlois Brothers and operated a grocery business. MacIsaac owned Riley's Chewing Tobacco Company and a credit collection agency in Prince Edward Island and New Brunswick. He was a member of the Charlottetown Board of Trade and the board of governors of the Charlottetown Hospital. MacLeod was a member of the Knights of Columbus and the Gyro Club. Andrew MacIsaac died 27 November 1988 at the Queen Elizabeth Hospital.

References
CPG 1959; PEI *Journal of the Legislative Assembly* 1959, p. 3; *Guardian* 28 November 1988.

MACISAAC, PETER A., dairy farmer; b. 10 February 1878 in Souris, son of Donald A. MacIsaac and Annie Ford; m. 22 November 1910 Mary Josephine McInnis, and they had nine children, five of whom died in infancy or late teens, and Hugh, Agnita, Waldren, and Helen; Roman Catholic; d. 9 January 1969 in Souris.

MacIsaac, a Liberal, was first elected to the Legislative Assembly in the general election of 1935 for 1st Kings. He was re-elected in the general election of 1939. He was defeated in the general elections of 1931 and 1943.

MacIsaac was educated at Souris School. From 1898 to 1902, he served as a Lieutenant in the 4th Regiment of the Canadian Artillery, and later with the 37th Field Artillery. MacIsaac was a dairy farmer in the Souris area. He was a member of the Souris Farmer Institute, the Egg and Poultry Association, and the Eastern Kings Exhibition Association. MacIsaac was a member of the Livestock division of the Prince Edward Island Marketing Board and the Maritime Chamber of Agriculture. He was a member of the Knights of Columbus and the Prince Edward Island Temperance Commission. Peter MacIsaac died 9 January 1969 in the Souris Hospital.

Mary MacIsaac, the daughter of Hugh McInnis, died in 1955.

References
CPG 1932, 1938, 1940, 1943, 1944; *Maritime Advocate and Busy East* April 1943; *Patriot* 10 January 1969.

MACKAY, DONALD NEWTON, farmer; b. 1 July 1868 in Springfield, son of William MacKay and Catherine Mallett; m. 5 December 1895 Flora Sutherland, and they had two children, Lemuel William and John Sutherland; United; d. 19 December 1943 in Charlottetown.

MacKay, a Liberal, was first elected to the Legislative Assembly in the general election of 1935 for 1st Queens. He was re-elected in the general election of 1939. He was defeated in the general election of 1943.

MacKay's granddaughter, Leone Bagnall*, daughter of John Sutherland, was a Conservative Member of the Legislative Assembly for 1st Queens from 1979 to 1993.

MacKay was educated at the local school. He was a successful farmer and a member of many farming organizations. MacKay was a supporter of the co-operative movement. An ardent proponent of temperance, he was a member of the Sons of Temperance and the Temperance Federation. Donald MacKay died 19 December 1943 at the Prince Edward Island Hospital.

Flora MacKay was the daughter of John and Agnes Sutherland of Stanley Bridge.

References
CPG 1943; *Maritime Advocate and Busy East* vol. 33 no. 8 March 1943; *Patriot* 20 December 1943.

MACKAY, HONOURABLE JOHN GEORGE,

farmer; b. 6 November 1893 in Albany, son of David MacKay and Elmira Harvey; m. 31 January 1918 Muriel Beatrice Boulter of Albany, and they had five children, John Howatt, Audrey Beryl, Lois Rita, Sutherland Bruce (died at 22) and Phillis (died at seven months); United; d. 21 October 1974 in Charlottetown.

MacKay, a Liberal, was first elected to the Legislative Assembly in a by-election held 4 July 1949 for 4th Prince. He was re-elected in the general elections of 1951, 1955, 1959, and 1962. In 1955 MacKay was appointed Minister without Portfolio. He was appointed Minister of Highways on 16 June 1955, and remained in this Ministry until 1959. From 1959 to 1966, MacKay served in Opposition, with the exception of a period of six months in 1962. Previous to the federal election in June 1962, MacKay resigned from the Legislative Assembly to run in the federal riding of Prince; he was defeated. Following his retirement from politics, MacKay served as Executive Assistant to the Minister of Public Works and Highways, George Ferguson*. During this time Ferguson became ill, and from 1967 to 1969 MacKay served as acting Minister of Public Works and Highways. On 6 October 1969, he was appointed Lieutenant-Governor, the first farmer to hold that position. MacKay served in this capacity until his death.

MacKay was educated in Albany. During the First World War, he enlisted in the Canadian Expeditionary Force and was assigned to the 10th Siege Battery. His military career ended when he was discharged for health reasons. MacKay returned to Albany, where he farmed hogs and potatoes. In 1928 he bought a larger farm and in 1945 again expanded the operation. Early in his career, MacKay became the Albany stock shipping agent for Swift Canadian. He also took a prominent part in farm organization work. MacKay served as president of the Tryon Dairy Company, the Tryon Farmers Institute, and for a time he was a director of the Prince Edward Island Swine Breeders' Association.

MacKay was an active member of his church and his community. He was an elder of the Tryon United Church for almost 50 years and Sunday school superintendent of Zion Baptist Church in Albany for many years. He was also a member of the Tryon Inter-Community Choral Club. George MacKay died 21 October 1974 at the Prince Edward Island Hospital, while serving as Lieutenant-Governor.

References
CPG 1950, 1961, 1966; HFER Prince p. 1; PEI *Journal of the Legislative Assembly* 1955 p. 1; *Guardian* 22 October 1974; *Maritime Advocate and Busy East* August 1955 p. 32; *Patriot* 21 October 1971.

MACKENZIE, WALTER GRANT, farmer and

business person; b. 1 July 1895 in Springfield, son of Robert MacKenzie and Margaret McLeod; m. first 21 December 1932 Eva Louise Simpson, and there were no children; m. secondly June 1955, Helen Johnstone, and there were no children; United; d. 21 October 1956 in Charlottetown.

MacKenzie, a Conservative, was first elected to the Legislative Assembly in the general election of 1931 for 1st Queens. He was re-elected in the general election of 1943. He was defeated in the general election of 1939. He served as a Minister without Portfolio in the James D. Stewart* Administration.

MacKenzie spent most of his life on the family homestead in Springfield, as a successful farmer specializing in the raising of Holstein cattle and purebred sheep. Later in life he moved to Charlottetown, where he worked as a salesman for Vere Beck and Son. He was also vice-president of the Prince Edward Island Mutual Fire Insurance Company. MacKenzie was a member of the Masonic Order and was a Past Master of the Prince Edward Lodge Number 14. He was a member of the Caledonia Club. Walter MacKenzie died 21 October 1956, as the result of an automobile collision 10 days earlier.

Eva MacKenzie, the daughter of J. Herbert Simpson of Bay View, was born in 1902 and died 6 October 1944.

References
CPG 1944; *Patriot* 22 October 1956; PARO: Lot 67 Cemetery Records.

MACKINLEY, RONALD, farmer, farm chemical

salesperson, and snow removal business person; b.

24 August 1947 in North River, son of John McKinley and Mildred Sellar of Argyle Shore; m. 2 August 1969 Anne Clarkin, and they had three children, Joanne MacKinley Curran, Jamie, and Jeff.

MacKinley, a Liberal, was first elected to the Legislative Assembly in a by-election held 2 December 1985 for 2nd Queens. He was re-elected in the general elections of 1986, 1989, and 1993. He was elected in the general election of 1996 and re-elected in the general election of 2000 for North River-Rice Point. MacKinley had been defeated in the general election of 1982 in 2nd Queens. He served on the Public Accounts Committee, the Agriculture Committee, and the Transportation and Public Works Committee. In the 2000 election, the Conservatives took 26 seats and the Liberals only one. MacKinley was the lone Liberal Member in the Legislature. Following the election, he became interim Leader of the Liberal party and Leader of the Opposition. Numerous sources, including Liberal party election advertisements, identify MacKinley as a politician willing to speak his mind in the interests of his constituents, and at times has been in conflict with his party and with government policy. MacKinley also chaired the Elliot River Community Improvement Committee.

MacKinley received his primary education at the school in York Point and later attended Charlottetown Rural High School. He is a farmer who grows potatoes as a partner in MacKinley Brothers and raises cattle. In the past, MacKinley has raised hogs and operated a dairy farm. He also operates a snow removal business. He was a director of the Prince Edward Island Federation of Agriculture, the Prince Edward Island Farm Centre, and the Prince Edward Island Potato Processing Council. MacKinley was a member of the Canadian Horticultural Council Labour Board and the Queens County Chair of the Prince Edward Island Potato Producers Association. He was a member of the federal Uniformity Legislation Committee. In 1984 MacKinley was nominated for the Jaycees' Outstanding Young Farmer in the Maritimes. He is a member of the Canadian Hereford Association and his cattle herd has won numerous awards. Ronald MacKinley and his wife live on the family farm in North River.

Anne MacKinley is the daughter of Bert and Catherine Clarkin from Lot 65.

References
CPG 1982-1983, 1986, 1998-1999; *Guardian* 19 June 1982, 21 March 1996, 29 March 1996, 15 November 1996; *Islandside.*

MACKINNON, Q.C., HONOURABLE DONALD ALEXANDER, school teacher and lawyer; b. 21 February 1863 in Uigg-Belfast, son of William MacKinnon and Katherine Nicholson; m. 17 October 1892 Adelaide Beatrice Louise Owen, and they had three children, Beatrice, Arthur, and a second son who died in childhood; Presbyterian; d. 20 April 1928 in Charlottetown.

MacKinnon, a Liberal, was first elected to the Legislative Assembly in the general election of 1893 for 4th Kings. He was re-elected in the general elections of 1897 and 1900. He served as Attorney-General from 1899 to 1900, resigning that year from the Legislative Assembly to run in the 1901 federal election for East Queen's. On 1 February 1901, the election in East Queen's was declared void. MacKinnon was elected to the House of Commons for East Queen's in a subsequent by-election held on 20 March 1901. In 1904 he was appointed Lieutenant-Governor for the province, and he served until 1910. In 1921 he was re-elected to the House of Commons for Queen's and served until 1925, at which point he retired from politics.

MacKinnon received his primary education at the Uigg Grammar School. At the age of 13, he passed the teachers' examinations. MacKinnon taught school in Springton for three years. He attended Prince of Wales College, and later law school at Dalhousie University. MacKinnon articled with the firm of Palmer and MacLeod — which included Premier Herbert J. Palmer* — and in 1887 he was admitted to the Bar. He practised law in Georgetown for the next 10 years, entering into a partnership with Alexander B. Warburton* in 1897. In 1900 MacKinnon was awarded the designation of Queen's Counsel.

In 1906 MacKinnon and Warburton co-authored *Past and Present of PEI*. MacKinnon also served as chairman of the Georgetown school trustees. Donald MacKinnon died 20 April 1928.

Adelaide MacKinnon died 16 April 1912 at the age of 41.

References
CDP p. 421; *CPG* 1897, 1899, 1905; Elections PEI; *Past and Present; Guardian* 21 April 1928; *Patriot* 21 April 1928; PARO: St. Peter's Cathedral Cemetery Records.

MACKINNON, DOUGALD, farmer and lobster cannery operator; b. 15 December 1886 in Mount Buchanan, son of John MacKinnon and Flora Caroline MacLeod; m. 1 September 1915 Mary

Sarah McWilliams, and they had two children, John Dougald and Marion; United; d. 21 August 1970 in Mount Buchanan.

MacKinnon, a Liberal, was first elected to the Legislative Assembly in the general election of 1935 for 4th Queens. He was re-elected in the general elections of 1939, 1943, 1947, 1951, and 1955. From 1939 to 1943, he served as a Minister without Portfolio in the Thane A. Campbell* Administration. On 15 June 1951, MacKinnon was sworn in as Minister of Public Works and Highways, and remained in this Ministry until 1955 when, on 16 June, he was appointed as Minister of Industry and Natural Resources and Minister of Public Works. The Ministry of Fisheries was added to his responsibilities in 1957. Together with his running mate, J. Walter Jones*, MacKinnon conceived the idea of the Wood Islands ferry service.

MacKinnon was educated in the Mt. Buchanan Public School. He owned and operated a farm. MacKinnon fished lobster with his father. He helped to organize the Number 6 Pinette River Co-operative Union, which assisted fishers in securing the highest prices for their lobster. He also operated the lobster cannery in Belfast. Dougald MacKinnon died 21 August 1970 at his home.

Mary MacKinnon was the daughter of Robert McWilliams.

References

CPG 1960; CWW 1955-1957 p. 675; PEI *Journal of the Legislative Assembly* 1943 p. 3, 1955 p. 3, 1957 p. 3, 1958 p. 3; *Maritime Advocate and Busy East* September 1941; *Patriot* 22 August 1970.

MACLEAN, JAMES RODERICK, merchant and notary public; b. 9 April 1842 in East Point, son of Alexander MacLean of East Point and Mary MacDonald; m. first 12 October 1870 Mary Armstrong Wightman, and they had three children, Charles Joseph Alexander, Wallace, and James; m. secondly ca. 1894 Marcella MacDonald, and they had three children, John, Mary Adele, and Alexandria Ronelda; Roman Catholic; d. 26 March 1903.

MacLean, a Liberal, was first elected to the House of Assembly in a by-election held in 1869 for 1st Kings. He was re-elected in the general elections of 1870, and 1872 in a by-election held 10 September 1873, and in the general elections of 1876, 1882, 1886, and 1890. He was elected to the Legislative Assembly in the general election of 1893. MacLean was defeated in the the general election of 1879. MacLean served on Executive Council

from 1872 to 1873. In 1891 he was appointed to Executive Council and served as Commissioner of Public Works.

In September 1873 MacLean was defeated in the special federal election held to elect members to the House of Commons for Prince Edward Island. MacLean supported free trade and government grants to Catholic schools.

His grandfather Charles emigrated from the North of Scotland to the Island around 1800, settling in East Point in 1805. MacLean resided there until November 1870. He purchased 173 acres in Souris and sold the 217-acre farm at East Point inherited from his father. MacLean owned a great deal of land, with buildings in Souris, two farms at New Zealand, a farm at Gowan Brae, and several other properties.

MacLean also served as a notary public and as a governor of Prince of Wales College. James MacLean died 26 March 1903.

Mary MacLean was born in Summerside, and her father, Joseph Wightman, was a Member of the Legislative Council. She died in January 1890. Ca. 1894 James MacLean married Marcella MacDonald, the daughter of Alexander MacDonald and Flora Campbell of Inlet. Captain LaVie of Souris had adopted and raised Marcella MacLean. When she was widowed, Marcella MacLean and her family remained in Souris until 1914, when they moved to Scotland. Marcella married a Major Thomas but left him in 1922 and reassumed the name MacLean.

References

CPG 1897; UPEI: Robertson Library: PEI Collection, Cheverie, pp. 44-47; PARO: St. Mary's Roman Catholic Church, Church Book 3.

MACLEAN, P.C., O.C., C.D., D.F.C., LL.D., HONOURABLE JOHN ANGUS, farmer; b. 15 May 1914 in Lewes, son of George Allan MacLean and Sarah MacLean; m. 29 October 1952 Gwendolyn Esther Burwash of Saskatoon, and they had four children, Jean, Allan, Mary, and Robert; Presbyterian; d. 15 February 2000 in Charlottetown.

MacLean, a Conservative, was first elected to the Legislative Assembly in a by-election held 8 November 1976 for 4th Queens. He was re-elected in the general elections of 1978 and 1979. On 3 May 1979, he was sworn in as Premier and President of the Executive Council. MacLean served as Minister Responsible for Cultural Affairs from 3 May 1979 to 1980. On 17 November 1981, he retired as premier, but remained a Member of the Legislative Assembly until 31 August 1982. One of the most significant duties Premier MacLean carried out was to lead the province's delegation during the First Ministers' Constitutional Conference.

Before entering provincial politics, MacLean served in the House of Commons. He was first elected in a by-election held 25 June 1951 for Queen's. He was re-elected in the federal elections of 1953, 1957, 1958, 1962, 1963, 1965, 1972, and 1974. He was defeated in the federal elections in 1945 and 1949. On 21 June 1957, MacLean was appointed a Member of the Privy Council and Minister of Fisheries; he served in this position until 22 April 1963. On 20 October 1976, a month after being elected leader of the province's Conservatives, he resigned from the House of Commons.

While an MP, MacLean was a delegate to the 1956 NATO Parliamentary Conference held in Paris and led the Canadian Delegation to the Colombo Plan Conference held in Tokyo in 1960. Subsequently, he led the Canadian Delegation at the United Nations Food and Agriculture Organization Conference held in Rome in 1961, and was a member of the Canadian-Japanese Ministerial Delegation which in 1963 travelled to Tokyo. In 1960 MacLean was a delegate to the 18th Parliamentary Conference in Westminster, England. Five years later, he attended the Commonwealth Conference held in Wellington, New Zealand. MacLean led the Canadian delegation to the Inter-Parliamentary Conference on European Co-operation and Security convened in Helsinki in 1973, and was a delegate to this organization's meeting the following year in Belgrade. In October 1981 he represented the province's Legislature at the 27th Commonwealth Parliamentary Association meeting that took place in Fiji. MacLean was a vice-president of the Canadian Branch of the Commonwealth Parliamentary Association.

MacLean's time as premier is best-known for the government's promotion of the theme of rural renaissance. The MacLean Administration's promotion of the theme of rural revival was, in part, a reaction to the modernizing effects brought upon the Island by the Comprehensive Development Plan. MacLean feared the Comprehensive Development Plan, which emphasized large-scale, government-driven development projects, was eroding the culture of rural life and its attached virtues of self-reliance and community. The MacLean government advocated development that was small in scale and appropriate to the province's rural heritage.

MacLean was a person of integrity who placed a value on candour, making it a central part of his political philosophy. Rob Dykstra, writing in *Atlantic Insight*, described the relationship between MacLean's values, his politics, and the people he represented. "MacLean's popularity stemmed partly from the fact that he exemplified some of the most cherished features of Island life." MacLean's frankness and pride of home was demonstrated on the national stage when he appeared as a guest on the long-running CBC talk show, *Front Page Challenge*. He commented that he considered himself an Islander first and a Canadian second. This irritated the show's panelists but gained him great admiration in his home province.

MacLean received his early education at Summerside High School and Mount Allison Academy. Later he returned to Sackville, New Brunswick, and graduated from Mount Allison University, and after this he studied at the University of British Columbia. MacLean served with the Royal Canadian Air Force (Reserve) from 1939 to 1947. During the Second World War, his plane was shot down behind enemy lines in the Netherlands. MacLean evaded capture for 10 weeks while making his way through Nazi-occupied Europe to the Allied lines. He was awarded the Distinguished Flying Cross in 1942 for his service with the RCAF. Following active service in the Second World War, he commanded the Test and Development Establishment from 1943 to 1945. From 1945 to 1947, MacLean worked for the Missing Research and Enquiry Unit as a Wing Commander. He also served as a president of the RAFES (Canadian Branch) and was a director with the RCAF Memorial Fund. His military service over, MacLean became a farmer.

MacLean was a member of the board of regents for Mount Allison University. From 1983 to 1987, he was a member of the Prince Edward Island Energy Corporation. MacLean was a member of the senior advisory board of the Maritime Provinces Education Foundation and the senior advisory board of the National Museum of Natural Sciences and National Museums of Canada. In 1986 he was the province's Commissioner to Expo in Vancouver. From 1992 to 1996, he served on the board of governors of the Prince Edward Island Museum and Heritage Foundation. In 1998 he completed *Making it Home*, memoirs of his life and career, which also chronicles his escape from behind enemy lines.

MacLean was a member of the United Services Officers Club, the Royal Canadian Air Force Association, the Masonic Lodge, the A.F. and A.M., and the Royal Canadian Legion. He joined the Greater Charlottetown Area Chamber of Commerce. MacLean was awarded an honourary doctor of laws degree from Mount Allison University in 1958 and from the University of Prince Edward Island in 1985. MacLean was a member of the Canadian Club-PEI, and in October 1982 was made an Officer of the Most Venerable Order of St. John Jerusalem. In 1992 he became an Officer of the Order of Canada. John Angus MacLean died 15 February 2000.

References
CDP p. 425; CPG 1977, 1981; CWW 2000 p. 796; HFER Queen's p. 2; MacDonald If You're Stronghearted pp. 345–46, 350–51; Atlantic Insight November 1981; Guardian 16 February 2000; 29 August 2002; Globe and Mail 19 August 1981; Patriot 13 November 1981.

MACLEOD, ANGUS, teacher and farmer; b. 1845, in Valleyfield, son of Alexander MacLeod and Catherine MacLeod; m. 13 January 1872 Jessie McDonald, and they had two children, Alex and Malcolm (died at two years and 10 months); Presbyterian; d. 4 February 1908 in Montague.

MacLeod, a Conservative, was first elected to the House of Assembly in the 1886 general election for 4th Kings. He was re-elected in the general election of 1890. He was defeated in the general election of 1893.

MacLeod was educated in Valleyfield, residing later in life at Brown's Creek in Montague. He was a teacher for 15 years, for a period including 1872 and 1876 to 1877, according to Board of Education records. Following his time as a teacher, he became a farmer. Angus MacLeod died 4 February 1908.

Though the names of MacLeod's parents are unknown, his ancestors came from the Scottish Highlands. Jessie MacLeod was born ca. 1849 and died 15 March 1923.

References
CPG 1887, 1891, 1897; Guardian 5 February 1908; Patriot 18 January 1872; PARO: MNI-Census 1891; Montague Funeral Home Records; Valleyfield United Presbyterian Cemetery Records.

MACLEOD, HECTOR LAWRENCE, carpenter, fisher, farmer, realtor, and contractor; b. 30 June 1944 in Ingonish, Nova Scotia, son of Walter MacLeod and Julia Hardy; m. 16 September 1967 Elizabeth Campbell, and they had two children, Sherri and Patti.

MacLeod, a Liberal, was first elected to the Legislative Assembly in the general election of 1993 for 1st Prince. He was re-elected in the general election of 1996 for the new electoral district of Alberton-Miminegash. He was defeated in the general election of 2000. MacLeod was a member of several Legislative Committees, including agriculture, forestry and environment, fisheries, intergovernmental affairs, and transportation and public accounts. In 1997 he was appointed chair of the Liberal caucus and party Whip. MacLeod served as the Opposition critic for forestry, fisheries, and the environment from 1996 to 2000.

MacLeod served on the Alberton Town Council from 1976 to 1979 and was Mayor from 1979 to 1989 and again from 1991 to 1993. He was president of the Federation of Municipalities of Prince Edward Island in 1988 and 1989, and the Prince Edward Island member for the Canadian Federation of Municipalities. MacLeod also served on the Housing Committee and the Rural and Small Town Committee of the Canadian Federation of Municipalities.

MacLeod received his education in Ingonish from 1949 to 1961. From 1966 to 1970, he worked as a heavy equipment operator, and as a contractor from 1970 to 1980. MacLeod fished from 1980 to 1990, and was a realtor from 1990 to 1993. He also spent some time farming, and is a carpenter by trade. Hector MacLeod lives in Alberton with his family.

Elizabeth MacLeod is the daughter of Robert Erskine Campbell*, who represented 1st Prince from 1962 until his death in 1992.

References
CPG 1996, 1998–1999; Guardian 31 October 1992, 8 March 1993, 5 November 1996.

MACLEOD, NORMAN, farmer, fisherman, merchant; b. 16 April 1867 in High Bank, son of Donald MacLeod and Janet MacLean; m., first, ca. 1898 Sarah Jane Bell, and there were two children, Alice and Hastings; secondly, Alexina "Lexie" MacSwain and there were no children; Church of Christ; d. 7 August 1964 in Montague.

MacLeod, a Conservative, was elected to the Legislative Assembly in a by-election held 14 January 1926 for 4th Kings. The by-election was called due to the death of the sitting member, Albert P. Prowse*.

MacLeod lived in High Bank at the end of MacLeod's Road or "Norman's Road," as it was known in the community. He also lived in Murray River. He was educated at the local school and for a short time attended Murray Harbour School. He farmed in High Bank and fished lobster with a sailboat near Pictou Island. He and his brother John Dan MacLeod established lobster canneries in Little Sands, Nova Scotia, and the Magdalen Islands. MacLeod operated a general merchandising business in Murray River. It was later operated by Charles Horton.

MacLeod was a man of remarkable intellect. His granddaughter remembers him memorizing astronomy. He had a photographic memory and, according to Dr. Malcolm Beck, whom he mentored, Norman would look at a page of the Bible in the morning before he went fishing, and then, while he fished, recite it from memory. At 87 years of age, he participated in a debate on church issues at the Church of Christ in Montague. MacLeod served as an elder and teacher at the Murray River Church of Christ. Norman MacLeod died 7 August 1964 at the Kings County Memorial Hospital in Montague.

Sarah Jane MacLeod, the daughter of Mr. and Mrs. James Bell of White Sands, was born in 1878. She died in 1904. Alexina "Lexie" MacSwain was born 10 August 1870 and died 9 June 1954.

References
Bonnell pp. 5, 7; *Guardian* 14 August 1964; Personal Inverviews: Dr. Malcolm Beck, Isabel Sabapathy.

MACLEOD, PETER B., farmer; b. 26 October 1930 in Lorne Valley, son of Malcolm MacLeod and Annie Palmer; m. 1 August 1953 Glenda Mae MacLeod, and they had four children, Judy, Barry, Donna, and Susan; Presbyterian; d. 29 May 2001 in Montague.

MacLeod, a Conservative, was first elected to the Legislative Assembly in the general election of 1982 for 3rd Kings. He was re-elected in the general election of 1986. He was defeated in the general elections of 1978, 1979, and 1989. In September 1988 MacLeod attended the Commonwealth Parliamentary Association Conference in Canberra, Australia.

MacLeod lived in Lorne Valley his entire life. He received his education at Lorne Valley School and became a farmer, taking over the family farm in 1948. MacLeod was a school trustee and served as chair of the Cardigan Consolidated School trustees. He was a member of the Cardigan Lions Club and served as president of that organization. Peter MacLeod died 29 May 2001 at the Kings County Memorial Hospital.

Glenda MacLeod is the daughter of Angus MacLeod and Annie MacInnis.

References
CPG 1979, 1980, 1989, 1990; *WWPEI* p. 91; *Guardian* 30 May 2001; Questionnaire to Former MLAs.

MACLURE, PRESTON DALZIEL, electrician and cattle breeder; b. 30 July 1913 in Murray Harbour North, son of George T. MacLure and Emma Dalziel; m. 12 August 1936, Margaret Graham, and they had one child, Evelyn; Presbyterian; d. 31 August 1972 in Dundas.

MacLure, a Conservative, was elected to the Legislative Assembly in the general election of 1966. He was defeated in the general election of 1970.

Though born in Murray Harbour North, MacLure resided in Montague for much of his life. He was an electrician by trade and worked on his own for a time, but eventually was employed by Langley Fruit Packers Limited and the Montague Hospital. At the time of his death, MacLure was on staff working on electrical maintenance for the Montague Hospital. Preston MacLure died in the morning of 31 August 1972 while attending the Dundas Plowing Match, where he intended to show his cattle in the Angus competition.

Margaret MacLure was from the community of Gaspereaux.

References
CPG 1970, 1971; *Patriot* 31 August 1972; PARO: Murray Harbour North Presbyterian Cemetery Records.

MACMILLAN, ANGUS D., merchant; b. 18 February 1839 in Wood Islands, son of Duncan MacMillan and Mary Shaw; m. 8 March 1871 Clara S. Janes-Cornish, and they had three children, Clara S. (died in infancy), Charlotte F., and Emma J.; Presbyterian; d. 1 January 1884.

MacMillan, a Liberal, was elected to the House of Assembly in 1882 for 4th Queens. He died while in office.

MacMillan's ancestors emigrated to PEI from Colonsay, Scotland. MacMillan was born in Wood Islands, and was educated at the local school. He resided in Wood Islands until his death on 1 January 1884.

Clara MacMillan was born in Labrador in 1852 and died 25 February 1883. MacMillan and his family lived in the house of John Cornish of Wood Islands, who was Clara MacMillan's adoptive father.

References
CPG 1883; Elections PEI; *Islander* 23 June 1871; PARO: MNI-Census 1881; Wood Islands Presbyterian Cemetery Records.

MACMILLAN, JOHN ROBERT SHAW, miller and fox rancher; b. 14 January 1882 in Alberry Plains, son of George MacMillan and Jemima Shaw; m. ca. 1923 Jessie MacLeod, and they had eight children, Frances, Jean, George, Marina, John, Frederick, Edna, and Florine; United; d. 1 November 1951 in Alberry Plains.

MacMillan, a Conservative, was first elected to the Legislative Assembly in the general election of 1923 for 4th Queens. He was defeated in the general elections of 1927 and 1931.

Shaw MacMillan was educated in the local school. He was a miller and had a fox ranch close to his residence in Alberry Plains. Shaw MacMillan died 1 November 1951 at his home.

Jessie McMillan was born 13 February 1901 and died 16 April 1973.

References
CPG 1924; *Patriot* 1 November 1951; PARO: Cherry Valley Christ Church Cemetery Records.

MACMILLAN, O.B.E., K.C.S.G., Q.C., M.D. (C.M.), F.R.C.S., F.I.C.S., F.A.C.S., L.M.C.C., S.G., HONOURABLE WILLIAM JOSEPH PARNELL, physician and surgeon; b. 24 March 1881 in Clermont, son of Joseph MacMillan and Mary L. Hogan; m. first 12 January 1909 Mary B. Macdonald, of Boston; m. secondly 3 May 1922 Letitia Macdonald (nee Roberts) of Boston, and they had six children, Mary Dorothea, Catherine Bernadette, Joseph, Stephen, Nora, and Allan; Roman Catholic; d. 7 December 1957 in Charlottetown.

MacMillan, a Conservative, was first elected to the Legislative Assembly in the general election of 1923 for 5th Queens. He was re-elected in the general elections of 1927, 1931, 1939, 1943, 1947,

and 1951. He was defeated in the general elections of 1935 and 1955. On 5 September 1923, he was appointed as a Minister without Portfolio in the government of J. D. Stewart.* He was sworn in as the province's first Minister of Education and Public Health on 14 August 1931. After assuming office, he was re-elected by acclamation. During the illness of Premier James Stewart*, MacMillan served as acting Premier. Upon Stewart's death in 1933, MacMillan became Premier as well as Provincial Secretary Treasurer on 13 October, and served as premier until 1935. He served as Leader of the Opposition from 1935 until he resigned from that position on 26 June 1950.

"Doctor W. J. P.," as he was known, entered politics "not with a political motive but to try and obtain a grant for his favourite charity," the Red Cross Society. However, he remained in the Legislature after he achieved this objective and served continuously until 1955, except for the period when the Liberals, under Walter M. Lea*, won every seat in the 1935 general election.

In 1957 MacMillan was appointed to the post of Lieutenant-Governor, but passed away two weeks after his appointment and before he was sworn in. The ceremony was to take place on 16 December.

MacMillan's government was associated, unavoidably, with the effects of the Great Depression. The harsh economic realities of this period contributed to the defeat of his government in 1935. Furthermore, MacMillan entered politics and the provincial government at a time "when finances were strained as a result of two fires which destroyed Prince of Wales College and Falconwood, the then provincial Mental Hospital." He had both buildings rebuilt and, at the same time, elevated Prince of Wales to junior college status. Perhaps MacMillan's greatest success was his procurement of a Carnegie Foundation endowment for establishing the provincial library system that still serves the Island. He also obtained money from the Carnegie Foundation for Prince of Wales College and St. Dunstan's University.

MacMillan received his early education in Clermont. He attended Kensington High School and Prince of Wales College. Upon graduation from McGill in 1908 with a medical degree, he received the Holmes Gold Medal and, in 1915, received an honourary Doctor of Laws degree from the same institution.

MacMillan chaired the Medical Board of the Charlottetown Hospital and served as president of the Children's Aid Society, the Red Cross Society, the Cancer Society, the Anti-tuberculosis League, and the Prince Edward Island Medical Association. He was City Health Officer and served on the Charlottetown School Board. For 22 years, MacMillan was a member of the Canadian Medical Council. He was a fellow and member of the board of governors of the American College of Surgeons and was also a Fellow of the Royal College of Surgeons and the International College of Surgeons. MacMillan was a long-time member of the Charlottetown Rotary Club, held high office in the Knights of Columbus, and was honourary chieftain of the Caledonia Club. He was awarded an Order of the British Empire for his work on the home front during the Second World War. W. J. P. MacMillan died 7 December 1957 at the Charlottetown Hospital.

Mary B. MacMillan and Letitia MacMillan were the daughters of Hugh S. Macdonald of South Boston, Massachusetts. Mary Dorothea MacMillan, a daughter, married Alban Farmer*, and Catherine Bernadette MacMillan, another daughter, married Charles St. Clair Trainor*.

References
CPG 1953; Premiers' Gallery; *Patriot* 7 December 1957.

MACNEILL, DANIEL FRANCIS, business person; b. 30 August 1885 in Summerside, son of James A. MacNeill* and Sarah Eliza MacNeill; m. Pearl Tamlyn, and they had 14 children, Francis*, John, Tanton, Hubert*, Gerald, Edward, Ronald, Gertrude, Margaret, Pearl, Dorothy, Anita, Kathleen (died in infancy), and Joseph (died in infancy); Roman Catholic; d. 24 September 1946 in Summerside.

MacNeill, a Conservative, was first elected to the Legislative Assembly in the general election of 1943 for 5th Prince. He was defeated in the general elections of 1935 and 1939. He died while sitting as a Member. MacNeill was also a long-time member of the Summerside Town Council, having served 14 years at the time of his death.

He came from a family with a long political history in the province. His father, and his brother Leonard Malcolm*, served as Members of the Legislative Assembly, and two of MacNeill's sons, Francis* and Hubert*, also served in the Legislature. All represented 5th Prince.

MacNeill became the proprietor of his family's farm machinery firm, James A. MacNeill and Sons, founded by his father. He also served as the deputy chief of the Summerside Fire Department. MacNeill spent a great deal of time promoting the welfare of the department and increasing its status in equipment and efficiency. Daniel MacNeill died 24 September 1946 in the Prince County Hospital.

Pearl MacNeill was from Summerside.

References
CPG 1946; *Patriot* 25 September 1946; *Summerside Journal* 26 September 1946; PARO: St. Paul's Roman Catholic Church Summerside Records Book.

MACNEILL, FRANCIS J. "PEG," teacher and school superintendent; b. 15 October 1912 in Summerside, son of Daniel Francis MacNeill* and Pearl Tamlyn; m. 31 January 1940 Anne Marie de la Garde of St. Isadore, Gloucester, England, and they had five children, Patricia, Mary Frances, Janice, Danny, and Donald; Roman Catholic; d. 12 July 2000 in Summerside.

MacNeill, a Conservative, was elected to the Legislative Assembly in a by-election held 26 November 1946 for 5th Prince. He was defeated in the general election of 1947. The by-election was held as a result of his father's death.

MacNeill came from a family with a long political history in the province. His grandfather James A.*, his father Daniel Francis*, his uncle Leonard Malcolm*, and his brother Hubert* were Members of the Legislative Assembly.

"Peg" MacNeill, as he was known, received his early education in Summerside, later attending Prince of Wales College in Charlottetown for two years. He received a Bachelor of Arts from St. Dunstan's College in 1935 and a Bachelor of Science from St. Francis Xavier University in 1936. In 1961 MacNeill received a Bachelor of Education degree from the University of New Brunswick. He began teaching a grade VI class in Summerside in April 1937 and continued to teach until the outbreak of the Second World War. He served overseas with the Cape Breton Highlanders and was discharged at war's end with the rank of Captain. Upon returning to the province, MacNeill went back to his pre-war teaching job. He taught classes in all subjects in grades XI and XII, which at the time were new grade levels in the Summerside school system. MacNeill was the first principal of Elm Street School and served as superintendent of all the Summerside schools, and later as the Superintendent of the Unit 2 School Board. When he retired from service in the school system in 1977, he had more than 40 years' experience.

MacNeill was a member of the Board of Directors of the Canadian Association of School Administrators, the Prince Edward Island Teacher's Federation and the Teachers Superannuation Board. He was president of the Summerside Branch of the Royal Canadian Legion, the Rotary Club and the Prince County Caledonia Club. MacNeill also was president of the Summerside Lobster Carnival and Livestock Exhibition. "Peg" MacNeill died 12 July 2000 at the Prince County Hospital.

Frances and Anne MacNeill were married in Dartmouth, Nova Scotia.

References
CPG 1947, 1948; *Journal-Pioneer* 7 April 1977, 13 July 2000; *Patriot* 27 November 1946.

MACNEILL, M.D., HUBERT BERNARD, physician and president of housing company; b. 4 March 1922 in Summerside, son of Daniel Francis MacNeill* and Pearl T. Tamlyn; m. 19 February 1952 Christine Mary Baker, and they had eight children, Sandra, Monica, Stephen, Robert, Richard, John, Carolyn, and Cynthia; Roman Catholic.

MacNeill, a Conservative, was first elected to the Legislative Assembly in the general election of 1959 for 5th Prince. He was re-elected in the general election of 1962. He was defeated in the general election of 1966. He was appointed Minister of Health in 1959. He served in that portfolio until 1965, when he was appointed Minister of Welfare and Labour.

MacNeill came from a family keenly interested in politics. His grandfather James MacNeill*, his father Daniel Francis, his uncle Leonard Malcolm MacNeill*, and his brother Francis J.* "Peg" all served in the Legislative Assembly, and each represented 5th Prince.

He received his primary education in Summerside, later attending Prince of Wales College. MacNeill served four years in the military during the Second World War, two of which were overseas. Following his service, he enrolled in medical school at Dalhousie University, from which he graduated with a medical degree. MacNeill began

medical practice in 1953. In 1958 he and four Summerside businesspeople started the Hillcrest Housing Company, a housing project for the use of Department of National Defence personnel stationed at CFB Summerside. The project was later expanded to other areas of Summerside. MacNeill was a director of the company and later became president. In 1983 he became manager of the Summerside Medical Centre. MacNeill was a member of the Royal Canadian Legion and the Knights of Columbus. Hubert Bernard MacNeill resides in Summerside.

Christine MacNeill is the daughter of Earl and Lily Baker.

References
CPG 1966, 1970; *Hillcrest Housing Limited* p. 7; PEI *Journal of the Legislative Assembly* 1965 p. 3, 1960 p. 2, 1966 p. 2; Questionnaire to Former MLAs.

MACNEILL, JAMES A., blacksmith and trader; b. 22 July 1854 in Travellers Rest, son of Malcolm MacNeill and Isabel McDonald; m. 4 August 1881 Sarah E., and they had eight children, Gertrude, Leonard*, Daniel Francis*, Willard, Pearl, Ella Mae, Ronald James, and Dunstan Joseph; Roman Catholic; d. 28 January 1927.

MacNeill, a Conservative, was first elected to the Legislative Assembly in the general election of 1908 for 5th Prince. He was re-elected in the general elections of 1912, 1915, 1919, and 1923. He was defeated in the general elections of 1900, 1904, and 1927. On 10 December 1910, he was appointed as Commissioner of Public Works in the Mathieson* Administration.

Two of MacNeill's sons served in the Legislative Assembly. Leonard* was elected in the general election of 1931 for 5th Prince and Daniel* was elected in the general election of 1944 for the same riding. Two of MacNeill's grandsons served in the Legislative Assembly. Francis "Peg"* was elected in 1946 for 5th Prince, and Hubert* was elected for the same riding in the 1959 general election, and again in 1962.

Prior to his career in provincial politics, MacNeill served for a number of years on the Summerside Town Council and was Mayor from 1901 to 1904. He was Chair of the Water Commission from 1906 to 1907 and Chief of the Fire Department from 1912 to 1916.

MacNeill was educated at the village school in Travellers Rest. He was associated with John

Harrington in the blacksmithing business under the name Harrington and MacNeill. The firm did a great deal of work on ships built in the Summerside area. He also served as the president of the Exhibition and Park Association. James MacNeill died 28 January 1927.

Sarah MacNeill was born 5 October 1855 and died 28 July 1954.

References
CPG 1916, 1928; Elections PEI; *Maple Leaf Magazine* May 1908; PARO: St. Paul's Roman Catholic Cemetery Records.

MACNEILL, M.D., C.M., JOHN FORBES, physician and publisher; b. 11 May 1870 in Long Creek, son of John Alexander MacNeill and Catherine MacKenzie; m. 23 September 1903 Ruby Darrach, and they had one daughter, Ruby; Baptist; d. 8 May 1962 in Summerside.

MacNeill, a Liberal, was first elected to the Legislative Assembly in a by-election held 30 August 1922 for 5th Prince. He was re-elected in the general election of 1927 and in a by-election held 12 October 1932. He was defeated in the general elections of 1923 and 1931. In August 1927 he was sworn in as a Minister without Portfolio in the Albert Saunders* Administration.

MacNeill was educated in public schools and at Prince of Wales College in Charlottetown. He operated drugstores in Montague and Summerside for a time before he went to McGill University in Montreal to obtain his medical degree. Upon returning to the Island, MacNeill established a practice in Summerside, which he maintained for 55 years. He served as president of the Medical Society of Canada and was involved in numerous Canadian medical organizations. He served as a Grand Master of the Masonic Order in Prince Edward Island. He and his family attended the United Baptist Church in Summerside. John MacNeill died 8 May 1962 at his home.

Ruby MacNeill, the daughter of Dr. D. Darrach of Kensington, was born 30 September 1878 and died 25 February 1963.

References
CPG 1929; Elections PEI; *Guardian* 31 August 1922; *Patriot* 8 May 1962; PARO: Summerside People's Protestant Cemetery Records.

MACNEILL, LEONARD MALCOLM, accountant; b. 11 December 1883 in Summerside, son of James A. MacNeill* and Sarah Eliza MacNeill; m. Elisabeth Regina Deagan, and they had six children, Leonore, Helen, Isabel, George, Virginia, and Hilda; Roman Catholic; d. 23 February 1932 in Summerside.

MacNeill, a Conservative, was elected to the Legislative Assembly in the general election of 1931 for 5th Prince. Upon his election, he was appointed Minister of Public Works and Highways, and he died while serving in this Ministry. Before entering provincial politics, MacNeill served as chairman of the Summerside Town Council's finance committee.

MacNeill came from a family with a long political history in the province. MacNeill's father James A.* and his brother Daniel Francis* both served as Members of the Legislative Assembly. Two of Daniel's sons, Francis "Peg"* and Hubert*, were also MLAs.

MacNeill was educated at Summerside High School. He was employed by the Town of Summerside, where he worked under Hugh J. Massey and became an accountant. MacNeill became associated with the firm of R. T. Holman Limited, where he worked for almost 30 years. In 1928, when he resigned, he was the chief accountant and one of the directors of the firm. His retirement was due to the failing health of his father, which resulted in MacNeill taking charge of the large machinery business his father had operated.

Outside of his private and political careers, MacNeill was actively involved in his community. He was a member of the Knights of Columbus. He also served as state deputy for the Prince Edward Island Council of the Summerside Trotting Park Association and the Charlottetown Gyro Club. Leonard MacNeill died on 23 February 1932.

Elisabeth MacNeill, the daughter of Phillip and Elisabeth Lacey Deagan, was born in 1885 and died in 1968.

References
CPG 1932; *Maple Leaf Magazine* April 1932; *Patriot* 24 February 1932; PARO: Census 1901; St. Paul's Roman Catholic Church Summerside Cemetery Records.

MACNEVIN, ALEXANDER J., general merchant and farmer; b. 20 September 1885 in Argyle Shore, son of John MacNevin and Ann Campbell; m. 1 September 1915 Perle Elnora McLeod, and there were no children; Church of Scotland; d. 25 August 1937 in Toronto.

MacNevin, a Conservative, was first elected to the Legislative Assembly in the general election of 1915 for 1st Queens. He was re-elected in the general election of 1923. He was defeated in the general election of 1919. According to the *Evening Patriot,* he was an able debater in the Legislature and a vigilant custodian of his constituents' interests. The *Evening Patriot* goes on to say that he was a keen businessman and had an exceptionally wide knowledge of agricultural problems.

MacNevin was educated in the local school and also attended Charlottetown Business College. For several years, he was a general merchant and farmer in Bonshaw. About 10 years before his death, he became a partner of the Canada Varnish Company Limited in Toronto. Alexander MacNevin died 25 August 1937.

Pearle MacNevin, the daughter of Colin McLeod who emigrated from Scotland in 1841, was born 1 April 1895.

References
CPG 1916, 1918, 1921, 1928; *Evening Patriot* 3 May 1921; PARO: Accession 3043/356; Argyle Shore Cemetery Records.

MACNUTT, FRANK LONGWORTH, farmer, insurance salesperson, and produce inspector; b. 29 April 1897 in Darnley, the son of Robert F. MacNutt and Lulu Cousins; m. 22 October 1944 to Gwendolyn B. MacLean, and they had two children, Isabel and Eleanor; Presbyterian; d. 20 September 1983 in Malpeque.

MacNutt, a Liberal, was first elected to the Legislative Assembly in the general election of 1951 for 3rd Prince. He was re-elected in the general election of 1955. He was defeated in the general elections of 1959 and 1962. One of MacNutt's opponents in the general election of 1951 was Hilda Ramsay. Ramsay was the first female candidate to campaign for a seat in the provincial legislature. She was a candidate for the CCF Party.

MacNutt received his early education in his native community of Darnley. Later in life, he moved to Malpeque where he owned a farm. MacNutt was also an insurance salesperson for Hyndman and Company Limited and for H. L. Sear Insurance Limited. From 1936 to 1946, he acted as the Fruit and Vegetable Inspector for the provincial government. MacNutt was a Member of the Keir Memorial Presbyterian Church and was active in church and community organizations. MacNutt died at his home in Malpeque on 20 September 1983.

On 22 October 1944, MacNutt married Gwendolyn B. MacNutt, the daughter of Roy E. MacLean.

References
CPG 1958, 1953, 1960, 1963; *Guardian* 24 October 1983; Elections PEI.

MACNUTT, PETER, farmer, merchant, and officeholder; b. 5 April 1834 in Darnley, son of Peter S. MacNutt and Mary Longworth; m. 30 January 1861 Anna Stewart, and they had five children, Annabella Emma, Mary M. Ella, Lucy Penelope, D. Preston, and C. Ernest; Presbyterian; d. 24 October 1919 in Charlottetown.

MacNutt, a Liberal, was first elected to the Legislative Assembly in the general election of 1897 for 4th Prince. He was elected in the general elections of 1900 and 1904 for 3rd Prince. Earlier in his political career, MacNutt was elected to the Legislative Council in a by-election in June 1882 for 2nd Prince. He was re-elected to the Legislative Council later in 1882 and again in 1890 for 2nd Prince.

MacNutt's early education took place in the local school in Darnley, and from there he went to Central Academy in Charlottetown. He was a successful businessperson and farmer. In 1857 he entered into a partnership with Dougald S. MacNutt in general merchandising at Malpeque. When Dougald died in 1888, MacNutt continued the business on his own. D. Preston entered into partnership with his father in 1902 and the business became known as MacNutt and Son. MacNutt retired from this enterprise in 1910, due to failing health.

Throughout his career, he held numerous public offices. In 1863 MacNutt was appointed as one of His Majesty's coroners for the Island. He served as a Commissioner of Small Debts until 1873, and as Prince County Sheriff from 1875 to 1877. MacNutt owned and operated a farm in Malpeque. In the local community he was considered one of the leading citizens of his day.

He was actively involved with his church, where he served for 30 years as the chair of the Managers of the Presbyterian Church in Malpeque. MacNutt served in the military as the Captain of the Malpeque Rifles, a company of the Prince County Regiment of the Volunteer Brigade. Peter MacNutt died 24 October 1919.

Anna MacNutt, the daughter of Thomas Stewart of Malpeque, was born ca. 1840.

References
CPG 1905; *Past and Present* pp. 341–42; *Islander* 15 February 1861; *Patriot* 25 October 1919; PARO: MNI-Hutchinson's pp. 170, 231, 240, 276; MNI-Census 1881.

MACNUTT, THOMAS, farmer; b. 4 December 1862 in Malpeque, son of James Maxwell MacNutt and Katherine Stewart; m. 1 July 1909 Sophie Carr of Campbellton, New Brunswick, and there were no children; United; d. 1942.

MacNutt, a Conservative, was first elected in a by-election held 30 August 1922 for 3rd Prince. He was re-elected in the general elections of 1923 and 1931. He was defeated in the general elections of 1927 and 1935. On 14 October 1933, he was named Minister of Agriculture.

MacNutt farmed for a living. He received his education at the local school, and attended Princeton United Church. Thomas MacNutt died in 1942.

Sophie MacNutt, the daughter of Mr. A. F. Carr, was born in 1876 and died 2 December 1932.

References
CPG 1924, 1934; *Maple Leaf Magazine* December 1932; PARO: Princetown United Church Presbyterian Records.

MACPHAIL, LIEUTENANT-COLONEL JAMES ALEXANDER "SANDY," engineer, professor, and university administrator; b. 25 January 1870 in Orwell, son of William Macphail and Catherine E. Smith; m. 10 May 1910 Agnes Mary Moray, and they had one child, Moray St. John; Church of Scotland; d. 13 January 1949.

Macphail, a Conservative, was first elected to the Legislative Assembly in a by-election held 15 November 1911 for 4th Queens. The by-election was necessary due to the appointment of F. L. Haszard* to the provincial Supreme Court. Macphail was re-elected in the general election of 1912. On 24 April 1915, his absence from the Legislative Assembly was excused due to his service in the war, and he was not a candidate in the general election of 1915.

Macphail received his early education in local schools and at Prince of Wales College in Charlottetown. He then attended McGill University in Montreal, where he earned a Bachelor of Science in Civil Engineering, going on to become a professor in the School of Mining at Queen's University in Kingston, Ontario. Macphail was appointed to the Department of Civil Engineering in 1904. He returned to Queen's after the First World War in 1919 and was appointed head of the Department of Civil Engineering, a post he held for 20 years. When Macphail retired in 1939, he was awarded an honourary degree. He was also awarded an honourary degree from McGill. He was the first recipient of the Medal for Meritorious Service to Queen's, awarded by the Montreal Branch of Queen's Alumni.

In the First World War, Macphail served as a commanding officer of the Canadian Officers Training Corps at Queen's. He was a Major in No. 5 Company of the Canadian Engineers. He formed the Queen's Company of Military Engineers and in 1914 was asked to assemble and proceed with this company to Valcartier. The company formed a nucleus from which contingent parts went overseas to serve mainly as engineers for the Canadian Air Force. During his time in the military, Macphail rose from Major to Lieutenant-Colonel. James Alexander Macphail died 13 January 1949.

Macphail was the brother of Sir Andrew Macphail, the noted physician and surgeon, agriculturalist, teacher, and writer. The Macphail Homestead is presently maintained by the provincial government as an historic site.

Agnes Macphail was the daughter of Archdeacon Macmorine of Kingston.

References
CPG 1912; Elections PEI; *Queen's Alumni Review* September/October 1970; PARO: Free Church of Scotland Book 4 p. 94; PARO: Macphail Family File.

MACPHAIL, C.M., HONOURABLE ROBERT LLOYD GEORGE, merchant; b. 22 March 1920 in New Haven, son of Robert Archibald MacPhail and Catherine C. MacLean; m. 8 January 1955 Helen MacDougall, and they had four children, Judith Anne, Lynn, Ferne, and Robert; Baptist; d. 2 July 1995 in Charlottetown.

MacPhail, a Conservative, was first elected to the Legislative Assembly in a by-election held 17 July 1961 for 2nd Queens. He was re-elected in the general elections of 1962, 1966, 1970, 1974, 1978, 1979, and 1982. He held the Ministries of Industry and Natural Resources, and Tourism and Development, from 16 June 1965 until 28 July 1966. During his time in Opposition, from 1966 to 1978, MacPhail was finance critic. From July 1976 until September of the same year, he served as interim Conservative leader. In the J. Angus MacLean* Administration, MacPhail was appointed Minister of

Finance and Chairman of the Treasury Board from 1979 until 1981. He was Minister of Development from 3 May 1979, until the department was phased out in 1980. On 21 October 1982, MacPhail was appointed Minister of Finance and the Chairman of the Treasury Board, as well as Minister responsible for Tourism. On 1 August 1985, he was appointed Lieutenant-Governor of Prince Edward Island.

MacPhail received his early education in New Haven, later attending Prince of Wales College. He followed in his father's footsteps by operating the family's store, R. A. MacPhail General Merchants, for 30 years. During this time, he also incorporated a farm supply business into the operation. MacPhail served for 14 years as director of the Provincial Exhibition Association and the Charlottetown Driving Park. Before school consolidation, he was a trustee of his local school. He was invested as a Knight of the Order of St. John of Jerusalem. Lloyd MacPhail was a member of the Charlottetown Rotary Club and a fellow of the Canadian Red Cross Society. On 1 March 1995, he received the Order of Canada. MacPhail was a member of the Clyde River Baptist Church where he served as deacon, Sunday school teacher, trustee, and congregational secretary. Lloyd MacPhail died 2 July 1995.

Helen MacPhail, the daughter of John W. MacDougall and Mary E. Beer of Argyle Shore, currently resides in the family home at Clyde River.

References
CPG 1990; *WWPEI* p. 1; *Guardian* 1 August 1985, 3 July 2001.

MACPHEE, Q.C., HUGH FRANCIS, lawyer; b. 8 December 1895 in Georgetown, son of Captain Hugh MacPhee and Eileen McKenna; m. 10 September 1923 Loretta Leonard, and they had two children, Mary and Eileen; Roman Catholic; d. 15 July 1957 in Charlottetown.

MacPhee, a Conservative, was first elected to the Legislative Assembly in a by-election held 14 January 1926 for 3rd Kings. He was re-elected in the general elections of 1931, 1939, and 1943. He was defeated in the general elections of 1927 and 1935. MacPhee served as Minister of Public Works and Highways from January 1926 until the general election of 1927, and again from 1931 until 1933 when he was appointed Attorney-General. MacPhee served in this position until the general election of 1935. In 1945 he resigned his seat in the Legislature to contest the federal election in King's unsuccessfully.

During the First World War, MacPhee enlisted in the Canadian Army and served in France with the 8th Artillery Siege Battery. Following his return, he was educated at St. Dunstan's College and Laval University. MacPhee was admitted to the Bar in 1922 and received the designation of King's Counsel in 1931. He was a partner in the firm of MacPhee and Trainor. During his legal career, MacPhee was one of the most prominent lawyers in the province.

MacPhee was actively involved in his community. He served as president of the Charlottetown Board of Trade and as a member of the governing bodies of St. Dunstan's University and the Charlottetown Hospital. MacPhee was a member of the Charlottetown School Board and the Knights of Columbus. Hugh MacPhee died 15 July 1957 in the Charlottetown Hospital.

Loretta MacPhee was the daughter of William Leonard of Cornwall.

References
CPG 1940; *Patriot* 16 July 1957; PARO: 1901 Census; Charlottetown Roman Catholic Cemetery Records.

MACPHERSON, LYNWOOD, farmer and business person; b. 21 September 1947 in Charlottetown, son of Callum MacPherson of Head of Montague and Evelyn Martin of Flat River; m. 17 November 1973 Mary Patricia Evans, and they had four children, Bethany, Jennifer, Susan, and Jeffrey; Presbyterian.

MacPherson, a Liberal, was first elected to the Legislative Assembly in the general election of 1986 for 4th Queens. He was re-elected in the general elections of 1989 and 1993. He was defeated in the general election of 1996 in the new electoral district of Belfast-Pownal Bay. On 21 May 1996, MacPherson was appointed Minister of Provincial Affairs and Attorney General. While a Member, MacPherson served as chair of the Intersessional Committee on Human Rights and served as vice-chair of the House Public Accounts Committee. He also served as a member of Policy Board and was a member of various Legislative Committees dealing with agriculture, health and social services, fisheries, industry, tourism and labour, and energy and forestry. MacPherson chaired the Electoral Reform Committee in the early 1990s.

MacPherson received his early education in

the Flat River School, and later attended Montague Regional High School. He was a tobacco farmer, and a shareholder and plant manager for Belfast Tobacco Growers Limited. MacPherson later became one of the first Island farmers to grow ginseng, at the time a new crop to the province. He served as a director of the Federal Enterprise Development Board and was a member of the Commodity Marketing Board. MacPherson was a member of the board of the Southern Kings and Queens Regional Services Centre, and a director of Eastern Ventures. He was the director of the Belfast Recreation Centre and a member of the Belfast Consultative Committee. Lynwood MacPherson is also a member of the Belfast Fire Department and a charter member of the Belfast Lions Club.

Mary MacPherson was born on 18 December 1947. She is the daughter of Joseph Evans and Rita MacQuillan of Tracadie Cross.

References
CPG 1996, 1997; PEI ECO 341/96; *WWPEI* p. 94; *Guardian* 2 February 1985, 15 March 1993, 16 August 1996.

MACRAE, MAJOR ANDREW BOSWALL, soldier, dairy farmer, and business person;

b. 14 September 1919 in Charlottetown, son of Frederick Taylor MacRae and Annie McGowan Boswall; m. 8 April 1941 Rena MacLean Jay, and they had one child, Andrew Ian; Presbyterian.

MacRae, a Conservative, was first elected to the Legislative Assembly in the general election of 1959 for 3rd Queens. He was re-elected in the general election of 1962. He was defeated in the general elections of 1955 and 1966. On 16 September 1960, MacRae was appointed Minister of Agriculture and served in that portfolio until 1966.

MacRae received his early education at Central Royalty School and went on to study at Prince of Wales College. At one time he lived in East Royalty. MacRae was a dairy farmer and he operated a business. A retired Major in the Canadian Army, he fought in the Second World War and the Korean War. He was a member of the Lake Superior Regiment from 17 July 1940 to 9 April 1946, where he rose to the rank of Captain. MacRae served in the United Kingdom and northwest Europe throughout the Second World War. When called to duty in Korea, he was part of the Royal Canadian Regiment from 1 August 1950 until 1 April 1953. By the time he retired, MacRae had earned the rank of Major. He is currently a member of the United Services Officers Club. Andrew MacRae and his wife live in Stratford.

Rena MacRae is the daughter of Crawford Jay and Eliza M. Jay.

References
CPG 1956, 1966, 1970; PEI *Journal of the Legislative Assembly* 1966 p. 3.

MACRAE, DANIEL ALEXANDER, business person;

b. in 1876 in Heatherdale; son of Angus MacRae and Annie Campbell; m. 1916 Alice May Gordon, and they had three children, Gordon, Jean, and Earl; d. 30 July 1964 in Charlottetown.

MacRae, a Liberal, was elected to the Legislative Assembly in a by-election held 4 July 1949 for 4th Kings.

MacRae was a businessperson who owned and operated a grist mill in Heatherdale. In the early 1940s, he operated an animal feed service in association with Shur Gain. The mills are no longer in service but his son, Gordon, continues to operate the family farm. Daniel MacRae died 30 July 1964 at the Prince Edward Island Hospital.

References
CPG 1950; *Patriot* 1 August 1964.

MADDIX, ROBERT JOSEPH, youth worker and civil servant;

b. 26 September 1960 in Wellington, son of René Maddix and Alice Gallant; m. 17 July 1982 Cathy Fraser, and they had two children, Keenan and Brody; Roman Catholic.

Maddix, a Liberal, was first elected to the Legislative Assembly in the general election of 1993 for 3rd Prince. He was elected in the general election of 1996 for the new electoral district of Evangeline-Miscouche. He was defeated in the general election of 2000. In 1997 he was named Opposition critic for economic development and tourism. During his time in the Legislature, he served on a number of Legislative Committees, including community affairs and economic development, agriculture, forestry and environment, social development, privileges, rules and private bills, and the Standing Committee on the Constitution of Canada. Maddix was also on the Community Consultative Committee. From 1999 to 2000, he served as Opposition House Leader.

Maddix received his early education in Evangeline and at the Evangeline Regional High School. From 1978 to 1979, he attended Université de Moncton, where he studied administration. From 1979 to 1980, Maddix was a student in the accounting technician program offered by Holland College. From 1980 to 1988, he worked at Jeunesse Acadien Limitée in Wellington. Maddix was employed as a tourism development officer in the Department of Tourism and Parks from 1988 to 1992. From May to September 2000, Maddix worked as an assistant to Joe McGuire, Member of Parliament for Egmont. He currently works as an economic development officer at Baie Acadienne in Wellington.

For some time Maddix has been actively involved in the province's Francophone community. He was the founding president of the Club Richelieu Evangeline and the first recipient of the Provincial Acadian Youth Award. Maddix received the Ordre de la Pléiadre for his contribution to the Francophone community. For several years, he worked as an organizer of the Prince Edward Island delegation to Les Jeux d'Acadie and has been active in community youth groups. Robert Maddix lives with his family in Abrams Village.

Cathy Maddix, a native of Summerside, was born on 31 December 1960. She is the daughter of Joseph Fraser of Summerside and Theresa Kilbride, originally from Portage.

References
CPG 1998-1999; *Guardian* 7 June 1989, 9 May 1996; Questionnaire to Former MLAs.

MALONEY, O.P.E.I., M.D., JOHN H., physician; b. 6 February 1918 in Barachois, Quebec, son of Val Maloney and Hildred McAuley; m. 27 December 1945 Marguerite Jobe, and they had five children, Peter, Leslie, Eric, Tara, and Valerie; Roman Catholic; d. 10 May 2001, in Charlottetown.

Maloney, a Liberal, was first elected to the Legislative Assembly in the general election of 1970 for 6th Queens. He was re-elected in the general elections of 1974 and 1978. On 25 June 1970, Maloney was appointed Minister of Health and Welfare and held this Ministry until 1972. He served as Minister of Industry and Commerce from 10 November 1971 to 2 May 1974, and as Minister of Development from 10 October 1972 to 2 May 1979. He also served as Minister of Education from 1978 to 1979. In the mid-1960s, Maloney was a central figure in a citizens' lobby group seeking the establishment of a new provincial university. In 1969 the provincial government created the University of Prince Edward Island.

Maloney studied at St. Francis Xavier University, and in 1942 received his medical degree from McGill University. From 1943 to 1946, he served overseas in the Royal Canadian Army Medical Corps. Maloney was the chief of obstetrics and gynaecology at the Charlottetown Hospital and helped establish the Charlottetown Clinic. He was a physician at the Queen Elizabeth Hospital and was a consultant at the Alberton and O'Leary hospitals.

Maloney had a lifelong interest in archaeology and devoted years of study to the Island's original inhabitants from 7000 or 8000 BC. He served on the federal task force that preceded the introduction of Medicare in Canada. Maloney was awarded a life membership in the Prince Edward Island Medical Society in 1987. He was a member of the Charlottetown School Board, the Advisory Committee of the Prince Edward Island Nursing Association, and the Premier's Task Force on Alcoholism and Extended Care. He served as chair of the federal Task Force: Methods of Delivery of Medical Care. In 1967 Maloney was awarded the Centennial Medal and was posthumously awarded the Prince Edward Island Order of Merit Medal in June 2001.

Maloney served as president of the Prince Edward Island Medical Society, the Prince Edward Island Mental Health Association, the Atlantic Association of Obstetrics and Gynecology, the Provincial Archaeology Board, and the Prince Edward Island Historical Society. He was honoraury treasurer of the Canadian Medical Association Committee on Economics and held a senior membership in the Canadian Medical Association. He worked and lived most of his life in Charlottetown. John Maloney died 10 May 2001.

Marguerite Maloney was born 20 March 1917 in Glace Bay, Nova Scotia. She was the daughter of James Lawrence Jobe and Mary Beatrice Jesso.

References
CPG 1978; *ECO* 727/78; *WWPEI* p. 95; *Guardian* 20 February 1979, 2 June 1990, 12 May 2001, 6 June 2001.

MARTIN, ALEXANDER, merchant, farmer, and teacher; b. 14 March 1842 in Springton, son of Alex Martin of Springton and Isabelle Martin; m. 8 February 1868 Anne McLeod, and they had six children, Maggie Belle, Rachel, Christy Ann, Albert John, Roderick M., and Isabella Catherine; Presbyterian; d. 13 April 1921 in Valleyfield.

Martin, a Conservative, was elected to the House of Assembly in a February 1884 by-election for 4th Queens. He was defeated in the general elections of 1886, 1890, and 1893. He was elected to the Legislative Council in the general election of 1886 for 2nd Queens. Despite his service in the Legislative Council, he was in favour of its abolishment, which occurred in 1893. Martin was elected to the House of Commons in 1896 for East Queen's, was defeated in 1900, and was re-elected for Queen's in 1904.

Martin was educated in the district school. He spent his early years in Springton, but later resided in Valleyfield, where he operated a general store from 1869 to 1905. For some time, Martin farmed in Springton and Valleyfield. He was a teacher for nine years, six of which were at the Valleyfield school. Alexander Martin died 13 April 1921.

Anne Martin, the daughter of Roderick McLeod of Uigg, was born ca. 1844 and died in March 1905.

References
CDP p. 354; *CPG* 1889; *Past and Present* p. 341; PARO: MNI-Census 1881.

MARTIN, DONALD CHARLES, teacher and lawyer; b. 1 February 1849 in Belfast, son of Peter and Sarah Martin; Presbyterian; d. 10 January 1888 in Charlottetown.

Martin, a Liberal, was first elected to the House of Assembly in the general election of 1882 for 4th Queens. He was re-elected in the general election of 1886. He died, quite suddenly, while in office.

Martin received his early education at the local school in Belfast. He attended Prince of Wales College in Charlottetown on a scholarship, and graduated as a grammar school teacher. Martin then went to Dalhousie University in Halifax. Throughout his education, he worked as a tutor to pay for his studies. Martin was a teacher in Alberton High School for five years before he began studying law with Hodgson and McLeod* of Charlottetown in 1875. Martin was called to the Bar in 1879. In that year he became a partner in the firm McLean and Martin, which became McLean, Martin and McDonald when Hector Charles McDonald* joined the firm. Donald Martin died 10 January 1888.

References
CPG 1885; Elections PEI; *Daily Examiner* 11 January 1888; PARO: St. John's Presbyterian Church Record; Martin Family File.

MARTIN, JOHN S., farmer; b. 2 August 1855 in Kinross, son of Samuel Martin and Sarah Campbell; m. 1 January 1875 Hattie MacKenzie of Charlottetown, and they had seven children, Annie C., Samuel, John William, Hugh, James B., Sarah, and Mary E.; Presbyterian/Church of Scotland; d. 29 June 1946.

Martin, a Conservative, was first elected to the Legislative Assembly in the general election of 1912 for 4th Queens. He was re-elected in the general election of 1915. He was defeated in the general election of 1919. On 29 March 1916, he was elected Speaker.

Martin received his education at the Uigg Grammar School and was a farmer in that community. John Martin died 29 June 1946.

Martin's wife, the daughter of F. John MacKenzie, was born 8 March 1864 and died 20 June 1942.

References
CPG 1918, 1920; PARO: Census 1901; Church of Scotland Cemetery Records.

MATHESON, ALEXANDER WALLACE, teacher, lawyer, and judge; b. 11 June 1903 in Bellevue, son of Archibald A. Matheson and Margaret MacPherson; m. 25 August 1937 Helen B. Farquharson, and they had five children, Frances Janet, Ellen Margaret (predeceased her father), James Alexander, Thomas Allan, and Andrew; United; d. 3 March 1976 in Charlottetown.

Matheson, a Liberal, was first elected to the Legislative Assembly in a by-election held 7 November 1940 for 2nd Queens. He was defeated in the general election of 1943, and from 1946 to 1947 served as Clerk of the Legislative Assembly. Matheson was elected in the general election of 1947 for 4th Kings. He was re-elected in the general elections of 1951, 1955, 1959, and 1962. He was sworn in as Minister of Health and Welfare on 12 March 1948, and served in that Ministry until 1953. Upon the appointment of Premier J. Walter Jones* to the Senate in 1953, Matheson was elected by the Liberal caucus as its new leader. He won the vote on the second ballot, defeating Walter Darby*, Douglas MacKinnon*, William Hughes*, and E. P. Cullen*.

Matheson was sworn in as the premier of

Prince Edward Island on 25 May 1953. His party was re-elected in the 1955 general election. From 1955 to 1959, Matheson held the positions of Premier, Advocate General, Attorney-General, and President of Executive Council. He was also Minister of Welfare and Labour in 1956 and 1958. He and the Liberals were defeated by the Conservatives, led by Walter R. Shaw*, in the general election of 1959. After having spent the last 24 years governing, the Liberals found themselves out of office. Ex-premier Matheson was said to have commented that at least now there would be a decent opposition. He remained as Leader of the Liberal Party and Leader of the Opposition following the 1959 general election. In September 1961, Matheson won an overwhelming vote of confidence from a provincial Liberal convention and continued to serve as Leader of the Opposition until 1966. He turned down an offer of a federal Cabinet portfolio, and a request to offer as a candidate in the 1961 federal election, in order to remain Leader of the Opposition. Matheson announced his retirement from politics on 9 March 1965. Following the election call in 1966, he returned to private life and to his private law practice.

Matheson was perhaps best remembered for the rural electrification program and an extensive rural paving program. He also demonstrated able leadership on behalf of the whole Maritime region in dealings with the federal government. "Big Alec," as he was known, believed in straight talk and was always upfront about his views and intentions.

Matheson received his early education at the Bellevue School, later attending Prince of Wales College in Charlottetown, after which he taught school for four years, first in Grandview and then in Valleyfield. Matheson then studied law in the firm of MacKinnon and McNeill in Charlottetown. He was admitted to the Bar in June 1933. Matheson practised law in Charlottetown, until he entered politics in 1940. During the Second World War, he held the rank of a Major in the Artillery Reserve in Charlottetown. After his political career ended, Matheson again entered private law practice until March 1967, when he was sworn in as a County Court Judge for Queens County. He served in this position until March 1974, when he resigned for health reasons.

Matheson was involved in many community organizations. He was a member of the Charlottetown Club, the United Services Officers Club, and the Garrison Officer's Mess. He was a member of the Trinity United Church in Charlottetown and of the Caledonia Club, as well as the Charlottetown Curling Club and the Belvedere Golf and Winter Club. Alexander Matheson died 3 March 1976 at the Livingstone-MacArthur Nursing Home in Charlottetown.

Helen Matheson was the daughter of Ernest W. Farquharson.

References

CPG 1941, 1965; *Provincial Premier Birthday Series 1873-1973*; *Maritime Advocate and Busy East* September 1948; *Patriot* 3 March 1976.

MATHESON, JOHN ARCHIBALD, merchant, farmer, and officeholder; b. 3 September 1844 in Black River, son of John and Ann Matheson; m. 30 July 1881 Emily Clowser of London, England, in Boston, and there were no children; Presbyterian; d. 20 March 1919 in Revelstoke, BC.

Matheson, a Liberal, was first elected to the House of Assembly in the general election of 1882 for 1st Prince. After his opponents protested that he was employed by the Post Office, and hence receiving a salary from the federal government, his election was declared void. Matheson was re-elected in a by-election held 17 April 1883, and in the general elections of 1886, and 1890. He was defeated in the general election of 1893.

Matheson received his early education in Brackley Point, and then attended Prince of Wales College in Charlottetown. In 1863 he moved to Alberton, where he was employed by George Howlan* in his general mercantile business. He then established his own fishing and general mercantile business, with stores in Miminegash and Campbellton. On 30 September 1880, Matheson retired from his post as Inspector of Fisheries so that he could enter politics. He continued his mercantile career until 1897. At various times in his career, Matheson held the positions of Justice of the Peace and postmaster. John Matheson died 20 March 1919.

Emily Matheson was born in 1848 and died 23 October 1914.

References

CPG 1891, 1897; *Journal of the House of Assembly of Prince Edward Island* 1883 pp. 8-9; *Guardian* 22 March 1919; PARO: MNI-Census 1891; Charlottetown People's Cemetery Records.

MATHESON, JOHN CLAUDE, teacher and farmer; b. 19 March 1935 in Forest Hill, son of Norman Matheson and Catherine Taylor; m. 23 March 1955 Mona Taylor, and they had five children, Claude, Floyd, Parker, Calvin, and Brent; United.

Matheson, a Liberal, was first elected to the Legislative Assembly in the general election of 1989 for 2nd Kings. He was re-elected in the general election of 1993. While in the Legislature, Matheson served on several Legislative Committees, including agriculture, fisheries, forestry, health and social services, environment, provincial affairs, natural resources, economic development, tourism, transportation, and public works.

Matheson received his early education in Forest Hill, and later attended Prince of Wales College in Charlottetown, where he earned a teacher's certificate. He also completed a number of courses at the University of Prince Edward Island. From 1953 to 1986, Matheson worked as a teacher and as an academic instructor in adult education at Holland College. While doing this, he helped operate the family farm in Forest Hill. In 1989 Matheson began working on the farm full-time, specializing in cattle. He was the director of the Prince Edward Island Soil and Crop Association and the Souris Soil and Crop Association. Matheson was the admissions chairperson for the Dundas Plowing Match and was a member of the St. Peters Co-op and the Morell Credit Union. He is a former president and secretary-treasurer of St. Peters Lions Club. Claude Matheson is a member of the Masonic Lodge and involved with the Central Kings Driving Park.

Mona Matheson is the daughter of Truelove Taylor and Bertha Taylor of Upton. Claude Matheson and his wife reside in Forest Hill.

References
CPG 1996; *Guardian* 15 April 1989; *Voice for Island Seniors* April 2002; Questionnaire to Former MLAs.

MATHESON, JOHN PHILIP, farmer; b. 14 August 1906 in Oyster Bed Bridge, son of Charles Lemuel Matheson and Martha Isabel Dixon; m. 7 August 1937 Florence Isabel MacRae, and they had two children, Margaret Elizabeth and Donald Charles; Presbyterian; d. 8 September 1990 in Charlottetown.

Matheson, a Conservative, was first elected to the Legislative Assembly in the general election of 1943 for 2nd Queens. He was re-elected in the general elections of 1947, 1959, and 1962. He was defeated in a by-election in 1940, and in the general elections of 1951, 1955, and 1966. Matheson was appointed Minister of Public Works and Highways on 17 September 1959, and remained in this Ministry until 1966. During his tenure, the second Hillsborough Bridge was completed, extensive highway construction was undertaken and the Shaw Building in Charlottetown was erected.

A resident of Oyster Bed Bridge, Matheson received his early education at Wheatley School, and later attended Prince of Wales College. When his education was finished, Matheson taught for a year before taking charge of the family farm, which he operated successfully until his retirement in 1982. After retirement, Matheson moved to West Royalty. During his farming career, he participated as a producer, director, and president of the New Glasgow Dairying Company, and he was a member of the Federation of Agriculture. Matheson was a member of the Board of Governors of the University of Prince Edward Island from 1972 to 1982, and served as chairman from 1982 until 1985. During his time as chairman, he participated in interprovincial negotiations for the construction of the Atlantic Veterinary College. He served as national president of the Canadian Good Roads Association, and in 1981 was made an honourary life member of the Transportation Association of Canada. He was a lifetime member of the Masonic Lodge and was a member of the Charlottetown Club. Matheson served as elder, secretary-treasurer, and clerk of session at Glasgow Road Presbyterian Church for 50 years. Philip Matheson died on 8 September 1990 at the Queen Elizabeth Hospital.

Florence Matheson was the daughter of Mary Isobel and William MacRae of Ebenezer. In 1973 she was given the Premier's Award for Distinguished Citizenship by Premier Alexander Campbell*, and was invested as an officer of the Order of Canada by H. M. Queen Elizabeth II in 1974.

References
CPG 1947, 1952, 1956, 1966; Zonta Club pp. 73–75; *Guardian* 10 September 1990; PARO: Marriage License Book #16 1882–1923 p. 41.

MATHIESON, DAVID LAIRD, lawyer; b. 5 March 1903 in Georgetown, son of John Alexander Mathieson* and Mary Alice Laird; m. first 17 June 1930 Louise MacKinnon, and they had one child,

John A.; m. secondly Elizabeth Jaggs of Vancouver, who had a daughter, Susan; Presbyterian; d. 15 February 1993 in Vancouver.

Mathieson, a Conservative, was elected to the Legislative Assembly in the general election of 1947 for 5th Queens. He was defeated in the general election of 1939 for 5th Kings and in the general election of 1951 for 5th Queens.

Mathieson came from a political family. His father served as premier and then Chief Justice of Prince Edward Island, and his mother was the daughter of David Laird*.

Mathieson was educated at Prince of Wales College in Charlottetown, at Dalhousie University in Halifax, and at McGill University in Montreal. He was called to the Prince Edward Island Bar in 1928, and practised law in the province from 1928 to 1939, and from 1945 to 1952 with Bell, Mathieson and Foster, a firm that included Reginald Bell*. In September 1952, Mathieson and his family moved to Edmonton, where he worked as a senior solicitor for Interprovincial Pipelines. In 1971 Mathieson and his family retired to Vancouver, where he was admitted to that province's Bar and did legal work on behalf of British Columbia's aboriginal peoples. David Mathieson died 15 February 1993.

Louise Mathieson was the daughter of Charles MacKinnon.

References
CPG 1941, 1951, 1953; *Guardian* 17 March 1993, 20 March 1993.

MATHIESON, K.C., HONOURABLE JOHN ALEXANDER, teacher, principal, lawyer, and judge;

b. 19 May 1863 in Harrington, son of Ronald Mathieson and Anne Stewart; m. 15 September 1896 Mary Alice Laird, and they had five children, Annie Louise (died at three years), Helen, Dora, Avila, and David Laird*; Presbyterian; d. 7 January 1947.

Mathieson, a Conservative, was first elected to the Legislative Assembly in the general election of 1900 for 4th Kings. He was elected in the general election of 1904 in 5th Kings. He was re-elected in the general elections of 1908, 1912, and 1915. He did not complete his final term, as he resigned in 1917 to accept the appointment as Chief Justice of the Prince Edward Island Supreme Court.

In 1903 the Conservative party named Mathieson as Leader of the Opposition and he served in that position for eight years. He became premier in 1911, when the Opposition Conservatives won two by-elections, thereby gaining the

majority in the Legislative Assembly. In the general election of 1912 he defeated the Liberals led by H. J. Palmer*. It was the first Conservative triumph in a general election since 1890. Mathieson's leadership and government received a positive endorsement, when the Conservatives won a second mandate in the 1915 general election. He continued as premier until resigning in 1917.

In 1912 Mathieson achieved one of his most significant victories as premier through his resolution of the subsidy issue with the federal government. He was a major driving force behind the campaign for ferry service between New Brunswick and the Island, which began operating in 1917. He introduced a new Automobile Act in 1913, despite serious opposition within his caucus. This legislation expanded the use of automobiles, which had been banned in 1908.

Premier Mathieson fought to have the British North America Act guarantee the province six seats in the House of Commons, and in 1914 he negotiated a satisfactory compromise with Prime Minister Borden ensuring four seats in the House of Commons, by virtue of an amendment to the British North America Act. As a result of the 1915 amendment, the Island's federal representation rose from three to four, with Queen's becoming a dual riding. This district elected two Members of Parliament until 1965.

In 1934 Mathieson served on the White Commission, a federal government initiative aimed at resolving the lingering economic disparity in the Maritime provinces. The Commission eventually recommended $275,000 per year. Mathieson refused to support the recommendations of the White Commission, convinced that the settlement offered to the Maritime provinces was inadequate.

Upon his death, a local newspaper, in tribute to the positive changes made in the province during his term in office, declared Mathieson the "maker of modern Prince Edward Island."

Mathieson attended the local school in Harrington. Following this he became a clerk. Later he attended Prince of Wales College, after which he taught for six years, first at DeSable for two years, then for 18 months in Manitoba, and lastly in Kensington. Mathieson was the principal of schools in both DeSable and Kensington. It was in the legal realm where Mathieson devoted most of his professional energy, and this process began when he studied law in Charlottetown with McLean and

McDonald. He was called to the Bar in 1894. Mathieson began practising law in Georgetown, and while living there served as a Member of the Georgetown Council and as a Lieutenant in No. 3 Company in the Georgetown militia. In 1905 he entered into a partnership with Aeneas A. MacDonald* in Charlottetown and began working in the capital. That same year, Mathieson was named King's Counsel. From 1906 to 1916, he was a partner in Mathieson, MacDonald and Stewart. James D. Stewart* was also a member of the firm. Mathieson was appointed Chief Justice of the Supreme Court in 1917, and served on the Bench until he resigned in 1943. John Mathieson died 7 January 1947.

Mary Mathieson was born 7 February 1867 and died 9 December 1945. She was the daughter of David Laird* and Mary Louisa Owen, both members of important political families in the province. Son David L. Mathieson* also served in the Legislative Assembly.

References

CPG 1915, 1916; Elections PEI; MacDonald *If You're Stronghearted* pp. 36, 53, 54; *MWOT* p. 741; *Past and Present* pp. 480–81; Polland p. 227; *Prominent Men* p. 531; *Provincial Premier's Birthday Series*; *Patriot* 10 December 1945; PARO: Sherwood Cemetery Records.

MCDONALD, Q.C., HECTOR CHARLES, lawyer, and judge; b. 3 May 1856 in Flat River, Belfast, son of John McDonald and Mary McKinnon; Presbyterian; d. 10 May 1914 in Charlottetown.

McDonald, a Liberal, was first elected to the House of Assembly in the general election of 1890 for 4th Queens. He was elected to the Legislative Assembly in the general election of 1893 for 4th Queens. He was re-elected in the general election of 1897. He was appointed to Executive Council as Attorney-General in 1897 under the Warburton* Administration, and was reappointed to the same position in August 1898 by Premier Farquharson*. McDonald resigned as Attorney-General in 1899 to accept an appointment as a County Court Judge for Queens County.

McDonald advocated the abolishment of the Legislative Council, serving as a member of the committee to draft a new constitution for the Legislative Assembly when the Council was abolished in 1893. He took a great interest in the promotion of a railway branch to Belfast, and was also a strong supporter of the bridge over the Hillsborough River in Charlottetown.

McDonald received his early education in Belfast. In 1876 he attended Prince of Wales College in Charlottetown, after which he studied at McGill University in Montreal, where he received a Bachelor of Arts in 1881 and a Bachelor of Civil Law in 1883. When he left McGill, McDonald returned to the Island where he studied law in the offices of McLean and Martin. One of the partners, Donald Martin*, was a member of the Legislature. McDonald was admitted as an attorney at law in 1885, and called to the Bar in 1886. He was designated Queen's Counsel in 1898, and served as a judge from 1899 until his death. George Inman* studied law with McDonald.

Besides his law career and political involvements, McDonald was involved in his community. He was a prominent Mason, a member of the St. John's Lodge A.F. and A.M. He was exalted to the Royal Arch and was Knighted in the Prince Edward Preceptory, and reached the 32nd degree in the A. and A.S. Rite. McDonald was a charter member of the Prince Edward Lodge Knights of Pythias. He also served as the Senior Grand Warden of the Grand Lodge of Prince Edward Island, Deputy Grand Master, and Grand Master. McDonald took an active interest in the militia, attending the Royal School of Artillery in Quebec, where he received a first class certificate. Hector McDonald died 10 May 1914.

References

CPG 1899; Elections PEI; *Patriot* 11 May 1914; *Guardian* 11 May 1914, 12 May 1914; PARO: MNI-Census 1891.

MCDONALD, MALCOLM, merchant, ship owner, and shipbuilder; b. 10 July 1836 in Uigg, son of Donald McDonald and Margaret Gordon; m. 30 September 1872 Grace Snelgrave, and they had two children, Annie and Harold; Presbyterian; d. 23 September 1902 in Charlottetown.

McDonald, a Liberal, was elected to the Legislative Assembly in the general election of 1900 for 3rd Kings. He was defeated in the general elections of 1882, 1893, and 1897. During his time in office, he served on Executive Council as a Minister without Portfolio. He died while sitting as a Member of the Legislative Assembly.

McDonald received his education at the Uigg School. From an early age, he was involved in mercantile pursuits. Early in his career, he worked in the store of Patrick Stevens of Orwell. Eventually McDonald moved to Montague Bridge. He established a shipbuilding and trading company with Captain Lewis John Westaway* in 1867 under the firm name Westaway and McDonald located in Georgetown. When Westaway died in 1885, McDonald continued to operate the business under the same name. In 1896 he was appointed an Agent for the Dominion Government's winter steamers docked in Georgetown. Malcolm McDonald died 23 September 1902.

Grace McDonald was the daughter of William Snelgrave of Charlottetown.

References

CPG 1901; *Patriot* 3 October 1872, 24 September 1902; PARO: MNI-Census 1881, 1891.

MCDONALD, MAYNARD FREEMAN, merchant and hotel keeper; b. 3 July 1876 in Montague, son of Norman J. McDonald and Annie McLeod; m. 24 September 1902 Nellie Westaway, and there were no children; Baptist; d. 14 April 1968 in Montague.

McDonald, a Conservative, was elected to the Legislative Assembly in the general election of 1923 for 4th Kings. He was defeated in the general elections of 1927 and 1931. McDonald served as one of the first mayors of the town of Montague before entering provincial politics, and also acted as a Justice of the Peace.

McDonald was educated at the local schools in Montague, and later attended Prince of Wales College in Charlottetown. He was a merchant and hotel keeper in Montague, operating the McDonald Hotel and General Store for many years. Maynard McDonald died 14 April 1968 at Riverview Manor.

Nellie McDonald, the daughter of Nathaniel and May Westaway, was born 6 May 1876 and died 15 September 1956.

References

CPG 1924, 1928, 1936; *Guardian* 15 April 1968, 16 April 1968.

MCDOUGALL, JOHN, shipbuilder; b. 28 February 1832 in Orwell, son of Donald McDougall and Eppy MacPherson; Roman Catholic; d. 1901.

John McDougall, a Conservative, was elected to the House of Assembly in the general election of 1882 for 3rd Kings.

McDougall was a prominent shipbuilder in Bridgetown. He operated a shipyard that built many ships, including some for William Welsh*. McDougall, William Welsh*, L. C. Owen*, and Robert Longworth were prominent in the large ship-building industry along Grand River East, now known as the Boughton River. They built primarily for the British market, where McDougall sold 11 vessels to customers in Great Britain. Other ships built by him were sent to Newfoundland. Although McDougall did not finance his own vessels, he had shares in at least 40 ships built in the Grand River area. On 5 June 1864, his shipyard was destroyed by fire. Despite the fire, McDougall launched a ship later that year. He remained active in the industry until the 1880s.

References

CPG 1883; Elections PEI; PARO: St. Alexis Roman Catholic Cemetery Records; MNI-Census 1861; MNI-Hutchinson's p. 141; MNI-Mercantile Agency Reference Book September 1876.

MCEACHEN, EMANUEL, farmer and justice of the peace; b. ca. 1816 in South Lake, son of Charles McEachen and Mary Beaton; Roman Catholic; d. 5 November 1875 in Charlottetown.

McEachen, a Conservative, was first elected to the House of Assembly in 1853 for 1st Kings. He was re-elected in a by-election in 1866, the general elections of 1870 and 1873, and in a by-election held in September 1873. He was defeated in the general elections of 1858, 1863, 1867, and 1872. Following the 1853 election, McEachen was appointed to Executive Council. He was removed from Executive Council when he struck Liberal Member William McGill in an anteroom of the Legislature. He eventually returned to Executive Council following the general election of 1870 and served until 1872 when the government of J. C. Pope was defeated. In 1873, when Pope and the Conservatives had returned to power, McEachen was appointed Commissioner of Public Lands. He served in the position until his death.

McEachen was well-known for his advocacy of publicly funded separate schools. At a time when most Roman Catholics in the Conservative party joined forces with the Liberals, he remained with his party. McEachen felt that religion, no matter what type, should be a part of education. He was also opposed to the Island joining Canada. While known for his temper, he was considered a kind man who bore few grudges. In addition to his political career, he served as a Justice of the Peace in 1864.

McEachen was born four months after the death of his father. Early in life, he took responsibility for the family farm of over 100 acres, supporting his mother and sisters. Emanuel McEachen died 5 November 1875.

References
CPG 1874; *DCB* X 1871–1880 pp. 472–73; PARO: MNI-Hutchinson's p. 247; McEachen Family File.

MCEWEN, Q.C., WALTER, lawyer; b. 31 January 1940 in Montague, son of Ted McEwen and Mary Burke; m. 11 September 1965 Myrna Nicholson, and they had three children, Scott, Shawn, and Jamie; Roman Catholic.

McEwen, a Liberal, was first elected to the Legislative Assembly in the general election of 1989 for 5th Prince. He was re-elected in the general election of 1993. On 15 April 1993, he was appointed Minister of Provincial Affairs and Attorney-General, and Minister Responsible for the Island Regulatory and Appeals Commission, the Workers Compensation Board, the Liquor Control Commission, the Human Rights Commission, Francophone Affairs, and Native Affairs. On 9 June 1994, McEwen was appointed Minister of Health and Social Services and Minister Responsible for the Health and Community Services Agency, the five Regional Health Boards, and the Prince Edward Island Housing Corporation.

McEwen received his secondary education at the Montague High School. He then attended St. Dunstan's University, where he earned a Bachelor of Science in 1965. After graduating he worked for a few years as a scientific equipment salesperson before returning to school. McEwen studied law at Dalhousie University and graduated in 1971. He moved to Toronto and was called to the Ontario Bar in March 1973. McEwen returned to the Island, where he articled with J. Melville Campbell. He was admitted to the Prince Edward Island Bar on 9 October 1973, and began a law practice in Summerside with the firm that later became Campbell and McEwen. In 1986 he was awarded the designation of Queen's Counsel. The firm eventually became Campbell, McEwen, Taylor and McLennan. He is currently in private practice in Summerside as counsel to the firm of Taylor and McLellan. He is also a member of the National Parole Board.

McEwen has been actively involved in his community for many years. He has served as president of the Summerside Boys and Girls Club, the Summerside Sheltered Workshop, and Junior Achievement of Summerside and Area. He was also a director of the Prince County Family Services Bureau, the Greater Summerside Chamber of Commerce, a Trustee of the Prince County Hospital, and an executive member of the Summerside and Area Minor Hockey Association.

References
CPG 1996; *Guardian* 10 October 1973, 27 October 1987 p. 3, 16 March 1993; *Journal-Pioneer* 10 October 1973;

MCFADYEN, MALCOLM, teacher, farmer, and merchant; b. 9 June 1838 in Lake Ainslie, Cape Breton, Nova Scotia, son of Edward McFadyen and Catherine McKinnon; Presbyterian; d. ca. 1883.

McFadyen, a Liberal, was elected to the House of Assembly in the 1882 general election for 4th Kings. He was defeated in the general elections of 1876 and 1879. He was also defeated in the 1878 federal election for King's County.

Born in Lake Ainslie, Cape Breton, McFadyen moved to the Island in August 1854. He was educated at Central Academy in Charlottetown. For nine years McFadyen was a school teacher. He was a farmer and a general merchant in Murray Harbour. According to *Meacham's Atlas*, McFadyen owned a lobster factory and was a shipbuilder and fisherman. Malcolm McFadyen died ca. 1883.

References
CPG 1879, 1880, 1883; *Meacham's Atlas*; PARO: MNI-Census 1881.

MCGOWAN, MAJOR DOUGLAS, business person; b. 18 November 1915 in Kilmuir, son of Malcolm Campbell McGowan and Jessie Murchison; m. first 12 October 1945 Elizabeth Margaret Watson of Toronto, and they had six children, Marlene, Anne, Rose Ellen, Dara, Denise, and Malcolm; m. secondly 1973 Irene Judson Harper, who had two sons, Dewar and Stephen Harper; Presbyterian; d. 25 October 1989 in Montague.

McGowan, a Conservative, was first elected to the Legislative Assembly in the general election of 1959 for 3rd Kings. He was re-elected in the general election of 1962. Before entering provincial politics, he had been Deputy Mayor of Montague from 1951 to 1955. McGowan's brother Neil Murdock* also served in the Legislative Assembly.

McGowan received his early education at Kilmuir School and West Kent School in Charlottetown. He attended Mount Allison University from 1935 to 1937. From 1932 to 1936, McGowan was a truck driver. After attending Mount Allison, he worked as a salesman and mechanic for McGowan Motors in Kilmuir. McGowan held the rank of Major with the Armoured Corps Division of the Canadian Grenadier Guards in the Second World War. In 1944 he received the Military Cross and in 1945 the Efficient Service Medal. McGowan also received the Royal Canadian Legion Medal of Merit and was the Honourary Lieutenant-Colonel of the Prince Edward Island Regiment. He commanded militia units in Montague and Souris from 1947 to 1953. Following the Second World War, McGowan established McGowan Motors in Montague. He retired as president of the company in 1975. McGowan served as chair of the board of trustees of Kings County Memorial Hospital. He also was president of the Montague Curling Club, and Chairman and Group Commander of Cubs and Scouts. Douglas McGowan died 25 October 1989.

References
COR 1989 p. 130; CPG 1966; WWPEI p. 102; Guardian 26 October 1989.

MCGOWAN, NEIL MURDOCK, merchant and automobile dealer;

b. 5 May 1903 in Kilmuir, son of Malcolm Campbell McGowan and Jessie Murchison; m. 1 February 1930 Lorna Ellen Weatherbie, and they had four children, Joan, Sidney, Jessie, and John; Presbyterian; d. 5 August 1983 in Montague.

McGowan, a Conservative, was elected to the Legislative Assembly in the general election of 1943 for 4th Kings. He was defeated in the general elections of 1935, 1939, and 1947. His brother Douglas* also served in the Legislative Assembly.

McGowan received his early education at the Kilmuir School, and later attended Mount Allison Academy, where he graduated in 1925 from the Commercial Program. He was president of McGowan's Limited general merchants from 1926 until his retirement in 1967, when the firm closed. He also was an automobile dealer. McGowan was a member of the Kings County Board of Trade and the International Order of Oddfellows Lodge. He was a member of the Caledonia Presbyterian Church, where he was an elder and clerk of session for many years. Murdock McGowan died 5 August 1983 at the Kings County Memorial Hospital.

Lorna McGowan was the daughter of Colo-

nel S. S. Weatherbie of Bellevue.

References
CPG 1939, 1940, 1946, 1948; Guardian 13 September 1983; PARO: Valleyfield United Presbyterian Cemetery Records.

MCINNIS, JAMES D., farmer;

b. 24 May 1855; m. 24 November 1873 Sarah J. McCormack of St. Georges, and they had six children, Frank, Margaret, John G., Joseph, Anastasia, and Jerome; Roman Catholic; d. 20 August 1917.

McInnis, a Liberal, was first elected to the Legislative Assembly in the general election of 1904 for 2nd Kings. He was re-elected in the general elections of 1908 and 1915. He was defeated in the general election of 1912. McInnis was appointed to Executive Council in the Haszard* Administration.

McInnis was educated in local schools. He resided on a farm at the Head of St. Peters Bay, and was a well-respected and successful farmer. James McInnis died suddenly on 20 August 1917, while serving as a Member of the Legislative Assembly.

Sarah McInnis, the daughter of Daniel McCormack and Margaret Walker, was born 8 April 1853 and died 30 November 1930.

References
CPG 1905, 1921; Elections PEI; Patriot 20 August 1917, 23 August 1917; PARO: Census 1901; St. Peters Bay Roman Catholic Cemetery Records.

MCISAAC, HILARY, farmer, shipbuilder, justice of the peace, probate commissioner, customs collector, and controller of navigation laws;

b. 1 November 1820 in St. Peters Bay, son of Dougald McIsaac; m. 1852, Sophia MacDonald, and they had nine children, James, Isabella, John A., Catherine F., Mary E., Sarah S., Bennet F., Clarah W., and Archibald; Roman Catholic; d. 23 August 1901 in Head of St. Peters Bay.

McIsaac, a Conservative, was first elected to the House of Assembly in the general election of 1873 for 2nd Kings. He was re-elected in the general elections of 1876. He was defeated in the general election of 1879. He served the Island as a member of the Board of Works.

McIsaac was educated in St. Peters Bay. His father had emigrated with his family to the Island from the Highlands of Scotland as a young boy, and they were early settlers of St. Peters. McIsaac was a farmer and, by one account, a prosperous and progressive agriculturalist. His success on the land did not prevent him from becoming a ship-builder in partnership with members of his family. Prior to Confederation, McIsaac was a customs collector and controller of navigation laws at the St. Peters Bay port. He also served as a Justice of the Peace and as a Commissioner for Probate of Wills. McIsaac lived in St. Peters Bay. Hilary McIsaac died 23 August 1901.

Sophia McIsaac was born in Little Pond ca. 1838 and died ca. 1894.

References
CPG 1879, 1880; Elections PEI; *Charlottetown Herald* 11 September 1901; *Watchman* 6 September 1901; PARO: MNI-Census 1881.

MCKAY, DONALD, merchant, trader, farmer, and officeholder; b. 13 January 1836 in New London, son of Donald and Jane McKay; m. 21 February 1861 Jane Matheson, and they had one child, Janet; Presbyterian; d. 2 January 1895 in Oyster Bed Bridge.

McKay, a Conservative, was first elected to the House of Assembly in 1876 for 2nd Queens. He was re-elected in the general elections of 1879, 1882, and 1890. He was defeated in the general elections of 1885 and 1893.

McKay was educated at local schools in his community. He operated a general store in Graham's Cross in Lot 21, did some trading of goods, and farmed. McKay was a Justice of the Peace and a Commissioner of Small Debt Court. He served as a member of the Board of Railway Commissioners. Donald McKay died 2 January 1895.

Jane McKay, the daughter of John Matheson of Wheatley River, was born in 1838.

References
CPG 1889, 1891, 1897; *Daily Examiner* 2 January 1895; PARO: MNI-Hutchinson's p. 152; MNI-Census 1881.

MCKINNON, HONOURABLE MURDOCH, farmer; b. 15 March 1865 in Brooklyn, son of Laughlin McKinnon and Mary McDonald; m. 21 October 1914 Perle Beecher Taylor, and they had one son, Francis P. T.; Presbyterian; d. 12 October 1944 in Charlottetown.

McKinnon, a Conservative, was first elected to the Legislative Assembly in the general election of 1897 for 4th Kings. He was not declared elected until 14 April 1898, as the two candidates for the riding received an equal number of votes. After a ruling by Justice E. J. Hodgson, McKinnon was declared the winner. McKinnon was defeated in the general election of 1900 by Alexander Bruce*, but after a recount he was declared re-elected. McKinnon was re-elected in the general elections of 1904, 1908, 1912, and 1915. He was defeated in the general election of 1919. He served as Commissioner of Agriculture and Provincial Secretary-Treasurer from 1912 to 1915. McKinnon was sworn in as Lieutenant-Governor on 8 September 1919 and remained in that position until 1924. During his time in this office, he made constitutional history when he refused to give assent to the Church Union Bill of 1923.

McKinnon received his early education at local schools, and then at Prince of Wales College in Charlottetown. In his early career, he was a farmer in Brooklyn. Murdoch McKinnon died 12 October 1944.

Perle Murdoch was the daughter of Dr. F. P. Taylor of Charlottetown.

References
CPG 1901, 1919, 1921; *CWW* 1936-1937 p. 753; Elections PEI; Wallace p. 471.

MCLAREN, M. D., L.R.C.S., L.R.C.P., PETER, physician and surgeon; b. 1841 in New Perth, son of James McLaren and Ann Stewart; Baptist; d. 1908.

McLaren, a Conservative, was elected to the House of Assembly in the general election of 1882 for 3rd Kings. He was defeated in the general election of 1886.

McLaren received his early education in local schools and at Prince of Wales College in Charlottetown. He attended medical school at McGill University in Montreal and graduated in 1869. He went on to complete further medical studies in Edinburgh and graduated in 1879. While in Edinburgh, he studied with Dr. Joseph Lister, who was then engaged in an early study on the causes of infections in surgery. McLaren was one of the first doctors in the province to adopt antisepsis in surgery. He practised first in Brudenell, and later in Montague, from 1871 until his death. Peter McLaren died in 1908.

References
CPG 1885, 1889; Elections PEI; Lea p. 29; *Meacham's Atlas*; Brudenell Pioneers p. 44; PARO: Brudenell Baptist Cemetery Records.

MCLAUGHLIN, ANTHONY, farmer and officeholder; b. 10 March 1844 in Mill Cove, son of James McLaughlin and Mary Phillips, both of Ireland; m. 2 July 1878 Clementina Carmichael, and they had eight children, John, Mary, Henry Dan, James T., Agnes, Ellen C., Rosanna, and Margaret; Roman Catholic; d. 27 November 1925.

McLaughlin, a Liberal, was first elected to the Legislative Assembly in the 1893 general election for 2nd Kings. He was re-elected in the general elections of 1897 and 1900. From 1891 to 1897, he served on Executive Council as a Minister without Portfolio in the Frederick Peters* Administration. From 1897 to 1898, McLaughlin served on Executive Council in the Alexander B. Warburton* Administration, and in 1898 on Executive Council in the Donald Farquharson* Administration.

McLaughlin was educated in the public school in Peakes Station, where he later worked as a farmer. He served as Bursar for the Prince Edward Island Hospital for the Insane and was a Magistrate for Kings County. Anthony McLaughlin died 27 November 1925.

Clementina McLaughlin, the daughter of Duncan Carmichael of Lot 49, was born ca. 1857. McLaughlin's parents came to the province in 1830.

References
CPG 1903; *Elections PEI*; *Past and Present*, pp. 530-31; PARO: Marriage Register 13 1873-1887 p. 30; Montague Funeral Home Records p. 95; MNI-Census 1891.

MCLEAN, ALFRED EDGAR, farmer and trader; b. 8 May 1868 in Southwest Lot 16, son of Roderick William McLean and Rachel McLean; m. 26 June 1895 Henrietta S. Stavert; Presbyterian; d. 28 October 1939 in Summerside.

McLean, a Liberal, was first elected to the Legislative Assembly in the general election of 1915 for 3rd Prince. He was re-elected in the general election of 1919. He was defeated in the general election of 1912. In 1921 he resigned from provincial politics to contest the federal seat of Prince. McLean was elected to the House of Commons in 1921, and was re-elected in 1925, 1926, 1930, and 1935. He was a Member of the House of Commons at the time of his death. McLean served for eight years on the Town Council in Summerside.

McLean was educated in the local schools, and later attended Summerside High School and Truro Agricultural College. He worked as a farmer and a trader, and was a director of A. E. McLean Silver Black Fox Company and president of Dominion Silver Fox Furs Limited. He was a director of the first National Fox Exchange and was a mem-

ber of the Masonic Order. Alfred McLean died 28 October 1939.

Henriette McLean, the daughter of Catherine McMurdo and William Stavert, was born 6 October 1873 and died 21 April 1906.

References
CDP p. 424; *CPG* 1912, 1915, 1916, 1919; *Guardian* July 1915; PARO: MNI-Census 1891; Census 1901; Kensington People's Cemetery Records.

MCLEAN, Q.C., ANGUS ALEXANDER, lawyer; b. 17 December 1854 in Belfast, son of William and Flora McLean; m. first 14 June 1882 Leah Yeo, and they had two children, Eric and Cecil Gower; m. secondly 24 October 1898 Frances H. Longworth, and there were no children; Presbyterian; d. 3 April 1943 in Charlottetown.

McLean, a Conservative, was first elected to the Legislative Assembly in a by-election held 15 March 1888 for 4th Queens. He was re-elected in the general election of 1890. He was defeated in the general elections of 1893, 1897, and 1900. McLean was defeated in federal by-elections for West Queen's on 15 January 1902, and Queen's on 16 February 1904. He was re-elected for Queen's in 1904, was defeated in 1908, and was re-elected in 1911. He served until the dissolution of the 12th Parliament.

McLean was educated at Prince of Wales College and at Harvard Law School in Boston. Following his formal education, he studied law in the office of W. W. Sullivan*. McLean was called to the Bar in 1878. He was a lawyer in the firm Sullivan McLean and Morrison, and later in the firm of McLean and MacKinnon. McLean was designated Queen's Counsel in 1894. He served as Clerk of the Legislative Assembly from 1879 to 1888. McLean was also comptroller of the Royal Northwest Mounted Police. Angus McLean died 3 April 1943.

Leah McLean, the daughter of John Yeo of Charlottetown, died in 1897. Frances McLean was the daughter of Henry Longworth.

References
CDP pp. 424-25; *CPG* 1899; *WWC* p. 649; PARO: MNI-Census 1891.

MCLEAN, HARRY DANIEL, merchant; b. 14 August 1877 in Souris, son of John McLean* and Matilda Jane Jury; m. 17 September 1902 Annie Mitchell of Amherst, Nova Scotia, and they had five children, Mary, John Robert*, Gordon, Margaret, and Helen; Presbyterian; d. 27 October 1962 in Charlottetown.

McLean, a Conservative, was first elected to the Legislative Assembly in a by-election held 5 January 1916 for 1st Kings. The seat was vacated by his father when he was appointed to the Senate. He was re-elected in the general elections of 1919, 1923, 1927, and 1931. He was defeated in the general election of 1935. McLean served as a Minister without Portfolio. He was sworn into the Executive Council of the Conservative government led by Premier James D. Stewart* on 29 August 1931, and again on 14 October 1933 under Premier William J. P. MacMillan*. McLean served as finance critic while in Opposition.

McLean's father was a Member of the Legislative Assembly for 20 years, and his son John would later serve as Speaker of the Legislative Assembly.

McLean received his education at Prince of Wales College. He and his family resided in Souris, where he had a successful career as a merchant. McLean was the director and secretary-treasurer of the firm Matthew and McLean Limited, and he specialized in the company's fisheries division. He was a successful sportsperson well-known in the Maritimes, particularly for his yachting victories. In July of 1962, Harry McLean became a resident of the Livingstone and MacArthur Nursing Home in Charlottetown, and lived there until his death on 27 October 1962.

Annie McLean, the daughter of Dr. Robert Mitchell, was born 2 February 1877 and died 23 August 1961.

References
CPG 1916, 1921, 1938; *CWW* 1936-1937 p. 758; *Patriot* 29 October 1962; PARO: Souris West Union Cemetery Records.

MCLEAN, HONOURABLE JOHN, teacher, merchant, and business person; b. 24 September 1846 in Mount Herbert, son of Daniel McLean and Sarah Currie; m. 5 June 1872 Matilda Jane Jury, and they had four children, Harry Daniel*, Roy, Rea Maude, and Winnie; Presbyterian; d. 20 February 1936 in Souris.

McLean, a Conservative, was first elected to the House of Assembly in the general election of 1882 for 1st Kings. He was re-elected in the general elections of 1886 and 1890. McLean was elected to the Legislative Assembly in the general election of 1900 for 1st Kings. He was re-elected in the general elections of 1908, 1912, and 1915. He was defeated in the general election of 1897. McLean resigned from the House of Assembly in 1891 and was elected in the federal election of that year for King's County. In 1904 he resigned from the Legislative Assembly and was defeated in the federal election for King's County later that year. In December 1915 he again resigned from the Legislative Assembly. McLean was appointed to Executive Council as a Minister without Portfolio from 5 December 1911 until his resignation. He was appointed to the Senate on 3 December 1915, where he remained until failing health forced him to resign in 1935.

McLean was educated in local schools and later at Prince of Wales College in Charlottetown. He was a teacher in Meadowbank from 1862 to 1864, then was a clerk with the Charlottetown firm of Heartz and Son from 1864 to 1869. In 1869 he became a partner in the firm of Matthew and McLean Limited Merchants in Souris. He was a manager at Dundas Starch Company. McLean was a director of numerous companies, including Bruce, Stewart and Company, *The Guardian*, Eastern Trust Company, Maritime Life Insurance Company, and the Denatured Alcohol Company.

McLean took an active role in his community. He served on the board of directors of the Prince Edward Island Hospital and was a member of the Charlottetown Club and the A.F. and A.M. Lodge. John McLean died 20 February 1936.

Matilda McLean, the daughter of John Jury, was born 12 June 1845. Harry McLean and his son John* both served in the Legislative Assembly.

References
CDP p. 425; *CPG* 1915; *Eminent Men* p. 481; *Patriot* 8 June 1872; PARO: MNI-Census 1881, 1891; Trinity Church Baptismal Records.

MCLEAN, JOHN ROBERT, merchant and company president; b. 1 January 1906 in Souris, son of Harry Daniel McLean* and Annie Mitchell; m. 12 October 1936 Marjorie Robina MacBeath, and they had two children, Pauline Anne and John Gordon; United; d. 9 October 1964 in Charlottetown.

McLean, a Conservative, was first elected to the Legislative Assembly in a by-election held 8 February 1940 for 1st Kings. He was re-elected in the general elections of 1947, 1959, and 1962. He was defeated in the general elections of 1939, 1943, 1951, and 1955. In 1959 he was appointed Speaker of the 49th General Assembly and, in 1963, Speaker of the 50th General Assembly.

McLean was the third generation in his family to serve 1st Kings. His father, and his grandfather John McLean*, had represented the same riding.

McLean received his early education in Souris. He received his post-secondary education at Pictou Academy in Nova Scotia. He worked at the Bank of Commerce for four years, before embarking on a mercantile career. Like his father, he became the president of the firm Matthew and McLean Limited. McLean was the secretary-treasurer of the Souris Skating Rink Company and a director of Associated Shippers Incorporated. He was a member of the Masonic Lodge. While still Speaker, John McLean died 9 October 1964 at the Prince Edward Island Hospital.

Marjorie McLean was the daughter of Donald MacBeath of Campbellton, New Brunswick.

References
CPG 1964; Elections PEI; *Guardian* 10 October 1964; *Maritime Advocate and Busy East* May 1943.

MCLELLAN, BERNARD DONALD, farmer and teacher; b. 3 November 1859 in Indian River, son of Angus J. McLellan and Matilda McDonald; m. 17 October 1881 Emily Costin, and there were no children; Roman Catholic; d. 11 April 1907.

McLellan, a Liberal, was first elected to the House of Assembly in a by-election held 15 March 1888 for 1st Prince. He was re-elected in the general election of 1890. He was defeated in the general election of 1893. McLellan served as Speaker from 1891 to 1893. He was elected to the House of Commons in a by-election held 13 April 1898 for West Prince, and was defeated in the 1900 federal election.

McLellan was educated at St. Dunstan's College and Prince of Wales College, and worked as a farmer and a school teacher for nine years. McLellan was the nephew of John Alexander MacDonald*, who also had been Speaker of the House. He lived in Palmer Road. Bernard McLellan died 11 April 1907.

Emily McLellan was the daughter of Michael Costin of Palmer Road.

References
CDP p. 427; *CPG* 1889; Elections PEI; *Meacham's Atlas*; PARO: MNI-Census 1881; McDonald Family File; Leard Files; St. Mary's Roman Catholic Church Records.

MCLELLAN, RODERICK JAMES, farmer; b. 11 April 1866 in St. Georges, son of Donald McLellan and Ann McIntyre; m. Mary MacCormack, and there were no children; Roman Catholic; d. 10 January 1953 in Montague.

McLellan, a Conservative, was elected to the Legislative Assembly in the general election of 1915 for 5th Kings. He was defeated in the general election of 1919.

McLellan was educated at the local school in St. Georges, after which he became a farmer in his native community. After his time in the Legislature, he served as administrator of the Old Age Pension Program for the province. McLellan was president of the St. Georges Branch of the St. Andrew's Society. Roderick McLellan died 10 January 1953 at the Kings County Hospital.

Mary McLellan was born in 1888 and died in 1966.

References
CPG 1916; *Guardian* 12 January 1953; PARO: MNI-Census 1891; St. Georges Roman Catholic Cemetery Records.

MCLEOD, Q.C., M.A., NEIL lawyer and judge; b. 15 December 1842 in Uigg, son of Roderick McLeod and Flora McDonald; m. 27 June 1877 Isabella Jane Adelia Hayden, and they had six children, Arthur, Adelia Flora, Jennie, Marie, Dorothy, and Mary; Baptist; d. 19 October 1915 in Summerside.

McLeod, a Conservative, was first elected to the House of Assembly in the general election held on 2 April 1879 for Charlottetown Royalty. He was re-elected in the general elections of 1882, 1886, and 1890. In March 1879, without being an elected representative, McLeod was appointed to the Executive Council position of Secretary-Treasurer by Premier W. W. Sullivan*. McLeod also served on Executive Council as a Minister without Portfolio.

When Premier Sullivan resigned in 1889 to accept the post of Chief Justice of the province, McLeod became Leader of the Conservative government. In the 1890 general election, McLeod and his party won 16 of 30 seats in the Assembly. In February 1891, three of McLeod's members (John MacLean*, Donald Ferguson*, and Patrick Blake*) resigned in order to contest that year's federal election, and left the Conservatives with 13 of 30 seats in the Assembly. Two of the subsequent by-elections were won by Liberals, James H. Cummiskey* for 3rd Queens and Alfred McWilliams* for 2nd Prince, with the third seat going to John Theophilus Jenkins*, an independent Conservative at odds with his party. The results gave the Liberals the majority and, as a result, McLeod tendered his government's resignation on 22 April 1891. McLeod served as Conservative Leader of the Opposition, until his appointment as a Judge in Prince County on 9 March 1893.

During his term as Leader of the Opposition, McLeod argued forcefully for the abolition of the Legislative Council as a means of reducing the deficit. In the debate that led to the amalgamation of the two Houses, McLeod moved, unsuccessfully, to eliminate the property qualification for voting and to have all Members elected through suffrage by all adult males. He died 19 October 1915, while serving on the bench.

McLeod received his early education in Uigg. Later he attended Horton Academy and Acadia University in Wolfville, Nova Scotia, where he received a Bachelor of Arts and a Master of Arts. Following his education at Acadia, he articled with a Charlottetown law firm and was admitted to the Bar in 1873. McLeod formed a partnership with Edward Jarvis Hodgson, which lasted for several years — Donald Martin* studied law with them — before joining Walter Morson* in the firm McLeod, Morson and McQuarrie in the 1880s. He was designated Queen's Counsel in 1891.

In 1892 MacLeod was appointed County Court Judge for Prince County and served until his death. In addition to his political and legal career, McLeod was a member of numerous community organizations, including trustee of the Provincial Institutions of the Mentally Ill and a Commissioner of the Poor House. Neil McLeod died 19 October 1915.

Isabella McLeod was the daughter of James and Maria Hayden of Vernon River.

References

CPG 1891; DCB XIV 1911-1920 pp. 726-27; MacKinnon *Life of the Party* pp. 67-69; Premier's Gallery; *Daily Examiner* 29 June 1877; PARO: MNI-Census 1881, 1891; Census 1901.

MCLEOD, ROBERT C.,

clerk, merchant, and farmer; b. May 1851, in Dunstaffnage, son of John Scott McLeod; m. 11 July 1883 Madge L. McRae, and they had five children, Lionel Stanley, Marion Louise, Henry, Margery Gordon, and A. Gwendolin (died at three years); Presbyterian; d. 5 April 1905.

McLeod, a Liberal, was elected to the Legislative Assembly in the general election of 1900 for 5th Prince. He was appointed to Executive Council in December of that year. Prior to his time in provincial politics, McLeod was a member of Summerside Town Council from 1880 to 1883, and he served as town chairman in 1883.

McLeod received his early education in Dunstaffnage. He moved to Summerside as a young man, and began working with R. T. Holman as a bookkeeper. Later, McLeod went into business for himself as a produce buyer. According to the 1881 Census, he lived in Summerside in the household of Alexander H. Allan and worked as a trader. Eventually he went into a partnership with John West to sell carriage and farm implements. Afterwards he bought out West's interest. The *Daily Patriot* obituary indicates McLeod accumulated considerable property as a result of his business success.

McLeod served as a manager of the Summerside Presbyterian Church for a number of years. He was the first president of the Summerside Board of Trade, and he continued to serve until his retirement from public life ca. 1904. McLeod was also a member of the school board in Summerside for about 10 years. During this time he served as chairman. Robert McLeod died 5 April 1905.

Madge McLeod, of Kingston, Ontario, and later Summerside, was born in 1853 and died in 1929. McLeod's father emigrated from Dumfrieshire, Scotland, as a boy.

References

CPG 1903; *Examiner* 20 July 1883; *Guardian* 6 April 1905; *Patriot* 5 April 1905; PARO: MNI-Census 1891; Census 1901; Summerside People's Protestant Cemetery Records.

MCLURE, WINFIELD CHESTER S.,

trader, haberdasher, wholesaler, fur merchant, fur farmer, publishing company president, and biscuit company president; b. 16 March 1875 in North Rustico, son of John McLure and Caroline McNeil Woolner; m. 25 June 1902 Lottie Evelyn Burhoe, and they had one child, Lena C.; Presbyterian; d. 18 June 1955 in Charlottetown.

McLure, a Conservative, was first elected to the Legislative Assembly in the general election of 1923 for 5th Queens. He was re-elected in the general election of 1927. He resigned in 1930. He was elected to the House of Commons in 1930 for Queen's, was defeated in 1935 and 1940, re-elected in 1945 and 1949, and defeated in 1953.

McLure received his early education at the local school. Later he attended Prince of Wales College and graduated with a provincial teaching certificate. Following college, he was a school principal in Alexandra, but after six years decided to open a men's clothing store. From there he moved into the wholesale business, and sold goods directly from the factory to retail stores. In 1910 McLure became a fur farmer, fur trader, and raw fur merchant. He was president and manager of C. McLure Fur Farms and manager of the Prince Edward Island Fur Sales Board. In 1919 he had the largest individual fox fur sale on record. His obituary recognized McLure as a major contributor to the province's fur industry. He was president of the Canadian Publishing Company Limited, the Imperial Biscuit Company, and the Charlottetown Selling Agencies. McLure was a member of the Oddfellows, the Masons, the Caledonia Club, and the Rotary Club. He was also a member of the Charlottetown Golf Club and the Abegweit Athletics Association. Chester McLure died 18 June 1955 at the Charlottetown Hospital.

Lottie McLure was the daughter of Theophilus Burhoe of Alexandra and Elizabeth Cousins.

References
Alexandra Women's Institute p. 26; *CPG* 1924, 1928; Elections PEI; *PPMP* pp. 135–36; *Guardian* 6 March 1919, 20 June 1955; PARO: Census 1901.

MCMAHON, Q.C., HONOURABLE GEORGE RUDOLPH, lawyer and judge; b. 30 May 1929 in Kensington, son of Peter Andrew McMahon and Emma Ruth MacKay; m. 20 September 1957 Gertrude Marie Ferguson, and they had four children, Lorraine, Marie, Marshall, and Patrick; Roman Catholic.

McMahon, a Conservative, was first elected to the Legislative Assembly in a by-election held 8 November 1976 for 5th Prince. He was re-elected in the general elections of 1978, 1979, 1982, and 1986. He was defeated in the general election of 1974. On 3 May 1979, McMahon was appointed Minister of Highways and Minister of Industry and Commerce and in 1980 he was appointed Minister of Public Works. On 17 November 1981, he was appointed Minister of Justice and Attorney General. On 28 October 1982, he became Minister of Justice and Minister of Labour. McMahon was ap-

pointed Minister of Community and Cultural Affairs on 3 November 1983, as well as Minister of Justice and Attorney General. He resigned his seat on 5 June 1986 to accept a position on the provincial Supreme Court.

McMahon received his secondary school education at Kensington High School and King Edward High School in Vancouver. He attended St. Dunstan's University and then law school at Dalhousie University. After graduating from Dalhousie in 1957, McMahon again returned to the Island, opening a private practice that year, which he maintained until 1979. He was a part-time Crown Prosecutor from 1959 to 1972. McMahon served on the board of directors of the Prince County Hospital and was a president of the Prince Edward Island Law Society.

Gertrude McMahon is the daughter of John Ferguson of Liverpool, Nova Scotia.

References
CPG 1986; ECO 1054/81, 842/83; *WWPEI* p. 103; *Guardian* 14 June 1986.

MCMILLAN, ANGUS, shipbuilder, bank director, and president; b. 29 October 1817 in Argyleshire, Scotland, son of Hugh McMillan and Catherine MacPherson; m. 26 February 1855 Mary Ross, and they had three sons and one daughter; Presbyterian; d. 13 March 1906 in Wheatley River.

McMillan, a Liberal, was first elected to the House of Assembly in a by-election held in 1868 for 5th Prince. McMillan was re-elected in the general elections of 1870, 1876, 1879, and 1890. He was defeated in the general elections of 1872, 1882, and 1886. McMillan was elected to the Legislative Assembly in the general election of 1893 for 5th Prince. He was re-elected in the general election of 1897. He served on Executive Council from 1878 to 1879 as a Minister without Portfolio. In 1891 he was again appointed to Executive Council, and to the position of Secretary-Treasurer and Commissioner of Public Lands. In 1900 McMillan retired due to his advanced age.

In provincial politics, McMillan was called "Honest Angus." Initially opposed to Confederation, he supported the building of the railway in the province, which eventually led to the Island joining Canada in 1873.

McMillian lived in Scotland for most of his childhood and received his early education there. He immigrated to the province with his family in

1834, and they settled in Wheatley River. In 1851 he began a shipbuilding career in his home community, and later started a shipbuilding business with his two brothers in Egmont Bay. Following this, he moved to Summerside to establish another shipyard. By the time McMillan left the shipbuilding business in 1884, he had constructed at least 58 vessels. He was also a merchant and used his ships to transport cargo for sale in Great Britain. The success of his business career was marked by his appointment in 1865 to the position of director, and eventually president, of the Summerside Bank. Angus McMillan died 13 March 1906.

Mary McMillan, the daughter of Malcolm Ross of Wheatley River, died in 1859.

References

CPG 1857; *DCB* XIII 1901-1910 pp. 666-67; Elections PEI; *PEI Journal of the House of Assembly* 1871 p. 2; *Patriot* 4 April 1906; PARO: Marriage Book 5 1852-1857 p. 435; MNI-Census 1881.

MCMILLAN, JOHN, farmer, businessperson, and sailor; b. 14 May 1851 at Hazelwood in Fairview, son of Captain Ewan McMillan and Isabella Matheson; m. 5 October 1882 Margaret Hamilton Reid, and they had seven children, Gladys, Louise, St. Clair, J. Cecil, Muriel, Alison, and Aimee Marguerite; Presbyterian; d. 1927.

McMillan, a Liberal, was first elected to the Legislative Assembly in the general election of 1904 for 2nd Queens. He was re-elected in the general elections of 1908 and 1915. He was defeated in the general election of 1912. He served on Executive Council from 1908 to 1911.

McMillan was educated at the local school and subsequently at Prince of Wales College in Charlottetown. He worked in agriculture, and owned 120 acres of farmland in Lot 65, where he lived and worked. McMillan spent a short period of time at sea, voyaging to Europe and the West Indies. He served as the director of Afton Hall Company and of the New Dominion Cheese Company. John McMillan died in 1927.

Margaret McMillan was the daughter of James A. Reid and Elizabeth Hamilton of Truro, Nova Scotia. She was born 10 November 1852 and died in 1941.

References

CPG 1908, 1916; Elections PEI; *Past and Present* pp. 466-67; PARO: Census 1901; St. Thomas Anglican Church Records.

MCNALLY, JOHN LEVI, public servant and retailer; b. 23 June 1914 in Donagh, son of John Patrick McNally and Louise Trainor; m. 6 August 1940 Roberta Weatherbie, and they had one child, Sharon Roberta; Roman Catholic; d. 28 September 1997 in Charlottetown.

McNally, a Liberal, was first elected to the Legislative Assembly in the general election of 1970 for 3rd Queens. He was re-elected in the general election of 1974. He was defeated in the general election of 1978. He was chair of the Building and Inspection Committee, and served on the finance and agriculture committees of the Legislature.

Levi McNally was educated in Donagh. He moved to Johnston's River and later to Bunbury. McNally worked with the Department of Transportation and Public Works for 23 years. He also worked as a retailer.

According to *The Guardian*, when asked what advice he would give young people today, McNally responded with a smile, "Get involved, and know your government." Levi McNally died 28 September 1997 at Beach Grove Senior Citizens' Home.

Roberta McNally is the daughter of Leo Weatherbie of Charlottetown.

References
CPG 1978; *Guardian* 16 April 1987, 30 September 1997.

MCNEIL, PETER ALOYSIUS, carpenter, construction company owner, and architect; b. 3 October 1917 in Dominion, Nova Scotia; son of James McNeil and Catherine MacCormack; m. 1941 Rose McVeigh of Inverness, Cape Breton, and they had six children, Peter Michael, Claire, Douglas, Donalda, Keith, and Sharon; Roman Catholic; d. 4 August 1989.

McNeil, a Liberal, was elected to the Legislative Assembly in a by-election on 23 November 1970 for 5th Queens. He was the first Chairman of the Village of Parkdale. He also served on a committee that established the Village of Sherwood.

McNeil was a native of Dominion in Cape Breton, Nova Scotia. He attended elementary and high school in Glace Bay, Nova Scotia. During his teen years, McNeil worked as a carpenter's helper and later as a farm labourer, followed by seven years as a carpenter's helper. During the Second World War, he served in the Royal Canadian Navy in the North Atlantic from 1941 to 1945. While serving with the Navy, he enrolled in an architectural course from the International Correspondence Schools. Later he worked for the Command Maintenance Office as a junior draughtsman under the Chief Architect for four years, while he studied architecture. At the end of the War, McNeill had not yet completed the six-year architect course and returned to the construction business as a carpenter, a carpenters' foreman, and as a construction superintendent. He later began his own construction company, which in 1952 employed 54 workers. However, his desire to work as an architect remained, and he applied for student membership in the Nova Scotia Association of Architects. The Association admitted him as a senior student, and he closed his construction business to work for a Halifax-based architectural firm, managing the Sydney office. In 1957 a love for Prince Edward Island and an association with the Bishop of Charlottetown lured McNeil to the province. He was the owner of Architectural Enterprises Incorporated in Charlottetown. In 1972, he was a founding member and first president of the Architects Association of Prince Edward Island. During his professional career, Peter McNeil designed many buildings in Nova Scotia and Prince Edward Island, including 20 churches, hundreds of senior citizens' units, schools, and recreational centres. Some of the province's buildings designed by McNeil were St. Paul's Church in Summerside, the Basilica Recreation Centre in Charlottetown, and St. Pius X Church in Parkdale. He was a member of the Architects Association of Prince Edward Island, the Specifications Writers of Canada, a Fellow of the Institute of Professional Designers, and a member of the Electric Service League of Prince Edward Island.

McNeil was a member of the Royal Canadian Legion. He was president of the Catholic Family Services Bureau, and served three consecutive terms as a director. Peter McNeil died on 4 August 1989 while a resident of Parkdale.

References
Guardian 5 August 1989, 3 October 1970, 24 November 1970; Prince Edward Island Architects Association Collection.

MCNEILL, WILLIAM SIMPSON, farmer, fisherman, highways commissioner, debt commissioner, and justice of the peace; b. 17 March 1814 in Cavendish, son of William McNeill and Eliza Bliss Townsend; m. 23 January 1839 Ann Maria Jones, and they had nine children, Jennie, Euphemia, Collin, Ellen L. Mannie, Mary, Emma, Annie, and Oliver; Presbyterian; d. 2 April 1902 in North Rustico.

McNeill, a Liberal, was first elected to the House of Assembly in 1866 for 2nd Queens. He was re-elected in the general elections of 1867, 1870, 1872, and 1873. He was defeated in the general election of 1876. Prior to Confederation, his father served in the House of Assembly for 25 years.

McNeill attended Central Academy in Charlottetown. He was a farmer and fisher, and he resided at Birkentree Farm in North Rustico. He served as Commissioner of Highways for District No. 5, as Commissioner for Recovery of Small Debts, and as Justice of the Peace. He was vice-president of the New London Agricultural Society and a captain in the militia with the New Glasgow Rifles. William McNeill died 2 April 1902.

Ann McNeill, the daughter of James Jones of North Rustico. She was born in London, England, in 1816 and died 30 November 1912.

References
CPG 1876; *Meacham's Atlas*; *Colonial Herald* 26 January 1839 p. 3; *Morning Guardian* 2 April 1902; *PEI Register* 30 June 1829; *Royal Gazette* 7 February 1843; PARO: MNI-Census 1841, 1881; MNI-Hutchinson's pp. 243, 275; McNeill Family File; Cavendish United Presbyterian Cemetery Records.

MCPHEE, ANGUS, farmer; b. 25 January 1869 in Riverdale, son of Duncan McPhee and Margaret Morrow; m. 6 April 1893 Drucella Rogerson, and they had 13 children, Louis Duncan, Margaret Jane, James Daniel, Frederick A., Thomas, Grace Bertha, Katie Belle, Malcolm Gordon, Leonard Angus, George Arthur, Richard Allen, Myrtle, and John Earl; Presbyterian; d. 1940.

McPhee, a Liberal, was first elected to the Legislative Assembly in the general election of 1927 for 2nd Queens. He was re-elected in the general election of 1935. He was defeated in the general election of 1931.

McPhee was educated in the Riverdale School and later worked in that area as a farmer. He was a member of the Masonic Order. Angus McPhee died in 1940.

Drucella McPhee, the daughter of Thomas Rogerson of Bonshaw. She was born in 1869 and died 8 February 1953.

References
CPG 1931; Elections PEI; PARO: Argyle Shore Cemetery Records.

MCPHEE, K.C., GEORGE WASHINGTON, teacher, lawyer and judge; b. 17 November 1880 in St. Catherines, son of Annie Rogerson *née* McPhee; m. first August 1911, Jennie M. Hodgson of Charlottetown, and they had one child, Elizabeth; m. secondly 7 July 1915 Flora Connor of Crystal City, Manitoba, and they had three children, George Fraser, Ian Archibald, and Mary Anne; Presbyterian, and later United; d. 23 November 1971.

McPhee, a Liberal, was elected to the Legislative Assembly in a by-election held 8 February 1911 for 2nd Queens. He was defeated in the general election of 1912. His by-election victory, brought about due to the resignation of Liberal William Laird*, was an important victory for the Liberals, as they were holding a 16-seat to 14-seat majority. Later that year, the Liberals would lose two by-elections and their majority.

In 1917, following a move to Saskatchewan, McPhee was defeated in the federal election in the riding of MacKenzie. In October 1925, he was elected to the House of Commons in the new riding of Yorkton, Saskatchewan, and was re-elected in 1926, 1930, and 1935.

Upon arriving in Saskatchewan, McPhee took part in the election campaign with the provincial Liberals. He played a role in the federal Liberal party beyond Saskatchewan's borders, campaigning federally in 1935 in Ontario and the Maritime provinces. McPhee took an active part in the provincial elections in New Brunswick. During a number of federal elections, he addressed more than 20 political conventions in Ontario. While a Member of the House of Commons, he was chair of the Private Bill Committee and was a member of the Committee on Banking and Commerce. In 1937 McPhee was one of the delegates of the Canadian Parliament to attend the Coronation of King George VI.

McPhee received his early education at the local school in St. Catherines. Later he attended Prince of Wales College and was trained as a teacher. From 1900 to 1905, he taught in Island schools. Following his time as a teacher, he studied law in the office of Weeks and Whear*, and was admitted to the Bar in 1910. Before leaving the Island, McPhee worked as a lawyer in Charlottetown. In 1914 he was appointed Chairman of the Board of License Commissioners for Saskatchewan, and from 1915 to 1918 served as Crown Prosecutor in Yorkton. In 1920 McPhee received the designation of King's Counsel. On 26 February 1940, he became a Judge of the District and Surrogate Courts for the judicial districts of Moose Jaw. In 1943 he was appointed chairman of the committee to deal with the restoration of organizations banned during the Second World War by the federal government. That same year, he was appointed as Rental Appeal Judge for southern Saskatchewan and served in this capacity until 1950. McPhee also served as president of the council of district judges of Saskatchewan.

McPhee was a member of fraternal organizations in Prince Edward Island and later in Moose Jaw. In Saskatchewan he was a member of the Canadian and Rotary Clubs, the Moose Jaw Lodge Number 3 and the A.F. and A.M. George McPhee died 23 November 1971, and he was buried in British Columbia.

Jennie McPhee was the daughter of S. F. Hodgson. Flora McPhee was the daughter of Archibald Connor and Mary Phillips.

References
CPG 1912, 1938; *CDP* p. 436; *HFER* vol. 2; Saskatchewan Yorkton p. 1; Blanchard *Islanders Away*, p. 277; *Guardian* 9 February 1911; *Leard Burial Sites*.

MCQUAID, Q.C., HONOURABLE MELVIN JAMES, barrister and judge; b. 6 September 1911 in Souris, son of John McQuaid and Annie Mullally; m. 15 September 1947 Catherine Handrahan, and they had three children, John, Mary-Jo and Peter; Roman Catholic; d. 16 January 2001 in Charlottetown.

McQuaid, a Conservative, was first elected to the Legislative Assembly in the general election of 1959 for 1st Kings. McQuaid was re-elected in 1st Kings in a by-election held 4 December 1972, and in the general election of 1974. He was defeated in the general elections of 1951, 1955, and 1962. He held the positions of Attorney-General and Advocate General, as well as Provincial Treasurer, from 16 September 1959 until 1962. McQuaid was Leader of the Conservatives in 1973, and served as Leader of the Opposition from 1973 until July 1976, when he was appointed to the Supreme Court. McQuaid was first elected to the House of Commons for King's in the 1965 federal election. He was re-elected in 1968 and 1970 for Cardigan but did not seek re-election in the fall of 1972, choosing instead to run provincially again.

McQuaid received his early education at Souris Elementary and Souris High School. He began his post-secondary education at St. Dunstan's College, and later received his Bachelor of Arts at St. Francis Xavier University in Antigonish, Nova Scotia, in 1936. McQuaid studied at Dalhousie University in Halifax and earned an LL.B. in 1937. In 1940 he was admitted to the Bar of Prince Edward Island. He established a law practice in Souris and continued working as a lawyer in the community when not serving in politics or the judiciary. He retired from his law practice in 1992. In 1939 he accepted the position of Town Clerk of Souris and continued in this capacity until 1957. McQuaid served as a Crown Prosecutor for two years and was appointed to the Supreme Court by Prime Minister Pierre Trudeau in 1976. He retired from the Supreme Court in 1981.

McQuaid was president of the Law Society of Prince Edward Island, a member of the Eastern Kings Board of Trade, a member of the Atlantic Provinces Economic Council, and a member of the National Parole Board. He was a charter member and secretary-treasurer of the board of directors in the construction of the original Souris hospital in 1945, and in the late 1980s co-chaired the financial campaign for the present Souris Hospital. McQuaid was a member of the local Retarded Children's Association and the Home and School Association. He served his home parish of St. Mary's Roman Catholic Church as a trustee, lector, and lay minister. He was a 4th degree member of the Knights of Columbus. Melvin McQuaid died 16 January 2001 at the Queen Elizabeth Hospital.

Catherine McQuaid, the daughter of Austin Handrahan of Tignish, predeceased her husband.

References
CDP p. 438; CPG 1976; WWPEI p. 105; Guardian 18 January 2001, 16 January 2002; Kings County Weekly 16 January 1982; Questionnaire to Former MLAs.

MCWILLIAMS, ALFRED, farmer, business person, mill owner, and officeholder; b. ca. 6 October 1840 in West Cape, son of David McWilliams and Sarah Wood; m. 1905, Clara Jane Winsloe of New Glasgow, and there were no children; Methodist; d. 1928, in West Cape.

McWilliams, a Liberal, was first elected to the House of Assembly in a by-election held April 1891 for 2nd Prince. He was elected to the Legislative Assembly in the general election of 1893 for 2nd Prince. He was re-elected in the general elections of 1897, 1900, 1904, 1908, and 1912.

McWilliams was educated in local public schools. He was a farmer, merchant, and shipbuilder, and he operated a mill. For 20 years he served as Postmaster for West Cape. McWilliams owned a 464-acre farm, which adjoined his home, as well as farms in neighbouring settlements. In total he owned 915 acres of farm land, and a grist mill, a carding mill, and a saw mill. Alfred McWilliams died in 1928.

Clara McWilliams was born ca. 1858 and died 10 September 1925. The couple were married in Maine.

References
CPG 1897, 1914; Meacham's Atlas; Daily Patriot 11 September 1925, 26 April 1928; PARO: MNI-Census 1891; McWilliams Family File; Bethel United Church Cemetery Records.

MELLA, M.A., HONOURABLE PATRICIA JANET, educator; b. 29 August 1943 in Port Hill, daughter of Frank Joseph MacDougall and Patricia Mary Hilda Callaghan; m. 27 June 1970 Angelo Mella and they had three children, Andrew, Michael, and Nancy; Roman Catholic.

Mella, a Conservative, was first elected to the Legislative Assembly in the general election of 1993 for 3rd Queens. She was elected in the general election of 1996 to the new electoral district of Glen Stewart-Bellevue Cove. She was re-elected in the general election of 2000. Mella was defeated in the general election of 1989 for 3rd Queens. Elected Leader of the Conservatives on 10 November 1990, Mella became the first woman in the province's history to be named leader of a political party. She had no seat in the Legislative Assembly until 1993, when she became the only Conservative member in the 31-seat Legislative Assembly. Mella resigned as Leader of the Opposition on 1 December 1995. On 27 November 1996, she was appointed Provincial Treasurer in the government of Premier Patrick Binns*.

Mella began her education at local schools and she obtained a high school diploma in 1961 at Kinkora High School. She attended St. Dunstan's University, where she obtained a Bachelor of Arts in 1965 and a Bachelor of Education in 1973. Mella studied at Catholic University of America in Washington, DC, where she earned a Master of Arts in 1967 and worked as a teaching assistant. She returned to Canada and accepted a position as a lecturer at Carleton University from 1967 to 1970, and at Queen's University from 1970 until 1972.

That same year, Mella moved back to the Maritimes, where she taught junior high school in Halifax. In 1979 she and her family moved to the Island where she taught junior and senior high school. In 1987 she obtained a teaching position at Charlottetown Rural Regional High School, and remained there until she became Leader of the Conservative party.

Mella served as Secretary of the Cardigan Riding Association and the Progressive Conservative Party. She was co-chair of the federal Progressive Conservative campaign in 1988. She was a member of the Bunbury-Southport-Crossroads Recreation Commission and the Local Advisory Council for Canadian Job Strategies for Employment and Immigration Canada. She has also served on committees relating to education and professional development through the Prince Edward Island Teacher's Federation. Mella is a past-president of the Charlottetown Christian Council and was a member of the Diocesan Pastoral Council for the Roman Catholic Diocese of Charlottetown. Patricia Mella and her husband currently reside in Stratford.

Angelo Mella, the son of Silvio and Josephine Mella of Romania, moved to Edmonton in 1951, and then to Ontario, where he joined the mathematics faculty of Carleton University. The couple met when Patricia Mella joined the faculty to teach sociology.

References
CWW p. 873; *Common Ground* vol. 9 no. 6, vol. 14 no. 5; *Guardian* 1 March 1993.

METHERALL, JOSEPH CHRISTOPHER, farmer; b. 16 April 1862 in Mill River, son of Thomas Metherall and Jane Gard; m. 27 February 1884 Sarah Gorill, and they had six children, Ethel, Hattie, Flossie, Sergeant, and another son and daughter; Methodist; d. 1947.

Metherall, a Liberal, was elected to the Legislative Assembly in the general election of 1919 for 1st Prince. He was defeated in the general election of 1923.

Metherall, though born in Mill River, lived in Alberton, where he received his education. In the early 1800s, his ancestors had emigrated to the Island to engage in shipbuilding, but he chose farming as his occupation. Joseph Metherall died in 1947.

Sarah Metherall, the daughter of John and Eleanor Irene Gorill of Cascumpec. She was born 10 October ca. 1862 and died in 1953.

References
CPG 1921, 1924; PARO: Census 1901; St. Peters Anglican and O'Leary United Church Baptismal Records; Cascumpec United Church Cemetery Records.

MILLER, CECIL ALLAN, train worker and police officer; b. 1896, in Marshfield, Massachusetts, son of James Allan Miller and Minnie Lane; m. 3 January 1922 Revola Fleet Stewart, and they had five children, Ruth Eleanor (died in infancy), Joan, Madge, Allan, and Glen; Presbyterian; d. 10 October 1988 in Charlottetown.

Miller, a Liberal, was first elected to the Legislative Assembly in the general election of 1966 for 3rd Queens. He was re-elected in the general elections of 1970 and 1974. He was defeated in the general elections of 1962 and 1978. From 1966 to 1970, Miller served as Minister of Industry and Natural Resources and Minister of Fisheries. He was elected Speaker on 2 June 1970. He was President of the Prince Edward Island Branch of the Canadian Parliamentary Association.

Miller's family moved to the Island in 1900. He was raised and educated in Charlottetown. In 1921 Miller settled in Frenchfort. Cecil Miller died 10 October 1988 at the Queen Elizabeth Hospital.

Revola Miller was born 29 April 1898 and died 10 May 1956.

References
CPG 1964, 1979; *Guardian* 11 October 1988, 12 October 1988, 25 March 1989; PARO: Marshfield St. Columbia Presbyterian Cemetery Records.

MILLIGAN, KEITH, teacher and farmer; b. 8 February 1950 in Inverness, son of Charles Bayfield Milligan of Northam and Reby Hazel MacKinnon of Inverness; m. 11 August 1978 Deborah Foley, and they had three children, Charles Christian, Olivia, and Dustin; Anglican.

Milligan, a Liberal, was first elected to the Legislative Assembly in a by-election held 2 February 1981 for 2nd Prince. He was re-elected in the general elections of 1982, 1986, 1989, and 1993. He was elected in the general election of 1996 in the new electoral district of Cascumpec-Grand River. Following the by-election victory in 1981, he was selected as interim leader and served as Leader of the Opposition until Joseph Ghiz* won the leadership convention held 24 October 1981. From 1982 to 1986, Milligan served as Opposition critic for education. When the Liberals formed the government in 1986, he was appointed Minister of Health and Social Services, and Minister Responsible for the Hospital and Health Services Commission; he held these Ministries until 1989. From 1989 to 1993, Milligan was Minister of Agriculture, and in 1993 was appointed Minister of Education and Human Resources. From June 1994 to 1996, Milligan served as Minister of Transportation and Public Works.

In 1996 Milligan was elected leader of the Liberal Party. Considered the underdog in the leadership race, Milligan received significant support from the grassroots, particularly from western Prince Edward Island. More than 5,000 Liberals attended the convention, held at the Field House, University of Prince Edward Island, and it was the largest ever political convention held in the province. On 10 October 1996, Milligan was sworn in as premier. Hoping to ride the wave of media coverage and interest created by the convention, he called an election for 18 November. The Liberals were defeated by the Conservatives and their newly elected leader, Patrick Binns*.

Milligan received his early education at the Inverness District School. He later attended O'Leary High School and was valedictorian of his graduating class in 1970. Milligan continued his studies at the University of Prince Edward Island, where he earned Bachelor of Arts and Bachelor of Education degrees. Following the completion of his education, he taught for two years in Regional Administrative Unit One. He was a silver fox and elk rancher, and served as manager of the West Prince Regional Services Centre.

Milligan was a junior arts representative on the University of Prince Edward Island Student Union. He has been associated with numerous community projects and initiatives, including the Tyne Valley Oyster Festival. Milligan has served as vice-president of the Tyne Valley Fire Hall, secretary of the Tyne Valley Community Sports Centre, secretary of the Stewart Memorial Health Centre, and as a member of the West Prince Community Advisory Board. He has been a member of the Canada Fox Breeders Association and the Prince Edward Island Fur Breeders Association. Keith Milligan and his family live in Tyne Valley.

Deborah Milligan is the daughter of John E. Foley of Bloomfield.

References
CPG 1998–1999; CWW 1997 p. 872; ECO 39/93, 138/93; WWPEI p. 106; Guardian 4 March 2000.

MONKLEY, GEORGE LORNE, public servant; b. 24 June 1914 in Summerside, son of Edward H. Monkley and Mae MacDonald; m. 23 December 1939 Edna Jane Champion, and they had three children, Edward, Errol, and Allen; United; d. 8 March 1997 in Charlottetown.

Monkley, a Conservative, was first elected to the Legislative Assembly in the general election of 1959 for 5th Prince. He was re-elected in the general election of 1962. He resigned from the Legislature in 1963.

Lorne Monkley was educated in local schools. In his early career, he worked as the secretary-treasurer of Amalgamated Dairies Limited. He was a Veteran of the Second World War, and retired as a Major from the Prince Edward Island Regiment. He was a director of the Hillcrest Housing Company, which was created for the use of Department of National Defence personnel stationed at CFB Summerside. Monkley was Clerk of the Legislative Assembly before entering politics. Following his political career, he was appointed Chairperson of the Civil Service Commission. Monkley served the province as Chief Electoral Officer. He was the first Islander to be elected as Superintendent of Insurance for Canada. He was a member of the Masonic Lodge, the Lions Club, and the Royal Canadian Legion. Lorne Monkley died 8 March 1997.

Edna Monkley was the daughter of Wesley Champion of Kensington.

References
CPG 1963, 1966; Hillcrest Housing Limited p. 7; Guardian 12 March 1997.

MONTGOMERY, DONALD, educator and school administrator; b. 3 May 1848 in Valleyfield, son of Malcolm Montgomery and Christine McDonald; m. 10 August 1887 Mary Isabella McPhail, and there were no children; United/Presbyterian; d. 14 May 1890 in Charlottetown.

Montgomery, a Conservative, was first elected to the House of Assembly in a by-election held September 1878 for 4th Queens. He was re-elected in the general election of 1879. He resigned on 25 September 1879 to accept the appointment of Chief Superintendent of Education.

Montgomery went to school in Valleyfield, later attending Prince of Wales College in Charlottetown for at least one year, where he placed first in his class. Montgomery attended the Island's

Normal School, and, by the early 1870s, was master of the Harrington grammar school. On 25 August 1874, he was appointed Master of the Normal School and Model School, where he focussed on training teachers. In September 1877, Montgomery was dismissed from this position by the L. H. Davies* coalition government, which believed he lacked the qualities necessary to transform the Normal school into a more professional institution. Montgomery moved to Montreal to study law at McGill.

On 25 September 1879, Premier W. W. Sullivan* selected Montgomery to be Chief Superintendent of Education. His duties were to enforce the Public Schools Act of 1877, to prepare annual reports on provincial education, to suggest improvements to the system, and to supervise publicly funded education. It is reported he carried out these tasks successfully. Montgomery classified Island schools according to the level of work done in each, introduced a uniform course of studies for each grade, and encouraged the improvement of school accommodations. He promoted continuing training and development for teachers. Montgomery helped establish the Provincial Education Institute, which held an annual two-day professional development convention for teachers in October. Montgomery served as its first president.

Montgomery played perhaps the single most important role in putting the Public School Act of 1877 into practice. When he died, while still Chief Superintendent, the province had a progressive educational system. Donald Montgomery died 14 May 1890.

References

DCB XI 1881 1890 pp. 601–03; *Daily Examiner* 15 May 1890.

MONTGOMERY, JOHN MALCOLM, farmer; b. 4 January 1843 in Princetown, son of James Townsend Montgomery and Rose McCary; m. 25 March 1882 Mary Emily McNeill, and they had four children, Annie S., Lucy R., Edith, and Charlotte G.; Presbyterian; d. 18 February 1895 in Malpeque.

Montgomery, a Liberal, was elected to the House of Assembly in the general election of 1890 for 3rd Prince. He was defeated in the general elections of 1886, 1893, and 1897. Montgomery served as Usher of the Black Rod in the Legislative Council from March 1887 to January 1890.

He received his early education at Fanning Grammar School in Malpeque. Before entering politics Montgomery was a farmer. John Montgomery died 18 February 1895.

Mary Montgomery was born ca. 1855.

References

CPG 1889, 1891, 1897; *Daily Patriot* 22 February 1895; PARO: Montgomery Family File; MNI-Census 1891.

MORRISSEY, CLARENCE FERDINAND, farmer and business person; b. 27 August 1876 in Tignish, son of Patrick Morrissey; m. 4 September 1910 Zita Catherine Kinch, and they had seven children, of whom three names are known, Claude, Annette, and Frances; Roman Catholic; d. 25 December 1960 in Charlottetown.

Morrissey, a Conservative, was elected to the Legislative Assembly in a by-election held 19 December 1945 for 1st Prince. He was defeated in the general election of 1947. In 1952 he served as one of the first Village Commissioners of Tignish.

Morrissey lived in Tignish his entire life. At 18, due to the death of his father, he helped provide for his mother and younger brothers and sisters. For many years, Morrissey owned and operated a large lobster packing plant in Black Marsh, just north of Tignish. He was also a successful fox farmer. Clarence Morrissey died 25 December 1960.

Zita Morrissey, the daughter of James Kinch, was born 14 February 1886 and died 20 January 1968.

References

C.F.'s Diary pp. 5, 9, 18a, 75a, 79a, 255a, 255b, 372a, 372b, 402a, 425a, 425b, 485b; *CPG* 1947, 1948; *Guardian* 27 December 1960, 10 March 1976; PARO: Saint Simon and Saint Jude Church Cemetery Records.

MORRISSEY, ROBERT JOSEPH, fisher; b. 18 November 1954 in Alberton, son of Bernard Morrissey and Marie O'Connor, both of Sea Cow Pond; Roman Catholic.

Morrissey, a Liberal, was first elected to the Legislative Assembly in the general election of 1982 for 1st Prince. He was re-elected in the general elections of 1986, 1989, and 1993. Morrissey was elected in the general election of 1996 in the new electoral district of Tignish-Deblois. On 2 May 1986, Morrissey was appointed Minister of Transportation and Public Works. He became Minister of Industry and Minister Responsible for the Prince Edward Island Marketing Agency in 1989. On 15 April 1993, Morrissey was named Minister of Economic Development and Tourism and Minister Responsible for Enterprise PEI. Following the 1996 general election, he held the positions of Opposition House Leader and Opposition critic for finance. While a Member, Morrissey served on the Standing Committee on Privileges, Rules and Private Bills, and the Standing Committee on Community Affairs and Economic Development. He was chair of the Standing Committee on Public Accounts.

Morrissey was educated at the Tignish Regional High School, Holland College, and at the University of Prince Edward Island. Beginning in 1973, he worked as a fisher out of Sea Cow Pond. Morrissey served as a trustee of the Unit 1 School Board and was chair of the West Prince Community Advisory Board. He was also vice-chair of the Parish Council of St. Simon and St. Jude, and an organizer of the Irish Moss Festival. Robert Morrissey is the great-great-great-grandson of Pierre M. Chiasson, the first Acadian to settle in the Tignish area.

References
CPG 1998-1999; WWPEI p. 109; Guardian 11 April 1986, 9 March 2000.

MORSON, WALTER AUGUSTUS ORMSBY, lawyer and officeholder; b. 24 December 1851 in Hamilton, Prince Edward Island, son of Richard Willock Morson and Elizabeth Codie; m. 14 October 1891 May Elizabeth DesBrisay, and they had three children, Arthur, Clifford, and Walter; Anglican; d. 9 September 1921.

Morson, a Conservative, was first elected to the Legislative Assembly in a by-election held 9 December 1902 for 3rd Kings. He was re-elected in the general elections of 1904 and 1908. He was defeated in the general election of 1900. In 1910 he resigned from the Legislature to accept the office of Deputy Prothonotary of the Supreme Court.

Morson received his early education in Hamilton. He studied law under Chief Justice W. W. Sullivan*, and was admitted to the Bar in 1877. Morson became a junior partner in the firm Sullivan, McLean and Morson in the same year. In 1879 he formed a partnership with Judge Neil McLeod* in Summerside under the name McLeod, Morson and McQuarrie, which lasted until 1903. At that time, he began a new partnership with Charles Gavan Duffy*, under the name Morson & Duffy. During his legal career he served as Protho-

notary and Clerk of the Crown.

Morson was a member of the board of trustees of the Prince Edward Island Hospital for many years. He also served on the branch of trustees of St. Peter's Cathedral. Morson was a member of the Masonic Order. In his early years, he was in the military, where he achieved the rank of Major. Walter Morson died 9 September 1921.

May Morson, the daughter of Theophilus and Dorcas DesBrisay, died 8 January 1928.

References
Elections PEI; Guardian 10 September 1921; Patriot 10 September 1921; PARO: MNI-Census 1891; St. Peter's Cathedral Cemetery Records.

MURPHY, MARION, teacher, secretary, farmer, and business person; b. 21 August 1941 in Albany, daughter of Marius Larsen and Nellie Heffel; m. 25 July 1964 Elmer Murphy of Millvale, and they had four children, Jo-Anna, Blaine, Faye, and Ray; Roman Catholic.

Murphy, a Liberal, was first elected to the Legislative Assembly in the general election of 1989 for 1st Queens. She was re-elected in the general election of 1993. She was defeated in the general election of 1986. During her time in the Legislature, Murphy served on numerous Legislative Committees, including community and cultural affairs, justice, and the Special Committees on the Constitution of Canada, Lands Protection, and the Legislative Assembly. She was also chair of the Special Committee on Election Expenses.

Murphy received her early education in Albany, Cape Traverse, and Augustine Cove schools, later attending Prince of Wales College in Charlottetown and the University of Prince Edward Island, where she studied to be a teacher. Murphy taught at various Island schools from 1958 to 1972. In 1973 she became the secretary at St. Anne's Elementary School, where she worked part-time until 1989. She was actively involved in the operation of the family farm and sawmill operation in Millvale with her husband Elmer.

Murphy has served as president of the Provincial Home and School Association, and as vice-president of the Canadian Home and School Association. She was instrumental in the establishment of the Small Farms Advisory Board and the Central Queens Funeral Co-operative. Murphy has been a director of the St. Anne's Community Centre Co-operative Association. Since 1975 she has been a 4-H Leader, and is actively involved with the Red Cross. Murphy served as president of the St. Anne's Catholic Women's League. She and her family are members of the St. Anne's Roman Catholic Church. She is currently President of the Association of Former MLAs. Marion Murphy and her husband Elmer reside in Millvale.

References
CPG 1987, 1996; *Guardian* 9 March 1993, 28 September 1996; *Journal-Pioneer* 13 February 1996.

MUSTARD, JOHN J., farmer and chair of the Workmen's Compensation Board; b. 24 January 1902 in Cardigan, son of John Mustard and Bell McKay; m. ca. 1940 Katherine Nicholson, and they had four children, John, Paul, Virginia and Gail; Presbyterian; d. 1 September 1981 in Charlottetown.

Mustard, a Liberal, was first elected to the Legislative Assembly in the general election of 1927 for 3rd Kings. He was re-elected in the general elections of 1935 and 1939. He was defeated in the general election of 1931. Mustard joined the armed forces in 1943 as an officer. He was a member of the Prince Edward Island Light Horse Regiment.

"Jack" Mustard attended Prince of Wales College and Nova Scotia Agricultural College. For the majority of his life, he was a farmer. He served as Chairman of the Workmen's Compensation Board for six years and retired in 1973.

Mustard's other assocations included membership in the Royal Canadian Legion, the Charlottetown Club, and the Masonic Lodge. He was committed to forestry projects and owned several acres of red pine trees, which he referred to as his "cathedral in the pines." He was a member of the Kirk of St. James in Charlottetown. Jack Mustard died 1 September 1981 in Charlottetown Hospital.

Katherine Mustard died in Charlottetown 4 July 2002 at the age of 88.

References
CPG 1940, 1944; CWW 1936–1937 p. 820; *Patriot* 3 September 1981; PARO: Lorne Valley St. Andrew's Cemetery Records.

MYERS, FRANK SHELDON, farmer; b. 22 February 1908, in Hampton, son of John H. Myers* and Adelaide Dixon; m. 12 December 1928 Florence May Profitt, and they had three children, Jean Borthwick, Francis Adelaide, and Sheldon Profitt; Anglican; d. 15 March 1975 in Crapaud.

Myers, a Conservative, was first elected to the Legislative Assembly in the general election of 1951 for 1st Queens. He was re-elected in the general elections of 1959, 1962, and 1966. He was defeated in the general elections of 1955 and 1970. In 1959 he was appointed Deputy Speaker and on 18 February 1965 became Speaker. Myers served in this capacity until 14 April 1966. Myers' father, John Myers*, served in the Legislative Assembly and the House of Commons.

Myers was educated in Hampton and was a farmer in this area. He served as chairman of the board of directors of the Riverside Hospital, was on the Board of Trade, and was a member of the Masonic Lodge. Frank Myers died 15 March 1975 at his home.

References
CPG 1952, 1958, 1970, 1971; Elections PEI; *Guardian* 17 March 1970.

MYERS, JOHN HOWARD, farmer; b. 23 September 1880 in Hampton, son of Abraham Myers and Annie McNeill; m. 16 December 1905 Adelaide Dixon, and they had 15 children, Frank Sheldon*, Borden, Lewis, Keith, Howard, Ralph, Norman, William, Arthur, Lulu, Laura, Mabel, Doris, Mildred, and Elizabeth; United; d. 12 October 1956 in Hampton.

Myers, a Conservative, was first elected to the Legislative Assembly in the general election of 1912 for 1st Queens. He was elected in the general election of 1923 for 4th Prince. He served as Minister of Agriculture and Provincial Secretary from 5 September 1923 until 10 September 1926 when he resigned from provincial politics. He was elected in the federal election for Queen's in 1926, and was defeated in 1930 and 1935.

Myers was educated at the local school and then at Prince of Wales College in Charlottetown. A prominent farmer in the Hampton area and throughout the province, he was active in agricultural associations for many years, and promoted agricultural interests both provincially and federally. Myers served as director of the Phoenix Farming Company and provided leadership in the dairy industry. John Myers died 12 October 1956, while helping with the potato harvest on a son's farm in Hampton.

Adelaide Myers was the daughter of John Dixon of DeSable. Frank Myers represented 1st Queens in the Legislative Assembly from 1951 to 1955 and again from 1959 to 1970.

References
CDP p. 385; CPG 1926; Elections PEI: *Guardian* 13 October 1956; *Patriot* 12 October 1956; PARO: Crapaud People's Cemetery Records.

N

NASH, FREDERICK JOHN, journalist, editor, and writer; b. 21 December 1862 in Halifax, son of Samuel C. Nash and Hannah Creelman; m. Emma Charlotte Miller, and they had two children, Isabel and Frederick; Presbyterian; d. 2 August 1929 in Charlottetown.

Nash, a Liberal, was elected to the Legislative Assembly in the general election of 1919 for 4th Queens. He was defeated in a by-election held 15 November 1911, and also in the general elections of 1912, 1915, and 1923. Nash served as a Minister without Portfolio in the John H. Bell* Administration. He served as President of the Young Liberal Association.

Nash was educated at the local school and Prince of Wales College in Charlottetown. He worked as a reporter, city editor, and associate editor. He was a marine reporter for a large Boston daily newspaper. Nash became editor of the *Daily Patriot* and the *Weekly Patriot* in November 1898, upon the resignation of David Laird* from this position. He was a well-respected writer, and served as correspondent for the *Toronto Globe* and for several leading liberal papers in Canada. Nash also served as the Island editor of the *Canadian Labour Gazette.* He gave numerous lectures and was regarded as one of the best platform speakers in the province. Nash took a great interest in education and served as a trustee and active member of the Charlottetown School Board. He was president of the Zion Presbyterian Church Literary Society and a member of the Charlottetown Board of Trade. Frederick Nash died 2 August 1929 while editor of the *Patriot.*

Emma Nash was the daughter of Lemuel Miller, principal of West Kent School in Charlottetown, and Margaret H. Lawson of Charlottetown. She was born 24 April 1872 and died 22 July 1931.

References
CPG 1921, 1924; *Past and Present* pp. 349–50; *Patriot* 3 August 1929; PARO: Charlottetown People's Cemetery Records.

NICHOLSON, JAMES, farmer; b. 16 October 1827 in Belfast, son of Samuel Nicholson and Flora MacLeod; m. 15 September 1855 Mary Jane Munroe, and they had seven children, A. John, Florence, F. Daniel, A. Samuel, Evangeline, Florence (died at two years and ten months), and Samuel I. (died at three years and five months); Presbyterian; d. 10 June 1905 in Eldon.

Nicholson, a Conservative, was first elected to the House of Assembly by acclamation in a by-election held 7 November 1878 for 4th Queens. He was re-elected in the general election of 1879. He was defeated in the general election of 1882. Later that year he was elected to the Legislative Council for 2nd Queens. In the general elections of 1886 and 1890, he was re-elected to the Legislative Council. Nicholson served as Leader of the Conservative party in the Legislative Council. He served on Executive Council from 1887 to 1891. Nicholson was a strong supporter of local industry and advocated protective tariffs.

Nicholson was born of Scottish parents and educated in Belfast. His father came to the Island from the Isle of Skye in 1803. In his early career, Nicholson had been a successful farmer and a temperance advocate. He was an elder in the Presbyterian Church and Superintendent of the Sabbath School. As a result of these involvements and his political service, Nicholson was well-respected within his community. James Nicholson died 10 June 1905.

Mary Nicholson was born in 1836 and died 14 March 1918.

References
CPG 1879, 1880, 1885, 1889; PARO: MNI-Hutchinson's p. 147; MNI-Census 1861, 1881, 1891; John's Presbyterian Church Records.

O

O'BRIEN, FRANCIS GERARD "JUNIOR", farmer; b. 15 December 1927 in Morell, son of Francis O'Brien of Morell and Emily Kenny of Morell Rear; m. 16 June 1953 Rosella Magennis, and they had 12 children, Gary, Francis, Leah, Rachael, Joan, Gerard, Theresa, Ivan, Robert, Linda, Olive, and Kenneth; Roman Catholic.

O'Brien, a Conservative, was first elected to the Legislative Assembly in the general election of 1982 for 2nd Kings. He was re-elected in the general election of 1986. He was chair of the Select Standing Committee on Transportation and also served on several Legislative Committees.

"Junior" O'Brien received his education at the school in Sinnott Road. He was a mink and beef farmer, and worked on the Prince Edward Island Fur Farm in Morell from 1966 to 1981. O'Brien was the director of the Morell Consumers' Co-op, the Morell Credit Union, and the Morell Chevy's Baseball Club. He is a volunteer for various community charities and is a member of the Knights of Columbus. Junior O'Brien and his wife reside in Green Meadows.

Rosella O'Brien was the daughter of Terrence and Marion Magennis of Elliotvale.

References
CPG 1989; *WWPEI* p. 111; *Guardian* 15 April 1986.

OWEN, LEMUEL CAMBRIDGE, business person and shipping magnate; b. 1 November 1822 in Charlottetown, son of Thomas Owen and Ann Campbell; m. 9 July 1861 Lois Welsh, and they had three children, William Edward Wallace, Lemuel Cambridge, and Marion Adele; Anglican; d. 26 November 1912.

Owen, a Conservative, was first elected to the House of Assembly in the general election of 1867 for 3rd Kings. He was re-elected in the general elections of 1870 and 1873. He was defeated in the general election of 1872. In 1870 Owen became Chairman of the Board of Works and, in Septem-

ber of that year, a member of Executive Council in the coalition government of Premier James C. Pope*, until Pope's defeat in 1872. In 1873 Owen was appointed to Executive Council for a second time under Pope, and in September of that year was selected as premier. He served in this position until his retirement in 1876, shortly before the election of that year.

Premier Owen's government was forced to deal with the immediate problems and issues produced by Confederation. These included the negotiations regarding assumption of the Island debt by Ottawa, the transfer of the railway to the federal government, and the final settlement of the land question. According to a fellow Member, A. J. MacDonald*, Owen was something of a figurehead, who deferred to Haviland on most matters. Owen, along with his Executive Council, which included Thomas Heath Haviland, Jr.*, as Colonial Secretary, Frederick de St. Croix Brecken* as Attorney-General, and William Wilfred Sullivan* as Solicitor-General, successfully dealt with those issues. However, in 1874 the issue of government funding of schools became central in the province, and Owen lost some members of his caucus. The alignments within the House of Assembly shifted from political parties to new alliances based on the school funding question. Owen retired from politics before the 1876 election.

Owen came from a wealthy and prominent family that controlled, along with the Chanters, Peakes, Yeos, and Popes, much of the Island's shipping and shipbuilding industry. He was educated at private schools and later at Central Academy in Charlottetown. Owen was involved in the family business. He began his career with James Peake, in James Peake and Company, a firm of merchants and shipbuilders that was perhaps the most successful of its generation. Owen established a number of agencies for off-Island merchants and manufacturers. He also served as the agent for Lloyd's of London.

In 1860 both Thomas Owen and James Peake died. Lemuel Cambridge Owen succeeded his father as Postmaster-General for the Island and carried on much of Peake's business with his new partner, William Welsh*. As Postmaster-General, Owen introduced a prepayment system for the mailing of letters and packages using postal stamps. He established regular mail service to and from the Island, and instituted a system which allowed for the interchange of money orders between Prince Edward Island and the United Kingdom. In 1861 the partnership between Owen and Welsh was sealed by the marriage of Owen to Welsh's youngest sister, Lois.

In 1862 Owen was appointed to serve as the commanding major of the Kings County regiment, a confirmation of his stature within the Island community. He served as a captain and volunteer with the militia responsible for Company D Rifles at Georgetown. Owen was a director of the Merchant's Bank, a director of the Steam Navigation Company, a director of the Marine Insurance Company, and a trustee of the Lunatic Asylum.

He refused to take any interest or part in the political activities of the province after his retirement. Instead, Owen devoted his time and energy to building his new family home on Longworth Avenue in Charlottetown and to his declining business interests. He died at the home of his son Lemuel Cambridge on 26 November 1912.

Lois Owen, daughter of Charles Welsh and Lois Bell, was born 4 September 1825 and died in 1903. Owen's sister Anna Louise MacDonald was married to Hugh Lord MacDonald*.

References
Cotton pp. 140–41; *CPG* 1876; *DCB* XIV 1911–1920 pp. 812–13; *Provincial Premiers Birthday Series 1873–1973*; PARO: Owen Family File.

P

PALMER, Q.C., HERBERT JAMES, lawyer and director; b. 26 August 1851 in Charlottetown, son of Edward P. Palmer and Isabella Phoebe Tremain; m. 19 October 1880 Ada Millicent Patena, and they had five children, Helen Isabel, Beatrice Adele, Philip Errol, Harold Leonard, and Charles Nevill Tremain; Anglican; d. 22 December 1939 in Charlottetown.

Palmer, a Liberal, was first elected to the Legislative Assembly in the general election of 1900 for 3rd Queens. He was re-elected in the general election of 1908. He was defeated in the general election of 1904, and in a by-election held 15 November 1911. The by-election, one of two held on the same date, came about due to Palmer's acceptance of the office of premier earlier in the year to replace Francis L. Haszard*, who was appointed to the Supreme Court. Palmer served as Attorney-General after the death of Premier Arthur Peters* in 1908.

In May 1911, upon Haszard's move to the Court, Palmer inherited a Liberal party that had been in power for more than 20 years. It had become unpopular and held only a small majority. Palmer was called upon to form the government. Seven months later, Palmer and fellow Liberal F. J. Nash* contested two by-elections, required by the constitution, and both were defeated. Due to the by-election results, the Conservatives became the new government. John Alexander Mathieson*, the Conservative leader, immediately called an election. In the 1912 general election, Mathieson defeated the Palmer-led Liberals. The 28-2 victory was historic as it marked the first Conservative triumph in a general election since 1890, and the first Conservative government since 1891. After years in power, the Liberal government had lost the approval of the electorate, and the provincial Conservatives were viewed as having more influence with the Conservative federal government.

Palmer attended local schools in Charlottetown, later studying at Prince of Wales College and King's College in Windsor, Nova Scotia. In 1872 and 1873, he studied law in his father's office, and upon his father's appointment to the County Court he moved to the office of Palmer and MacLeod, where Robert Shaw* also studied. Palmer was admitted to the Bar in 1876 as an attorney, the same year he became a notary. In 1877 he became a barrister, and joined the partnership Palmer, MacLeod and MacLeod. In 1891 Palmer established his own legal practice and was designated Queen's Counsel in 1898. Following his political career, Palmer returned to the practice of law, and for a time practised with Michael Farmer*. He was appointed a director of the Prince Edward Island Telephone Company. H. James Palmer continued to practise law until his death on 22 December 1939.

Palmer's father, Edward D. Palmer, was Chief Justice of Prince Edward Island and a Father of Confederation. Palmer's mother was a native of Quebec, and the daughter of Charles Patena.

References

CPG 1909, 1912; MacDonald *If You're Stronghearted* p. 52; Premiers Gallery; *Patriot* 23 December 1939; PARO: MNI-Census 1881, 1891; St. Paul's Anglican Church Records; Sherwood Cemetery Records.

PATON, JAMES, merchant and business person; b. 5 June 1853 in Paisley, Scotland, son of Alexander Paton and Elizabeth McKechnie; m. first 22 January 1880 Eva Melcora Anderson, and they had one child, Cora E.; m. secondly 21 September 1887 Florence Gertrude Brown, and they had three children, Isobel Evelyn, Beatrice G., and James Rowland, m. thirdly July 1912, Susan Barrett, and there were no children; Methodist; d. 16 September 1935 in Charlottetown.

Paton, a Conservative, was elected to the Legislative Assembly in the general election of 1915 for Charlottetown Royalty. He was defeated in the general elections of 1897, 1900, and 1919. Before entering provincial politics, Paton served on Charlottetown City Council from 1902 to 1906, and was Mayor of Charlottetown from 1906 to 1908.

Paton was educated at Moores Public School and Nelson High School, both in Paisley, Scotland. At the age of 13, he went to work at Robertson and McGibbon, the leading drapers of Paisley, where he was employed for six years. In 1872 Paton came to the Island. He clerked in Charlottetown for four years, after which he entered into partnership with W. A. Weeks. In 1888 Paton became the sole owner of this business and changed the name of the firm to James Paton and Company. He travelled to Britain to make purchases for his business. In his lifetime, he crossed the Atlantic over 100 times.

Paton was actively involved in numerous community organizations. He was a member of the Methodist Church, where he served as a steward and a trustee. He was a director of the Caledonia Club in Charlottetown and a charter member of the Charlottetown Board of Trade, where he served as president. He was also involved in the Provincial Exhibition Association, serving as both a director and as president. James Paton died 16 September 1935 at his home.

Eva Paton, the daughter of John Anderson of Sackville, New Brunswick, died 27 April 1885. Florence Paton, the daughter of William and Isabella Jane Brown of Charlottetown, was born 6 October 1863 and died 31 March 1911. Susan Paton, the daughter of James and Sarah Barrett of Charlottetown, was born 31 December 1872.

References

CPG 1916, 1922; *Past and Present* p. 658; *Examiner* 22 January 1880; *Patriot* 17 September 1935; PARO: Census 1901; Baptismal Record, Trinity United Church book 2 pp. 119, 155; Marriage Register 13 1870–1887 p. 514; Charlottetown People's Cemetery Records.

PERRY, J. RUSSELL, federal public servant and service station operator; b. 1 June 1915 in Palmer Road, son of William T. Perry and Evelyn Poirier; m. Rosetta Gallant, and they had seven children, David, Donald, Marina, Joanne, Peggy, Betty Ann, and Paula; Roman Catholic; d. 23 January 1981 in Charlottetown.

Perry, a Liberal, was first elected to the Legislative Assembly in the general election of 1970 for 1st Prince. He was re-elected in the general elections of 1974, 1978, and 1979. On 15 March 1976, he was appointed as Speaker, and served from 6 June 1978 to 29 June 1979. Perry was a member of several select standing committees including those on fisheries, transportation, and tourism. While Perry served 1st Prince, the Mill River Golf Course, five new schools, the first Regional Services Centre in the province, a veterinary clinic, a grain elevator, and numerous housing projects were built by government. He felt his greatest accomplishment in politics was his involvement in a development at Tignish Run, where he provided assistance to 40 homeowners, enabling them to secure title to their land. With these titles clear, the homeowners could apply to the government for the Home Improvement Grants available.

Perry received his early education at the local school and later attended Summerside High School and St. Dunstan's College. After being discharged from the Armed Forces following the Second World War, he served for 12 years as a protection officer with the federal Department of Fisheries in the Tignish area. He later operated a service station. He and his family lived for a time in Nail Pond, and in 1956 they moved to Tignish.

Perry was a member and chairman of the Tignish Village Commission, and chairman of the Tignish Consolidated School District. He was a member and president of the Royal Canadian Legion Branch No. 6 and president of the Prince Edward Island Air Cadet League, as well as a director of the National Air Cadet League. Russell Perry died 23 January 1981 at the Queen Elizabeth Hospital.

Rosetta Perry was the daughter of John A. Gallant and Jane Handrahan. She died in Alberton on 27 February 2002.

References

CPG 1981; *Eastern Graphic* 15 September 1982; *Guardian* 16 April 1979, 28 January 1981, 28 February 2002.

PERRY, STANISLAUS FRANCIS, teacher, justice of the peace, and farmer; b. 7 May 1823 in Tignish, son of Pierre Poirier and Marie-Blanche Gaudet; m. 11 April 1847 Margaret Carroll, and they had ten children, Peter, Ann, John, Veronica, Stanislaus, Joseph, William, Mary, Daniel, and Marguerite; Roman Catholic; d. 24 February 1898 in Ottawa, and was buried in Tignish.

Perry, a Liberal for the majority of his political career, was first elected to the House of Assembly in the general election of 1854 for 2nd Prince. He was re-elected in the general elections of 1858 and 1859 for 3rd Prince. He was re-elected in the general elections of 1870 and 1873, in a by-election held in 1879, and in the general elections of 1882 and 1886, all in 1st Prince. Perry was defeated in the general election of 1867 in 1st Prince. In 1863, prior to the general election of that year, the Liberal Party asked Perry to step aside in favour of James Warburton. In the spring of 1873, while a member of the coalition government, Perry was appointed Speaker and served until he resigned from the House of Assembly in 1874. In 1887 Perry again resigned from the House. A Liberal for much of his career, in August 1870, Perry and most of the Catholic Liberals left the party to support J. C. Pope* because Liberal Premier Haythorne refused to give grants to Catholic schools.

During the 1860s, Perry was opposed to Confederation, but eventually changed his position on union with Canada. He was defeated in the special federal election in September 1873 as a Liberal for Prince County, won the 1874 federal election, and was defeated in the 1878 and 1882 federal elections. Following a second career in provincial politics, Perry was re-elected federally in 1887 and 1891. In the 1896 federal election for West Prince, Perry was defeated by Edward Hackett. The election in West Prince was declared void due to a breach in the law. As a result, a by-election was held in 1897, and Perry was successful. He died before the end of his term.

Perry was the first Island Acadian to hold a seat in both the Prince Edward Island Legislature and the House of Commons. He was also the first Acadian to be appointed Speaker of the House of Assembly. He was criticized within the Acadian community for his perceived lack of support for French-language education. He boycotted the Acadian national convention in 1884, and encouraged his constituents to do the same. He was upset because the convention was held in Miscouche, not Tignish. Although he was on the committee organizing the event, he was not consulted on the convention's location.

Perry attended elementary school in Tignish, and St. Andrews College for three years of study in the English language. He could not write in French. In his words, "I got anglified when I was young so much that even my name is English..." In 1843 Perry began teaching, receiving his first class teaching certificate the following year. Around this time, he anglicized his name from Poirier to Perry. Perry farmed to support his family. In 1851 he was appointed a Justice of the Peace. He was a Commissioner for Small Debts and the Acknowledgement of Deeds. He left teaching in 1854 for politics. Stanislaus Perry died 24 February 1898 in Ottawa.

Margaret Perry was the daughter of John Carroll and Ann Horan. Veronique and Anne Perry were, respectively, the mother of Angus L. MacDonald, a premier of Nova Scotia, and the mother of Joseph Alphonsus Bernard*, a Member of the Legislative Assembly of Prince Edward Island who would also serve as Lieutenant-Governor of the province.

References
Acadians pp. 91, 118; *Acadiens* p. 95; *CPG* 1880, 1887; *DCB* XII 1891–1900 pp. 836–38; Elections PEI; *Examiner* 1 March 1898; *Island Magazine* No. 43; *Patriot* 1 March 1898; PARO: Marriages 1844–1852 p. 261; MNI-Census 1881; MNI-Hutchinson's pp. 181, 241.

PETERS, Q.C., ARTHUR, lawyer; b. 29 August 1854 in Charlottetown, son of James Horsfield Peters of New Brunswick and Mary Cunard of Halifax; m. 25 September 1884 Amelia Jane Stewart, and they had four children, Catherine, James, Arthur Gordon, and Margaret Allison; Anglican; d. 29 January 1908 in Charlottetown.

Peters, a Liberal, was first elected to the House of Assembly in the 1890 general election for 2nd Kings. He was elected to the Legislative Assembly in the general election of 1893. He was re-elected in the general elections of 1897, 1900, and 1904. In the 1904 general election, Peters and his opponent, Harry D. McEwen, received an equal number of votes. A by-election was called in 1905 to resolve the impasse and Peters was elected by acclamation. He was appointed Attorney-General in 1900 and held that post until 1901. Chosen as party leader in 1901, Peters became premier in December 1901 and served until 1908. He led the Liberals to victory in the 1904 general election.

As was the case for many of the premiers who preceded him, Peters' term was marked by the dominant themes of post-Confederation Prince Edward Island: representation in the House of Commons, the inadequate subsidy from the federal government, and the quality of winter communication between the Island and the mainland. On the representation question, he argued that the province, because of its smallness, should be entitled to more seats than provided for in the British North America Act. At this time, the province had four seats in the House of Commons, while at the time of Confederation it had six. A resolution to the question eluded Premier Peters, but he continuously and forcefully made the Island's case to Ottawa.

The level of subsidy from Ottawa was a nagging concern for Peters. Since entering Confederation in 1873, the province had struggled to raise sufficient revenue to provide government services to Islanders. Continually the federal government had been urged to increase its subsidy to ensure the province stayed solvent. In 1906, at the federal-provincial conference, Peters and the other premiers made some progress in this area, but it was not until February 1908, shortly after his death, that an increase in the subsidy to the province was officially announced.

Peters also took on the challenge of improving travel to the mainland. Although the Island population was increasingly in favour of building a tunnel below the Northumberland Strait, his attention focused on urging the federal government to improve the ferry service. On 30 April 1903, following another bad winter, Peters' Administration demanded a third and more efficient steamer, as the *Minto* and the *Stanley* were frequently stuck in ice. After his death, the federal government responded to the province's demand and Premier Peters' urging. In 1909 the *Earl Grey*, a much more powerful steamer than the *Stanley* and the *Minto*, was put in service and helped to defuse the campaign for the construction of the tunnel.

Peters' brother Frederick* served as premier from 1891 until 1897. He won two electoral victories as leader, including the 1897 general election.

Peters was born in Charlottetown and lived at Elmwood, a house which still stands within the older section of Brighton. During his childhood, he was educated in Charlottetown by private tutors. Later he attended Prince of Wales College, and King's College in Halifax, Nova Scotia, where he obtained an Arts degree. After a period in the law office of Edward Jarvis Hodgson in Charlottetown, Peters read law in England, working with the esteemed instructor G. Brough Allen, and later Richard Everard Webster. He returned to the Island and was called to the Bar in 1878. A year later, he was admitted to the Bar in England. Following his return from Great Britain, ca. 1887, he joined his brother Frederick in law practice in Charlottetown. He became a partner in Peters, Peters and Ings. At some point, Albert Saunders*, another future premier, articled with this firm. Peters was designated Queen's Counsel in 1898. Arthur Peters died 29 January 1908.

Amelia Peters was the daughter of Charles Stewart, a former Member of the House of Assembly for 2nd Kings. She was born 11 June 1857 and died 12 May 1913. Peters' father was a provincial Supreme Court Judge. Peters' mother was the daughter of Sir Samuel Cunard, founder of the Cunard Steamship Line.

References
CPG 1908; *DCB* XIII pp. 834–36; Elections PEI; MacDonald *If You're Stronghearted* pp. 40–41; Premier's Gallery; *Daily Examiner* 25 September 1884; *Daily Patriot* 30 January 1908; PARO: MNI-Census 1891; St. Peter's Anglican Cathedral Cemetery Records.

PETERS, Q.C., FREDERICK, lawyer; b. 8 April 1852 in Charlottetown, son of James Horsfield Peters and Mary Cunard; m. 19 October 1886 Bertha Susan Hamilton Gray, and they had five children, Frederick, Helen, Noel, Gerald, and Jack; Anglican; d. 29 July 1919 in Prince Rupert, British Columbia.

Peters, a Liberal, was first elected to the House of Assembly in the general election of 1890 for 3rd Queens. He was defeated in the general election of 1882 in Charlottetown Royalty. Peters was elected to the Legislative Assembly in the general election of 1893. He was re-elected in the general election of 1897. Upon the resignation of the Neil McLeod* government, Peters was appointed Premier and Attorney-General in April 1891. In the general election of 1891, Peters was elected by acclamation. He served until 1897, and despite leading the Liberals to victory in the general election of that year, by a margin of 19 seats to 11, Peters moved to British Columbia. He continued to serve as a member in the Prince Edward Island Legislative Assembly until 1900, even though he was no longer a resident. In 1899 the Prince Edward Island Liberals had a small majority government. Determined to maintain it, Premier Farquharson* tried to convince Peters to return to the Island, to ensure a majority and to buy time, but Peters never returned to the Legislative Assembly.

During Peters' term as premier, one of his most significant initiatives was the enactment of a bill to change the Legislature from two houses, the Legislative Council and the House of Assembly, to one house, the Legislative Assembly, in 1893. Premier Peters abolished both Houses and created a Legislative Assembly, in which members served as either Councillors or Assemblymen.

Peters received his early schooling in Charlottetown. He attended Prince of Wales College and St. Dunstan's College, before leaving the province to further his education. In 1871 he received a Bachelor of Arts degree from King's College in Halifax, Nova Scotia. Later he studied at the Inner Temple and Lincoln's Inn in London, England, and was called to the English Bar in 1876. That same year, he was called to the Bars of Nova

Scotia and Prince Edward Island.

Peters' legal career began in Charlottetown. He tutored William Stewart* in the law, forming a partnership with him. Peters' younger brother Arthur*, who served as premier from 1901 to 1908, joined him in the law practice of Peters, Peters and Ings ca. 1887. As well, Albert Saunders*, another future premier, articled with the firm. In 1894 Peters was designated Queen's Counsel, and in 1896 he was appointed as senior counsel for the Canadian government before the Bering Sea Claims Commission. Peters moved to Vancouver in 1897, where he and Sir Charles Hibbert Tupper established the firm of Tupper and Peters, and eventually to Prince Rupert, where he continued his practice. In 1911 he served as the city solicitor for Prince Rupert. Peters also served as president of Prince of Wales College and, in 1896, as the vice-president of the Canadian Bar Association. Frederick Peters died 29 July 1919, outliving his sons Gerald and Jack who were killed in the First World War.

Bertha Peters was a daughter of Colonel John Hamilton Gray of Charlottetown, a Father of Confederation. Frederick Peters' father, a native of New Brunswick, was a Prince Edward Island Supreme Court Judge. Peters' mother, a native of Halifax, was the daughter of Sir Samuel Cunard, founder of the Cunard Steamship Line.

References
CPG 1883, 1891, 1899; DCB 1st ed., Wallace; Elections PEI; MacDonald If You're Stronghearted pp. 24-25; MacKinnon Life of the Party p. 68; Premiers Gallery; Daily Examiner 20 October 1886; Prince Rupert Daily News 30 July 1919; PARO: MNI-Census 1891; St. Paul's Anglican Church Records.

PHILLIPS, FORREST WILLIAM, farmer and land appraiser; b. 1 July 1887 in Ellerslie, son of Thomas Henry Phillips and Eleanor Agnes Williams; m. 14 August 1907 Gertrude MacArthur, and they had six children, Vera, Olive, Evelyn, Thomas, Albert, and Malcolm (died at 10 years); United; d. 8 July 1972 in Summerside.

Phillips, a Liberal, was first elected to the Legislative Assembly in a by-election held 17 September 1946 for 2nd Prince. He was re-elected in the general elections of 1947, 1951, and 1955. In 1949 Phillips was appointed Speaker of the Legislative Assembly, and in 1951 was again appointed to this position, subsequently serving in this capacity until 1955. On 3 April 1956, he became Minister of Welfare and Labour, but retired from the Minis-

try due to illness. Phillips returned to serve as a Minister without Portfolio for a short time before finally leaving political life.

He received his education at the Ellerslie School, and for some time remained in his home community, where he farmed for a living. In 1916, however, Phillips moved to Mount Royal, where he continued to farm. In addition to farming, from 1936 to 1940, he was a part-time land appraiser for the Canadian Farm Loans Board and worked in the Board's office from 1940 to 1945. He returned to Mount Royal to manage his brother's frost-proof warehouse in O'Leary, remaining there until September 1946. Forrest Phillips died 8 July 1972 at Prince County Hospital in Summerside.

Gertrude Phillips was the daughter of A. E. MacArthur of Enmore. She was born 27 May 1889 and died 22 November 1964. Vera Phillips married Joshua MacArthur*, who served in the Legislative Assembly from 1970 to 1976.

References
CPG 1958; Speakers of the Legislative Assembly for PEI 1873-1999; Journal-Pioneer 10 July 1972; Guardian 11 July 1972; PARO: Knutsford Methodist Cemetery Records.

PINEAU, HENRY J., farmer and lobster canner; b. 22 January 1863 in Bloomfield, son of Joseph Pineau and Bathilde Doiron; m. 10 May 1887 Mathilde Doiron in Palmer Road, daughter of Jean Thibodeau and Françoise Perry; they had at least five children: Joseph Emmanuel, Marie Célina, Mathilde Anne, Jean Jérôme, and Pierre Cyrille; Roman Catholic; d. 18 February 1904 in Miminegash.

Pineau, a Conservative and later a Liberal, was elected to the Legislative Assembly in a by-election held 25 July 1899 for 1st Prince. During the years 1899 and 1900, Pineau was a central figure in the House, as the Liberal government attempted to maintain a slim majority. A sitting Conservative, Pineau, who had been conspicuously absent for a number of months, at a crucial moment switched to the government side.

The crisis for the Liberals began during the 1899 legislative sessions, when Joseph Wise* broke ranks with the government and voted with the Conservatives. Premier Donald Farquharson* made efforts to persuade him to resign his seat. Wise agreed to do this if a by-election was held before the spring 1900 session. The by-election did not go ahead and Wise withdrew his resignation. During the 1900 session, on 8 May, his resignation was announced in the House, but this was immediately followed by Wise defiantly taking his seat. Amidst pandemonium, his vote with the Conservatives, which would have defeated the government, was not recognized by Speaker James Cummiskey*. The next day, Wise attempted to take his seat while the Speaker entered the refuted resignation into the record. Wise refused to withdraw when asked, and then was removed from the Legislative Assembly by the Sergeant-at-Arms, assisted by the House Messenger. He was locked in the Speaker's room until the House adjourned. When order was restored, Farquharson held on to power, as Pineau had switched his political allegiance to the Liberals.

Pineau went to school in Cascumpec and Bloomfield. He farmed and ran a fishing establishment in Miminegash for a number of years.

Henry Pineau died 18 February 1904 in Miminegash.

References

Acadiens p. 94; Elections PEI; MacDonald *If You're Stronghearted* pp. 24–25; PARO: Marriage Register No. 13 1870–77 p. 438; MNI-Census 1891; Census 1901; St. Anthony's Church, Bloomfield Parish, Book 2 p. 148; Profit Funeral Register, Alberton Vol. I 1895-1945.

POOLE, WILLIAM AITKEN, farmer and merchant; b. 1 September 1831 in Murray Harbour, son of John and Ann Matilda Poole; m. 17 April 1860 Christina Leslie, and they had four children, John Leslie, Matilda, George, and William E.; Methodist/Presbyterian; d. 28 August 1903 in Lower Montague.

Poole, a Conservative, was elected to the House of Assembly in the general election of 1879 for 4th Kings. He was defeated in the general election of 1882.

Poole farmed in Lower Montague and was a merchant in the firm of W. A. Poole & Co. According to the obituary in the *Patriot,* he was one of the most respected residents of Lower Montague in his time. William Poole died 28 August 1903.

Christina Poole was born in 1831 and died on 1 March 1893.

References

CPG 1881 p. 377; *Patriot* 29 August 1903; PARO: MNI-Census 1861, 1881, 1891; Methodist Register, Murray Harbour p. 921; Marriage License Book #7 1856–1863; Montague Funeral Home Records 1889–1963 p. 7.

POPE, GEORGE DALRYMPLE, officeholder; b. 1867, in Charlottetown Royalty, son of James Colledge Pope* and Eliza Dalrymple Pethick; m. Ethelwyn Calhoun, and they had three children, Arthur D., George Reginald, and Mrs. Louis Romcke; Anglican; d. 28 October 1927 in Ottawa.

Pope, a Conservative, was elected to the Legislative Assembly in a by-election held 14 January 1926 for 5th Prince. He was defeated in the general election of 1927.

Pope's father, James Colledge Pope*, was premier from 1865 to 1867, 1870 to 1872, and from April 1873 to September 1873. George Reginald Pope's son, Peter Pope*, was also a Member of the Legislative Assembly.

Pope was educated at the Ottawa Model School in Ontario and at Prince of Wales College in Charlottetown. He was the Comptroller of Revenue in the Department of the Interior. George Pope died 28 October 1927.

Ethelwyn Pope was born in 1868 and died in 1951.

References

CPG 1926, 1928; PARO: Pope Family File; St. Paul's Church Baptismal Records Book 1 p. 99; St. John's Anglican Records.

POPE, P.C., HONOURABLE JAMES COLLEDGE, entrepreneur, landed proprietor, shipowner, and land agent; b. 11 June 1826 in Bedeque, son of Joseph Pope and his first wife Lucy Colledge; m. 12 October 1852 Eliza Pethick, and they had eight children, Percy, George Dalrymple*, James C., Florence, Lucy, William, and two others; Methodist and later Anglican; d. 18 May 1885 in Summerside.

James Pope, a Conservative, was first elected to the House of Assembly in a by-election held on 1 June 1857 for 3rd Prince. He was re-elected in the general elections of 1859, 1863, and 1870 for 4th Prince, in the general elections of 1872 and 1873 for Charlottetown Royalty, and in a by-election held in January 1875 for 5th Prince by acclamation. He was defeated in a by-election held in 1868 for 5th Prince and in the general election of 1876 for Charlottetown Royalty.

Pope served on Executive Council in 1859, and as premier from 1865 to 1867, from 1870 to 1872, and in 1873 from April to September.

In September 1873, Pope resigned from the House of Assembly to contest, successfully, the special federal election for the riding of Prince County held on 17 September of that year. After a short return to provincial politics in 1875 and 1876,

Pope was re-elected to the House of Commons in a by-election held 22 November 1876 for Queen's County. He was again re-elected to the House of Commons for Queen's County in the federal election of 1878, and in a by-election after accepting office on 9 November 1878. On 19 October 1878, he was appointed a Member of the Privy Council, where he served as Minister of Fisheries until 1881, when he took a leave of absence from Cabinet.

During Pope's time as premier, he negotiated the final terms of the union of Prince Edward Island with Canada, giving him the distinction of serving as both the last premier of the colony and the first premier of the new province. He also participated in the debate over absentee land ownership. Pope was a benevolent land owner, and a major player in the campaign to transfer title of lands to the Island tenantry. Nonetheless, Premier Pope summoned troops from Halifax in mid-1865 to suppress the Tenant League, which resisted the collection of land rents. This move was an issue in the 1867 general election, which the Conservatives lost. Pope did not contest the general election of 1867.

Pope felt that a railway was a necessity if the Island was to keep pace economically. He introduced the Railway Bill, which was one of the factors that led Prince Edward Island into Confederation. While he was publicly against Confederation, there is evidence that he was, at times, sympathetic to union with Canada. Pope was a central figure in the school debate. Nonetheless, his position on public funding for denominational schools changed. On occasion, when in Opposition, he advocated funding for denominational schools. As Premier he found reasons not to provide funding, stating that the issue was too divisive for action at that particular time. In 1870, Pope's position on the school question created divisions among the Liberal Members. The Liberal Members of Roman Catholic faith crossed the floor to create a Liberal-Conservative coalition under Pope's leadership, defeating the Liberal government led by Robert Haythorne. Pope had pledged to provide government funding for Catholic schools. To the dismay of the Liberals who crossed the floor, he did not deliver on the pledge. In 1876 Pope allied himself with a number of Liberals and Conservatives in a coalition referred to by their opponents as the Denominationalists or the Sectarian School Party. The Denominationalists were in favour of government assistance to denominational schools. The Free School Party or the Non-Sectarian School Party, led by eventual Premier Louis Henry Davies*, supported free non-denominational schools in the 1876 general election. Pope's stand was a significant factor in his defeat in Charlottetown Royalty in the 1876 election.

Educated first in Bedeque, at the age of 14 Pope went to Saltash, England, to attend school. Upon his return to Bedeque, he entered the family business, later establishing his own store in Summerside. Pope owned shipyards in Bedeque and Summerside. James Pope ranked third among Island shipowners of the 1800s in number, and total tonnage, of ships owned. In 1851 he served as Collector of Customs for Bedeque. Pope's other business enterprises included agriculture, fishing, real estate, the carrying trade, retailing, and money-lending. He owned the telegraphic link between Summerside and New Brunswick. He was a land agent for his own land holdings and for other proprietors. Pope owned a farm in Lot 27, where he kept a large herd of cattle. He speculated in cargoes of produce. Undoubtedly, he was one of the most prominent economic figures on the Island in his time. It seems, however, that a devotion to politics may have led to the neglect of his numerous business interests, and resulted in heavy personal financial losses.

Pope came from a family involved in politics. His father was a Member of the House of Assembly, as well as a Speaker. His elder brother William Henry also was a Member of the House of Assembly and was one of the Fathers of Confederation. James Pope died 18 May 1885, and was survived by his father, his wife, and five of his eight children. His son George Dalrymple* was a Member of the Legislative Assembly, as was Pope's great-grandson Peter MacArthur Pope*.

Eliza Pope was the daughter of Thomas Pethick and Henrietta Webster.

References

CDP p. 469; *DCB* XI 1881-1890 pp. 699-705; *Island Story* pp. 137-40; *Provincial Premiers Birthday Series 1873-1973; Examiner* 18 May 1885; PARO: Pope Family File.

POPE, PETER MACARTHUR, businessperson; b. 1 September 1933 in Summerside, son of George Reginald Pope and K. Adele MacArthur; m. January 1958, Georgie E. Lockhart, and they had three children, Nancy, David, and James; Anglican.

Pope, a Conservative, and for a short time an Independent Conservative, was first elected to the Legislative Assembly in the general election of 1979 for 5th Prince. He was re-elected in the general elections of 1982 and 1986. Pope was defeated in the general elections of 1974 and 1978. On 12 February 1985, he resigned from the Conservative caucus to sit as an Independent, because he felt the Summerside area was being neglected by the provincial government. Pope felt that government was being centralized in Charlottetown, and his efforts toward decentralization were not being supported by the government caucus. On 28 May 1985, he rejoined caucus as a result of a promise from Premier James M. Lee* to deal with his decentralization concerns. Pope believed Summerside required more economic development, job opportunities, and a more equitable share of provincial government spending. He was also an advocate of Maritime Union. He felt strongly that Summerside would do better economically if the three Maritime provinces were politically united, as there would be less government centralization in Charlottetown. Pope was appointed Minister of Transportation and Public Works on 13 August 1985, until the defeat of the Lee Government in 1986. On 7 January 1987, Pope resigned his seat in the Legislative Assembly.

Pope is a descendant of former members James C. Pope* and George Dalrymple Pope*.

Pope received his early education in Summerside and graduated from Summerside High School. Later he attended Acadia University. Following this, Pope became a car dealer and, in time, president of Pope Properties Limited. He was a member of the Rotary Club of Summerside and the Summerside Chamber of Commerce. He also owned harness racehorses. Peter Pope resides in Summerside.

Georgie Pope was the daughter of James Lockhart of Malpeque.

References

CPG 1978, 1979, 1987; *ECO* 396/85; *WWPEI* p. 116; *Atlantic Insight* November 1980; *Guardian* 19 April 1979, 29 May 1985; *Journal-Pioneer* 12 February 1985, 7 January 1987; PARO: Pope Family File.

PRATT, RODERICK BRUCE, farmer and salesperson; b. 21 January 1927 in St. Peters, son of Chester Charles Pratt and Olive Branch Anderson; m. 23 November 1949 Mary Irene Matheson, and they had five children, Halbert, Barbara Jean, Malcolm, Janet, and Roderick; United; d. 19 September 2001 in Charlottetown.

Pratt, a Conservative, was first elected to the Legislative Assembly in the general election of 1978 for 2nd Kings. He was re-elected in the general elections of 1979, 1982, and 1986. On 17 November 1981, Pratt became Minister of Highways and Public Works and served in this position until 3 November 1983, the same date he was appointed Minister of Fisheries and Labour. He served in that Ministry until 1986. He was a member of the Treasury Board.

During his time in the Legislature, "Roddy" Pratt was known as an outspoken advocate for his constituents and for causes he felt important. At one point, he launched a one-person filibuster to protest the government's funding of The Island Nature Trust. In 1984 Pratt was a representative of the Canadian government at the funeral of Indira Gandhi in India. As Minister of Fisheries, he oversaw an expansion in the fishing industry and was supportive of the Island lobster processing industry. Pratt obtained 16 crab industry licenses for the province from the federal government and cited this as a personal highlight of his career.

Pratt received his early education in St. Peters. Later he attended Fredericton High School and the Union Commercial College. Pratt operated a family farm in St. Peters, where first he raised beef, and, in 1970, he grew potatoes. He was also a farm supply salesperson and the crop manager at Dundas Farms. Pratt was president of the Potato Producers Association and a member of the Federation of Agriculture. He had a keen interest in educational matters and served as a trustee of the St. Peters School and as a member of the building committee for area schools. Pratt was a member of the St. Peters Lions Club and served as its president. He was a member of the Royal Canadian Legion and St. Peters United Church. Roddy Pratt died on 19 September 2001 at the Queen Elizabeth Hospital in Charlottetown.

Mary Pratt, the daughter of Clifton and Jean Matheson, was born on 2 February 1928. Clifton Matheson was a station agent and the family lived in many Island communities, including Freetown and Hunter River. Mary and Roddie Pratt celebrated their 50th wedding anniversary in the fall of 1999.

References

CPG 1979, 1989; *ECO* 1054/81; *WWPEI* p. 117; *Guardian* 31 March 1978, 19 April 1978, 8 November 1984, 12 April 1986, 20 September

2001; *Patriot* 14 April 1989.

PROUD, GEORGE ALBERT, utility company employee, deputy mayor, cab driver, carnival hawker, investment consultant, and director; b. 9 April 1939 in Charlottetown, son of Peter W. Proud and Margaret Beairsto; m. 3 August 1963 Elizabeth Ann Lawlor, and they had three children, Michael Peter, David George Walter, and Geoffrey Lyndon; Roman Catholic.

Proud, a Liberal, was first elected to the Legislative Assembly in the general election of 1974 for 5th Queens, He was re-elected in the general election of 1978. He was defeated in the general election of 1979. In 1974 Proud was appointed Minister Responsible for Housing Corporation and the Status of Women. He was appointed Minister of Labour and Minister of Municipal Affairs and Provincial Secretary in 1978. In the 1988 federal general election, Proud successfully ran for Hillsborough, and was re-elected in 1993 and 1997. In February 1989, he was appointed labour critic for the Opposition. Proud was appointed critic for Veterans Affairs in September 1990. He served on the Standing Committee on Labour, Employment and Immigration, and the Standing Committee on National Defence and Veterans Affairs. In September 1995, Proud was elected chair of the Standing Committee on National Defence and Veterans Affairs. He was named Parliamentary Secretary to the Minister of Veterans Affairs in July 1997. Proud was a member of the Canadian NATO Parliamentary Association and was a member of the Commonwealth Parliamentary Association. From 1984 to 1986, he was Deputy Mayor and a member of Town Council in Pine Point, Northwest Territories.

Proud received his primary education at the school in York. Later he attended St. Dunstan's University. From 1968 to 1969, he studied at Prince of Wales College. Proud also went to the Atlantic Regional Labour Education Centre and the Labour College of Canada. He worked for Maritime Electric as a linesman and line area foreman, as well as a property and fleet supervisor. In 1978 Proud worked as a cab driver and with the Bill Lynch Carnival. From 1980 to 1985, he was employed by the Northern Canada Power Commission in the Northwest Territories, advancing to the position of plant manager in 1985. In 1986 he moved back to Charlottetown and worked in the investment field. The following year, Proud returned to Maritime Electric. In 2001 he was appointed a Director of the Canadian Transport Commission.

Proud was recording secretary and vice-president of the International Brotherhood of Electrical Workers Local 1432. He was a president of the Prince Edward Island Federation of Labour and vice-president of the Canadian Labour Congress. He also served as a member of the board of governors of the University of Prince Edward Island. Proud was a member of the executive of the Prince Street Home and School Association and the Charlottetown Minor Hockey Association. He was a member of the Lions Club. George Proud lives in Ottawa.

References

CPG 1975, 1997, 1998-1999; *Guardian* 17 April 1979, 27 September 1988, 17 May 1997, 3 July 1997, 12 October 2000; *Queens County Telecaster and Commentator* 5 November 1975; Interview: Michael Proud.

PROWSE, ALBERT PERKINS, merchant, exporter, and dealer; b. 24 December 1858, son of Samuel Prowse* and Eliza Willis; m. 29 November 1881 Williamina A. Kirkland of Kingston, Kent County, New Brunswick, and they had 10 children, Louisa E. W., William F., Edith H., Preston S., Albert S., Lemuel G., Joseph B., Vivia, Gerald R., and Ada L.; Methodist; d. 20 June 1925.

Prowse, a Conservative, was first elected to the Legislative Assembly in a by-election held in 1899 for 4th Kings. He was re-elected in the general elections of 1904, 1908, 1912, 1915, and 1923. He was defeated in the general elections of 1897 and 1919.

Prowse received his early education in local schools, before attending Wesleyan Academy in Charlottetown for two years. He was a successful merchant, dealing in and exporting fish, lobster, and produce at Murray Harbour. He entered business with his father, Samuel Prowse*, in 1872. At the age of 24, Prowse was made a partner in the family business. His brother William became a partner four years later. For 11 years, father and sons were partners in the firm of Prowse and Sons. After Samuel retired, the business continued on under the direction of his children, and under the same name, until 31 December 1902, when William retired and sold his interests to Albert Prowse. From this point, Prowse worked alone, although the business maintained the same name. When he died on 20 June 1925, Albert Prowse was a sitting Member of the Legislative Assembly.

Williamina Prowse, the daughter of John Kirkland and Helen Easton, was born in 1861 and died in 1938.

References
CPG 1918, 1925, 1926; Elections PEI; *Past and Present* pp. 430–31; *Patriot* 31 December 1925; PARO: Census 1901; Murray Harbour South Beachpoint Cemetery Records.

PROWSE, LEMUEL EZRA, merchant and business person; b. 2 February 1858 in Charlottetown Royalty, son of William and Helen Prowse; m. 23 July 1879 Frances Josephine Stanley of Nova Scotia, and they had four children, of whom three names are known, Herbert, Georgina M., and Thomas William Lemuel*; Methodist; d. 11 December 1925 in Ottawa.

Prowse, a Liberal, was first elected to the Legislative Assembly in the general election of 1893 for Charlottetown Royalty. He was re-elected in the general election of 1897. In the federal election of 1908, Prowse was elected to the House of Commons for Queen's, and was defeated in 1911.

Prowse was educated in local schools in Charlottetown. He was a merchant, and the president of Prowse Brothers Limited, one of the largest businesses on the Island. In 1915, his son, T. W. L. "Bill" Prowse, joined the firm in the role of secretary-treasurer, becoming president and general manager in 1930. Prowse Brothers Limited was one of the best-known mercantile enterprises of the Atlantic provinces. Lemuel Prowse died 11 December 1925.

Frances Prowse was born in 1860 and died in 1938. T. W. L. "Bill" Prowse* was a Member of the Legislative Assembly and later became Lieutenant-Governor.

References
CDP p. 478; CPG 1899; CWW 1910 p. 188; PARO: Cornwall United Church Book 3 p. 1; 1891 Census; Charlottetown People's Cemetery Records.

PROWSE, HONOURABLE SAMUEL, merchant, justice of the peace, court commissioner, and cabinetmaker; b. 23 August 1835 in Charlottetown Royalty, son of William Prowse of Charlottetown Royalty; m. first 17 October 1856 Eliza Willis, and they had two children, Albert P.* and Elizabeth; m. secondly 4 February 1861 Louisa Jane Willis, and they had two children, William and Samuel; also fathered a son, Frederick Smallwood (died in 1861 at six years and seven months) by a woman

surnamed Wells previous to his first marriage; Methodist; d. 14 January 1902 in Charlottetown.

Prowse, a Conservative, was first elected to the House of Assembly in the general election of 1867 for 4th Kings. He was re-elected in the general elections of 1876, 1879, and 1886, and in a by-election held 31 July 1882. He was defeated in the the general elections of 1873 and 1882.

Prowse was appointed to Executive Council in 1876 as a member of the L. H. Davies* coalition government, which was formed due to the debate regarding secular or denominational schools. He served on Executive Council as a Minister without Portfolio from 1876 to 1878, from 1879 to May 1882, and from July 1882 to 1889. In 1878 Prowse resigned from cabinet, and in 1889 he resigned from the House of Assembly. Later that year he was appointed to the Senate, where he served until his death.

Born and educated at Charlottetown Royalty, Prowse moved to Murray Harbour to run a general store and a cabinet-making business, Prowse and Sons, with two of his children, William and Albert. Aside from his business interests, he also served as a Justice of the Peace and Commissioner for Taking Affidavits in Supreme Court.

Eliza Prowse was born ca. 1835 and died 10 March 1860. Louisa Prowse, Eliza's older sister, was born ca. 1831 and died in 1907.

References
CDP p. 478; CPG 1880, 1883; Elections PEI; *Meacham's Atlas*; PARO: Marriage License Book #4 1851–65; Marriage Book #7 1856–1863 p. 42a; MNI-Mercantile Agency Reference Book 1876; MNI-Census 1881, 1891; Montague Funeral Home Records; Murray Harbour South Cemetery Records.

PROWSE, HONOURABLE THOMAS WILLIAM LEMUEL, businessperson; b. 31 August 1888, son of Lemuel E. Prowse* and Frances J. Stanley; m. 4 February 1913 Annie Martyn, and they had four children, Lemuel E., Doris H., Margaret F., and Fairlie C.; Presbyterian; d. 2 November 1973 in Charlottetown.

Prowse, a Liberal, was first elected to the Legislative Assembly in the general election of 1935 for 5th Queens. He was re-elected in the general election of 1943. He was defeated in the general elections of 1939 and 1947. He served as a Minister without Portfolio from 1935 to 1939 in the Walter Lea* and Thane Campbell* governments, and again from 1943 to 1947 in the J. Walter Jones* Administration. Before entering provincial politics, from

1922 to 1930 Prowse served on Charlottetown City Council as the representative for Ward 5, then served as Mayor from 1930 to 1932. He served as Lieutenant-Governor from 1950 to 1958. In his day, Prowse was one of the most popular Lieutenant-Governors the province had ever had. He was known simply as "Bill."

Prowse's father, Lemuel Prowse*, served as both a Member of the Legislative Assembly and a Member of the House of Commons.

T. W. L. "Bill" Prowse was educated at West Kent Elementary School, at Sydney Academy in Nova Scotia, and at Prince of Wales College in Charlottetown. He worked for the Royal Bank of Canada from 1907 to 1915. In 1915 Prowse joined the family business, Prowse Brothers Limited, as secretary-treasurer, and in 1930 he was made president and general manager. Prowse Brothers Limited was one of the best-known mercantile enterprises of the Atlantic Provinces.

Outside his business and political life, Prowse was actively involved in his community. He was a member of the Rotary and Abegweit Clubs, as well as the Knights of Pythias and the Masonic Order. Prowse was a member of the Provincial Exhibition and Driving Park Association, the Charlottetown Exhibition Association, the Charlottetown Board of Trade, and the Charlottetown Club. T. W. L. "Bill" Prowse died 2 November 1973.

Annie Prowse was the daughter of John B. Martyn of Ripley, Ontario.

References
CPG 1938, 1940, 1944, 1947, 1948; *Guardian* 9 August 1971; *Patriot* 3 November 1973; *Maritime Advocate and Busy East* February 1951; Maritime Reference Book p. 64.

RAMSAY, FREDERICK CARR, farmer; b. 22 September 1901 in Montrose, son of Bertram H. Ramsay and Martha Isabel Wright; m. 19 July 1950 Aaltjje Van Der Bor, and they had seven children, Carolyn Kay, Ronald Lindsay, Crystal Ann, Donald McDowell, Alie-Ann, Freddie, and David; United/Jehovah's Witness; d. 28 September 1986 in O'Leary.

Ramsay, a Liberal, was first elected to the Legislative Assembly in the general election of 1943 for 1st Prince. He was re-elected in the general elections of 1947 and 1955. He was defeated in the general election of 1951.

Ramsay was educated at the local school in Alberton, and he also attended the Charlottetown Business College. He returned to his birthplace, where he farmed for a living. He was listed as a member of the United Church in the 1958 *Canadian Parliamentary Guide*, and by the end of his life had become a Jehovah's Witness. Fred Ramsay died 28 September 1986 at the O'Leary Community Hospital.

Aaltjje Ramsay was the daughter of Cornelius Van Der Bor of Hilversum, Holland.

References
CPG 1958, 1960; *Journal-Pioneer* 30 September 1986.

READ, JOSEPH, merchant, shipowner, and master mariner; b. 31 October 1849 in Summerside, son of Ephraim Read and Rosara Chappell; m. 27 September 1877 Sarah Carruthers of Bedeque, and they had two children, John and George; Unitarian; d. 6 April 1919 in Ottawa.

Read, a Liberal, was first elected to the Legislative Assembly in the general election of 1900 for 4th Prince. He was re-elected in the general elections of 1904 and 1908. Following the 1908 election, which he won by two votes, he was defeated in July 1909 because of a discrepancy over the eligibility of some voters. Other accounts state he resigned to allow for a by-election. Read was defeated in the subsequent by-election held 6 August 1909, by a margin of three votes. He was appointed as a Minister without Portfolio in the Executive Council on 10 October 1904 and served until he resigned in January 1905. In the 1917 federal election, he ran successfully for Prince, and died while a Member of the House of Commons.

An issue of particular concern to Read was the number of provincial representatives in the House of Commons. Following Confederation, the province had six Members of Parliament, but due to a decrease in the Island's population and an increase in the population of the rest of Canada, provincial representation in the Commons had been decreased to five seats in 1892, and to four in 1904. Read made a reasoned and well-argued speech in the Legislature in March 1909, urging Ottawa to restore provincial representation to the level it was when the Island first joined Canada. Despite his efforts and the plea of the provincial government, the number of Island Members of Parliament was reduced to three in 1911.

A lifelong resident of Summerside, Read studied at Summerside High School, after which he travelled to Liverpool, England, where he attended Ion's Nautical Academy. Early in his adult life, he became a sailor, and eventually gained the status of master mariner. For many years, he commanded some of the largest ships owned by John Lefurgey*. Read later sailed his own ship, a barque named the *Charles E. Lefurgey*. Following his time at sea, he became a produce merchant, and owned Joseph Read and Company Limited in Summerside. Although he was ultimately a success in the business world, Read suffered a business failure. In a tribute to Read's integrity, delivered in the House of Commons, D. D. MacKenzie, Leader of the Opposition, recounted how Read had gone back to sea to make enough money to pay all his creditors, though the laws of insolvency did not require him to do so.

Read's other involvements included serving as the president of the local and Maritime Board of Trade. He was also shipping master and port warden in Summerside. Read appreciated history, and despite his busy life in politics and business contributed to the book *Past and Present of Prince Edward Island* (1906). Joseph Read died 6 April 1919.

Sarah Read was born ca. 1840 and predeceased her husband by several years. Read's mother was born in Nova Scotia.

References
CDP p. 484; *CPG* 1905, 1909, 1910; *CWW* 1910 p. 190; Elections PEI; *Guardian* 8 April 1919, 12 April 1919; *Patriot* 1 March 1909, 7 April 1919; *Summerside Journal* 16 April 1919; PARO: RG 19 Vital Statistics Marriage Records Vol. 9 1871–1878; MNI-Census 1891.

REID, C.M, O.P.E.I., LL.D., HONOURABLE MARION LORETTA, educator; b. 4 January 1929 in North Rustico, daughter of Michael Doyle and Josephine Loretta Whelan; m. 1949, Lea Reid, and they had eight children, Maureen, Colleen, Kevin, Bethany, Mary Lee, David, Andrew, and Tracey; Roman Catholic.

Reid, a Conservative, was first elected to the Legislative Assembly in the general election of 1979 for 1st Queens. She was re-elected in the general elections of 1982 and 1986. She was defeated in the general election of 1989. In 1979 Reid was appointed Deputy Speaker, making her the first woman in provincial history to serve in this position. On 18 March 1983, she became the first female Speaker of the Legislative Assembly. From 1986 to 1989, Reid was Opposition House Leader. As a Member, she served on various committees, including the Standing Committee on Education, the Standing Committee on Agriculture, and the Standing Committee on Tourism and Parks. Reid was a delegate to Commonwealth Parliamentary Association conferences in Canada, Kenya, Westminster, and the Isle of Man. On 16 August 1990, she was sworn in as the first female Lieutenant-Governor in the Island's history.

Reid has lived in North Rustico, Hope River, and Charlottetown. She received her early education at North Rustico and Stella Maris Schools. Reid attended Prince of Wales College from 1944 to 1946, obtaining a first class teaching license. In 1972 she took a leave from teaching and returned to the University of Prince Edward Island to obtain a Certificate Five teachers license. During her education, Reid won the John H. Bell debate prize, the Lord Strathcona prize, and a Scholarship for Academic Excellence. She was a teacher for 21 years, and for the last three was principal of St. Ann's Elementary School. Reid was an active member in teaching and professional organizations. From 1970 until 1977, she was a member of the board of governors and secretary of the Prince Edward Island Teacher's Federation. Reid served on the curriculum committee, the teacher recruitment team, the negotiation strategy committee, and the status of women committee of the Prince Edward Island Teacher's Federation.

Reid had an interest in many community activities. She was a member of the Charlottetown Zonta Club, President and Life Member of the Stirling Women's Institute, a leader in 4-H work, a founding member of the Queen Elizabeth Hospital Foundation, a member of the Board of Governors of the Confederation Centre of the Arts, and a member of the Wanda Wyatt Scholarship Foundation. Reid has chaired the Premier's Action Committee on the Prevention of Family Violence. She has served as an honourary patron of Laubach Literacy of Canada, the Prince Edward Island Royal Canadian Legion, the Girl Guides of Canada, the Prince Edward Island Council of Scouts Canada, and she was presented a life membership in the PEI Wildlife Association. Other honours include an appointment to the Order of Canada in 1996, the Prince Edward Island Medal of Merit in 1997, an honourary Doctorate of Laws from the University of Prince Edward Island, the Paul Harris Fellow Award by the Charlottetown Rotary Club, the Toastmasters International Communications and Leadership Award (District 45), and the Rural Beautification W. R. Shaw Award. Reid was invested in 1991 as Dame of Grace in the Order of St. John of Jerusalem. In 1992, Reid received the 125th Commemorative Medal. On 28 March 2001, she was the first Island recipient of the Canadian Red Cross Humanitarian Award. Marion Reid currently resides in Stanley Bridge.

Lea Reid was the son of Leander Reid and Florence Turner of Hope River. He died on 6 July 1999.

References
CPG 1990, 1993; *CWW* 2000 p. 1052; *WWC* 1993 p. 681.

REID, SAMUEL EDWARD, bookkeeper, woolen manufacturer, merchant, farmer, dairy manager, and justice of the peace; b. 14 November 1854 in St. Eleanors, son of James Reid of Donegal, Ireland, and Charlotte Dawson of Tryon; m. 29 December 1880 Melvina (Lea) Ellis, and they had three children, E. Ryerson, B. Arthur, and Helen Lea; Methodist; d. 8 March 1924 in Boston.

Reid, a Liberal, was first elected to the Legislative Assembly in a by-election held 2 February 1899 for 4th Prince. He was re-elected in the general elections of 1900 and 1904, and in a by-election held 23 February 1905 as a result of being appointed to office. Reid served as Speaker from March 1901 to December 1904. In 1905 he was made Secretary-Treasurer and Commissioner of Agriculture.

Reid attended St. Eleanors and Summerside public schools. Sources list his residences as St. Eleanors and Charlottetown, but it is also likely that he lived for some time in Tryon, given his business interests in the community. For three years, he worked as a bookkeeper for his brothers J. D. and J. C. Reid, general merchants in Summerside. Following this he founded and, for 30 years, operated the Tryon Woolen Mills, which produced woolen tweeds, blanketing, and flannels. Reid remained secretary of the operation after it became a joint stock company in 1880. His brother, J. D., remained as president. Reid operated a farm and organized the Tryon Dairying Company, serving as manager for 10 years. He also served as a Justice of the Peace. Samuel Reid died 8 March 1924.

Melvina Reid died 1 April 1942 in Stoneham, Massachusetts. Reid's father-in-law, William Lea, was from Tryon.

References
CPG 1908, 1909; Elections PEI; *Maple Leaf Magazine* June 1942; *Patriot* 9 March 1924, 10 March 1924; *Summerside Journal* 20 January 1881, 19 March 1924; PARO: Marriage Register RG 19 series 3 subseries 3 volume 10 1878–1888; MNI-Census 1891; Summerside People's Protestant Cemetery Records.

RICHARD, JOSEPH HECTOR, fisher, carpenter, and sawmill operator; b. 5 January 1903 in St. Felix, son of Joseph Stanislaus Richard and Victoria Buote; m. 24 September 1924 Mélina Doucette, and they had 11 children, Gerard, Rita, Joseph, Ann, Alphonse, Alice, Arthur, Angela, Hubert, Victor, and Emily; Roman Catholic; d. 16 January 1994 in Alberton.

Richard, a Liberal, was elected to the Legislative Assembly in the general election of 1947 for 1st Prince. He was defeated in the general election of 1951.

Born in St. Felix, and later a resident of Howlan, Richard worked as a fisher and carpenter, and also operated a sawmill. According to his obituary, he derived great pleasure from fishing and being on the sea. He operated one of the last schooners to travel between the Island and New Brunswick. Joseph Richard died 16 January 1994 at the Western Hospital in Alberton.

Mélina Doucette was the daughter of Joseph Doucette and Eulalie Gallant. She died on 13 December 1999 at the Western Hospital in Alberton.

References
Acadiens p. 96; *CPG* 1951, 1953; *Journal-Pioneer* 5 October 1983, 17 September 1984, 3 February 1994, 13 December 2000.

RICHARDS, JAMES WILLIAM, merchant and shipowner; b. 31 May 1850 in Swansea, Wales, son of Captain William Richards and Susan Yeo; m. 4 October 1909 Ella E. Myers, and there were no children; Episcopalian; d. 9 March 1915 in Ottawa.

Richards, a Conservative in his early career, was first elected to the House of Assembly in a by-election held September 1873 for 2nd Prince. He was re-elected in the general elections of 1876, 1879, 1882, and 1886, and was elected as a Liberal in 1890. As a Liberal he was elected to the Legislative Assembly in the general election of 1893 and was re-elected in the general elections of 1897, 1900, and 1904. Richards served on Executive Council as a Minister without Portfolio from 22 April 1891 to November 1904. He resigned his seat to become a candidate for Prince in the 1904 federal election, but was defeated. In the federal elections of 1908 and 1911, Richards was elected to the House of Commons for Prince. During his career as a provincial politician, Richards was a strong supporter of the Land Purchase Act and the School Act.

Richards was educated at Prince of Wales College and St. Dunstan's University in Charlottetown. He then attended commercial school in Saint John. After completing his studies, Richards returned to the Island where he began his business career in Bideford. There he operated mercantile and industrial businesses with his father. His younger brother John Richards* also served in the Legislature.

James Richards died 9 March 1915 in Ottawa, while serving as a Member in the House of Commons, and was buried in Bideford.

References
CDP p. 490; *CPG* 1874, 1877, 1908; *Meacham's Atlas*; *Past and Present* pp. 499–500; *Maple Leaf Magazine* April 1915; PARO: Marriage License Book 16 p. 130; Richards Family File.

RICHARDS, JOHN, farmer and stock breeder; b. 4 October 1857 in Port Hill, son of Captain William Richards and Susan Yeo; m. 1 October 1884 Isabel Alice Broad, and they had one son, Kenneth; Anglican; d. 8 March 1917 in Los Angeles, California.

Richards, a Liberal, was first elected to the Legislative Assembly in the general election of 1908 for 2nd Prince. He was re-elected in the general election of 1912. He served as Provincial Secretary-Treasurer and Commissioner of Agriculture in the Haszard* Administration from 1908 to 1912. When the Liberal government was defeated in the 1912 general election, Richards was re-elected and chosen as Leader of the Opposition.

Richards was educated first in local schools and then at St. Dunstan's College in Charlottetown. He attended the Collegiate School and King's College in Windsor, Nova Scotia. In his early career, Richards was associated with his father in shipbuilding and produce export. He was a successful and prominent farmer and stock breeder. He was one of the leading stock breeders in Canada, specializing in Shorthorn and Aberdeen Angus cattle. He also raised purebred Clydesdales and Standard Bred Horses. Richards owned and operated one of the largest farms in Prince County. He was also a successful pioneer of oyster culture on the Island.

Richards was a founder of the Provincial Exhibition Association and one of its honoured directors, and a director of a number of Canadian stock breeding associations. He was a director and one of the largest shareholders of the Steam Navigation Company, and held the position of a director of the Charlottetown Driving Park Association and the Standardbred Association of Canada. John Richards died 8 March 1917 while visiting Los Angeles with his wife.

Isabel Richards, the daughter of T. C. Broad of St. Eleanors, was born 31 March 1858 and died 18 March 1937. John Richards' older brother, James William Richards*, also served in the Legislative Assembly.

References
CPG 1915; *Daily Examiner* 2 October 1884; *Guardian* 10 March 1917; *Maple Leaf Magazine* April 1937; *Patriot* 9 March 1917; PARO: Census 1901; St. James Anglican Church Records.

ROBERTSON, ALEXANDER D., merchant and farmer; b. 5 March 1849 in West River, son of James Robertson of Kingsboro and Mary Jarvis of Guysborough County, NS; m. 24 February 1887 Bertha Lydia Fraser, and they had six children, Alexander, Bessie, Rhoda, Martha, Ralph, and Theodore; Baptist; d. 2 January 1921.

Robertson, a Liberal, was elected to the House of Assembly in a by-election held 19 April 1891 for 1st Kings. He was elected to the Legislative Assembly in the general election of 1893. He was defeated in the general election of 1897.

He received his early education in local schools and then at the Charlottetown Normal School. He was a merchant and farmer in the Red Point area. Alexander Robertson died 2 January 1921.

Bertha Robertson, the daughter of Donald Fraser, was born ca. 1863 and died in 1950.

References
CPG 1891, 1897; Elections PEI; *Guardian* 21 July 1987; PARO: MNI-Census 1891: Robertson Family File.

ROBERTSON, M.D., HONOURABLE JAMES EDWIN, doctor and surgeon, b. 8 October 1840 in New Perth, son of Peter Robertson and Annie McFarlane; m. 11 November 1878 Elizabeth McFarlane, and they adopted one son; Baptist; d. 30 October 1915 in Montague.

Robertson, a Liberal, was first elected to the House of Assembly in 1870 for 4th Kings. He was re-elected in the general elections of 1872, 1876, and 1882. He was defeated in the general election of 1879. Robertson served on Executive Council as a Minister without Portfolio from 1872 to 1873, from 6 September 1876 to August 1878, and from 12 September 1878 to 10 March 1879. He resigned his seat in 1882.

Although Robertson was elected to the House of Commons in 1882 for King's County, he was declared not duly elected on the grounds that at the time of the election he was a Member of the House of Assembly. After resigning from the Assembly, Robertson was re-elected to the House of Commons on 26 April 1883 and in 1887, and he was defeated in 1891. Robertson was appointed to the Senate on 7 February 1902, where he served until 15 April 1915. James Robertson died on 30 October of that year.

Robertson was educated at local schools and at Central Academy in Charlottetown. He attended medical school at McGill University in Montreal, following which he practised medicine in Montague.

Elizabeth Robertson was born in 1844.

References
CDP p. 495; Currie pp. 217-19; *CPG* 1880, 1883; *Meacham's Atlas*; PARO: MNI-Census 1881.

ROBERTSON, JOHN FERGUSON, clerk, merchant, and ship broker; b. 10 July 1841 in Charlottetown Royalty, son of Alexander Robertson and Margaret Ferguson; m. 23 November 1869 Margaret Heatherington of Richibucto, New

Brunswick, and they had one child, John F.; Presbyterian; d. 25 October 1905 in Charlottetown.

Robertson, a member of Free School Coalition, was elected to the House of Assembly in the general election of 1876 for 4th Queens. Following the election, he served on Executive Council. For a number of years, he served as the Auditor under the Coles government.

Robertson was a lifelong resident of Charlottetown, who lived on Richmond Street West at the time of his death. In the early part of his career, he worked as a clerk for Duncan Mason and Company. Soon after that, he became a partner and manager of the shipbuilding firm James Duncan and Company. Once James Duncan and Company suspended its operations, Ferguson commenced ship brokering in Charlottetown. Due to his many years in the marine trade, Robertson was considered an authority on shipping matters throughout the province. John Robertson died 25 October 1905.

Margaret Robertson, the daughter of S. B. Heatherington of Richibucto, New Brunswick, was born ca. 1846. Both Robertson and his wife were first-generation Maritimers as Robertson's father was born in Scotland while Margaret Robertson's parents were born in England.

References
CDP p. 597; *CPG* 1877; *Islander* 26 November 1869; *Patriot* 27 October 1905; PARO: MNI-Census 1881, 1891; St. James Church, Book 1, p. 3; Charlottetown People's Cemetery Records.

ROBINSON, HONOURABLE BREWER WAUGH, soldier, fox rancher, and mill and bakery owner; b. 9 January 1891 in Summerside, son of George W. Robinson and Lucy Waugh; m. 24 September 1919 to Ethel R. Mills, and there were no children; United; d. 20 January 1949 in Summerside.

Robinson, a Conservative, was elected to the Legislative Assembly in the general election of 1939 for 5th Prince. Before entering provincial politics, Robinson was Mayor of Summerside from 1936 to 1937. He was appointed to the Senate in April 1945.

Robinson received his education at Summerside High School and at the Commercial College. Soon after completing his education, he moved to Western Canada, where he worked for several years in the Union Bank of Canada. Upon the outbreak of the First World War, Robinson returned home and was one of the first from Summerside to enlist. He joined the 2nd Battery, Canadian Heavy Artillery, and went overseas in 1915, where he served until the end of the war. In 1919 Robinson returned to Summerside and entered the fox ranching business with his father. He also became involved in the family bakery, Robinson's Bakery Limited, as manager.

In 1942, while still serving as a Member of the Legislative Assembly, Robinson again went overseas as a member of the Canadian Legion War Services. He remained there until the end of the Second World War, and moved up to the position of deputy head of the Canadian Legion War Services in London, England. In April 1945, while still overseas, Robinson was informed of his appointment to the Senate, where he served until his death.

Besides his extensive military and political engagements, Robinson was actively involved in his community. He was Mayor of Summerside from 1936 to 1937. He served as president of the Summerside Board of Trade and was a member of both the Rotary and the Masons. Robinson was a prominent member of the Summerside branch of the Royal Canadian Legion and was honourary president of the branch at the time of his death. He was also a director of the Prince Edward Island Fur Pool Limited. Robinson was keenly interested in sports. He served as president of the Prince Edward Island Hockey League and also as president of the Summerside Curling Club. Brewer Robinson died 20 January 1949 at his home.

Ethel Robinson was the daughter of W. A. Mills of Halifax.

References
CDP p. 498; *CPG* 1943; *Guardian* 21 January 1949; *Patriot* 20 January 1949; *Summerside Journal* 20 January 1949.

ROGERS, BENJAMIN, merchant and business person; b. 1 September 1836 in Kinleith, Carmarthen, Wales, son of Jonah Rogers and Hannah Thomas; m. 13 November 1866 Mary L. Treneman of Rochester, New York State, and they had four children, Benjamin, Carrie M., George J., and Thomas D.; Methodist; d. 21 January 1911 in Charlottetown.

Rogers, a Liberal, was first elected to the Legislative Assembly in the general election of 1893 for Charlottetown Royalty. He was re-elected in the general election of 1897. Rogers served on Executive Council as a Minister without Portfolio in the

Warburton* Administration in 1897, and again in the Farquharson* Administration in 1898.

Rogers immigrated to the Island with his family ca. 1839, settling in Bedeque, where he was educated in the local schools. In 1854, at the age of 19, he began to work as an employee of Thomas W. Dodd. Rogers had a keen business sense, and within five years Dodd made him partner. In 1892 Rogers bought out Dodd's interest in their business. In 1904 the business was converted into Rogers Hardware Company Limited, one of Charlottetown's best-known and most successful businesses. Rogers served as president of Rogers Hardware until his death on 21 January 1911.

Besides his business interests, Rogers was identified with many of the leading enterprises of the day in the province. He was president of the Prince Edward Island Telephone Company, vice-president of the Steam Navigation Company, and president of the Patriot Publishing Company. He was involved with the Free and Accepted Order of Masonry, serving for some time as the Grand Master of the Grand Lodge of Prince Edward Island.

Mary Rogers, the daughter of Richard Treneman who came from England, was born 7 June 1847 and died 13 February 1923. Rogers lived with his family on Prince Street, and their residence was called Fairholm. The subject's son, Benjamin Rogers, had a daughter, Helena, who married R. Reginald Bell*, who was a member of the Legislative Assembly.

References
Eminent Men pp. 277–81; *Past and Present*, p. 521; *Guardian* 23 January 1911; *Patriot* 21 January 1911; PARO: Charlottetown People's Cemetery Records.

ROGERS, HONOURABLE BENJAMIN, bookkeeper, merchant, farmer, and officeholder; b. 7 August 1837 in Bedeque, son of Joseph Rogers and Margaret James; m. first 20 February 1862 Susannah Abella Hubbard, and they had six children, Francis G., Frederick C., Charles R., Addie Y., Sibella Maggie, and Reginald Hiber; m. secondly 1898, Annie M. Hunter, and there were no children; Presbyterian; d. 16 May 1923 in Alberton.

Rogers, a Liberal, and for a short time an Independent, was first elected to the Legislative Assembly in the general election of 1893 for 1st Prince. Running as an Independent, he defeated Liberal A. J. Matheson and Conservative A. F Birch. He was re-elected in the general election of 1900.

He was defeated in the general elections of 1863, 1872, 1897, and 1915. Rogers was elected to the Legislative Council in 1878 for 1st Prince. He was re-elected in 1882 and 1886.

Rogers served on Executive Council in the administrations of Frederick Peters*, Alexander B. Warburton*, and Donald Farquharson*. He was appointed Provincial Secretary of the Treasury and Commissioner of Agriculture in 1900. Rogers was appointed Lieutenant-Governor in 1910 and served until 1915. Following his term as Lieutenant-Governor, he served as leader of the Liberal Party.

Rogers served as Leader of the Opposition in the Legislative Council from 1883 to 1886, and as President of Legislative Council from 1891 to 1893.

Rogers was educated in Bedeque. Upon completing his studies, he accepted a clerkship in Summerside, after which he worked as a bookkeeper for James C. Pope* until 1858. In that year, he moved to Alberton and opened his own business, taking over the business of his brother David. Upon the opening of his Alberton store, Rogers decided against the sale of alcoholic beverages, even though this would most likely mean a serious loss of trade. Rogers continued this policy throughout his life and career. Benjamin Rogers died 16 May 1923.

Susannah Rogers, the daughter of Captain William Hubbard of Tignish, was born ca. 1836 and died 12 July 1897. Annie Rogers was the daughter of James Hunter.

References
CPG 1879. 1885, 1889, 1893, 1901, 1915; MacLeod p. 79; *WWC* 1914 p. 797; *Examiner* 14 December 1893; *Guardian* 16 May 1923; PARO: *Rogers Family Chronicle*; MNI-Census 1881, 1891; MNI-Hutchinson's pp. 135, 240, 241, 258, 272, 276, 282.

ROGERS, DAVID, merchant and shipbuilder; b. 15 November 1829 in Llanstephen, Carmarthen, Wales, son of Joseph Rogers and Margaret James; m. first 20 March 1861 Annie Hester Gourlie, and they had five children, Arthur, Helen, Willie, Caroline, and Winnifred; m. secondly 17 June 1886 Rosina Gertrude Brine, and there were no children; Anglican; d. 22 October 1909 in Summerside.

Rogers, a Conservative, was elected to the House of Assembly in the 1890 general election for 5th Prince. He was defeated in the general election of 1893. He served on Executive Council from 1890 to 1891.

Rogers' family immigrated to the Island in

1831. He was educated at the local school in Freetown. At the age of 19, Rogers was employed with N. J. Brown in St. Eleanors. In 1851 he was employed for some time with William McEwen, and later at the mercantile and shipbuilding establishment of James C. Pope*. In 1856 he established a business in Alberton, which was later operated by his brother Benjamin Rogers*. Circa 1858, Rogers became a partner with Pope, whom he bought out some years later. For the remainder of his commercial career, Rogers conducted his own business, which he carried out in a general store on Water Street in Summerside.

Rogers was the first Mayor of Summerside, from the time of its incorporation in 1877, until 1883. Rogers was also the president of the Literary Society. David Rogers died 22 October 1909.

Annie Rogers, the daughter of James A. Gourlie, was born in 1843 in New Brunswick and died in 1884. Rosina Rogers, the daughter of the Reverend R. T. Brine, was born ca. 1853 and died in 1931.

References

CPG 1891, 1897 p. 397; *Daily Examiner* 21 June 1886; *Islander* 29 March 1861; *Summerside Journal* 27 October 1909; PARO: *Rogers Family Chronicle*; MNI-Census 1881, 1891; MNI-Hutchinson's p. 133.

ROSS, JOHN STEWART, farmer and fisher; b. 24 November 1902 in Flat River, son of Magnus Ross and Sarah Stewart; m. first 15 July 1931 Bessie MacRae of White Point, and they had four children, Kathleen, Lona, Elizabeth, and Connie; m. secondly 1981 Florence MacAulay MacKenzie, and there were no children; Presbyterian; d. 5 April 1999 in Eldon.

Ross, a Liberal, was first elected to the Legislative Assembly in the general election of 1959 for 4th Queens. He was re-elected in the general elections of 1962, 1966, and 1970.

"Stewart" Ross was educated in Flat River. He was a successful farmer and a lobster fisher for over 50 years in that community. Ross was a member of the St. John's Presbyterian Church in Belfast and the Masonic Lodge. Stewart Ross died 5 April 1999.

Bessie Ross died in 1978. Florence Ross died in 1988.

References

Elections PEI; *Guardian* 5 April 2000.

ROSSITER, LEO FRANCIS, merchant and farm machinery dealer, realtor, and chair of Workers Compensation Board; b. 13 January 1923 in Morell, son of J. Ernest Rossiter and Catherine Clarkin; m. 17 October 1946 Anna Pierce, and they had six children, Jaqueline, Gerald, Eugene, Melvin, Elijah (deceased 1954), and Hanna (deceased 1964); Roman Catholic; d. 25 October 1996 in Charlottetown.

Rossiter, a Conservative, was first elected to the Legislative Assembly in the general election of 1955 for 2nd Kings. He was re-elected in the general elections of 1959, 1962, 1966, 1970, 1974, 1978, and 1979. In 1959 he served as Minister of Industry and Natural Resources and Minister of Fisheries. From 1965 to July 1966, Rossiter was Minister of Fisheries and Minister of Municipal Affairs. He was again appointed as Minister of Fisheries in May 1979, and also served as Provincial Secretary from May 1979 to 1980. In 1980 Rossiter became Minister of Labour. He resigned from politics upon his appointment as Chair of the Workers Compensation Board on 1 November 1981. Rossiter also served as Opposition critic for housing, fisheries, public works, and highways. He was chair of the Morell Village Commission for several terms.

Rossiter was educated in Morell and at St. Dunstan's University. For 20 years, he operated a general store and a farm machinery dealership. He was the general manager of Dingwell and Rossiter Limited. Rossiter also operated Rossiter Realty. He served two terms as the provincial representative on the council of governors of the Canadian Centre for Occupational Health and Safety, and was appointed president of the Association of Workers Compensation Boards for Canada.

Rossiter was a 4th degree member of the Knights of Columbus, and was an associate member of the Navy Officers Club of Charlottetown and the United Officers Service Club. In 1978 he received the Queen's Silver Jubilee Medal. In 1984 he received investiture into the "Most Venerable Order of the Hospital of St. John of Jerusalem" as a Serving Brother, by Governor General Madame Jeanne Sauve. Leo Rossiter died 25 October 1996 at the Queen Elizabeth Hospital in Charlottetown.

Anna Rossiter was the daughter of Elija Pierce of Elmira.

References

CPG 1981; *CWW* 1983 p. 980; PEI *Cabinet Biographic Summary* 1980; *Guardian* 31 March 1978, 31 October 1981, 24 February 1984, 5 August 1987, 20 October 1996.

ROWE, MANOAH, farmer, merchant, shipbuilder, and customs collector; b. ca. 1813, in England; m. Penelope Rowe of Prince Edward Island, and they had one child, Minney; Methodist; d. 12 May 1899.

Rowe, a Liberal, was elected to the House of Assembly in the general election of 1873 in 4th Kings.

Rowe came to the Island in 1832. Besides being a farmer, he was involved in a number of mercantile activities in the Montague area. He operated a general store in Montague Bridge, and was a general importer, shipbuilder, and customs collector in Montague. He also operated a country tavern in the Montague area. While in his twenties, Rowe was a member of the Young Men's Temperance Society.

Records indicate that for a period of time Rowe lived in Summerside. Later, certainly by 1880, he made his home in Montague Bridge. His numerous economic interests in the Montague area indicate that at some time previous to residing in Summerside he may have lived near Montague. Manoah Rowe died 12 May 1899.

Penelope Rowe was born ca. 1825 and died 13 September 1907. Her parents emigrated to the Island from England. The 1881 Census indicates that Minney Rowe was born in New Brunswick.

References
CPG 1874; *Meacham's Atlas*; *Royal Gazette* 14 May 1839 p. 3; PARO: MNI-Hutchinson's p. 157; MNI-Mercantile Agency Reference Book 1876; MNI-Census 1881, 1891; License book #6 pp. 166–67, 170–71; Montague Funeral Home Records.

S

ST. JOHN, JOHN BRENTON, farm produce dealer and exporter, and director of fish factory; b. 11 January 1910 in Souris, son of Patrick St. John and Anastasia MacAulay; m. 25 August 1941 Edna Campbell, and they had one child, George Kevin; Roman Catholic; d. ca. 1959.

St. John, a Liberal, was first elected in a by-election held 18 July 1949 for 1st Kings. He was re-elected in the general elections of 1951 and 1955. In 1951 he was appointed as a Minister without Portfolio and served in that capacity until 1953. St. John was Deputy Speaker from 1954 until 1959. He was defeated in the general election of 1959.

St. John attended the local schools in Souris, as well as St. Dunstan's College. He was a director of Griffins' Fisheries and worked as a dealer and exporter of farm produce. St. John served on the Souris Town Council for nine years. He was a member of the Souris Board of Trade and the Fisheries and Game Association.

Edna St. John was the daughter of John D. Campbell and Bridget MacNeill of Poplar Point.

References
CPG 1950, 1959.

SAUNDERS, K.C., HONOURABLE ALBERT CHARLES, lawyer and judge; b. 12 October 1874 in Summerside, son of Charles B. Saunders and Margaret MacKenzie; m. 1902, Leila Zwicker Graves, and they had four children, Reginald, Mrs. Floyd Cleveland, Mrs. Harold Schurman, and Mrs. Myron Stoll; Church of England; d. 18 October 1943 in Summerside.

Saunders, a Liberal, was first elected to the Legislative Assembly in the general election of 1915 for 2nd Prince. He was re-elected in the general elections of 1919, 1923, and 1927. He served as Leader of the Opposition from 1923 to 1927. In the general election of 1927, the Liberals, led by Saunders, defeated Conservative Premier James D. Stewart*. Saunders was sworn in as the sixteenth premier on 12 August 1927. On 20 May 1930, he resigned to accept appointment to the position of Master of Rolls and Justice of the Supreme Court of Prince Edward Island. Saunders first entered the political arena in Summerside where he served as Mayor for four terms before entering provincial politics.

The Conservatives campaigned in the election of 1927 on a platform to repeal the Prohibition Act. Saunders and the Liberals were in favour of prohibition. The Conservatives wished to regulate the distribution of liquor by placing it under government control. The Conservative Prohibition policy was clearly against public opinion and they were defeated. During Saunders' first session as Premier, the Legislature passed a bill designed to make the enforcement of the Prohibition Act more effective. His government was also responsible for the revision of the public school curriculum and an increase in teachers' salaries. During his time as premier, significant road construction was carried out throughout the province.

Upon his death, the *Patriot* noted that Saunders, the son of a harness maker, was unaided by wealth or influence in his rise to premier. He possessed a great capacity for painstaking concentration on the task at hand, a quality that allowed him to achieve great success in both the legal and political communities of the province.

Saunders was educated at Summerside schools and at Prince of Wales College in Charlottetown. Upon graduating from Prince of Wales, he studied law in the Summerside firm of James E. Wyatt*. Saunders moved on to article with Peters, Peters, and Ings in Charlottetown, a firm that included Frederick Peters* and Arthur Peters*, both premiers. After Saunders was called to the Bar on 3 October 1899, he opened his own office in Summerside. He was recognized as one of the leading criminal lawyers in the province. In the 1920s, Saunders formed a partnership with Thane Alexander Campbell*, who would also become a premier of the province. In the early 1940s, Saunders presided at the trial that resulted in the last executions in the province. Albert Saunders died 18 October 1943 at his home.

References
CPG 1928; Elections PEI; Graves p. 413; MacKinnon *Life of the Party* pp. 88-89; *Provincial Premiers Birthday Series 1873-1973*; *Patriot* 18 October 1943, 19 October 1943; PARO: MNI-Census 1891.

SAVILLE, GEORGE EDWARD, farmer, fisher, shipper, newspaper correspondent, and lecturer; b. 18 November 1880 in St. Georges, son of Edward S. Saville and Elizabeth J. Howlett; m. first Alberta Huestis of Charlottetown, and they had one son, Robert; m. secondly 31 December 1914 Maggie C. Chaffey, and there were no children; Baptist; d. 6 May 1961 in Charlottetown.

Saville, a Liberal, was first elected to the Legislative Assembly in the general election of 1935 for 5th Kings. He was re-elected in the general elections of 1939, 1943, 1947, 1951, 1955, and 1959. He was defeated in the general elections of 1927 and 1931. In the general election of 1959, there was a tie vote between Saville and Leslie Hunter. A recount revealed that a ballot for his opponent had been marked with a ballpoint pen instead of a pencil. The Returning Officer awarded the seat to Saville. He died while a Member of the Legislative Assembly.

Saville received his education in the local schools at St. Georges and Annandale. Early in his career, he farmed and fished. Beginning in 1897, and for many years after, Saville was a correspondent for the *Guardian* and the *Evening Patriot.* He began lecturing at the age of 14 on the subject of politics, among other subjects. Saville was also the Annandale shipper for the Potato Growers Association. He was a member of the Forresters and the Loyal Orange Association. Saville was a founder of the Daimeny Society in Dundas and an officer of the Kings County Order of Royal Scarlet Knights. George Saville died 6 May 1961 at the Prince Edward Island Hospital.

Alberta Saville died in 1902. Maggie Saville was the daughter of Joseph Chaffey of Little Pond.

References
CPG 1936; *Guardian* 8 May 1961.

SCHURMAN, ROBERT CLAYTON, radio station owner and sportscaster; b. 5 December 1925 in Melrose, Massachusetts, son of Benjamin Colin Schurman and Grace Lavinia Rankin; m. 6 August 1945 Lois Eleanor Macdonald, and they had three children, Marsha, Brent, and Paul; United; d. 15 January 1973 in Summerside.

Schurman, a Liberal, was elected to the Legislative Assembly in the general election of 1970 for 4th Prince. He was appointed Minister of Community Services on 24 September 1970, and Minister of the Environment and Tourism on 1 December 1971. He served as Minister Responsible for Communications from 1971 to 1972.

Schurman's family moved from the United States to Summerside when he was six years old. He attended Summerside Elementary and Summerside High School. In 1947 Schurman began his radio career as an announcer for CGHS, which later became CJRW. In 1952 he was named general manager of CJRW and, in 1953, vice-president. He acquired control of the station in 1957 and became president and general manger. Schurman also worked as a sportscaster for CJRW, and for 12 years could be heard broadcasting various sporting events from many Maritime centres. He often served as a Master of Ceremonies for civic, provincial, and regional functions. In 1986 he was posthumously inducted into the Canadian Broadcast Hall of Fame.

Schurman served as an elder and finance chairman of Trinity United Church in Summerside, and was a choir member and soloist with his church. He served as president of the Prince Edward Island Tuberculosis League, vice-president of the Prince Edward Island Music Festival Association, government liaison and a member of the Confederation Trust. In 1973 he was chair of the Prince Edward Island Centennial Commission. He was a member of the Summerside Industrial Commission, and was a president and chairman of the board of the Waterfront Development Corporation, a president of Summerside Y's Men's Club, a member of the Royal Canadian Legion and the Masonic Lodge, as well as a volunteer with the Canadian Cancer Society.

An accomplished athlete, Schurman excelled in baseball and hockey, and was inducted posthumously into the Prince Edward Island Sports Hall of Fame. He contributed to the development of sport in the Summerside area, as a volunteer with the Summerside Recreation Commission and the Summerside Minor Hockey Association. He also helped organize the annual international friendship hockey series between Natick, Massachusetts, and Summerside. Robert Schurman died 15 January 1973 at the Prince County Hospital.

Lois Schurman, the daughter of Norman MacDonald, was born in St. Eleanors.

References
CPG 1973; *Journal-Pioneer* 16 January 1973, 18 July 1973, 3 November 1986; *Patriot* 16 January 1973.

SCRIMGEOUR, JOHN GOW, farmer, trader, ship-builder and sawmill operator; b. 9 September 1842 in Glasgow, Scotland, son of John Scrimgeour and Mary Gow; m. May 1881, Charlotte Sencabaugh, and they had one child, John William; Presbyterian; d. 21 August 1917 in Cardigan.

Scrimgeour, a Liberal, was first elected to the House of Assembly in a the general election of 1876 for 3rd Kings. He was defeated in the general election of 1873. Scrimgeour resigned in 1878. In 1886 he was elected to the Legislative Council, until its abolishment in 1893. While in the Legislative Council, he served as Usher of the Black Rod.

Scrimgeour lived on Burnside Farm in Cardigan Bridge, a property which was one of the largest farming lands in eastern Prince Edward Island. He owned approximately 500 acres. A trader, Scrimgeour was listed as the proprietor of a country store in Cardigan Bridge in 1874. He was also a shipbuilder and owner of Burnside Mills, which manufactured lumber and shingles. Besides his interests in community affairs, he was also a Freemason. John Scrimgeour died 21 August 1917.

Charlotte Scrimgeour was the daughter of Jacob Sencabaugh of Charlottetown and Murray Harbour and Charlotte Dixon of Scotland. She was born ca. 1835 and died in 1917. Scrimgeour's parents were born in Perthshire, Scotland. His father arrived on the Island in 1843, with Scrimgeour and his mother following a year later.

References
CPG 1876, 1889; *Meacham's Atlas*; *Past and Present* pp. 484–85; PARO: MNI-Census 1891; Montague Funeral Home Records, p. 76; St. Andrew's Presbyterian Church Records.

SCULLY, PAUL ALPHONSUS, store clerk and general store owner-manager; b. 25 January 1885 in Souris West, son of Thomas Scully of Ireland and Mary A. Howlett; m. 8 August 1910 Mary A. McInnis, and they had nine children, Stephen W., Thomas Gerard, Joseph, Adolphus, Lucy, Geraldine, Agnes, Constance, and Bernadette; Roman Catholic; d. 5 June 1931 in Georgetown.

Scully, a Liberal, was elected to the Legislative Assembly in the general election of 1927 for 5th Kings. On 4 August 1930, he was appointed as a Minister without Portfolio.

Scully, a native of Souris West, was educated in Souris. While still a boy, Scully began his mercantile career as a clerk with Sterns, Son & Company. He was employed with Archibald Currie and later, ca. 1915, joined J. J. Hughes and Company. In 1919 Scully became manager of the company and later a shareholder. Later he moved to Georgetown, and for a number of years was a partner in Scully and Delory, with Fred Delory. He was a prominent member of the Kings County Board of Trade, and was a member the Knights of Columbus. Paul Scully died 5 June 1931, while serving as a Member of the Legislative Assembly.

Mary Scully, the daughter of Joseph and Katie McInnis of Souris, was born 16 September 1882 in Souris and died in 1951 in Georgetown.

References
CPG 1930, 1931; *Maple Leaf Magazine* August 1931; *Patriot* 5 June 1931; PARO: MNI-Census 1891; St. James Roman Catholic Cemetery Records.

SHARPE, GEORGE SHELTON, fisher, fox breeder, lobster packer, and oyster farmer; b. 28 September 1876, son of George W. Sharpe and Martha Ennis; m., Bessie MacKay, and there were no children; Presbyterian; d. 13 March 1942 in Tyne Valley.

Sharpe, a Conservative, was first elected to the Legislative Assembly in a by-election held 21 October 1930 for 2nd Prince. He was re-elected in the general election of 1931. He was defeated in the general elections of 1927, 1935, and 1939. On 29 August 1931, Sharpe was appointed to Executive Council as Minister of Agriculture and Provincial Secretary-Treasurer. He was re-elected by acclamation after assuming the above offices. Upon the death of Leonard M. MacNeill*, he became Minister of Public Works and served in that Ministry until 1935. He was defeated in the federal election of 1925 in the riding of Prince.

A resident of Bideford, Sharpe was involved in a number of occupations. He was a fisher and a lobster packer, and for many years he farmed oysters and in 1908 began cultivating private oyster beds. Sharpe served as president of the National Silver Fox Breeders Association from 1929 to 1931. George Sharpe died 13 March 1942 at his home.

Sharpe's father was a native of Scotland. Bessie Sharpe was born in 1877 and died in 1965.

References
CPG 1933, 1936, 1941; *HFER* vol. 7 Prince p. 2; *Patriot* 14 March 1942; PARO: MNI-Census 1891; Census 1901; Tyne Valley Cemetery Records.

SHAW, CYRUS, farmer; b. 25 January 1850 in New Perth, son of Robert Shaw and Jane Williams; m. 27 December 1883 Penelope Partridge, and they had one child, Jenny; Presbyterian; d. 27 September 1900.

Shaw, a Conservative, was first elected to the House of Assembly in the general election of 1886 for 3rd Kings. He was re-elected in the general election of 1890. He was elected to the Legislative Assembly in the general election of 1893 for 3rd Kings. Shaw was re-elected in the general election of 1897. He was a leader of the Conservative Party. Shaw's brother Robert Shaw* was a Member of the House of Assembly.

Shaw attended Prince of Wales College, and his academic ability was recognized when he won a provincial scholarship in 1866. Despite this success, he concluded his education after two years, and began operating the family farm of 200 acres. In 1868 he was a member of the Lily Lodge in 1868. Cyrus Shaw died 27 September 1900.

Penelope Shaw, the daughter of Richard Partridge, was born in England in 1847 or 1848 and died 31 August 1925. Shaw's father was a native of Colonsay, Scotland. The elder Shaw first emigrated to Nova Scotia and later to the Island.

References
CPG 1889 p. 219; Currie p. 121; Elections PEI; *Past and Present* p. 493; *Examiner* 31 December 1883; PARO: MNI-Census 1891; Montague Funeral Home Records.

SHAW, ROBERT, lawyer; b. 2 September 1845 in New Perth, son of Robert Shaw and Jane Williams; m. 5 December 1873 Florence M. J. Yuill, in Truro, NS, and they had three children, Joseph, Lottie G. and Robert (died at 18 months); Presbyterian; d. 22 March 1882 in Charlottetown.

Shaw, a Conservative, was elected to the House of Assembly in the general election of 1879 for 3rd Queens. He served as a member until his death. Shaw's brother Cyrus Shaw* was a member of the House of Assembly.

Shaw was educated at Central Academy and Prince of Wales College in Charlottetown. He attended Dalhousie University in Halifax, where he received a Bachelor of Arts with first class honours. At his graduation, Shaw received first prizes in Classics, Mathematics, History, and Ethics. On returning to the Island, he studied law in the office of Palmer and MacLeod, where Herbert Palmer* also studied. In 1870 Shaw was called to the Bar. Robert Shaw died 22 March 1882.

Florence Shaw, the daughter of Gregor Yuill of Truro, Nova Scotia, was born in 1853.

References
CPG 1880; Currie p. 164; *Examiner* 15 March 1881; *Patriot* 23 March 1882; *Islander* 19 December 1873; *Summerside Journal* 30 November 1882; PARO: MNI Census 1861, 1881.

SHAW, O.C., M.B.E., LL.D., WALTER RUSSELL, livestock field worker, livestock supervisor, farmer, and civil servant; b. 20 December 1887 in St. Catherine's, son of Alexander Crawford Shaw and Isobel Maynard; m. 1 June 1921 Margaret MacKenzie of Victoria, and they had three children, Margaret Eileen, Norma Katherine, and Walter Maynard; United; d. 29 May 1981 in Charlottetown.

Shaw, a Conservative, was first elected to the Legislative Assembly in the general election of 1959 for 1st Queens. He was re-elected in the general elections of 1962 and 1966. He was defeated in the general election of 1955 for 3rd Kings. In 1957 he was elected Leader of the Conservative party. On 1 September 1959, Shaw led the Conservatives to victory, winning 22 seats to the Liberals' eight. Premier Shaw served in that office and as President of Executive Council from 17 September 1959 to 28 July 1966. After more than three years as Leader of the Opposition, he announced his retirement on 13 December 1969, and in 1970 he retired from political life.

Shaw's political career, which followed a long career as a civil servant, was paradoxical, particularly given the provincial political culture of the late 1950s and 1960s. He was a bureaucrat and a farmer, able to successfully resolve the incompatibilities of these two worlds by means of his popularity and his public rhetoric which appealed to rural Islanders. The fact that the two occupations in which he was engaged were accomplished with sincerity gave Shaw integrity. He was also regarded as a great speaker and frequently made an eloquent defence of Island values.

When he assumed power, the Island was on the threshold of an unprecedented period of industrial and cultural development. Shaw was well-suited to be premier at this time, given the comfort level he had in rural areas and in managing the affairs of the province. He had to deal with the challenge of stimulating economic growth, while at the same time trying to preserve the traditional values that many Islanders valued. In the general election of 1962, Shaw became the first Conservative premier to win two consecutive terms since 1915.

In 1959 the Conservative campaign platform

advocated a commitment to progress, which included a plan to build a causeway connecting Prince Edward Island and New Brunswick. Shaw felt that the role of his Administration was to assist in the process of narrowing the social and economic gap between Islanders and other Canadians. He understood the importance of agriculture and fishing to the economy. The dilemma he faced was that the Island had relied heavily on agriculture and fishing, yet reliance on these industries had not allowed the province to achieve economic parity with other provinces. The question became how best to allow the primary industries to grow. Shaw's answer was to invest government money in the food processing industry and to revitalize the shipbuilding industry.

In 1961 Shaw's government assisted in the construction of Seabrook Frozen Foods in New Annan and in 1963 the Administration invested in Langley Fruit Packers in Montague. These food processing plants met with some success, particularly in comparison to another government-supported initiative, the Gulf Garden fish plant in Georgetown. The Shaw administration granted financial support to Bathurst Marine to also locate a shipbuilding operation to Georgetown. Due in part to mismanagement by the owner, both Gulf Garden and Bathurst Marine were bankrupt by 1967. In total, the province had invested $9.35 million in Georgetown without realizing the economic benefit for which the government strived.

There were many other notable initiatives of the Shaw Administration. The regional high school system was established, a new provincial administration building was constructed, and the provincial civil service had its salaries and employment conditions improved.

Shaw received his primary education at the school in St. Catherine's. Later he attended Prince of Wales College and the University of Toronto, where he earned a Bachelor of Science in Agriculture. He attended the Nova Scotia Agricultural College and excelled at livestock judging, public speaking, and athletics.

While still a young man, Shaw participated in the harvest excursions to Western Canada, and during the First World War served with the 9th Siege Battery. From 1916 to 1919, he worked for the Department of Agriculture, and from 1919 to 1922 he edited an agricultural paper for Garden City Publishing in Ste-Anne-de-Bellevue, Quebec. In 1922

Shaw returned to the Island to work as a livestock field worker and later a livestock superintendent with the province's Department of Agriculture. During his tenure of service as Deputy Minister of Agriculture, numerous reforms and improvements were launched under his direction or as a result of his influence. Shaw was responsible for launching the Prince Edward Island Federation of Agriculture and served as its general secretary. He also was a member of the board of directors of the Canadian Federation of Agriculture. He was the president of the Canadian Horticultural Council and chairman of the Council's Potato Committee. He was a member of the National Agricultural Advisory Committee. Shaw retired as Deputy Minister of Agriculture in 1954. While working in the civil service, he operated a farm in Clyde River.

Shaw was a member of the Masonic Lodge, the Foresters, and the Y's Men's Club, and served as Chief of the Island Clans. He was a member of the Rural Development Council of Prince Edward Island and a director of the Prince Edward Island Heritage Foundation.

Shaw received many honours and was decorated by royalty on three occasions. In 1935 he received the Jubilee Medal, in 1950 he was awarded a Member of the British Empire and Citation, and a few years later he received a Coronation Medal. In 1971 Shaw became an Officer of the Order of Canada. He received honourary degrees from St. Dunstan's University and Mount Allison University, as well as the Canada Medal of Merit. In 1975 Shaw's memoirs, *Tell Me The Tales*, were published. In 1980 he was inducted into the Canadian Agricultural Hall of Fame, and he stated that "he counted his induction into the Canadian Agricultural Hall of Fame as the most gratifying of all his awards." Walter Shaw died 29 May 1981.

Margaret Shaw was the daughter of Alexander MacKenzie of Victoria West.

References

CPG 1970; Forester pp. 127–28; Ledwell pp. 48–55; MacDonald *If You're Stronghearted* pp. 263, 265; *Provincial Premiers Birthday Series 1873–1973*; Shaw; *Atlantic Insight* 3 (2) March 1981; *Charlottetown Monthly Magazine* February 1984; *Globe and Mail* 14 December 1969; *Guardian* 30 May 1981; *Journal-Pioneer* 17 December 1971, 23 May 1980, 30 May 1981; *Maritime Advocate and Busy East* August 1954; PARO: MNI-Maritime Reference Book p. 88.

SIMPSON, ALBERT EDWIN, farmer; b. 28 December 1866 in Hamilton, Lot 18, son of William McNeil Simpson and Sophia Clarke; m. 4 July 1905

Florence L. Davidson, and there were no children; Protestant; d. 14 January 1947 in Parkdale.

Simpson, a Conservative, was elected to the Legislative Assembly in the general election of 1912 for 2nd Kings.

Simpson received his education at Guelph Agricultural College, and worked as a farmer on the Island. Albert Simpson died 14 January 1947.

Florence Simpson, the daughter of James L. Davidson of St. Peters, was born in 1876 and died in 1960.

References
CPG 1915; Elections PEI; *Guardian* 15 January 1947; PARO: Midgell Cemetery Records.

SIMPSON, GEORGE WOODSIDE, farmer; b. 10 December 1858 in Bay View, son of John and Barbara Simpson; m. 23 August 1888 Catherine Taylor, and they had two children, Lilla and Laura; Presbyterian; d. 21 October 1906.

Simpson, a Liberal, was first elected to the Legislative Assembly in the general election of 1900 for 1st Queens. He was re-elected in the general election of 1904. On 15 April 1903, he was appointed to Executive Council.

In the summer of 1906, Simpson was nominated as one of the Liberal candidates for Queen's in the federal election, but he died before he could contest the seat.

Simpson was educated in Hope River. He worked as a farmer and as a school trustee, and was active in the temperance movement. George Simpson died 21 October 1906 while a member of Executive Council.

References
CPG 1905; Elections PEI; *Patriot* 23 October 1906; PARO: Marriage License Book 16 1887-1923 p. 36.

SINCLAIR, SR., PETER, farmer and justice of the peace; b. 18 November 1819 in Glendaruel, Cowal Peninsula, Argyll, Scotland, son of Peter Sinclair and Mary Crawford; m. 5 February 1879 Margaret M. MacMurdo, and they had 10 children, John E., Adeline, Janette, James Norris, Archibald MacMurdo, Mary, Peter, Jr.*, Margaret, Winnifred, and Amy Ann; Presbyterian; d. 9 October 1906 in Summerfield.

Sinclair, a Liberal, was first elected to the House of Assembly in the 1867 general election for 1st Queens. He was re-elected in the general elections of 1870, 1872, 1873, 1882, 1886, and 1890.

He was defeated in the general election of 1858. He was elected to the Legislative Assembly in the general election of 1893. He was re-elected in the general election of 1897. Sinclair served on Executive Council from 1868 to 1871, and was reappointed to Executive Council in 1872 when he was also elected Government House Leader. At this time, he was appointed a member of the Board of Works. From 1868 to 1871, Sinclair served as a member of the Board of Education. From 1871 to 1897, Sinclair served on Executive Council in the Frederick Peters* Administration, and again in the Donald Farquharson* Administration from 1897 to 1898.

In 1873 Sinclair resigned from the Assembly to contest, successfully, the special federal election in September 1873 for Queen's. He was re-elected by acclamation in the 1874 federal general election.

Sinclair was a proponent of requiring absentee landowners to sell their land to their tenants, and an advocate of free schools and of temperance. He strongly believed that decisions on matters such as Confederation and the Railway should be made by consulting the citizens of the province in a vote on the issue.

Sinclair moved to the Island in 1840 with his mother, after his father died in 1830. His mother purchased a farm in Lot 67 and the family named it Summerfield, after their family home in Scotland. Sinclair was instrumental in the development of the farm. Sinclair was educated in Scotland before moving to the Island. Peter Sinclair died 9 October 1906.

Margaret Sinclair, the daughter of Archibald MacMurdo of New Annan, was born in 1852 and died 14 December 1932. A son, Peter Sinclair, Jr.*, served in the Legislative Assembly and the House of Commons.

References
CPG 1899; *CDP* p. 533; *DCB* XIV 1911-1920 pp. 954-56; *Past and Present* pp. 471-72; *Patriot* 10 October 1906, 23 October 1906; PARO: MNI-Hutchinson's p. 245; MNI-Census 1881; Andrew's Funeral Home Records.

SINCLAIR, JR., PETER, farmer; b. 13 November 1887 in Springfield, son of Peter Sinclair, Sr.*, and Margaret M. MacMurdo; m. 23 December 1909 Joanna ("Anna") Campbell, and they had seven children, Scott Campbell, Margaret Winnifred, Donald William, Peter, Caroline, Isabel, and Albert;

United; d. 9 March 1938 in Ottawa.

Sinclair, a Liberal, was first elected to the Legislative Assembly in the general election of 1927 for 1st Queens. He was defeated in the general election of 1931. On 20 February 1928, Sinclair was appointed to Executive Council as a Minister without Portfolio. In the federal election of 1935, Sinclair was elected for Queen's. He died while serving as a Member of the House of Commons.

Sinclair's father, Peter Sinclair*, served in the House of Assembly, the Legislative Assembly, and the House of Commons.

Sinclair was educated at the public school in Springfield. He farmed there in his early career before moving to Charlottetown with his family. He was a member of the Masonic Order and the United Church of Canada. Peter Sinclair, Jr., died on 9 March 1938.

Joanna Campbell, the daughter of William Campbell of Graham's Road, was born 18 July 1885 and died 9 July 1975.

References
CPG 1931; CWW 1936-1937 p. 997; *Past and Present* p. 471; *Patriot* 9 March 1938; PARO: Summerfield United Church Cemetery Records.

SINNOTT, M.D., C.M., JOSEPH CYRIL, physician; b. 7 May 1922 in Morell, son of Patrick R. Sinnott and Margaret Sinnott; m. 23 August 1951 Willa Coreen FitzGerald, and they had six children, Patrick, Maureen, Sheila, Marylou, Bethany, and Leah; Roman Catholic; d. 6 October 1987 in Charlottetown.

Sinnott, a Conservative, was elected to the Legislative Assembly in the general election of 1966 for 5th Kings. He was defeated in the general election of 1970. Sinnott served on several Legislative Committees including education, public health, transportation, and public accounts. He was a candidate for the leadership of the party with Ivan Kerry and George Key, the eventual winner. Sinnott served as President of the provincial Conservative party from 1983 to 1985, and Vice-President of the Progressive Conservative Party of Canada from 1977 to 1983. He was a candidate for national Vice-President for the Atlantic Region in 1983. Sinnott was a member of the Progressive Conservative Club at McGill University, and on his return to the Island became a member of the provincial party. He also served as aide-de-camp to the Honourable William J. MacDonald, Lieutenant-Governor.

"Cy" Sinnott began his education at the

local school in Bristol. He then attended Prince of Wales College and St. Dunstan's University, graduating with a Bachelor of Science *summa cum laude* in 1949. In 1953 Sinnott graduated with a medical degree from McGill University, and spent the next five years in post-graduate work there and at the Montreal General Hospital. In 1957 he was awarded a diploma in internal medicine and Master of Science in medical investigation. Later that year, Sinnott was named a Fellow of the Royal College of Physicians and Surgeons for Canada.

Sinnott served as president of the United Services Officers Club and was a member of the Royal Canadian Legion, the Royal Canadian Air Force Association, the Knights of Columbus, and the Rotary Club. He was president of the Prince Edward Island branch of McGill Alumni. In the Royal Canadian Air Force during the Second World War, he achieved the rank of Flight Engineer. From 1942 to 1945, he served as Flight Lieutenant and was later promoted to Squadron Leader.

Sinnott and his wife lived in Montreal, and later moved to Charlottetown where they raised their family and he practised internal medicine at the Charlottetown Clinic. Cyril Sinnott died 6 October 1987 at the Queen Elizabeth Hospital.

Willa Sinnott is the daughter of Henry J. FitzGerald.

References
CPG 1970, 1971; *Guardian* 5 November 1959, 22 January 1983, October 1987.

SMITH, HAROLD PERCY, farmer and insurance broker; b. 25 March 1907 in Pownal, son of Captain Wallace Smith and Adelaide Jardine; m. 25 January 1933 Hazel MacEachern, and they had seven children, Winston, Donald, James, Ronald, Ian, David, and Marilyn; United; d. 28 September 1982 in Pownal.

Smith, a Liberal, was first elected to the Legislative Assembly in a by-election held 10 September 1953 for 4th Queens. He was re-elected in the general elections of 1955, 1959, 1962, and 1966. He was defeated in the general election of 1970. On 23 November 1966, Smith was appointed to the position of Deputy Speaker. During his political career, he supported the expansion of the road paving program to assist farmers in the marketing of farm produce and stressed the need for a stable market for farm products.

Smith was born in Pownal and was a lifelong resident of the community. He attended the Pownal School and continued his education by taking agricultural courses throughout his life. As a farmer, Smith took a great interest in grain-growing, for which he won national prizes. He worked with his brother Edison in the shipping and poultry business, and for a time was employed as an insurance broker with Bus Peake and A. R. MacInnis Ltd. In keeping with his agricultural interest, Smith served as the director of the Dundas Plowing Association and the secretary-treasurer of the Queens County Plowing Association. In his community he was a scoutmaster, and served in various positions in his home church, Pownal United, including the board of stewards and clerk of the session. Harold Smith died 28 September 1982 at his home in Pownal.

Hazel Smith, the daughter of James MacEachern and Etna MacEachern, survives her husband.

References
CPG 1954, 1970, 1972; *Guardian* 30 September 1982.

SMITH, MATTHEW, farmer, resort owner, and lime company president; b. 15 July 1843 in Crapaud, son of George Smith and Anne Wiggington; m. 30 August 1870 Sarah Elizabeth Lea, and they had eight children, William L., G. Edgar, Annie B., Harriet G., Stewart D., Claud M., Helen M., and Edna L.; Methodist; d. 1 March 1909 in Charlottetown.

Smith, a Liberal, was first elected to the Legislative Assembly in the general election of 1900 for 1st Queens. He was re-elected in the general elections of 1904 and 1908. On 30 October 1900, Smith was appointed to Executive Council as a Minister without Portfolio. At the time of his death, he was Speaker of the Legislative Assembly.

Smith was educated at the local school in Crapaud. He was a farmer and the proprietor of Pleasant View Summer Resort, a popular vacation spot for summer tourists. Smith served as a trustee and secretary of the school board for over 25 years. He was involved in his church, serving as a steward for more than 30 years and as Sunday School superintendent for over 20 years. He was well-known for the promotion of religion, temperance, and education. Matthew Smith died suddenly on 1 March 1909 while serving as Speaker of the Legislature.

Sarah Smith, the daughter of William Lea of Tryon, was born in 1848 and died in 1922.

References
CPG 1909, 1910; Elections PEI; *Past and Present* pp. 390-91; *Guardian* 2 March 1909; PARO: Crapaud People's Cemetery Records.

SOLOMAN, ROGER, teacher and school principal; b. 16 May 1939, in Georgetown, son of G. Walter Soloman and Lucy Scully; m. 27 December 1965 Sheila Graham, and they had four children, Paulette, Terry, Kimberly, and Frank; Roman Catholic.

Soloman, a Liberal, was elected to the Legislative Assembly in the general election of 1993 for 1st Kings. While a member, Soloman served on a number of Legislative committees. He chaired the Special Committee on Proposed Tax Harmonization in 1996. Soloman also served as Campaign Chair for Cardian MP Lawrence MacAulay and, in 1996, for Keith Milligan*.

Soloman earned a Bachelor of Science from St. Dunstan's University in 1963 and a Bachelor of Education from the University of Prince Edward Island in 1971. Later he attended the University of New Brunswick and St. Francis Xavier University, where he received a Master of Education in 1977. Following his graduation from St. Dunstan's University, Soloman served as a Lieutenant in the Royal Canadian Navy. He served on the HMCS *Bonaventure* in the Canadian contingent of the United Nations Forces in Cyprus from 1963 to 1964. For 32 years beginning in 1964, Soloman was a teacher in the Souris schools. He taught math and science and was the principal of both Souris Consolidated and Souris Regional High. He was a member of the Board of Governors of the PEI Teacher's Federation. Soloman served as chair of the Souris West Community Council. He operates De Roma Cottages, a small cottage operation on the Brudenell River.

Soloman was a member of the Souris Curling Club, member and president of both the Royal Canadian Legion in Souris and the Lions Club, and was a volunteer with the United Appeal and Flowers of Hope Campaign. He volunteered with the Souris Minor Hockey Association, Scouts Canada, and the Souris Sea Cadets. Roger Soloman and his wife live in Souris West.

Sheila Soloman is the daughter of Guy Graham of Murray Harbour North and Martha French.

References
CPG 1996; *Guardian* 15 February 1993, 6 March 1993.

STEWART, BRUCE LOWELL, teacher, fuel oil salesperson, fisher, town councillor, and mayor; b. 5 October 1916 in Murray Harbour, son of John Ernest Stewart and Alfreda Jordan; m. 6 June 1941 Florence Christene MacDonald, and they had three children, Joan Alfreda, Alan Bruce, and David Gordon; Baptist; d. 5 May 1991 in Souris.

Stewart, a Liberal, was first elected to the Legislative Assembly in the general election of 1966 for 1st Kings. He was re-elected in the general elections of 1970 and 1974. On 7 February 1969, he was appointed Minister of Health. From 1969 to 1970, he served as Minister of Municipal Affairs, and served as Minister of Industry and Commerce from 1 June 1970 to 1971. Stewart was Minister of Fisheries from 1 June 1970 to 1972, and Minister of Labour from 24 September 1970 to 2 May 1974. On 10 October 1972, he became Minister of Social Services and Minister of Health, and he served in those Ministries until 2 May 1974, on which date Stewart was named Minister of Public Works and Minister of Highways. He served in this position until the fall of 1976, when he became ill. After an eight-month recovery period, in April 1977 Stewart returned to the Ministry of Public Works and remained there until 27 April 1978. He indicated that poor health and his doctor's advice dictated his decision to retire from politics in 1978.

Stewart's victory in 1966 occurred in a special election for 1st Kings held following the general election on 30 May. William A. Acorn* had won the Liberal nomination for 1st Kings for the general election, but died during the campaign. As a result of his death, the vote for councillor and assemblyman for 1st Kings was deferred until 11 July 1966. The Liberals won both seats and formed the government with a total of 17 seats to the Conservatives' 15 seats.

Stewart considered four initiatives in particular as his most significant contributions as a public servant. While he served as a Member of the Legislative Assembly, the Souris area benefitted from the establishment of the Eastern Kings Regional Services Centre, the introduction of the Magdalen Islands ferry service, the construction of a million-dollar wharf on the Souris waterfront, as well as the construction of Colville Manor nursing home. Stewart was also a councillor and mayor for the town of Souris. His fondest memory in politics was the role he played in implementing Medicare in the province.

Stewart received his primary education at the Murray Harbour School. From 1933 to 1934, he attended Prince of Wales College and received a teacher's license. Later he studied at McGill University. Stewart began his working life as a teacher and taught for six years. He also worked as an agent for Imperial Oil and as a fisher. Stewart spent some time in the service of the military.

Beyond politics, Stewart was involved in a number of community activities. He served as president of the Souris Branch Royal Canadian Legion and as provincial chairman and Dominion representative of the Royal Canadian Legion. Stewart was a board member of the Protestant Children's Home, chairman of the Souris Hospital Board, and president of the organization known later as the Association for Community Living. During the celebrations of the 70th Anniversary of the Town of Souris, Stewart served as chair of the organizing committee. He was also a member of the board of directors of the United Way. Bruce Stewart died 5 May 1991 in the Souris Hospital.

Florence Stewart, the daughter of Alan Neil MacDonald, was born in Heatherdale.

References

COR 1991 p. 188; CPG 1967, 1970, 1978; ECO 289/78; WWPEI 1986 p. 132; Guardian 13 July 1973, 22 January 1982, 6 May 1991.

STEWART, C.D., D.S.O., E.D., LIEUTENANT-COLONEL JOHN DAVID, businessperson; b. 21 August 1910 in Georgetown, son of James David Stewart* and Barbara Alice Westaway; m. 16 March 1935 Constance Creelman McArthur, and they had four children, Judith Beattie, Barbara Lois, Heather Marion, and Patricia Jane; Presbyterian; d. 5 December 1988 in Charlottetown.

Stewart, a Conservative, was first elected in the general election of 1959 for 5th Queens. He was re-elected in the general elections of 1962 and 1966. He was defeated in the general election of 1970. Following the 1959 election, Stewart became Provincial Secretary. In 1961 he was also appointed as Minister of Tourist Development and of Municipal Affairs. He served in both positions until 1965.

Before his provincial political career began, Stewart was a member of the Charlottetown City Council from 1946 to 1951, and was Mayor of Charlottetown from 1951 until his retirement in 1958. He was elected president of the Federation of Mayors and Municipalities of Canada in 1955.

Stewart's father, James David Stewart*, served as premier from 1923 to 1927, and again from 1931 to 1933.

Early in his life, Dave Stewart lived in Georgetown, but he later resided in Charlottetown. He attended West Kent School in the capital city. Stewart was a prominent business person who held senior positions with various companies. He was chairman of the Georgetown Shipyard Incorporated, president of Northumberland Ferries Limited, president of Charlottetown Petroleum Products Limited, and president of Stewart Motors Limited. He also was director of Industrial Enterprises Incorporated, a member of the advisory board of the Canada Permanent Trust Company, and a member of the board of broadcast governors of the Canadian Broadcasting Corporation.

A veteran of the Second World War, Stewart had a distinguished military career. He served in France, Belgium, Holland, and Germany. Stewart joined the Prince Edward Island Highlanders as a Private in 1928 and held the rank of Captain in the Canadian Army in 1939. He subsequently joined the North Nova Scotia Highlanders as a Major and went overseas where, in September 1943, he was made a Lieutenant-Colonel. Stewart was given command of the Argyll and Sutherland Highlanders of Canada. With only nine days of combat experience, on 10 August 1944, near Cannes, France, he and his men were ordered to take Hill 195. Stewart manoeuvred all 400 Argyles through enemy lines unscathed. He was ultimately awarded the Distinguished Service Cross and Efficiency Decoration, and his name was mentioned in dispatches. Stewart was a member of various clubs, including the United Services Officers Club, the Charlottetown Club, the Green Gables Golf Club, and the Charlottetown Curling Club. J. David Stewart died in a Charlottetown nursing home on 5 December 1988.

Constance Stewart was the daughter of Senator Creelman McArthur* and Hannah Lois Beattie of Summerside.

References

COR 1988 p. 166; CPG 1970, 1972; CWW 1973-1975 p. 957; PEI *Journal of the Legislative Assembly* 1960 p. 3, 1961 p. 3, 1965 p. 3; *WWPEI* p. 132; *Guardian* 6 December 1988, 16 May 1989.

STEWART, K.C., JAMES DAVID, lawyer; b. 15 January 1874 in Lower Montague, son of David

Stewart and Lydia Ayers; m. Barbara Alice MacDonald Westaway and they had seven children, Roma, Nell, Marjorie, Lillian, James A., James David*, and Maude; Presbyterian; d. 10 October 1933.

Stewart, a Conservative, was first elected to the Legislature in a by-election held July 1917 for 5th Kings. He was re-elected in the general elections of 1919, 1923, 1927, and 1931. In 1921 he was elected Leader of the Conservative party and became Premier and Attorney-General after defeating the government of Premier John H. Bell* in 1923. Stewart served in this capacity until 1927, when his party was defeated. When the Conservatives were re-elected in 1931, he once again served in the roles of Premier and Attorney-General.

With the 1923 election, Stewart became the fifteenth premier of the province, and when he won re-election in 1931 he was the only party leader since the Island joined Confederation to return as premier after being defeated. Throughout his two terms as premier, Stewart fought for a higher subsidy for the province and attempted to advance the cause of Maritime rights in Ottawa. In the general election of 1927, Stewart and the Conservative Party were defeated because they promised to repeal Prohibition, an idea which a majority of Islanders rejected.

Stewart received his early education in Lower Montague and later attended Prince of Wales College and Dalhousie University. Stewart taught school for several years before beginning his law career. He read law with Mathieson and MacDonald. John Mathieson* was premier from 1911 to 1917, and Aeneas MacDonald* also served in the Legislature. Stewart was called to the Bar in 1906. At some point James Augustine Macdonald* read law with Stewart. In 1917 Stewart was appointed King's Counsel. He was a partner in Mathieson, MacDonald and Stewart in Georgetown and Charlottetown from 1906 until 1916. From 1917 to 1928, he practised law without a partner. From 1928 to his death, he was a partner in the firm Stewart and Lowther. Stewart served as vice-president of the Bar Association in 1927. He served as chair of the Board of Falconwood Hospital. Stewart was an active member of the A.F. and A.M. and served as Provincial Grand Master 915. He was also a member of the Charlottetown Golf Club. James Stewart died 10 October 1933 while in office. He was one of only three Island premiers, including Arthur Peters* and

Walter Lea*, who died while serving as premier.

Barbara Stewart, the daughter of John and Catherine Westaway of Georgetown, was born 2 June 1879 and died 28 September 1968 in Charlottetown. His son David Stewart* represented 5th Queens in the Legislative Assembly from 1959 to 1970.

References
CPG 1933; *Prominent Men* p. 41; PARO: MNI-Census 1881; People's Cemetery Records.

STEWART, WALTER FITZ-ALAN, farmer and fox rancher; b. 11 July 1885 in Strathgartney, son of Robert Bruce Stewart and Anne Warburton; m. 12 January 1933 Marion Lea, and they had three children, Anne Warburton, Barbara Fitz-Alan, and Mary Lea; Anglican; d. 5 February 1956.

Stewart, a Liberal, was first elected to the Legislative Assembly in the general election of 1927 for 1st Queens. He was re-elected in the general elections of 1935, 1939, 1943, 1947, 1951, and 1955. He was defeated in the general election of 1931. He served as Speaker in 1931 and again from 1942 to 1943. In 1944 he was appointed Minister of Agriculture. He was appointed the Minister of Welfare and Labour in January 1956 and served until January 1957.

Stewart received his early education at Bonshaw Public School, and later attended Prince of Wales College and the Ontario Agriculture College in Guelph, Ontario. He resided in Strathgartney and was a farmer and fox rancher. Stewart served as the honourary president of the Junior Farmers Movement of Prince Edward Island and was an officer of the Ayrshire Breeders Association. He was a member of the Agricultural Institute of Canada and the Freemasons. Stewart served as a Lieutenant in the 105th Regiment from 1915 to 1930. Walter Fitz-Alan Stewart died 5 February 1956.

Marion Stewart, the daughter of Walter Maxfield Lea* and Helena Esma Maude Mary Rogerson, was born 5 October 1900 and died 5 February 1956. Her father was premier from 1930 to 1931 and again from 1935 to 1936. Her paternal grandfather was William Charles Lea*.

References
CPG 1936; *CWW* 1936-1937 p. 1036; *Provincial Premiers Birthday Series 1873-1973*; *Patriot* 9 February 1956 p. 1; PARO: RG Vital Stats Box M, Marriage License; Census 1901; St. John's Anglican Cemetery Records.

STEWART, WILLIAM ALLAN, merchant; b. 28 November 1871 in Charlottetown, son of Daniel Stewart and Sarah Jane Cameron; m. 30 September 1904 Eliza Blanche Simpson, and they had two children, Allan S. and Marjorie B.; Presbyterian; d. 14 April 1962 in Charlottetown.

Stewart, a Conservative, was first elected to the Legislative Assembly in the general election of 1931 for 5th Queens. He was re-elected in the general election of 1939. He was defeated in the general elections of 1935 and 1943. Stewart also served on the Charlottetown City Council.

Stewart was educated at public school in Charlottetown and lived there throughout his life. A merchant, he was both a director and departmental manager of Moore and MacLeod. He later became honourary president of the company and held this title until he died. Stewart was a long-serving chairman of trustees of the Protestant Orphanage. He was past-president and charter member of the Charlottetown Rotary Club. He became a life member of the Oddfellows, a member of the Masonic Lodge, and a member of the Charlottetown Club. William Stewart died 14 April 1962 in Charlottetown at the Prince Edward Island Hospital.

Eliza Stewart was the daughter of James Simpson of Bayview.

References
CPG 1940, 1944; *Guardian* 16 September 1962.

STEWART, WILLIAM DUNBAR, merchant and bookkeeper; b. 15 August 1839 in New Perth, son of Peter Stewart and Lizzie MacIntyre; m. 1866 Thomasina Amelia Pidgeon, and they had four children, Frank H., Gertrude B., William F., and Harold; Presbyterian; d. ca. 1879.

Stewart, a Liberal, was first elected to the House of Assembly in the general election of 1873 for 1st Queens. He was re-elected in the general election 1876. He was defeated in the general election of 1879. Stewart was appointed Commissioner of Public Works in 1876 and, following his appointment, was returned to the House of Assembly by acclamation.

Stewart was a resident of at least three Island communities. Born in New Perth, he resided in New London ca. 1866 and in Charlottetown ca. 1879. Stewart worked as a bookkeeper in Margate ca. 1864 and as a commission merchant while serving in the House of Assembly. William Stewart died ca. 1879.

Thomasina Stewart, the daughter of Ann McLeod and James Pidgeon of French River, was born 18 February 1839. Her father was born in Great Torrington, Devonshire, England.

References

CPG 1879, 1880; Elections PEI; Pollard p. 203; PARO: License granted 2 and 4 January 1866, Marriage License Books 1863–1871 and 1866–1870; MNI-Census 1881; MNI-Hutchinson's p. 156; St. Mark's Anglican Church Records, Kensington, Record Book 2 p. 35.

STEWART, K.C., WILLIAM SNODGRASS, lawyer and judge; b. 13 February 1855 in Marshfield, son of Alexander and Florence Stewart; m. 27 September 1892 Annie Augusta Beer, and there were no children; Presbyterian; d. 11 February 1938 in Charlottetown.

Stewart, a Conservative, was first elected to the Legislative Assembly in the general election of 1912 for 5th Queens. Before this he had been defeated in the 1893 general election for 3rd Queens, and in the 1908 general election for 2nd Queens. He was also defeated in the federal arena, in the 1900 federal election by L. H. Davies* in West Queen's. Stewart served as a Minister without Portfolio in the Mathieson* Administration from 1912 to 1914, when he resigned his seat to accept an appointment as a Queens County Judge.

Stewart received his early education at the district school in Marshfield. He attended Prince of Wales College in Charlottetown, studied at Dalhousie University in Halifax for one term, then entered McGill University in Montreal where he earned a Bachelor of Arts with First Class Honours and the Chapman Gold Medal. He left McGill in 1878 to study law under Frederick Peters* in Charlottetown, and was admitted to the Bar in 1883. That year he moved to Summerside, where he worked for several years as a partner in the Peters firm. Eventually Stewart moved back to Charlottetown to open his own practice. Stewart was made Judge of the County Court of Queens on 22 July 1914, and, on the death of the Honourable W. W. Sullivan*, became Judge of the Admiralty Court. He retired from the bench in February 1930.

After his retirement, Stewart entered municipal politics and in 1932 became Mayor of Charlottetown. He served in this position until the election of 1934. Stewart was well-known and well-

respected in the province. Late in life he continued to express his views through letters and opinion pieces in the Island press. William Stewart died 11 February 1938.

Annie Stewart was the daughter of Henry Beer*, also a mayor of Charlottetown, and Amelia Ings. She died 11 February 1938.

References

CPG 1897, 1901, 1909, 1914; *Patriot* 12 February 1938; PARO: MNI-Census 1881, 1891.

STRONG, O.B.E., M.C., V.D., K.C., LIEUTEN-ANT-COLONEL ERNEST HENRY, lawyer and judge; b. 26 September 1886 in Crapaud, son of C. Edward Strong and Sarah Davis Ellison; m. first Loretta MacNeill, and they had two children, Edward Wilkinson and Elizabeth Davis; m. secondly 12 August 1931 Clara Wilkinson of O'Leary, and there were no children; Baptist; d. 7 August 1961 in Summerside.

Strong, a Conservative, was elected to the Legislative Assembly in the general election of 1943 for 5th Prince. He was defeated in the general elections of 1947, 1951, and 1957 for 4th Prince, and in the general election of 1955 for 2nd Prince. In 1945 Strong resigned to run in that year's federal election for Prince; he was defeated by 75 votes.

His grandfather, William G. Strong, was a member of the Legislative Council for eight years and served as government leader in the Council for three years. Strong's brother Heath Edward* was elected to the Legislative Assembly in the general elections of 1931 and 1943, and he served as Speaker from 1931 to 1935.

Although he was born in Crapaud, Strong resided for the majority of his life in Summerside. He attended Summerside High School and Prince of Wales College, after which he articled with Judge Albert C. Saunders*. Strong was admitted to the Bar on 25 June 1912. He served as Stipendiary Magistrate in Summerside from 1931 to 1958, and also was appointed as a Deputy Judge in Juvenile Court in that community.

A member of the Royal Canadian Legion, Strong enlisted for overseas service in December 1915. He served with the 105th Prince Edward Island Battalion and 26th New Brunswick Battalion in England, France, Belgium, and Germany during the First World War. Strong won the Military Cross and other military honours. Between the First and Second World Wars, he was active in a peacetime unit and in the early 1930s was the commanding officer of the Prince Edward Island Highlanders. In 1939 he retired from the military with the rank of Lieutenant-Colonel. Ernest Strong died 7 August 1961 in Summerside at the Prince County Hospital.

Loretta Strong was born 1 April 1886 and died 21 December 1928. Clara Strong was the daughter of J. C. Wilkinson of O'Leary.

References
CPG 1945, 1947, 1948, 1952, 1957, 1962; *HFER* 1993 p. Prince 1; *Meacham's Atlas*, *Journal-Pioneer* 7 August 1961; *Patriot* 7 August 1961; PARO: Summerside People's Protestant Cemetery Records.

STRONG, K.C., HEATH EDWARD, lawyer and news reporter; b. 21 August 1882 in Summerside, son of C. Edward Strong and Sarah Davis Ellison; m. 4 November 1925 Ethel Louise Sinclair, and there were no children; Presbyterian; d. 26 November 1950 in Summerside.

Strong, a Conservative, was first elected to the Legislative Assembly in the general election of 1931 for 4th Prince. He was re-elected in the general election of 1943. He was defeated in the general elections of 1935, 1939, and 1947. From 1931 to 1935, he served as Speaker.

His grandfather, William G. Strong, was a member of the Legislative Council for eight years and served as government leader in the Council for three years. Strong's brother Ernest Henry* was elected to the Legislative Assembly in 1943 for 5th Prince, but resigned to run, unsuccessfully, as the Conservative candidate for Prince in the 1945 federal election.

Strong received his early education in Summerside and later attended Prince of Wales College in Charlottetown. He was appointed to the Bar on 7 May 1907. Strong worked in Summerside for many years as a lawyer, and was appointed King's Counsel on 11 December 1924. He served as president of the Prince Edward Island Bar Association and provided legal services to the Children's Aid Society. Strong was a director of the Prince Edward Island Protestant Orphanage. For several years, he assumed the role of Summerside correspondent for the *Patriot*. At the time of his death on 26 November 1950, Heath Strong was president of the board of managers of the Presbyterian church in Summerside.

Ethel Strong, daughter of Neil Sinclair of Summerside. She was born ca. 1887. She died 8 May 1987.

References
CPG 1936, 1940, 1944, 1948; *Journal* 4 June 1987; *Patriot* 27 November 1950; PARO: Summerside People's Protestant Cemetery Records.

SULLIVAN, JOHN P., farmer, merchant, and store owner; b. 23 April 1843 in New London, son of William Sullivan and Mary McArthy, both of County Kerry, Ireland; m. first 9 September 1873 Ellen MacDonald; m. secondly 17 July 1877 Helen MacDonald; Sullivan had one daughter, Ellen; Roman Catholic; d. 30 September 1898 in Charlottetown.

Sullivan, a Conservative, was elected to the House of Assembly in the general election of 1890 for 2nd Kings. He was defeated in the general election of 1893. He was the brother of William Wilfred Sullivan*, a premier and Chief Justice of Prince Edward Island.

Sullivan operated a general merchandise business in St. Peters for many years, and farmed in that area. John Sullivan died suddenly on 30 September 1898 while travelling to Charlottetown.

Sullivan's first wife, Ellen, died 16 February 1875. Helen Sullivan died in November 1900.

References
CPG 1897; *Daily Examiner* 18 July 1877; *Daily Patriot* 30 September 1898, 1 October 1898 p. 3; PARO: St. Augustin Roman Catholic Church Book 6 p. 77; MNI-Census 1881, 1891; MNI-Mercantile Agency Reference Book September 1876; Marriage Register 1871–1878; St. Peters Bay Roman Catholic Cemetery Records; St. Andrew's Roman Catholic Cemetery Records.

SULLIVAN, Q.C., HONOURABLE SIR WILLIAM WILFRED, journalist, lawyer, and judge; b. 6 December 1843 in New London, son of William Sullivan and Mary McArthy, both of County Kerry, Ireland; m. 13 August 1872 Alice Maud Mary Newberry, and they had six children, Adele M. M., Alice M. M., W. F. Cleaver, Wilfred C. P., Faustina M. L., and Louis Arthur; Roman Catholic; d. 30 September 1920 in Memramcook, New Brunswick, and was buried in Charlottetown.

Sullivan, predominantly a Conservative, but a Liberal during his early career, was first elected to the House of Assembly in the 1872 general election for 1st Kings. He was re-elected in the general elections of 1873, 1876, 1879, 1883, and 1886. He was defeated in an 1869 by-election for 1st Kings, in the 1870 general election for 3rd Queens, and in another by-election for 1st Kings in 1871. He served on Executive Council in Premier Robert Poore Haythorne's Administration from April to June of 1872, until resigning over a disagreement about the provincial railway. In 1873 he was appointed Solicitor-General in the coalition government of Conservative James C. Pope*. When Pope's Denominationalists were defeated in the 1876 general election by the Free School Party of L. H. Davies*, Sullivan continued to oppose the Public Schools Act of 1877. From 1876 to 1879, he served as Leader of the Opposition. In the general election of 1879, Sullivan defeated Davies and became Premier and Attorney-General, a position he held until 1889.

Sullivan was the first Island premier to win three consecutive elections. His 10-year term as premier was a record until Alex Campbell's 12-year stint in the 1960s and 70s. Premier Sullivan was concerned primarily with provincial finances. The Davies government had been unable to balance the budget and, when it attempted to impose taxation through the Assessment Act of 1877, the electorate reacted angrily. Having joined Confederation for the financial stability and security it offered, Islanders were indignant at the possibility of direct taxation by the provincial government. In the 1879 campaign, Sullivan promised to do away with direct taxation and to deal with the province's financial problems by requesting more support from the Federal government. This effort would allow him to balance the budget and eliminate the need for direct taxation in the province. His plan pleased the electorate, and Sullivan was elected with the largest majority ever recorded in the Assembly to that time.

The Sullivan Administration made many changes to provincial spending patterns. Sullivan eliminated the secret ballot, reverted to statutory labour (compulsory) on the roads, cut the pay of Members of the Assembly, reduced the number of offices and the salaries in the civil service, eliminated some of the jurors on civil cases, and amalgamated the institutions of higher learning in the province. Despite his repeated appeals to the federal government for revenue supplements after he abolished the direct tax in 1882, Sullivan was unable to balance the budget. Unwilling to reintroduce the direct tax and unable to secure adequate funds from the federal government, the Sullivan Administration was forced to borrow large sums of money to cover the cost of its operations. Ultimately, Sullivan was able to gain an increased subsidy to the province from the federal government.

In 1889 Sullivan left office to accept the appointment of Chief Justice of the Supreme Court of Prince Edward Island on 13 November 1889. His brother John Sullivan* served in the House of Assembly from 1890 to 1893.

Sullivan was educated at Central Academy in Charlottetown and at St. Dunstan's College. Following his schooling, Sullivan was one of the editors at the Charlottetown *Herald*, and continued to write for the newspaper in the early years of his law career. He completed his law apprenticeship with Joseph Hensley and was admitted to the Bar on 29 June 1867. He was a partner in the law firm of Sullivan and McNeill. He was also a partner in Sullivan and Morson. In 1876 Sullivan was designated as Queen's Counsel.

On 29 June 1914 Sullivan was appointed a Knight Bachelor. In 1917 he resigned his judicial positions due to ill health. William Sullivan died 30 September 1920, while residing with one of his daughters.

Alice Sullivan, the daughter of John Fenton Newberry and Adella Travaglini of London, England, and Sienna, Italy, was born in 1846 and died in November 1908.

References

CPG 1876; *DCB* X 1871–1880 pp. 981–83; *Eminent Men,* pp. 720-24; *MWOT* 1898 p. 985.

SUTHERLAND, JAMES MILLER, lawyer; b. 30 June 1853 in Park Corner, son of John S. Sutherland and Marion Miller; m. 14 January 1875 Isabella Henderson, and they had three children, Marion, Ella, and Sinclair Gordon; Presbyterian; d. 1921.

Sutherland, a Liberal, was first elected to the House of Assembly in the general election of 1886 for 1st Queens. He was re-elected in the general election of 1890. He resigned in 1891.

Sutherland attended Prince of Wales College. In March 1877, he was called to the Bar. His residence during his years in the House of Assembly was listed as Charlottetown, although he represented 1st Queens, the district where he lived during his childhood. James Sutherland died in 1921.

Isabella Sutherland was born ca. 1847. Sutherland's parents were natives of Scotland and immigrated to the Island in 1844.

References

CPG 1889, 1891; Elections PEI; PARO: #81 Zion Presbyterian Church Records Book 1 p. 5; MNI-Census 1881, 1891; Sutherland Family File.

SUTHERLAND, WILLIAM GEORGE, farmer and mill owner; b. 17 October 1866 in New London, son of James Sutherland and Mary A. Whitehead; m. 19 November 1890 Ina M. MacIntyre, and they had four children, Annie A., George M., Margaret M., and Jennie; Presbyterian; d. 2 May 1921.

Sutherland, a Liberal, was elected to the Legislative Assembly in the general election of 1919 for 4th Kings. He died while in office.

Sutherland received his education in New London's public school. He had a number of occupations in his lifetime, beginning as a farmer and then spending some time performing masonry work on the Hillsborough Bridge. Finally Sutherland bought Montague Mills, a successful milling business situated at the head of the Montague River. He was a member of the International Order of Oddfellows. William Sutherland died 2 May 1921.

Ina Sutherland was the daughter of Captain James MacIntyre. She was born in New London 12 October 1870 and died 29 August 1962.

References
CPG 1921; *Patriot* 3 May 1921, 6 May 1921; PARO: Montague Funeral Home Records; Lower Montague United Cemetery Records.

T

TANTON, WILFRED, barrister; b. 21 February 1880 in Summerside, son of William Tanton and Sophia C. Jamieson; m. 4 January 1918 Lillian Swabey Cox, and there were no children; Anglican; d. 21 April 1951 in Charlottetown.

Tanton, a Conservative, was elected to the Legislative Assembly in the general election of 1923 for 1st Prince. He was defeated in the general elections of 1927 and 1931.

Tanton received his education in the local school and later attended Prince of Wales College. He practised law in Alberton. Keenly interested in the affairs of his community he served as Mayor of Alberton from 1939 to 1944. From 1914 to 1917, he served as Stipendiary Magistrate to Prince County. He was a member of the Masonic Fraternity of A.F. and A.M. Wilfred Tanton died 21 April 1951.

Lillian Tanton, the daughter of Doctor Frank Cox of Morell, was born in 1885 and died in 1969.

References
CPG 1924, 1925, 1934; *Patriot* 21 April 1951; PARO: Charlottetown People's Cemetery Records.

THOMPSON, GORDON MAX, farmer and tourism operator; b. 24 February 1914 in North Tryon, son of Gordon Warren Thompson and Lena Lillian MacDonald; m. 12 October 1937 Doris Marie Crosby, and they had three children, Marlene, John Donald, and Ralph Crosby; United; d. 13 May 1985 in Charlottetown.

Thompson, a Liberal, was elected to the Legislative Assembly in the general election of 1966 for 4th Prince.

Max Thompson received his early education in the Warren Grove School, and later attended the Royal School of Cavalry in St. John's, Quebec, and the Graham School of Scientific Breeding in Kansas City, Mississippi. He farmed and operated a tourism business. Thompson was director and president of the Crapaud Creamery Company Limited and owner of the Birch Haven Farm in Victoria. He was active in the Crapaud Exhibition Association and was the first president of the Prince Edward Island Association of Exhibitions; he continued to serve in that role for 25 years. Thompson was a director of the Dairy Farmers of Canada from 1959 to 1960, of the Holstein-Friesian Association of Canada from 1956 to 1958, and president of the Crapaud-Victoria Board of Trade from 1956 to 1958. He also served as director of the Maritime Board of Trade from 1956 to 1966. Thompson served on the Board of National Farm Products Marketing Council and served as chairperson of the Board of the Prince Edward Island Marketing Development Centre and the Prince Edward Island Marketing Council. He was chairman of the Board of Trustees of the Englewood Regional High School. Thompson was a member of the Victoria United Church, the True Brothers Masonic Lodge Number Eight in Crapaud, and the Crapaud Curling Club, and was a fundraising chairperson for the Canadian Heart Foundation. Max Thompson died 13 May 1985 at the Queen Elizabeth Hospital.

Doris Thompson was the daughter of H. D. Crosby.

References
CPG 1970; *Guardian* 14 May 1985.

TRAINOR, K.C., HONOURABLE CHARLES ST. CLAIR, lawyer and judge; b. 8 December 1901 in Albany, son of Thomas Trainor and Annie Greenan; m. first 24 August 1938 Catherine Bernadette MacMillan, and they had three children, Elaine Bernadette, Dr. Charles St. Clair, and Father Joseph Leo; m. secondly 10 June 1968 Annie Maud MacGuigan Noonan; Roman Catholic; d. 19 June 1978.

Trainor, a Liberal, was first elected to the Legislative Assembly in the general election of 1935 for 5th Queens. He was defeated in the general elections of 1931 and 1939.

Trainor received his early education in the Searletown School. He graduated from St. Dunstan's College with a Bachelor of Arts in 1923, and then studied law under Mark R. MacGuigan*. On 30 November 1927, he was called to the Bar. Trainor continued to work with MacGuigan and eventually the two formed a partnership, MacGuigan and Trainor. He was designated King's Counsel in 1938. Trainor served as the prosecutor for Queens County from 1939 to 1942. In 1942 he was appointed Judge of the Kings County Court, where he served until 1949. On 22 December 1949, he was appointed Judge of the Queens County Court where he served until 1967. On 7 November of that year, Trainor was elevated to the province's Supreme Court, and became its Chief Justice 9 July 1970.

Aside from his active law career, Trainor was involved in numerous community initiatives. From 1965 to 1969, he served as chairperson of the Board of Governors of St. Dunstan's University. In 1969, when St. Dunstan's University and Prince of Wales College merged, through to 1978, he served as chairperson of the Board of Governors of the University of Prince Edward Island. Trainor served as chairperson of the Public Utilities Commission from October 1946 to January 1968, and also served as chairperson of the Veterans Land Act Advisory Board. From 1953 to 1956, Trainor was Deputy Commissioner of the War Claims Commission. He was a member of three different Commissions of Inquiry under the Public Inquires Act. Trainor was an executive member of the Federation of Prince Edward Island Home and School Association, as well as a member of its Examining Board. From 1956 to 1968, he served on the Charlottetown School Board. Trainor was a member of the Prince Edward Island branch of the Canadian Red Cross Society and the Canadian Mental Health Association. He helped found the Prince Edward Island Polio Foundation and acted as chairman of the Canadian National Institute for the Blind. He also was a 4th degree member of the Knights of Columbus. C. St. Clair Trainor died 19 June 1978.

Catherine Bernadette Trainor was the daughter of W. J. P. MacMillan*, a premier, and his second wife, Letitia Macdonald. She died in 1965. Her sister, Mary Dorothea, married Alban Farmer*. Annie Maude Trainor Noonan died 10 March 1994.

References
CPG 1936, 1940; *Topics* 30 June 1978 pp. 1-2; UPEI: Robertson Library: PEI Collection.

U

UNDERHAY, JOHN COLLIER, farmer, land surveyor, and justice of the peace; b. 15 January 1829 in Bay Fortune, son of William Underhay and Marianne Withers; m. 17 September 1856 Rosaline Craswell, and they had eight children, William H., Minnie, Frederick Withers, May Mary, Edward Whalen, Ada, Ethel Maude, and Lillian; Presbyterian (raised Anglican); d. 23 October 1919.

Underhay, a Liberal in his early career and later a Conservative, was first elected to the House of Assembly in the general election of 1879 for 1st Kings. He was elected in the general election of 1886 for 2nd Kings, and re-elected in the general election of 1890. He was defeated in the general election of 1882 for 2nd Kings. In 1874 he was defeated in the general election for Legislative Council for 1st Kings. Underhay believed in responsible government, free schools, and tenant land ownership. He eventually joined the Conservative party, as he felt it more fully represented the principles of the old Liberal party of Prince Edward Island.

Educated at local schools, Underhay completed his studies with Robert Black Irving, then one of the Island's best mathematicians. He worked as a farmer and land surveyor in Bay Fortune. At the age of 24, he was appointed a Justice of the Peace, the youngest ever on the Island. Underhay was given credit for his assistance in implementing the Canada Temperance Act. Of the 50 judgements he made on the Act, not one was set aside or reversed by higher courts. He served as a Commissioner of the Court for the Trial of Small Debts at Bay Fortune, and acted as the presiding judge until the creation of the County Courts.

Though raised an Anglican, Underhay joined the Presbyterian faith, serving as secretary-treasurer of the Bay Fortune Presbyterian Church and taking an active part in its construction. He was a longtime trustee for the area's school district. He became a member of the Order of Good Templars in 1868, and in 1870 became the Grand Chief of the Island. In 1884 he was a delegate to the Washington session of the Right Worthy Grand Lodge. Underhay was a leader in the temperance movement. John Underhay died 23 October 1919.

Rosaline Underhay was the daughter of the Honourable James Craswell and Harriet Withers Heal. She was born in 1837 and died 23 June 1910.

References
CCB pp. 415–16; PARO: Bay Fortune United Church Cemetery Records.

W

WALKER, ANDREW, human resources manager; b. 5 January 1954 in Summerside, son of Kenneth and Willene Walker; m. 1 September 1979 Carol Ann MacLanders, and they had five children, Luke Andrew, Rebecca Anne, Victoria, Hannah, and Michaela; Presbyterian.

Walker, a Conservative, was elected to the Legislative Assembly in a by-election held 10 November 1986 for 5th Prince. He was defeated in the general election of 1989. In the Legislature, Walker was Opposition critic for justice, labour, community and cultural affairs, and environment. In June 1988 he was a candidate for the Conservative party leadership. He served as Treasurer of the 5th Prince Progressive Conservative Association and President of the Prince Edward Island Progressive Conservative Party Association.

"Andy" Walker received his secondary education at Summerside High School, and later attended prep school at Phillips Exeter Academy. In 1976 he obtained a Bachelor's degree with a major in political science and physics at Dartmouth College in Hanover, New Hampshire. He attended Cornell University in Ithaca, New York, and in 1980 graduated from law school at Dalhousie University. In 1981 Walker began practising law in Summerside and became a partner in the firm Walker and Aylward. He served as president of the Law Foundation of Prince Edward Island, and was a member of the articling and admissions committee and the discipline committees of the Law Society of Prince Edward Island. He is currently employed as human resources manager at M. F. Schurman Company Limited in Summerside.

Walker served as chairman of the board of managers of the Presbyterian Church in Summerside. An accomplished distance runner, he finished third in the Canadian Olympic Trials in 1976 for the 3,000-metre steeplechase. He was an all-Ivy League champion in distance running twice.

Andrew Walker resides in Summerside.

References
CPG 1987, 1989, 1993; *Guardian* 14 June 1988, 18 April 1989, 22 December 1995.

WARBURTON, K.C., D.C.L.,
ALEXANDER BANNERMANN, lawyer, judge, and author; b. 4 April 1852 in St. Eleanors, son of James Warburton and Martha Compton Green; m. first 23 August 1883 Helen Margaret Davies of St. Eleanors, and there were no children; m. secondly 25 October 1889 Isabella Cogswell Longworth of Charlottetown, and they had three children, Olga, Mrs. J. Holroyd, and Morah Frances; Anglican; d. 14 January 1929 in Charlottetown.

Warburton, a Liberal, was first elected to the House of Assembly in a by-election held 29 May 1891 for 1st Queens. He was defeated in the general election of 1890 for Charlottetown Royalty. He was elected to the Legislative Assembly in the general elections of 1893 and 1897. Following the unexpected resignation of Frederick Peters* in 1897, Warburton became premier in October of that year. On 1 August 1898, he resigned as premier and as a Member of the Legislative Assembly to accept a judicial appointment to the Court of Kings County. As a result of urging from members of the Liberal party, on 21 October 1904, Warburton resigned from the Bench to become a candidate in that year's federal election for Queen's. Despite being defeated, he reoffered in the 1908 federal election and was elected. Warburton was defeated in the 1911 and 1917 federal elections. He served as Mayor of Charlottetown from 1901 to 1904.

Warburton was born in Summerside and attended public school there. He attended St. Dunstan's for two years. Later he attended King's College in Windsor, Nova Scotia, and received a Bachelor of Arts degree. While at King's College, he won the Williams Engineering Prize and the Welsford Scholarship for ranking first in the first-year class. In 1876 Warburton was awarded a Bachelor of Law degree, and he received a Doctor of Law degree in 1897, both from King's College. Warburton also studied at the University of Edinburgh for one year, concentrating on Arts and Classics.

Warburton began law studies in London, England, where he was tutored by the famous instructor, Walter Wren, as well as by M. G. Baugh, noted special pleader at the Inner Temple. Later, upon his return to the Island, he continued his studies with L. H. Davies*. On 6 July 1878, Warburton was admitted to the Bar and established a law practice in Charlottetown. In 1882 Warburton and Francis Conroy became law partners. He later became a partner with C. R. Smallwood, at another period a partner with Donald A. MacKinnon*, and later with D. Edgar Shaw. Following a career in provincial politics, in 1898 Warburton was appointed as a judge with the Kings County Court where he served until resigning in 1904. In 1920 he returned to the Bench when he was appointed Judge of Probate, and remained there until his death.

Warburton was also an author and lecturer. He wrote *A History of Prince Edward Island 1534–1831*, and was an editor with D. A. MacKinnon and one of the authors of *Past and Present*. For a number of years he was one of the chief political editorial writers for the *Patriot*. Warburton was among the first Islanders to promote school consolidation and wrote a series of provocative essays to point out its advantages. He was a director of Patriot Publishing Co. and Eastern Assurance, a member of the Charlottetown school board, secretary of the Prince Edward Island Exhibition Association, and a vice-president of the Dominion Forestry Association. Warburton was also a central figure in the campaign to plant trees in the city of Charlottetown. As a result of his efforts and those of his colleagues, over 800 trees were planted, beginning in 1884. Alexander Warburton died 14 January 1929.

Warburton's father came to the Island in 1834 from Garry Hinch, Portartington, in Queens County, Ireland. He, too, was a public figure in the province, serving as Treasurer and in 1851 as Colonial Secretary. A prominent Reform (Liberal) politician in the mid-1800s, James Warburton was one of the leading proponents in the campaign for responsible government for Prince Edward Island.

Helen Warburton, the daughter of Daniel and Catherine Davies, died 22 July 1884. Isabella Warburton, the daughter of John Longworth and Elizabeth Tremaine, was born 11 July 1859 and died 28 November 1945.

References
CDP pp. 591–92; *CPG* 1899; Elections PEI; *Meacham's Atlas*; *Past and Present* pp. 352–54; *Provincial Premiers Birthday Series*; MacDonald *If You're Stronghearted* p. 67; Cotton pp. 38, 46; *Examiner* 16 November 1885; *Journal-Pioneer* 14 August 1973; *Patriot* 14 January 1929; *Royal Gazette* 5 April 1852; PARO: Marriage Register RG 19 Vital Statistics series 3 subseries 3 vol. 5 1882–1923; MNI-Census 1891; Charlottetown People's Cemetery Records; Foxley River Anglican Cemetery Records; Sherwood Cemetery Records.

WARBURTON, M.D., JAMES, physician and surgeon; b. 30 June 1855 in Conway, son of Honourable James Warburton and Martha C. Green; m. 13 July 1887 Louisa May Hobkirk, and they had three children, Helen Martha, James Arthur, and Eric; Anglican; d. 9 February 1928 in Montreal.

Warburton, a Liberal, was first elected to the Legislative Assembly in a by-election held 16 March 1904 for 5th Queens. He was re-elected in the general elections of 1904 and 1908. Warburton served as President of the provincial Liberal Association.

Before entering provincial politics, Warburton was elected Mayor of Charlottetown in 1897. He was re-elected in 1900 by acclamation, and was re-elected by a large majority a third time in 1902. During his three successive terms, a system of concrete sidewalks and a sewage system were established in the city.

Warburton received his early education in local schools, before attending St. Dunstan's College in Charlottetown. He also attended Prince of Wales College and then Windsor College in Halifax. In 1880 he graduated from the medical department at the University of Edinburgh, Scotland.

Warburton first practised medicine in Fifeshire, Scotland, for two-and-a-half years. In 1882 he returned to the Island and established a medical practice in Charlottetown. Warburton continued to practise medicine until two weeks prior to his death, which occurred while on a trip to Montreal for a medical consultation and an operation. James Warburton died 9 February 1928.

Louisa Warburton, was the daughter of Dr. William H. Hobkirk of Charlottetown. She was born ca. 1855 and died in 1913.

References
CPG 1909; *Past and Present*, pp. 512–13; *Examiner* 13 July 1887; *Guardian* 10 February 1928; PARO: MNI-Census 1891.

WEDGE, Ph.C., HENRY W., pharmacist, property owner, and sheep breeder; b. 27 December 1908 in Summerside, son of John P. Wedge and Adele Arsenault, both originally from Mont Carmel; m. firstly 25 September 1935 Marie L. Delaney, and they had two children, J. H. Richard and Carol Ann; m. secondly, in Moncton, September 1962, E. Marie Condrick of Boston, and there were no children; Roman Catholic; d. 15 June 1972 in Halifax.

Wedge, a Conservative, was first elected to the Legislative Assembly in the general election of

1959 for 3rd Prince. He was re-elected in the general elections of 1962 and 1966. He was defeated in the general election of 1970. On 17 September 1959, Wedge was appointed Minister of Welfare and Labour, and served as Minister of Health from 1965 until 28 July 1966. He was named Islander of the Year for 1965 for launching a program dedicated to housing for senior citizens. One of the results of this program was the construction of Summerset Manor in Summerside.

Before beginning his provincial political career, Wedge was an alderman in Summerside from 1938 to 1950. From 1950 to 1956, he served as Mayor of Summerside. During his years in the Mayor's office, a number of buildings were erected in Summerside, including the Summerside High School auditorium and the Summerside Junior High School. As well, Queen Elizabeth Park was constructed and the Civic Stadium project was begun.

Wedge received his early education in Summerside. He attended St. Dunstan's College, and later Dalhousie University, where he graduated from the pharmacy program in 1935. Wedge began his pharmacy career at Enman Drug Company in Summerside, and later became the majority shareholder and manager. He was one of the principals of Hillcrest Housing Corporation and owned Wedge Realties. Wedge was active in promoting and preserving the Acadian culture. He was president of the PEI Pharmaceutical Society, president of the Summerside branch of the La Société St-Thomas-d'Aquin, and La Société l'Assomption, a member of the Board of Governors of St. Dunstan's University and president of the Alumni, and was founding member of the Acadian Museum. Wedge was a sheep breeder and contributed to the Egmont Bay and Mont Carmel Exhibitions. He was a member of the Knights of Columbus and achieved the distinction of serving as Grand Knight. He was also an active member of the Kinsmen Club. Henry Wedge died 15 June 1972 at Victoria General Hospital.

Marie Wedge, the daughter of Dr. Mark Delaney and Marie Cosgrove of Wellington, died on 13 September 1961.

References
Acadiens p. 96; *CPG* 1970, 1971; *Journal-Pioneer* 15 June 1972, 26 June 2000, 21 July 2000; *Guardian* 16 June 1972.

WELSH, WILLIAM, merchant, shipowner, and importer-exporter; b. 22 November 1822 in Lot 49, son of Charles Welsh and Lois Bell; m. 31 January 1854 Maria Jones Pethick, and there were no children; Anglican; d. 22 June 1905 in Charlottetown.

Welsh, an Independent Liberal, was first elected to the House of Assembly in a by-election held September 1873 for 4th Queens. He was re-elected in the general election of 1876. He resigned from the House of Assembly in 1878. Welsh was elected to the House of Commons in 1887 for Queen's County, and was re-elected in 1891. He was defeated in the federal election of 1896 for East Queen's.

Welsh received his education at Central Academy in Charlottetown. He was a merchant and shipowner, in partnership with Lemuel C. Owen*, in the firm Welsh and Owen. This firm acted as an importer-exporter for the Island in the late 1860s until the late 1870s. John McDougall* built some vessels for Welsh. William Welsh died 22 June 1905.

Maria Welsh, the daughter of Thomas Pethick and Henrietta Webster, was born in 1828 and died 15 July 1890. William Welsh's younger sister, Lois, was married to Lemuel Cambridge Owen*.

References
CDP p. 597; *DCB XIV* pp. 812-813; Bremner, *Memories of Long Ago* p. 40; *Daily Examiner* 16 July 1890; *Islander* 3 February 1854; PARO: Marriage License book 5 1852-57 p. 342; MNI-Census 1881.

WESTAWAY, LEWIS JOHN, merchant, sea captain, and ship owner; b. 12 November 1821 in Georgetown, son of Roger Dart Westaway of Devonshire, England, and Damaris Watts, of Charles, Plymouth, England; m. Ann Westaway, and there were no children; Anglican; d. 23 November 1885 in Georgetown.

Westaway, a Liberal, was elected to the Legislative Assembly in the 1876 general election for Georgetown and Royalty, defeating Archibald J. MacDonald by one vote. He was defeated in the general election of 1879. His win in 1876 over Archibald J. MacDonald* was historic as it was the only loss MacDonald suffered in 12 elections.

Westaway lived in Georgetown throughout his life. He was a merchant, ship owner, and a sea captain who sailed out of Georgetown. In 1880, according to *Meacham's Atlas*, he partnered with Malcolm McDonald* in the company Westaway and McDonald, of Georgetown. It is likely that Westaway's business ventures were profitable, as a family account states he was a rich man. At one time, he had accumulated $2 million worth of money and property. The family account further states that he owned large sailing ships, steamers, hotels, houses, a foundry, and a shipyard. Lewis Westaway died 23 November 1885.

Ann Westaway was born in Glasgow, Scotland, ca. 1830 and died 23 February 1878.

References
CPG 1877, 1880; Meacham's Atlas; *Daily Examiner* 23 February 1878 p. 3; PARO: MNI-Census 1881; MNI-Hutchinson's p. 127; MNI-Mercantile Agency Reference Book 1876; Westaway Family File; St. Paul's Anglican Church Records; Trinity Anglican Cemetery Records.

WHEAR, JOHN FREDERICK, lawyer, post office inspector, and postmaster; b. 1 January 1867, son of John Whear and Margaret Barnard; m. 5 September 1895 Florence J. Murchison, and they had two children, Marion B. and Constance C.; Methodist; d. 1951.

Whear, a Liberal, was elected to the Legislative Assembly in the general election of 1900 for 5th Queens, and was appointed to Executive Council. He resigned his seat in 1904. In 1900 Whear was elected to the Charlottetown City Council for Ward Four, and in 1902 was elected for Ward Five.

Whear received his early education in local public schools, before attending Prince of Wales College in Charlottetown. He studied law in the office of L. H. Davies*. Whear was admitted to the Bar in January 1890. He practised in Davies' firm until 1901, when he began his own law firm. He later formed a partnership with Major W. A. Weeks under the name Weeks and Whear. George McPhee* would later article with the firm. Whear continued his work as a lawyer until he was appointed Postmaster of Charlottetown and Post Office Inspector for the province. John Whear died in 1951.

Florence Whear was the daughter of James and Ann Murchison of Point River, Belfast. She died in 1961.

References
CPG 1903; Elections PEI; *Past and Present* pp. 357-58; PARO: Sherwood Cemetery Records.

WIGMORE, THOMAS, farmer; b. 7 August 1877 in Graham's Road, son of Henry Wigmore and Mary Ramsay; m. 30 January 1907 Katie Bertram, and they had eight children, Fred, Cecil, Hazen, Christine, Elmer, Edna, Adelaide, and Mildred; United; d. 16 June 1958 in Kensington.

Wigmore, a Conservative, was elected to the Legislative Assembly in the general election of 1931 for 1st Queens. He was defeated in the general election of 1935.

Wigmore moved from Graham's Road in 1930, to a farm in Pleasant Valley. In 1948, when he retired from farming, he moved to Kensington. In 1955 Wigmore was appointed town magistrate and Justice of the Peace. He retired from these positions in 1958, due to failing health. Wigmore was a member of the A.F. and A.M. of Stanley Bridge, as well as the L.O.L. of Breadalbane. He also was a member of the Kensington United Church. Thomas Wigmore died 16 June 1958 at his home.

Katie Wigmore died 12 September 1978.

References
CPG 1933; *Guardian* 12 September 1978; *Patriot* 16 June 1958; PARO: Pleasant Valley Floral Hills Cemetery Records.

WILLIAMS, JOHN ELLIOT, lobster fisher, boat builder, and boat designer; b. 5 September 1920 in Beach Point, son of Elliot L. Williams and Katie Jane MacLeod; m. 11 September 1940 Annie Giddings, and they had seven children, Olive, Kenneth, Ernest, Charles, Miriam, Lily, and Perry; Church of Christ; d. 4 June 1988 in Charlottetown.

Williams, a Conservative, was elected to the Legislative Assembly in the general election of 1978 for 4th Kings. He was defeated in the general election of 1979.

"Johnnie" Williams was educated in Beach Point. He had a varied career, which began as a general merchant in the 1940s. Williams enlisted in the Royal Canadian Navy during the Second World War, to work as a shipwright. He received the Voluntary Service Medal. Following the war, Williams returned to Beach Point and became a fisherman, carpenter, plasterer, and eventually a well-known boat builder, working at this last venture from the early 1950s until his death.

He was a member of the board of directors of the Georgetown Shipyard. Williams was vice-president of the Murray Harbour Library and president of the Montague Regional High School Band Parents Association. John Williams died 4 June 1988 at the Queen Elizabeth Hospital.

References
CPG 1979, 1980; WWPEI p. 139; *Eastern Graphic* 8 October 1986; *Guardian* 25 June 1988.

WISE, JOSEPH, farmer and livestock exporter; b. 14 October 1834 in North Milton, son of Joseph Wise and Grace Ryder; m. first 29 March 1866 Jane Essery, and they had one child, Caroline Penelope; m. secondly 20 February 1883 Sophia MacKinnon, and they had four children, Frederick, Henry, Fannie, and Albert; Presbyterian; d. 21 February 1909 in Charlottetown.

Wise, a Liberal, was elected to the House of Assembly in the general election of 1886 for 2nd Queens. He was first elected to the Legislative Assembly in the general election of 1893. He was re-elected in the general election of 1897. Wise was defeated in the general election of 1890.

In 1899 and 1900, Wise proved a key player in the Liberal government's effort to maintain their slim majority. During the 1899 legislative sessions, he broke with them to vote with the Conservatives. The government, led by Premier Farquharson*, tried to persuade him to resign, which he agreed to do if a by-election was held before the spring 1900 session. The by-election was not held and, as a result, Wise withdrew his resignation. Nonetheless, on 8 May 1900, his resignation was announced in the House. This was immediately followed by Wise defiantly taking his seat. In the uproar that followed, his vote with the Conservatives, which would have defeated the Government, was not recognized by Speaker James Cummiskey*. The following day, Wise attempted to take his seat, but the Speaker entered the refuted resignation into the record. When asked to withdraw, Wise refused. He was dragged out of the Legislature by the Sergeant-At-Arms, assisted by the House Messenger, then locked in the Speaker's room until the House adjourned. When order was restored, Farquharson maintained his majority when Conservative Henry Pineau*, who had been conspicuously absent for a number of months, switched to the government side.

Throughout his life, Wise lived in North Milton where he was educated in the local school. He spent his lifetime farming in Milton and also exported livestock to England. Wise served as Grand Master of the Grand Orange Lodge of Prince Edward Island. Joseph Wise died 21 February 1909.

Jane Wise died 16 August 1871. Sophia Wise was born ca. 1843. Joseph Wise's father, born in Devon, England, immigrated to the Island in 1827.

References
CPG 1891, 1899; Elections PEI; *Meacham's Atlas*; MacDonald *If You're Stronghearted* pp. 24-25; *Patriot* 22 February; PARO: RG 19

Marriage Register series 3 subseries 3; Marriage Record Book No. 13 1870–1887; MNI-Census 1891; St. Paul's Anglican Church Records; Union Road Cemetery Records.

WOOD, LEONARD J., farmer and trader; b. 27 July 1865, at Mt. Herbert, son of Leonard Wood and Margaret Irving; m. 3 May 1889 Jessie May Stewart, and there were no children; United; d. 13 April 1957.

Wood, a Conservative, was first elected to the Legislative Assembly in the general election of 1904 for 3rd Queens. He was re-elected in the general elections of 1915 and 1923. He was defeated in the general election of 1919. On 12 January 1916, he was appointed as a Minister without Portfolio in the Mathieson* and Arsenault* Administrations. On 5 September 1923, he was again appointed Minister without Portfolio, this time in the Stewart* administration.

Wood received his education in the local school, and was a farmer and a trader in Hopeton. Leonard Wood died 13 April 1957.

Jessie Wood was the daughter of Charles and Sarah Stewart. She was born 8 January 1870 at Mt. Albion, Lot 48. She died 13 December 1959.

References
An Island Family p. 52; CPG 1909, 1917, 1923, 1924; *Guardian* 15 April 1957; PARO: MNI-Census 1891; Census 1901; Mount Herbert United Church Cemetery Records.

WOOD, MATTHEW WORLAND, farmer; b. 2 March 1879 in Mount Herbert, son of Robert and Margaret Wood; m. first 15 August 1902 Ethel Catherine Wood, and they had three children, Matthew Roland (died in infancy), Helen, and Lisle (predeceased her father); m. secondly Maude MacPherson, and there were no children; Baptist; d. 10 May 1969 in Charlottetown.

Wood, a Conservative, was elected to the Legislative Assembly in the general election of 1931 for 3rd Queens. He was defeated in the general elections of 1935, 1939, 1943, 1947, and 1951. Wood was sworn in as a Minister without Portfolio on 29 August 1931. He served under Premier James Stewart* until 1933, and then under Premier W. J. P. MacMillan* from 1933 to 1935.

Wood lived in Mount Herbert and later at Crossroads, until 1966 when he moved to a nursing home in Charlottetown. He was a buyer and shipper of cattle, chiefly to Newfoundland. Wood was also one of the pioneers in the silver fox industry on the Island, and won many trophies for his foxes. He served as a judge at fox shows. Matthew Wood died 10 May 1969. He was survived by his daughter Helen and his second wife Maude.

Ethel Wood was born 18 January 1881 and died 18 January 1934.

References

CPG 1932, 1936, 1940, 1944, 1947, 1952; *Guardian* 12 May 1969; PARO: Marriage License Book 16 1882-1923 p. 100; Census 1901.

WRIGHT, HORACE, farmer and fox rancher; b. 7 January 1879 in Bedeque, son of Thomas Wright and Mary Alice Hooper; m. 20 June 1904 Minnie May Ross, and they had four children, William Ross, Winnifred Isabel, Horace Melvin, and John Sydney; United; d. 21 January 1951 in Charlottetown.

Wright, a Liberal, was first elected to the Legislative Assembly in the general election of 1927 for 4th Prince. He was re-elected in a by-election held February 1936, and in the general elections of 1939, 1943, and 1947. He was defeated in the general election of 1931. He served as a Minister without Portfolio under premiers J. Walter Jones* and Thane Campbell*. He served as President of Executive Council in 1943. Wright was defeated in the federal election of 1921 as a Progressive candidate.

A strong supporter of Prohibition, Wright fought strenuously against the Cullen Amendment, which would have allowed liquor to be sold without the prescription of a doctor. He threatened to resign as Minister if the bill was passed. However, when the bill was passed, Wright did not resign.

Wright was educated at the local school and at Prince of Wales College in Charlottetown. Immediately following the completion of his education, Wright taught for three years, but decided not to pursue a career in education. He chose instead to become a farmer. Wright owned a large and prosperous farm in Middleton. He was also a fox rancher. Horace Wright died 21 January 1951.

Minnie Wright, the daughter of Daniel Ross, was born 27 August 1880 and died 24 January 1953.

References

CPG 1928; HFER Prince p. 1; PEI *Journal of the Legislative Assembly* 1943 p. 3; *Patriot* 22 January 1951; PARO: Lower Bedeque Cemetery Records.

WYATT, JAMES EDWARD "NED," lawyer: b. 24 September 1860 in Charlottetown, son of William and Randal Wyatt; m. Cecilia Lefurgey of Summerside and they had three children, Dorothy Randal, Wanda Lefurgey, and Ivan Edward; Anglican and Presbyterian; d. 4 May 1932.

Wyatt, a Conservative, was first elected to the Legislative Assembly in the general election of 1908 for 5th Prince. He was re-elected in the general election of 1912. He was defeated in the general elections of 1904 and 1915, and in a by-election held 30 August 1922. In March of 1912, Wyatt was elected Speaker of the Legislative Assembly. Wyatt was defeated in the federal election of 1926 in the Prince County riding.

"Ned" Wyatt, though born in Charlottetown, lived much of his life in Summerside. He was educated at Prince of Wales College. Following a five year period in which he studied law with E. J. Hodgson, Wyatt was admitted to the Prince Edward Island Bar on 2 November 1883. In the Charlottetown *Examiner*, he was commended for a good performance on his Bar admission exam. He then entered legal practice with J. E. Lefurgey in Summerside. J. E. Lefurgey was his wife's brother and the son of John Lefurgey*, a successful shipbuilder and merchant, and a Conservative Member of the House of Assembly. Much of the legal work of the firm involved the management of the affairs of John Lefurgey. Wyatt had legal offices in both Summerside and Charlottetown.

Wyatt's daughter, Wanda, was the first female law student in the province. James Wyatt was a central figure in enabling this possibility for his daughter, as he supported a bill that allowed women the opportunity for the first time. Wyatt's firm also sponsored her application for admission to law school, and provided an office in which to article. Wanda Wyatt became a heritage advocate and philanthropist. Ned Wyatt died 4 May 1932.

Cecilia Wyatt, the daughter of John Lefurgey and Dorothea Read of Summerside, was born in 1864. She died in 1937. Ivan Edward Wyatt, James and Cecilia's son, died in 1898 at the age of two years.

References

CPG 1908, 1914, 1916, 1923; Elections PEI; Kessler; *Maple Leaf Magazine* September 1932; PARO: MNI-Census 1891; Summerside People's Cemetery Records; Leard Files.

Y

YEO, JAMES, merchant, shipbuilder, and ship owner; b. 31 October 1827 in Port Hill, son of Honourable James Yeo and his second wife, Damaris Sargent, of Kilkhampton, England; m. 25 January 1854 Sarah Jane Glover, and they had four sons and two daughters, of whom the only known name is Herbert; Anglican; d. 13 February 1903 in Wellington.

Yeo, a Liberal, was first elected to the House of Assembly in the general election of 1872 for 2nd Prince. He was re-elected in the general election of 1873. Yeo served on Executive Council from 1872 to 1873. Yeo resigned from the Assembly in 1873 to successfully contest, in Prince County, the special federal election held 29 September. He was re-elected to the House of Commons in 1874, 1878, 1882, and 1887.

Yeo came from a family actively involved in politics. His father was a Conservative Member of the House of Assembly, as well as a member of both the Executive and Legislative Councils. Yeo's brother John* was a Member of the House of Assembly from 1859 to 1891, a Member of the House of Commons from 1891 to 1898, and a Member of the Senate from 1898 to 1924.

Yeo was educated at a grammar school in Charlottetown. He was a prominent merchant, shipbuilder, and ship owner on the Island. The Yeo firm of Port Hill was among the largest mercantile establishments in the province. James Yeo died on 6 December 1916.

Sarah Yeo, the daughter of William Glover, was born in 1833 and died on 19 January 1912.

References
CDP p. 612; *Daily Examiner* 19 January 1912; *Islander* 27 January 1854; *Patriot* 14 February 1903; PARO: Birth Records, Church of England, Richmond Book 1; Yeo Family File.

YEO, HONOURABLE JOHN, farmer and merchant; b. 29 June 1837 in Port Hill, son of Honourable James Yeo and his second wife, Damaris Sargent, of Kilkhampton, England; Anglican; d. 14 December 1924 in Port Hill.

Yeo, both a Liberal and a Conservative, was first elected to the House of Assembly in the 1858 general election for 2nd Prince as a Conservative. He was re-elected in the general elections of 1859, 1863, 1867, 1870, 1872, 1873, 1876, 1879, 1882, 1886, and 1890. Yeo was appointed to Executive Council in 1870. He was elected Speaker in 1871, a position he held when the Island entered Confederation in 1873. In that year, Yeo was appointed to Executive Council, and was reappointed in 1876 as a member of the Free Schools Party coalition led by L. H. Davies*. He served on Executive Council until 1879. Yeo remained with the Liberals and was for many years Leader of the Opposition.

Upon the retirement of Yeo's brother James* from the House of Commons in 1891, Yeo resigned his seat in the Assembly and was elected to the House of Commons for Prince County. When the riding was divided, in 1896, he was re-elected for East Prince. In 1898 Yeo was appointed to the Senate and served there until his death on 14 December 1924.

Yeo's family was involved in politics. His father was a Conservative Member of the House of Assembly, as well as a member of both the Executive and Legislative Councils. Yeo's brother James*, a Liberal, was returned to the House of Commons from 1876 until his retirement.

Yeo was the fifth child of his father's second marriage. He was educated in England, but returned to the Island while a young man. Upon his return, Yeo was associated with his father in numerous enterprises. After the death of his father in 1868, Yeo assumed management of his various business and agricultural interests. The Yeo firm at Port Hill was among the largest mercantile establishments in the province. Yeo also continued his father's shipbuilding business and was a capable farmer. He was known as one of the most successful stock raisers in the province.

Apart from political and business involvements, Yeo was active in his community. He served as the first Grand Master of the Free Masons in Prince Edward Island, a position he held from 1875 until 1889.

References
CDP p. 612; *CPG* 1876; *Standard Dictionary* pp. 559–60, 984; *Past and Present* pp. 498–99; PARO: Leard Files .

YOUNG, CHARLES FRANK ROSS "JOHNNY," businessperson; b. 1 September 1931 in Red Point, son of Major Ralph Young and Nellie Mossey; m. 27 July 1955, Helen MacLean of Kingsboro, and they had four children, Bonnie, Lynda, Ross*, and Shelley; Baptist; d. 7 March 1990 in Red Point.

Young, a Liberal, was first elected to the Legislative Assembly in the general election of 1978 for 1st Kings. He was re-elected in the general elections of 1979, 1982, 1986, and 1989. He served as Deputy Speaker and Party Whip. In 1986 Young was appointed Minister of Fisheries, and served in this Ministry until 1989. The position meant a great deal to Young, as his family had a strong background in the fishery. In 1990 Young served constituents from his bedside, until only hours before his death from cancer. In the by-election held after his death, his seat in the Legislature was filled by his son Ross, who served in the Legislature until 1996.

Young, or "Johnny," as he was called, received his education in Red Point, North Lake, and Montague, following which he spent a few years working in Montague and Toronto. In 1952 he returned to Red Point where he began operating an Esso Service Station. Young was a farm equipment dealer for Massey Ferguson. He also operated a service station in Souris for a number of years. In 1970, Young, along with his wife, and his sister Doris, began operating the Sea Breeze Motel and Restaurant in Kingsboro.

Along with numerous political and business involvements, Young was involved in his community. He served as a trustee of the Red Point School Board from 1956 to 1974. Young was president of the Eastern Kings Community Improvement Committee and a founding director of the Eastern Kings Fire Department. He held the position of president of the Souris Lions Club and was active in both the 1st Kings and Cardigan Liberal Associations. He was a member of the East Point Baptist Church. Johnny Ross Young died 7 March 1990.

References
CPG 1990; *Guardian* 1 March 1990, 7 November 1991; *Journal-Pioneer* 10 March 1990.

YOUNG, ROSS, sales manager and financial security advisor; b. 20 March 1962 in Souris, son of "Johnny" Ross Young* and Helen Rae MacLean; m. 30 December 1994 Mary Rita Sullivan, and they had three children, Laura Victoria, John Ross, and Jay Sullivan; Protestant.

Young, a Liberal, was first elected to the Legislative Assembly in a by-election held 18 March 1991 for 1st Kings. He was re-elected in the general election of 1993. He was defeated in the general election of 1996 in the new electoral district of Souris-Elmira. The 1991 by-election was called due to the death of Young's father, "Johnny" Ross Young, who represented 1st Kings from 1978 to 1990. In 1994 Young introduced a private member's bill which laid out the current electoral districts first used in the 1996 general election.

Young received his early education at Souris Regional High School. In 1984 he graduated with a Bachelor of Arts degree from Mount Allison University in Sackville, New Brunswick. During his time at Mount Allison, Young played on the football team. He was an AUAA all-star, a CIAU all-star, and served as co-captain and assistant coach of the team. Following university, he managed a Wacky Wheatley's store, one of Atlantic Canada's largest electronic and carpet retailers. In 1989 he joined the Atlantic Television Network as an account executive in Saint John. In 1991 he attended the University of Prince Edward Island. Young is currently a financial advisor with Freedom 55 Financial in Charlottetown.

Young was a member of the Kings County Exhibition Association, the Souris Ski Club, and the Souris Curling Club. He coached the Eastern Kings Wildcat football team and was a board member of the Prince Edward Island Tackle Football Program. He was a board member with Prince Edward Island United Way and with the John Howard Society. From 2000 to 2002, Young co-chaired the annual Canadian Mental Health fundraising golf tournament. He is a board member of Junior Achievement of PEI, president of Mount Allison 5th Quarter Club, and secretary-treasurer of the Former MLAs Association. Young is also chair of the Junior Achievement Tuna Tournament, which was revived in 2000. Ross Young and his family live in Vernon River.

Mary Sullivan Young was born 4 May 1959.

References
CPG 1991, 1996, 1997; *Guardian* 26 January 1984, 20 February 1991.

Afterword

Prince Edward Island's transition from a 32-seat to a 27-seat Legislature

It is an honour to have the opportunity to provide some history on the transition from a 32-seat to a 27-seat Legislature on Prince Edward Island. I undertake this endeavour from the perspective of someone who served in both the 32-seat Assembly and the 27-seat Assembly, and as a member of the Electoral Boundaries Commission that led to the establishment of 27 single-member districts in the Prince Edward Island Legislature in 1994.

To provide a backdrop to our present circumstances, it should be pointed out that the first Prince Edward Island House of Assembly was elected 4 July 1773. It consisted of 18 members who were elected on a colony-wide basis by adult Protestant males. In 1830 the franchise had been extended to Roman Catholics. By 1838, the Assembly was increased to 24 members elected in four dual-member constituencies in each of the three counties. In 1856 the Assembly was further expanded to 30 members elected in five dual-member districts in each county. Members of the Assembly were elected with virtually universal male suffrage.

The Legislative Council, the upper house of the Prince Edward Island Legislature, generally represented property-owning interests, and initially consisted of 12 members appointed by the governor. In 1859 it was expanded to 17 members. An act was proclaimed in 1861, which made the Legislative Council an elected body and reduced its membership to 13. They were elected in two dual-member constituencies in each county and a single-member constituency in the Charlottetown area. Councillors were to be elected by male residents who were 21 years of age and owners of real property valued at more than £100 currency.

Following Confederation, Canadian provinces began to eliminate their Legislative Councils.

To this end, the Legislative branch in Prince Edward Island underwent major institutional reform in 1893. After years of prolonged and sometimes acrimonious debate, the Assembly and Legislative Council were combined to form one chamber. The new Legislative Assembly incorporated features of both parent institutions. Like the pre-1893 Assembly, the new Assembly consisted of 30 members who were to be elected in 15 dual-member districts. There were five districts assigned to each of the three counties. The two Members of the Legislative Assembly in each district were designated as assemblyman or councillor, with each position to be contested separately. The Assemblyman was to be elected by popular franchise (i.e., males of voting age) and the Councillor by property franchise (i.e., males of voting age, but with minimum property qualifications). This distinction between assemblyman and councillor recognized the practice, prior to 1893, whereby the House of Assembly was elected by popular franchise and the Legislative Council by property franchise. Women received the right to vote in provincial elections in 1922.

One of the unique features of the property franchise was that a property holder could vote in any electoral district in which he held property. Such an elector, with property in a district valued at greater than $325, was entitled to vote for both the Assemblyman and Councillor candidates. This meant an individual, with the necessary property, could vote in up to 15 electoral districts and cast up to 30 ballots.

Following the 1893 reforms, some of the constituencies attempted to provide representation for both Protestants and Roman Catholics. Dual-member districts permitted a practice of electing a Protestant and a Roman Catholic in many of the "mixed" districts, thereby providing assurances that the voices of both religious groups would be reflected in the Legislative Assembly and government. In districts of one religion, both members were generally of that faith. Political parties were able to reinforce this practice by generally selecting individuals of the same religious affiliation to contest either the assemblyman's or councillor's seat. The practice also prevented religion from colliding with party affiliation in claims, or voters' loyalties. It helped remove religion from elections, but kept it in politics. In dual-member districts where the Acadians were a majority, the system also accommodated representation of the minority Acadian population who were predominantly Roman Catholic. The electoral districts of 1ˢᵗ and 3ʳᵈ Prince traditionally elected a Member of the Legislative Assembly of Acadian background.

After 1893, the Prince Edward Island Legislative Assembly and the electoral system remained largely unchanged until 1961, when the provincial government appointed a Royal Commission on Electoral Reform. Because of an ever-widening gap in voter population between the largest district (5ᵗʰ Queens) and the smallest district (5ᵗʰ Kings), the Commission recommended that the district of 5ᵗʰ Kings be eliminated and that there be created an additional dual-member district in Charlottetown called 6ᵗʰ Queens.

The electoral re-districting proposed by the Royal Commission invited much debate. The general approach taken was to remove a district in one county (5ᵗʰ Kings) and add a district in the neighbouring county (6ᵗʰ Queens). The vast majority of districts in the province remained unaffected. This proposal was greeted by strong resistance from the residents of 5ᵗʰ Kings, who felt they were being deprived of representation. The Legislature, in the end, opted to maintain 5ᵗʰ Kings as an electoral district and create an additional district in the Charlottetown area, thus increasing the Legislative Assembly to 32 members. The Legislature also abolished the property franchise for councillor seats. The abolition of the property franchise eliminated the only distinction between the assemblyman's and councillor's seat. In the 1966 election, all Islanders enjoyed their first opportunity to participate in the election of the 32 Members. The Legislative Assembly revisited the issue of electoral boundaries in 1974, by establishing the Electoral Boundaries Committee, but absolutely nothing came of it.

In spite of the creation of an additional dual-member district in Charlottetown, the voter population among districts continued to vary significantly. Between 1966 and 1993, the voter population in all districts grew, as did the overall voter population in the Province. In 1966 the average number of voters per district was 3,535. In 1993 that average had grown to 5,759. Keeping in mind the average, note that in 5ᵗʰ Queens in 1966 there were 7,591 voters (114.4 per cent above the average) while 5ᵗʰ Kings had 1,551 voters (-56.1 per cent below the average). In 1993, in the district of 5ᵗʰ Queens, there were 12,682 voters (120.2 per cent

above the average), while 5ᵗʰ Kings had 1,995 voters (-65.4 per cent below the average). With the exception of 5ᵗʰ Prince, all the districts that were above average were growing further above the average, while the districts that were below were growing further in the negative column. The already wide variances among districts were becoming even greater.

It is against that backdrop of relatively modest changes in 1962, and no action whatsoever in 1974, that the Electoral Boundaries Commission undertook its task in 1993. Electoral boundary reform in Prince Edward Island over the past century had been relatively modest, and the province had no convention or legal mechanism that might trigger electoral reform. The Charter of Rights and Freedoms, however, became part of the Canadian Constitution in 1982, providing the basis for three important Supreme Court of Canada decisions, which, in effect, said the change was necessary. The core of the court's ruling was that an electoral system that dilutes one citizen's vote unduly, as compared with another citizen's vote, runs the risk of providing inadequate representation to the citizen whose vote is diluted.

In court action initiated by the City of Charlottetown and Don MacKinnon, currently a Member of the Legislative Assembly, the Supreme Court of Prince Edward Island found that the existing electoral distribution in the province provided inadequate representation to a large percentage of the voters due to the significant variances in population in the electoral district.

Change was inevitable. What had to be worked out was the extent of the change that was to take place. The first decision that had to be made was whether the dual-member ridings should be maintained or changed to single-member districts. People felt that the abolition of the property vote in the 1960s rendered the distinction between the position of assemblyman and councillor meaningless.

Those favouring a move to single-member districts tended to be of the view that conditions for maintaining dual-member districts no longer existed. In 1893 dual-member districts were used to accommodate the distinction that was being made between property owners and non-property owners. In later years, the dual-member districts also, at times, provided for the practice of nominating both a Roman Catholic and Protestant in the 16 electoral districts. By 1993, people generally felt that these considerations were no longer needed.

Single-member districts were also presented as being beneficial to the electoral re-districting exercise. The practical argument for single member-districts is that the larger number of ridings and their resulting smaller geographic area can make the exercise of redistribution much easier in the future. There was also the feeling that single-member ridings promote clear lines of accountability between the constituent and elected official. On the basis of extensive public input, and the recommendation of the Electoral Boundaries Commission, the Legislative Assembly accepted the notion of single-member districts.

The final issue that had to be resolved was the number of members of the Legislative Assembly. At the time, the call to reduce districts appeared to rest on the sense that the province was over-represented at all levels of government. The early 1990s were also marked by government downsizing and reform. People felt that the Legislative Assembly should show some leadership by reducing its size. By the time the recommendations of the Electoral Boundaries Commission reached the floor of the Legislature, the real sticking point was the extent of a diminished presence for Kings County as well as the number of seats. Members wanted to avoid the perception of a rural-urban split. As a result of much discussion around variance and the plight of Kings County representation, the Assembly increased Kings County representation from three to five members, and reduced the overall makeup of the Assembly from 30, the number originally proposed by the Commission, to 27.

Finally, in 1994, after many commissions and much debate, the Prince Edward Island Legislature passed legislation that provided Islanders with the first significant and comprehensive electoral reform over the past century. This electoral reform will certainly change the political makeup of our great province. I believe it is all for the better, but only time will provide the true test of my sentiments.

Paul Connolly

Prince Edward Island General Elections

Date	Result
April 1873	Conservatives 18 Liberals 12
10 August 1876*	Free School Coalition 19 Conservatives 11
2 April 1879	Conservatives 24 Liberals 6
1 May 1882	Conservatives 21 Liberals 9
30 June 1886	Conservatives 18 Liberals 12
30 January 1890	Conservatives 16 Liberals 14
13 December 1893	Liberals 23 Conservatives 7
21 July 1897	Liberals 19 Conservatives 11
12 December 1900	Liberals 21 Conservatives 9
7 December 1904	Liberals 22 Conservatives 8
18 November 1908	Liberals 16 Conservatives 14
3 January 1912	Conservatives 28 Liberals 2
16 September 1915	Conservatives 17 Liberals 13
24 July 1919	Liberals 24 Conservatives 6
26 July 1923	Conservatives 25 Liberals 5
25 June 1927	Liberals 24 Conservatives 6
6 August 1931	Conservatives 18 Liberals 12
23 July 1935	Liberals 30
18 May 1939	Liberals 26 Conservatives 4
15 September 1943	Liberals 20 Conservatives 10
11 December 1947	Liberals 24 Conservatives 6
26 April 1951	Liberals 24 Conservatives 6
25 May 1955	Liberals 27 Conservatives 3
1 September 1959	Conservatives 22 Liberals 8
10 December 1962	Conservatives 19 Liberals 11
30 May 1966 & July 1966	Liberals 17 Conservatives 15
11 May 1970	Liberals 27 Conservatives 5
29 April 1974	Liberals 26 Conservatives 6
24 April 1978	Liberals 17 Conservatives 15
23 April 1979	Conservatives 21 Liberals 11
27 September 1982	Conservatives 22 Liberals 10
21 April 1986	Liberals 21 Conservatives 11
29 May 1989	Liberals 30 Conservatives 2
29 March 1993	Liberals 31 Conservatives 1
18 November 1996	Conservatives 18 Liberals 8 New Democrats 1
April 17 2000	Conservatives 26 Liberals 1

* The general election of 1876 was not a clear contest between the traditional parties, Liberal and Conservative, but rather a contest between the Denominationalists (under the Conservative banner) and the Free Schoolers. The dominant issue was the role the provincial government would play in funding public and/or sectarian schools. A number of Protestant Liberals combined with a number of Protestant Conservatives to form the Free School Coalition, while the remaining Conservatives and some Liberal Catholics were referred to as the Denominationalist Coalition.

Premiers of Prince Edward Island

from the Grant of Responsible Government in 1851

Pre-Confederation 1851-1873

1. George Coles - Liberal	1851
2. John Holl - Conservative	1854
3. George Coles - Liberal	1855
4. Edward Palmer - Conservative	1859
5. John H. Gray - Conservative	1863
6. James Colledge Pope - Conservative	1865
7. George Coles - Liberal	1867
8. Joseph Hensley - Liberal	1869
9. Robert P. Haythorne - Liberal	1869
10. James Colledge Pope - Conservative	1870
11. Robert P. Haythorne - Liberal	1871
12. James Colledge Pope - Conservative	1873

Post-Confederation 1873-2001

James Colledge Pope - Conservative	April-September 1873
13. Lemuel Cambridge Owen - Conservative	1873 - 1876
14. Louis Henry Davies - Liberal, Free Schooler	1876 - 1879
15. William Wilfred Sullivan - Conservative	1879 - 1889
16. Neil McLeod - Conservative	1889 - 1891
17. Frederick Peters - Liberal	1891 - 1897
18. Alexander Bannermann Warburton - Liberal	1897 - 1898
19. Donald Farquharson - Liberal	1898 - 1901
20. Arthur Peters - Liberal	1901 - 1908
21. Francis Longworth Haszard - Liberal	1908 - 1911
22. Herbert James Palmer - Liberal	May - December 1911
23. John Alexander Mathieson - Conservative	1911 - 1917
24. Aubin Edmond Arsenault - Conservative	1917 - 1919
25. John Howatt Bell - Liberal	1919 - 1923
26. James Donald Stewart - Conservative	1923 - 1927
27. Albert Charles Saunders - Liberal	1927 - 1930
28. Walter Maxfield Lea - Liberal	1930 - 1931
29. James Donald Stewart - Conservative	1931 - 1933
30. William Joseph Parnell MacMillan - Conservative	1933 - 1935
31. Walter Maxfield Lea - Liberal	1935 - 1936
32. Thane Alexander Campbell - Liberal	1936 - 1943
33. John Walter Jones - Liberal	1943 - 1953
34. Alexander Wallace Matheson - Liberal	1953 - 1959
35. Walter Russell Shaw - Conservative	1959 - 1966
36. Alexander Bradshaw Campbell - Liberal	1966 - 1978
37. Wilfred Bennett Campbell - Liberal	1978 - 1979
38. John Angus MacLean - Conservative	1979 - 1981

39. James Matthew Lee - Conservative   1981 - 1986
40. Joseph Atallah Ghiz - Liberal   1986 - 1993
41. Catherine Sophia Callbeck - Liberal   1993 - 1996
42. Keith Milligan - Liberal   October - November 1996
43. Patrick George Binns - Conservative   1996 to present

Lieutenant-Governors
of the Province of Prince Edward Island

Name	*Date of Appointment*
Honourable W. C. F. Robinson	10 June 1873
Honourable Sir Robert Hodgson	4 July 1874
Honourable Thomas H. Haviland	14 July 1879
Honourable Andrew A. Macdonald	1 August 1884
Honourable Jedediah S. Carvell	2 September 1889
Honourable George William Howlan	21 February 1894
Honourable P. A. McIntyre	23 May 1899
Honourable Donald A. MacKinnon, K.C.	3 October 1904
Honourable Benjamin Rogers	1 June 1910
Honourable Augustine Colin MacDonald	2 June 1915
Honourable Murdock MacKinnon	8 September 1919
Honourable Frank Richard Heartz	8 September 1924
Honourable Sir Charles Dalton	29 November 1930
Honourable G. desBrisay DeBlois	28 December 1933
Honourable Bradford LePage	1 October 1939
Honourable Joseph Alphonsus Bernard	30 May 1945
Honourable T. William L. Prowse	4 October 1950
Honourable F. W. Hyndman	31 March 1958
Honourable William J. MacDonald	1 August 1963
Honourable J. George MacKay	6 October 1969
Honourable Gordon L. Bennett	24 October 1974
Honourable J. Aubin Doiron	14 January 1980
Honourable Lloyd G. MacPhail	1 August 1985
Honourable Marion L. Reid	16 August 1990
Honourable Gilbert R. Clements	30 August 1995
Honourable Léonce Bernard	29 May 2001

Bibliography

Archival and Manuscript Collections

Public Archives and Records Office, Charlottetown. PARO

Collections cited include:

Accession 2323: George Leard Files

Accession 3043: Charles Winfield Matheson fonds.

Accession 3466/XHF83.7083: Charlottetown Manuscript.

Accession 3979: Colonel Henry Beer Biography

Accession 4289: Genealogies of Prince Edward Island families.

Census Returns—indexed in Master Name Index with the exception of 1901, which can be accessed through *Index for the 1901 Census of Prince Edward Island.* 4 vol. P.E.I. Genealogical Society, 1998. Microfilmed copies of the original returns are also available.

Church Records—these are assigned individual accession numbers; most are available on microfilm; see the Index to Church Records available at PARO; some church records are indexed in the Master Name Index.

Family Files—file folders of various materials comprised of genealogical notes, pedigree charts, family group sheets, newspaper clippings, correspondence, etc. Documents have been compiled and contributed by genealogical researchers.

Index to Baptisms Prior to 1896

Index to Deaths Prior to 1906

Montague Funeral Home Register—also indexed in the Master Name Index.

Prince Edward Island Genealogical Society.

Cemetery Transcripts—also indexed in the Master Name Index.

Master Name Index—a card catalogue index created by Prince Edward Island Heritage Foundation staff, and volunteers of the P.E.I. Genealogical Society. Includes cemetery tombstone transcriptions; census returns; marriage records; some church records; manuscripts; government records such as Commission books; funeral home records; newspapers; business directories such as Hutchinson's (1864) and the Mercantile Agency Reference Book (1876); Meacham's 1880 Atlas; many community histories and biographies etc. In 1992, the genealogical collections formerly housed at the P.E.I.

Museum and Heritage Foundation, including the Master Name Index, were transferred to the Public Archives and Records Office.

RG 6.1 Supreme Court
    Series 19: Bar Admittances

RG 19: Vital Statistics
    Series 3: Marriage records
        subseries 1: license cash-books
        subseries 3: marriage registers
        subseries 5: marriage bonds

U.P.E.I. - Robertson Library - P.E.I Collection

Unpublished student essays:

Barbour, Kevin. *Senator George Hilton Barbour.* U.P.E.I, Charlottetown, 1987.

Cheverie, Leo. *East Point: The First Two Hundred Years 1719 to 1919.* UPEI, Charlottetown, 1981.

Rankin, Robert Allan. *A Biographical Sketch of Sir Charles Dalton - Foxman.* UPEI., Charlottetown, 1974.

Vertical File - Biography: "A Message From Hon. Barry Clark, Progressive Conservative Leadership for the 80's". - news release; *"PC News"* - published by the Committee to Elect Frederick Driscoll, 1981.; Trainor, St. Clair (Charles)

Other Manuscript Collections

Prince Edward Island Architects

Association - Biography of Peter MacNeill

Personal Collection of

Waldron Leard - MLA Files etc.

Personal Collection of Danny Keoughan

Author's Personal Collection - Questionnaire to Former MLAs

Newspapers, Magazines and Journals

Atlantic Advocate

Atlantic Insight Magazine

Beacon

Canada and the World

Canadian Annual Review

Canadian Magazine

Canadian Parliamentary Review

Charlottetown Herald; also *Herald*

Charlottetown Monthly Magazine

Colonial Herald and Prince Edward Island Advertiser

Common Ground: The News and Views of PEI Women Constitutionalist

County Line Courier, merged with *Queen's County Telecaster* and *Commentator* to form the *Monitor*

Examiner, also *Examiner and General Intelligencer*, *Examiner and Semi-Weekly Intelligencer*, *Daily Examiner* and *Charlottetown Examiner*

Eastern Graphic

Guardian; also *Daily Guardian, Morning Guardian, Charlottetown Guardian, Guardian of the Gulf*

Island Argus; also *Weekly Examiner* and *Island Argus*

Island Farmer

The Island Magazine

Islandside

Journal-Pioneer, also *Summerside Journal and the Pioneer*

Kings County Weekly

The Maple Leaf Magazine

The Maritime Advocate and Busy East

Patriot; also *Daily Patriot, Island Patriot, Prince Edward Island Patriot, Charlottetown Patriot, Evening Patriot* and *Weekly Patriot*

Pioneer, also *Alberton Pioneer*

The Prince Edward Island Magazine

Prince Edward Island Register

Prince Edward Islander, also *Islander*, or *Prince Edward Island Intelligence and Advertiser*

Royal Gazette

Queen's Alumni Review

Topics

The Watchman

Weekly Examiner, see *Island Argus*

West Prince Graphic

Publications

Agricultural Institute of Canada. *Who's Who in the Agricultural Institute of Canada.* Ottawa: The Institute, 1948.

Alexandra Women's Institute. *A Short History of the District of Alexandra, Prince Edward Island.* Alexandra: Alexandra Women's Institute, 1965.

Allen, C.R. *Illustrated historical atlas of Prince Edward Island : From surveys made under the direction of C. R. Allen.* Belleville, ON. : Mika Silk Screening, 1972. Reprint of *Illustrated historical atlas of the province of Prince Edward Island : From surveys made under the direction of C. R. Allen.* Philadelphia : J. H. Meacham, 1880.

The Arrival of the First Scottish Catholic Emigrants in Prince Edward Island and After: Memorial Volume, 1772-1922. Summerside, P.E.I.: Journal Publications, 1922.

Arsenault, Aubin Edmond. *Memoirs of the Hon. A.E. Arsenault: Former Premier and Retired Justice, Supreme Court of Prince Edward Island.* [P.E.I.: n.p., 1951].

Arsenault, Georges. *The Island Acadians: 1720-1980.* Moncton : Les Éditions d'Acadie, 1987. Reprint, Charlottetown, P.E.I.: Ragweed, 1999.

The Atlantic Guidebook: A Guide to the Governments of New Brunswick, Nova Scotia, Prince Edward Island and Newfoundland. Edited by Anne Levy-Ward. Don Mills, ON. : Corpus Information Service, 1988.

The Bell History. Compiled by Nathan Bell and Jean Carruthers. Carleton, PEI: the authors, n.d.

Birch-Noye, Marlene. *The Parish of Port Hill.* Charlottetown, P.E.I.: [the author], 1991.

Blanchard, J. Henri. *The Acadians of Prince Edward Island, 1720-1964.* Charlottetown, P.E.I.: [the author], 1964.

Blanchard, J. Henri. *Acadiens de L'île du Prince Edouard.* [PEI]: L'Imprimerie Acadienne, 1956.

Blanchard, J. Wilmer. *Islanders Away:* Vol. 1. Summerside, P.E.I.: J. Wilmer Blanchard, 1992.

Bonnell, Ann. *Little Sands Cemetery : Prince Edward Island.* 11 July, 1998, <**http://www.rootsweb.com/~pictou/lilsands.htm** > (5, April 2002).

Boswell, Ruth et al. *An Historical Compilation of Victoria By the Sea: our legacy and trust.* [PEI: the authors], 1973.

Bremner, Benjamin. *An Island Scrapbook: Historical and Traditional.* Charlottetown, P.E.I.: Irwin Printing , 1932.

_____. *Memories of Long Ago: Being a Series of Sketches Pertaining to Charlottetown in the Past.*

Charlottetown, P.E.I.: Irwin Printing, 1930.

A Bridge to the Past: Wilmot Valley 1784-1979. [Wilmot, PEI]: Wilmot Valley Historical Society, 1980.

By the Old Mill Stream: History of Wellington 1833-1983. Edited by Allan Graham and Mary Graham. Wellington, PEI: Wellington Senior Citizens' History Committee, 1983.

Callbeck, Lorne. *My Island, My People.* Charlottetown, P.E.I.: Prince Edward Island Heritage Foundation, 1979.

Canada. Veterans Affairs Canada. *Canadian Virtual War Memorial.* February 28, 2001, <http://www.vac-acc.gc.ca/generalsub.cfm? source=collections/virtualmem> (April 6, 2002).

Canada's Smallest Province: a History of P.E.I. Edited by Francis W. P. Bolger. Charlottetown, P.E.I.: Prince Edward Island Centennial Commission, 1973.

The Canadian Biographical Dictionary and Portrait Gallery of Eminent and Self Made Men: Volume 2: Quebec and the Maritime Provinces. Chicago: American Biographical Publishing Co., 1881.

Canadian Directory of Parliament, 1867-1967. Edited by J. K. Johnson. Ottawa: Public Archives of Canada, 1968.

The Canadian Men and Women Of The Time: A Handbook of Canadian Biography. Edited by Henry James Morgan. Toronto: W. Briggs, 1898. 2nd ed. 1912. Title varies.

The Canadian Parliamentary Guide. Quebec, 1862-63; Montreal, 1864-74; Ottawa, 1875-1988; Toronto, 1989- . Editor and title varies. Bilingual from 1982/83: *The Canadian Parliamentary Guide/Guide Parlementaire Canadien.*.

Canadian Publicity Company. *Prominent People of the Maritime Provinces.* Saint John, N.B.: J. & A. McMillan, 1922.

Canadian Who's Who: A Handbook of Canadian Biography of Living Characters. Toronto: Trans-Canada Press, 1910- .

The Capital List: A Biographical Record of Leadership in the Nation's Capital. Edited by Terrence McLaughlin and Ellen Wathen. Ottawa: Capital List Ltd., 1978.

Centenary celebration and unveiling of monument erected to the memory of the Brudenell pioneers : Brudenell Island, July 16, 1903. Charlottetown, P.E.I. : *The Guardian,* 1946.

C.F's Diary 1913-1952. Edited by Annette M. Judge. Summerside, P.E.I.: Williams and Crue, 1977. -diary of Clarence Ferdinand Morrissey.

Challenged to be the church in unity: an historic review of the United Church of Canada on Prince Edward Island, 1925-1985. Edited by Rev. Garland C. Brooks. Charlottetown, P.E.I.: United Church History Committee, 1988.

Checklist and Historical Directory of Prince Edward Island Newspapers: 1787-1986. Compiled by Heather Boylan. Charlottetown, P.E.I.: Public Archives of Prince Edward Island, 1987.

Cotton, William Lawson. *Chapters In Our Island Story.* Charlottetown, P.E.I.: Irwin, 1927.

Cornelius Howatt: Superstar! Edited by David Weale and Harry Baglole. Summerside, P.E.I.: Williams and Crue, 1974.

Currie, Mildred, et al. *New Perth: Link With the Past, 1803-1995.* New Perth, PEI: New Perth History Committee, 1995.

A Cyclopaedia of Canadian Biography : being chiefly men of the time. A collection of persons distinguished in professional and political life; leaders in the commerce and industry of Canada, and successful pioneers. Edited by George MacLean Rose. Rose's National Biographical Series. 2 vols. Toronto: Rose Publishing, 1886-88.

Dewar, Lloyd George. *A History of My Family and the Family Farm at New Perth, Prince Edward Island: and a Short History of New Perth.* Summerside, P.E.I.: Williams and Crue, 1976.

Dictionary of Canadian Biography. 14 vols. to date. Regular edition. Toronto: U of T. Press, 1966- .

An Encyclopaedia of Canadian Biography: Containing Brief Sketches and Steel Engravings of Canada's Prominent Men. Montreal: Canadian Press Syndicate, 1907.

Encyclopedia Canadiana. Edited by John E. Robbins. 10 vols. Ottawa: Canadiana Co., 1957-58. Also 1975 edition. Toronto: Grolier. Edited by Kenneth H. Pearson.

Feehan, John A. *An Island Family: The Feehans.* Hantsport, N.S.: Lancelot Press, 1986.

Forester, Joseph E. and Anne D. Forester. *Silver Fox Odyssey: History of the Canadian Silver Fox Industry.* Charlottetown, P.E.I.: Canadian Silver Fox Breeders Association and PEI Department of Agriculture, [1980].

Fraser, Alice. *The Aitkens of Kings County, Prince Edward Island.* [P.E.I.: the author], 1974.

Glen, Elizabeth A. *A Genealogy of the Family.* Bonshaw, PEI: the author., 1992.

Glen, William M. and Elizabeth A. Glen. *Bonshaw: A Stroll Through Its Past.* Bonshaw, PEI: the authors, 1993.

Graves, Ross. *William Schurman : Loyalist of Bedeque, Prince Edward Island and his descendants. Vol. 1* Summerside, P. E. I.: H. B. Schurman, 1973.

Green, Alice. *Footprints on the Sands of Time: a History of Alberton.* Summerside, P.E.I.: Williams and Crue, 1980.

Highlights of the Cardigan Area. Edited by Beth Brehaut. [Cardigan: the author, 1987].

Hillcrest Housing Limited: the First 25 Years 1958-1983. Summerside, P.E.I.: Alfa-Graphics, 1983.

The History of Margate, Prince Edward Island. [Margate, PEI]: Margate Women's Institute, 1973.

A History of Southport and district including Rosebank, Keppoch and Kinlock. Edited by Jim Hornby. Summerside, P.E.I.: The History Committee of the Southport Women's Institute, 1982.

History of the Federal Electoral Ridings 1867-1992. 2nd ed. 7 vols. Ottawa: Library of Parliament, 1993. - Vol. 7: "New Brunswick, Nova Scotia, Prince Edward Island, Newfoundland, Appendices, Indexes". Vol. 2: Saskatchewan, Manitoba, Yukon, Northwest Territories.

Jardine, Donald E. *Jardines of Atlantic Canada. Vol. 1* Halifax, N.S.: Atlantic Provinces Branch of the Jardine Clan Society, 1997.

Kessler, Deirdre. *A century on Spring Street : Wanda Lefurgey Wyatt of Summerside, Prince Edward Island (1895-1998).* Charlottetown, P.E.I.: Indigo Press, 1999.

Lea, R. G. *Island medicine: a historical review.* Charlottetown., P.E.I.: Prince Edward Island Medical Society, 1984.

Leard, George A. *Historic Bedeque: The Loyalists at Work and Worship in Prince Edward Island - a History of Bedeque United Church.* Bedeque, P.E.I.: Bedeque United Church, 1973.

Leard, Waldron and Susan Leard. "Burial Sites of Interesting People on Prince Edward Island: Historic sites and monuments". In *The Island Register.* 1 January, 2002, <**http://www.islandregister.com /burials/ip1.html**> (6 April 2002).

Ledwell, Frank and Reshard Gool. *Portraits & Gastroscopes: A Collection of Square Deals, Gastroscopes and Personalities.* Charlottetown, P.E.I.: Square Deal Publications, 1972.

MacDonald, Edward. *If You're Stronghearted: P.E.I. in the 20th Century.* Charlottetown, P.E.I.: Prince Edward Island Museum and Heritage Foundation, 2000.

_____. *New Ireland: the Irish on Prince Edward Island.* Charlottetown, P.E.I.: Prince Edward Island Museum & Heritage Foundation, 1990.

MacKinnon, Wayne E. *J. Walter Jones: The Farmer Premier.* Summerside, P.E.I.: Williams and Crue, 1974.

_____. *The Life of the Party.* Summerside, P.E.I.: Prince Edward Island Liberal Party, 1973.

MacLeod, Ada. *Roads to Summerside: the story of early Summerside and the surrounding area.* Ed. Marjorie McCallum Gay. Summerside, P.E.I.: [the author], 1980.

MacNevin, Mrs. Lorne. *Past and Present: a History of Brae.* Summerside, P.E.I.: Williams and Crue, 1979.

Mahar, Katelyn. *"Daniel J. MacDonald".* *Eastern Kings Consolidated School.*
     <http://www.edu.pe.ca/easternkings/danielj.htm> (April 11, 2002).

Maritime Reference Book: biographical and pictorial record of prominent men and women of the Maritime provinces. Halifax, N.S.: Royal Print & Litho, 1931.

The Maritimes: Tradition, Challenge & Change. Edited by George Peabody et. al. Halifax, N.S.: Maritext Ltd, 1987.

Past and Present of Prince Edward Island: Embracing a Concise Review of its Early Settlement, Development and Present Conditions, Written by the Most Gifted Authors of the Province. Edited by D. A. MacKinnon and A. B. Warburton. Charlottetown, P.E.I.: B. F. Bowen, [1906].

Pollard, James B. *Historical Sketch of the Eastern Regions of New France: From the Various Dates of Their Discoveries to the Surrender of Louisburg, 1758; Also Prince Edward Island Military and Civil.* Charlottetown, P.E.I.: J. Coombs, 1898.

Premiers Gallery. Official Website of the Government of Prince Edward Island. <http://www.gov.pe.ca/premiersgallery/> (March 27, 2002).

Prince Edward Island.
     House of Assembly.
          Journal. Charlottetown, 1788-1893, except 1798-1805 when none were printed. Title varies.
          Department of Justice. *Annual Report,* 1978-1981.
     Elections PEI.
          Legislative Assembly: Province of Prince Edward Island. Rev. 8 April, 1998. - partial contents: "Alphabetical Listing of MLAs 1873-1996"; "Election Results from 1873-1996"; "Speakers of the Legislative Assembly of PEI: 1873-1999"; "General Assemblies and Sessions 1773-1996";" Premiers of Prince Edward Island"; "Women in Island Politics". - see also Official Website of the Government of Prince Edward Island. Elections PEI. http://www.gov.pe.ca/election/index.php3

Executive Council. *Orders.* 1972-1996.

Island Information Services. *PEI Cabinet Biographic Summary,* 1980.

Provincial Premiers Birthday Series 1873-1973. Charlottetown, P.E.I.: The Prince Edward Island 1973 Centennial Commission., 1973.

Prominent Men of Canada, 1931-32. Edited by Ross Hamilton. Montreal: National Publishing, [1932-]

Remember Yesterday: a History of North Tryon, PEI 1769-1992. Edited by Hazel and John Robinson. Albany, PEI: North Tryon Historical Association, 1993.

Rogers, Evan Benjamin, and Claudia Hester Rogers. *A Rogers Family Chronicle: Emigration from Wales; Settlement in Canada; Dispersal.* Charlottetown, P.E.I.: Rogers Hardware Company, 1991.

Shaw, Walter. *Tell Me The Tales.* Charlottetown, P.E.I.: Square Deal Publications, 1975.

A Standard Dictionary of Canadian Biography: the Canadian Who Was Who. Edited by Charles G. D. Roberts and Arthur L. Tunnell. Volume I, 1875 to 1933. Toronto: Trans Canada Press, 1934.

Stamp, Robert M. *Canadian Obituary Record: a Biographical Dictionary of Canadians Who Died.* Toronto: Dundurn Press, 1988-92.

Townsend, Adele. *Ten Farms Become a Town: A History of Souris 1700-1920.* Ed. Ann Thurlow. Souris, P.E.I.: The Town of Souris, 1986.

Tuplin, Frank F. *Origin of Silver Foxes on P.E. Island in 1887.* n.p: n.p., n.d.

Wallace, W. Stewart. *Dictionary of Canadian Bi-*

ography. Toronto: MacMillan., 1926. 3rd edition, 1963. Title varies: *The MacMillan Dictionary of Canadian Biography*.

Who's Who in Canada: An Illustrated Biographical Record of Men and Women of the Time. Toronto[etc.]: International Press Ltd.[etc.], [1910-] Title, subtitle, and editor varies.

Who's Who in Canadian Law. Edited by Evelyn Davidson. 6 vols. Toronto: Trans-Canada Press, 1981-87.

Who's Who on PEI. Edited by John Barrett. Charlottetown, P.E.I.: Walt Wheeler Publications, 1986.

Zonta Club of Charlottetown. *Outstanding Women of Prince Edward Island*. Summerside, P.E.I.: Williams and Crue, 1981.

Interviews
Dr. Malcolm Beck
Alfred Blanchard
Jean Blanchard
Irene Burge
Carl Delaney
Waldron Leard
Ivan MacArthur
Michael Proud
Isabel Sabapathy